"A comprehensive and insightful look into the threat of domestic terrorism. The authors remind us to lead the fight rather than simply react to one of the most dangerous conflicts our nation faces. Highly recommended!"

— **Bob Paudert**, *Police Chief, Retired, for West Memphis, Arkansas*

"This compendium accomplishes the vital goal of summarizing, examining, analyzing, and explaining terrorism in America in a way that is as seamless and succinct as its title might suggest. As an analyst, researcher, writer, and instructor on terrorism, I keep this book on my desk for frequent consultation. It is logically presented, digestible, and above all, useful."

— **Captain Christopher Ward**, *Intelligence & Policy Analyst, FDNY Center for Terrorism & Disaster Preparedness; Instructor, Wilmington University*

"This book provides a comprehensive examination of theoretical explanations, motivating factors, recruitment strategies, and the role of cyberspace in fueling terrorism both in the United States and abroad—[and] a thought-provoking discussion on ending terrorism…in our national and global landscapes."

— **Claudia San Miguel**, *Associate Professor of Criminal Justice/Dean of the College of Arts & Sciences, Texas A&M International University*

Terrorism in America

Offering a fresh perspective on the changing face of terror attacks, *Terrorism in America* focuses on domestic groups, examining the beliefs, actions, and impacts of American-based terrorists and terror organizations. Editors Robin Maria Valeri and Kevin Borgeson and their contributors draw on theories from criminology, psychology, and sociology to explore the ideologies of right-wing, left-wing, and religious-extremist groups—how and why they convert followers, recruit financially, and take extreme action against others. No competing text offers such in-depth and nuanced coverage of the radical ideologies behind these attacks, or the ensuing fear domestic terrorism creates, as well as the strategies to combat violent extremism.

A core text for domestic terrorism courses and an excellent supplement for any counterterrorism or homeland security course, *Terrorism in America* brings its singular focus to the growth and evolution of terrorism in the United States. Interviews, case studies from the field, and chapter themes make this a highly readable text for criminal justice, psychology, sociology, and homeland security students, professors, or practitioners.

Robin Maria Valeri, PhD, Professor of Psychology, St. Bonaventure University and Volunteer Fire Fighter, earned her BA from Cornell University and her MA and PhD from Syracuse University.

Kevin Borgeson, PhD, Associate Professor of Criminal Justice and Research Fellow for the Center for Holocaust and Genocide Studies, Salem State University, earned his BA from Bridgewater State College and his PhD from Northeastern University.

Together they have co-edited *Hate Crimes: Victims, Motivations and Typologies* and are the co-authors of *Skinhead History, Identity and Culture* as well as several chapters and articles, including "Sticks and Stones: When the Words of Hatred Become Weapons" in *Global Perspectives on Youth Gang Behavior, Violence, and Weapons* and "Masculine Identities within the Skinhead Movement" in *Advances in Sociology Research*.

Terrorism in America

Edited by Robin Maria Valeri
and Kevin Borgeson

Routledge
Taylor & Francis Group

NEW YORK AND LONDON

First published 2018
by Routledge
711 Third Avenue, New York, NY 10017

and by Routledge
2 Park Square, Milton Park, Abingdon, Oxon, OX14 4RN

Routledge is an imprint of the Taylor & Francis Group, an informa business

© 2018 Taylor & Francis

Library of Congress Cataloging-in-Publication Data
Names: Valeri, Robin Maria, editor. | Borgeson, Kevin.
Title: Terrorism in America / edited by Robin Maria Valeri and Kevin Borgeson.
Description: 1 Edition. | New York : Routledge, 2018. | Includes bibliographical
    references and index.
Identifiers: LCCN 2017060859 (print) | LCCN 2018004449 (ebook) |
    ISBN 9781315456010 (master) | ISBN 9781138202085 (hardback) |
    ISBN 9781138202092 (pbk.) | ISBN 9781315456010 (ebk)
Subjects: LCSH: Terrorism—United States.
Classification: LCC HV6432 (ebook) | LCC HV6432 .T499 2018 (print) |
    DDC 363.325—dc23
LC record available at https://lccn.loc.gov/2017060859

ISBN: 978-1-138-20208-5 (hbk)
ISBN: 978-1-138-20209-2 (pbk)
ISBN: 978-1-315-45601-0 (ebk)

Typeset in Times New Roman
by Apex CoVantage, LLC

Visit the eResources: www.routledge.com/9781138202092

This book is dedicated to all past and current first responders. In an emergency, you are the first on scene and you rush in, often at great risk to yourself, to save the lives of others. Thank you for the selfless, life-saving services you provide to your communities. And, to my husband, for your love and support.

—Robin

This book is dedicated to my wife Pam and Stephen Angelo. Without their support and feedback, this project would never have got off the ground. I would also like to dedicate this book to Michael E. Brown, an incredible mentor, and friend.

Contents

Contributors

Joel A. Capellan is an Assistant Professor of Law and Justice Studies at Rowan University. He received his PhD in Criminal Justice from the CUNY Graduate Center in 2016. Prior to his doctoral studies, Professor Capellan received an MA in Social Science research from the University of Chicago and a BA from Buffalo State College. Professor Capellan specializes in statistics and spatial analysis. Substantively, his research interests are wide. He has conducted and published research on state-sponsored repression, segregation, mass public shootings, lone wolf terrorism, policing bias, and criminological and sociological theories. Currently, he is devoting most of his attention to the study of mass public shootings in the United States.

Mark Hamm is a former prison warden from Arizona and currently a professor of Criminology at Indiana State University and a Senior Research Fellow at the Center on Terrorism, John Jay College of Criminal Justice, City University of New York. In the 1980s and 1990s, he wrote widely about right-wing extremists in the United States and on subjects as diverse as apocalyptic violence, cop killer rap, and ethnography and terror. His books include *The Age of Lone Wolf Terrorism* (2017), *The Spectacular Few: Prisoner Radicalization and the Evolving Terrorist Threat* (2013), *Terrorism as Crime*: *From Oklahoma City to Al-Qaeda and Beyond* (2007), *In Bad Company*: *America's Terrorist Underground* (2002), *Apocalypse in Oklahoma*: *Waco and Ruby Ridge Revenged* (1997), and *American Skinheads*: *The Criminology and Control of Hate Crime* (1993). Professor Hamm received three major grants from the National Institute of Justice: one to study crimes committed by terrorist groups, one to study terrorist recruitment in American correctional institutions, and the other to study lone wolf terrorism in America.

Michael Loadenthal is a Visiting Professor of Sociology and Social Justice at Miami University of Oxford, Ohio, and the Executive Director of the Peace and Justice Studies Association. He completed his PhD in Conflict Analysis at George Mason University (2015) and earned an MLitt at the Centre for the Study of Terrorism and Political Violence at the University of St Andrews (2010). Dr. Loadenthal has taught courses on political violence, terrorism, and sociology at Georgetown University, George Mason University, the University of Cincinnati, the University of Malta, and Jessup Correctional Institution. Dr Loadenthal has served as the Dean's Fellow for George Mason's School for Conflict Analysis and Resolution, a Practitioner-in-Residence for Georgetown's Center for Social Justice, and a Research Fellow at Hebrew Union College's Center for the Study of Ethics and Contemporary Moral Problems. His work has been published in a variety of venues, including *Critical Studies on Terrorism, Journal for the Study* *of Radicalism, Perspectives on Terrorism, Journal of Applied Security Research, Journal of Feminist Scholarship, Journal of Radical Criminology, Anarchist Developments in Cultural Studies*, and other social movement and political theory journals and books.

Tom Monahan is a retired 30-year veteran of the Las Vegas Metropolitan Police Department, where he spent the majority of his career investigating violent sex crimes, homicides, and terrorism. Since retirement, he has contracted with the U.S. Department of Homeland Security and traveled to Afghanistan as part of the U.S. Department of State Antiterrorism Assistance Program. He holds a Bachelor's degree from Boston University and a Master's degree from the Naval Postgraduate School.

Thomas R. O'Connor is a criminologist and Associate Professor at Austin Peay State University, where he directs the Institute for Global Security and teaches in the Criminal Justice/Homeland Security Program. He holds a PhD from Indiana University of Pennsylvania, a Master's from the University of Illinois, and a Bachelor's from Knox College. He combines 20 years of teaching experience with 10 years of practical experience, and has authored works on terrorism, mass murder, serial killing, cybercrime, and white collar crime.

Christopher J. Wright teaches terrorism-related courses in the Criminal Justice Department's Homeland Security Concentration at Austin Peay State University. His research has looked at the ways in which radical Islamists use the Internet, and he has trained FBI recruits on the subject. He has also researched extensively on the effect of foreign fighter returnees on domestic terrorism. He has a PhD from the University of Southern California, has been married for 25 years to his lovely wife, Kim, and is the father of four.

Introduction

Robin Maria Valeri and Kevin Borgeson

THE current book examines terrorism in the United States of America. In this book, we go beyond a discussion of domestic terrorism, which the Federal Bureau of Investigation (FBI, September 7, 2009) has described as "Americans attacking Americans based on U.S.-based extremist ideologies," to include terrorist attacks by Americans that are motivated by extremists or extremist ideologies whose roots stem from individuals or ideologies outside the United States. Therefore, how Americans have been impacted by terrorist groups, including Islamic extremists based outside the United States, is discussed.

The book is divided into four parts. Part I examines theories of terrorism and the major right-wing and left-wing terrorist groups. In Chapter 1, O'Connor discusses the major political, criminological, sociological, and psychological theories of terrorism. In Chapter 2, Borgeson discusses right-wing terrorist groups with a focus on white nationalists and militia groups. The chapter includes a discussion regarding why people join these groups. Loadenthal, in Chapter 3, traces the history of Leftist political violence occurring in the United States over the past century before turning to a discussion of militant underground networks fighting for environmental and animal liberation and the rise of the anti-globalization movement. Loadenthal closes the part with a compelling discussion of the government's efforts to derail these groups following the terrorist attacks of September 11, 2001.

Part II explores three of the major ideologies that have motivated terrorist activities in the United States. Borgeson, in Chapter 4 explains the beliefs underlying Christian Identity and how these beliefs have been used to justify the actions of white supremacists. In Chapter 5, Wright explores Salafi jihadism, which represents a minority view within Islam but has been used to justify violent Islamism around the world, including inspiring Americans to take up arms and engage in terrorism. In Chapter 6, Valeri discusses the Sovereign Citizens Movement, an anti-government movement that encourages adherents to take back their sovereign status through unlawful and sometimes violent actions.

In Part III, the authors examine the recruitment tactics of terrorist organizations and analyze their effectiveness. In Chapter 7, Valeri examines terrorist propaganda, with an emphasis on the crucial role cyberspace plays in spreading terrorist ideologies. Valeri applies psychological theories to understanding how and why terrorists are able to recruit new members and then discusses alternative to banning hate speech. In Chapter 8, Capellan draws on research from the work-performance literature to explore the reasons why an individual becomes a lone wolf terrorist. Hamm, in Chapter 9, explores the role prison can play in the recruitment of terrorists.

Part IV examines the fall-out from terrorism. In Chapter 10, Monahan and Valeri discuss the resulting fear caused by acts of terrorism and how that fear influences the decisions of individuals, businesses, and governments. Finally, in Chapter 11, an End to Terrorism, the book closes with some thoughts on the role of cyberspace in the proliferation of terrorism and strategies for ending terrorism.

REFERENCE

Federal Bureau of Investigation (FBI) (September 7, 2009). Domestic Terrorism in the Post-9/11 Era. Retrieved from www.fbi.gov/news/stories/2009/september/domterror_090709

Part I

Roots of Terrorism

Chapter 1

The Criminology of Terrorism
Theories and Models

Thomas R. O'Connor

Overview

- Theories, motives, and causality
- Anarchism, fascism, and religion
- Rational choice and globalization
- Sociology, psychology, and psychiatry
- Biology and physiology
- Traditional criminological theories
- Unique criminological theories

This chapter discusses the major criminological theories of terrorism, or those theories that offer insights into what might be called explanations of terrorist behavior as criminal conduct. Explanations, as opposed to understandings, are designed to provide scientifically valid guides to research and, sometimes, policy. Theory-driven policy is rare, but far more common is theory-driven research. A good theory has practical uses if it provides, for example, some fairly clear ideas about what are the independent variables (the causes) and the dependent variables (the effects). Criminological theory is mostly about attempting to correctly identify the causes of behavior, and often this quest takes us into the realm of concepts we cannot see or observe directly. It helps if the concepts in a theory have clear meanings so researchers can test them by collecting and analyzing data that prove or disprove a theory. Admittedly, not all theories are inherently testable, and few offer crystal-clear meanings, but the job of explanation is never easy. By reviewing those theories that have stood the test of time, this chapter hopes to encourage more interest in theories of terrorism, the development of which is urgently needed.

Most of the major theories of terrorism are derived from theories of collective violence in the field of political science. Indeed, prior to the emergence of criminal justice as a separate discipline in the early 1970s, it can be safely said that political science pretty much had a monopoly over theories of terrorism, followed perhaps by the disciplines of religion, economics, sociology, and psychology. Criminological theories have also certainly had a role to play with some relevance. We will begin, first, with the theories of politically motivated collective violence—with the goal of providing an objective overview of theoretical concepts, causal factors, and models connecting cause and effect. The underlying concern should be to answer the questions, "Why does terrorism occur?" or "What causes it?," rather than pass judgment or assess any of the theories at this point. With the political theories, it is often the case that the form of governance is held to be the main cause of terrorism, and with the other theories, a number of subcultural and personality factors are usually found to be at work. With other theories, such as sociology, the interplay between social movements and societal response is often looked at to help explain terrorism.

It should be noted that theory is more than the study of motive. In criminology, theories tend to take on more than the explanation of offender mind-sets and behavior. They often tackle issues such as victimology and criminal justice system response. Motive itself is frequently ignored in the prosecution of terrorists (Smith, 1994; Smith, Damphousse, Jackson, & Karlson, 2002). Justice itself is often evasive. Sentencing variations in bringing terrorists to justice occur mostly because of "structural-contextual" effects (when components of criminal justice work at odds with one another), because of "liberation" effects (when judges and juries nullify the law or follow their own sentiments), or because of justiciability issues (prosecutors decide not enough evidence exists to prosecute a case). Inconsistencies in sentencing affect the ability to collect research data because an unindicted or acquitted terrorist is not, legally, a terrorist. For this reason, and others, terrorism databases have limitations. However, analyses using such databases afford opportunities to test theories, tease out relevant variables or factors, do comparative theory testing, and so on—all of which help the larger purpose of theory development. It should be remembered, as the following theories are reviewed, that a strict legalistic conception of who is or is not a terrorist makes for a more rigorous approach. Just because somebody shares some of the ideas mentioned as causal factors in this chapter does not make them a terrorist. A court of law determines if a person is a true terrorist, and any theory that can explain court behavior as well as terrorist behavior definitely has some added value.

The Political Theory of Anarchism as a Theory of Terrorism

Terrorism is most definitely not a form of governance, but anarchism is. Most anarchists reject terrorism in its vanguard varieties (for nationalist or religious purposes), but in a theoretical sense, anarchism justifies terrorism as a form of criminal action that attacks the values of an organized, complacent society. Anarchism is a theory of governance that rejects any form of central or external authority, preferring instead to replace it with alternative forms of organization such as shaming rituals for deviants, mutual assistance pacts between citizens, syndicalism (any nonauthoritarian organizational structure that gives the greatest freedom to workers), iconoclasm (the destruction of cherished beliefs), libertarianism (a belief in absolute liberty), and plain old rugged individualism. An extreme form of it is called nihilism, which holds that all truths, values, and organizational structures are meaningless and that chaos is preferable to anything else, so one might as well destroy everything. Not all anarchists are nihilists, but they do share some compatibilities. Anarchism is often referred to as the 19th-century root of terror-ism, the term first being introduced in 1840 by Pierre-Joseph Proudhon. Anarchism is defined as the rejection of the state, of any form of coercive government, and of any form of domination and exploitation. It involves the notion of free and equal access to all the world's resources to enable positive freedom (freedom to) in place of negative freedom (freedom from, or the basis of most constitutional rights).

As a theory, anarchism holds a unique place in history because it was the first revolution-ary movement to come up with systematic ideas about the purpose of agitation. The reader will surely recognize some of these ideas as terrorist tactics, but it's important to first understand them in the context of anarchism. Proudhon contributed the idea of finding the "moment," as when the moment is ripe for revolutionary action. Another anarchist, Mikhail Bakunin, popular-ized the idea of "propaganda by deed," or letting your actions speak for themselves—which was a theory originally developed by Carlo Pisacane, an Italian revolutionary who argued that ideas spring from deeds and not the other way around. Over the years, this notion has evolved into a fairly coherent philosophy of the bomb as part of a propaganda campaign to stimulate awareness and sympathy with the cause, and in this respect has been noted as a defining feature of terror-ism (Georges-Abeyie & Hass, 1982). Bakunin's ideas strongly influenced anarchism because his concept of propaganda by deed also included a prohibition against large-scale group action (it being better, he thought, for anarchist action to be individualized or done in small groups). Most anarchists operate on the principle of leaderless resistance, or acting on your own, with little knowledge or support of the groups to which they may belong. Another anarchist, Sergei Nechaev, who was an associate of Bakunin's, glorified the "merciless" aspect of destruction, but it was Bakunin who laid out the six steps necessary to destroy a social structure. These steps are paraphrased as follows:

Select targets that hold significance

- Kill the intelligensia (kill those who are intelligent and influential in society).
- Kidnap the rich and powerful (those who yield the biggest ransoms).
- Infiltrate the politicians (to find out their secrets and discredit them).
- Help the guilty criminals (to confuse society over justice and punishment).
- Defend the loudmouths (those who make dangerous declarations).
- Nurture the supporters (help fellow travelers who believe in societal destruction).

Major anarchist figures, such as Karl Heinzen and Johann Most, contributed the idea that murder, especially murder-suicide, constituted the highest form of revolutionary struggle. Both advocated the use of weapons of mass destruction (WMD). Other anarchists contributed additional ideas, such as Peter Kropotkin's notion of "propaganda by word," or radicalizing the public by use of subversive publications. Anarchism (like fascism) has also had some influential female figures such as Emma Goldman (1869–1940), who comes to mind as an early founder of free speech (the American Civil Liberties Union, or ACLU) and sexual liberation movements. Minor figures in the history of anarchism—such as Charles Gallo, Auguste Vaillant, Émile Henry, and Ravachol (François Claudius Koenigstein)—advocated the idea that to have the most effect, the targets must be innocents (in places such as crowded dance halls or shopping centers) or symbols of economic success (for example, banks and stock exchanges). It may be worth noting, in passing, that the famous Italian criminologist Cesare Lombroso developed his notion of the "born criminal" in part by being called in to examine the physical features of some minor anarchists who were really nothing more than criminals justifying their behavior with anarchist talk.

Between 1875 and 1912, anarchists alone or in small groups managed to assassinate or attempt to assassinate the leaders of nine different countries, including the United States (President William McKinley in 1901). These crimes were just the best-known acts of anarchism because anarchists were also involved in numerous ordinary crimes such as theft, robbery, murder, kidnapping, assault, and bombing. The most famous incident was the Haymarket riot in Chicago in 1886. During these peak years for classic anarchism, May Day celebrations became famous as all-out, crime-rampant days. Police departments around the world became convinced there was an international conspiracy, and suspicious foreigners were locked up by the hundreds in many countries. Perfunctory trials were held, and many defendants were hanged or deported. The most famous of these trials was the 1920 case of Nicola Sacco and Bartolomeo Vanzetti, who were more antiwar and labor activists than anarchists. Anarchism in the classical sense was largely erased from the face of the earth by 1917 via a number of factors: the rise of communism and fascism (both of which are opposed to anarchism), strong xenophobic deportation (Red Scare) laws in democratic countries, and the fact that classic anarchism never became an organized movement. Twentieth-century terrorist groups that emerged later and claimed an ancestry with anarchism include the Japanese Red Army, the British Angry Brigade, the German Baader-Meinhof Gang, the Weathermen in the United States, and the Mexican Zapatista movement (Kushner, 2003). During the Spanish Civil War in the 1930s, something called anarcho-syndicalism developed, which is a loose confederation of various protest groups. Those who call themselves anarchists today (see Purkis & Bowen, 1997) are more likely to be environmentalists or part of the antiglobalization movement, and they target such institutions as the World Bank, International Monetary Fund (IMF), or World Trade Organization (WTO).

For purpose of balance, it is important to point out that much anarchist thought does not support terrorism. It has historically supported terrorism, and even today might support assassination, but there are only weak analytical links between the two, most strongly with the concept of propaganda by deed. A significant number of anarchists are pacifists. Anarchists hold to a doctrine that the utopian ideal of anarchy must first be created in the act of self-liberation from oppressive and coercive relationships. You don't blow up the relationship as terrorists do; instead, you convince others that grounds for the existing relationship must be blown up. Anarchism is not really about mad bombing or chaos, as it is often portrayed. Terrorists target people, whereas anarchists target things such as institutions and structures. Bakunin did not want the death of people but the destruction of things and positions of authority. Only small minorities of terrorists have ever been anarchists, and only small minorities of anarchists have ever been terrorists.

In fact, there is an area of study called anarchist criminology, a controversial subfield of critical criminology that celebrates the fact that anarchism really has no workable definition (Tifft, 1979; Ferrell, 1997). Anarchist criminology advocates the abolishment of criminal justice systems. It argues that much harm has been committed in the name of reasonableness, and anarchist criminology is committed to promoting the unthinkable and unreasonable. Like other subfields of critical criminology, anarchist criminology views the state as an inherently oppressive entity, and anarchist justice advocates not only social justice (equal access to all resources), but also the protection of diversity and differences among people (Ferrell, 1999).

The Political Theory of Fascism as a Theory of Terrorism

Fascism is the one form of government with the most disagreement about a definition for it. Passmore (2002) attempts a definition based on two ideas: extreme nationalism and shameless racism. The word "fascism" comes from the Latin *fasces*, which means to use power to scare or impress people. It generally refers to the consolidation of all economic and political power into some form of superpatriotism toward a cult of personality figure and a devotion to endless war with one's enemies. Benito Mussolini, who practically invented the term in 1922, said that fascism is the merger of state and corporate power, but Mussolini's version was based on the idea of an indomitable power and an attempt to resurrect imperial Rome. Adolf Hitler said fascism is the clever and constant application of propaganda so that people can be made to see paradise as hell and the other way around. Hitler's brand of fascism drew upon philosophical reflections by Hegel, Nietzsche, and Spengler, and also drew upon Nordic folk romance from Wagner to Tacitus. Japanese fascism involved racism, fanaticism, historical destiny, and a mixture of Bushido, Zen and Shinto Buddhism, emperor worship, and past samurai legends.

Fascism has close similarities to nativist populism (the favoring of established inhabitants over newcomers) in that both exploit the inherent weaknesses of democracies thru demagoguery (appeal to the lowest common denominator), fearmongering, scapegoating, and manipulation of the masses via promulgation of conspiracies. While both fascism and populism tend to rely upon the twin tactics of calling for immediate action (against perceived security threats) in conjunction with accusing opponents (of disloyalty or worse), it is usually fascism that is most associated with naturally evolving into a dictatorship. This is because almost all forms of fascism try to control the thought, belief, and speech processes of society by shutting down any attempts at reasoned deliberation or discourse.

So-called Islamofascism can be traced to the time period of the birth of Nazi "national socialist" fascism in 1928, when the Muslim Brotherhood, purported parent organization of numerous terrorist groups, was formed in reaction to the 1924 abolition of the caliphate by the Turks. Islamofascism draws heavily upon Muslim Brotherhood pamphleteers, as well as the Koran, the career of Saladin, and the tracts of Nasserites and Baathists. The term "Islamic Fascism" is a better term to use, best describing the agenda of contemporary radical extremists who happen to believe in Islam. Fascism is almost always reactionary. In one sense, it is born out of insecurity and a sense of failure, but in another sense, fascism thrives in a once-proud, humbled but ascendant, people. Envy and false grievance are the trademarks of reactionary movements. Believers hold many kinds of conspiratorial delusions that setbacks were caused by others and can be erased through ever more zealotry. Fascist leaders love conspiracies and lies, and little they say can or should be trusted. Their followers are equally obdurate.

Fascism frequently supports terrorism at home and abroad. Charismatic leaders are usually given supreme powers to crack down on dissidents, peacemakers, and anyone who doesn't abide by the "cult of the individual," which worships a he-man mentality and the party line. With the frequent wars and militaristic ventures that come with fascism, an effort is made to demonize the enemies as subhumans that deserve extinction. These enemies are also made into scapegoats for all a nation's past problems. Fascism appeals to the frustrations and resentments of a race of people who think they ought to have a bigger place at the global table. When combined with an anti-Western slant, fascism becomes a means of social identity (Pan-Africanism, Pan-Arabism, Islamofascism) as well as a facilitator of antiglobalistic terrorism.

Frustrated fascists who fail to gain control in their own countries have historically turned to terrorism. They are quite likely to turn to domestic terrorism or genocide because they do not believe that citizen rights are bestowed merely because someone inhabits a country. In other words, they do not believe that all humans are possessed of equal rights, and they betray their superiority complex in this regard and in the rest of the world as well. "Foreign" families and businesses (as fascists define them) are usually targeted for extermination by fascists. The enemies who are seen as the greatest threat are usually those whom fascists see as corrupting or poisoning family and property relations.

Fascism is full of ironies and contradictions. On the one hand, it is antimodern in its glorification of the land, a return to country life, and its fascination with peasant dress or costume. On the other hand, it is pro-modern in its worship of military technology, favoritism of big business, mass mobilization of people, promotion of commercialized sport, and surprisingly liberal attitude toward the involvement of women in the movement (at the same time supporting a patriarchal "right" kind of role for a woman). Sexual orientations other than heterosexual are looked down upon. Science and scholarship take on interesting twists under fascism. "Hard" sciences such as biology and chemistry usually advance significantly, especially in areas like genetic research and engineering. "Soft" sciences—for example, sociology and psychology—usually become usurped into mumbo-jumbo pseudoscientific talk about a glorified folk culture and reasons for hating the enemy.

Just as anarchists have their May Day (May 1) celebrations, fascists also tend to celebrate anniversaries. Many terrorists, of course, have been known to time their attacks to coincide with the date of a historical event or birthday of someone special to them. For example, with ecoterrorism, that day is October 16, which coincides with United Nations World Food Day, and is usually when fast food restaurants are targeted for vandalism. However, the most important date in the history of terrorism is April 19. A number of significant events happened on that date. Right-wing domestic terrorist groups call it "Militia Day" because it was when the siege at Waco ended, it was when surveillance began at the Ruby Ridge compound in Idaho, and it marks the anniversary of the Oklahoma City bombing of the Murrah Federal Building. Neo-Nazi groups celebrate April 19 because it was the day German Nazis started wiping out Jewish ghettos across Europe, as well as the following day being Adolf Hitler's birthday. Both domestic and international terrorists who herald themselves as "freedom fighters" trace at least part of this justification to the American Revolution, which started on April 19, 1775, at the Battle of Lexington.

The Philosophical Theory of Religion as a Theory of Terrorism

More than one criminologist has pointed out that the disciplines of theology, religion, and philosophy have important things to say about terrorism (Stitt, 2003; Kraemer, 2004). It is also a fact that about a quarter of all terrorist groups and about half of the most dangerous ones on earth are motivated primarily by religious concerns (Hoffman, 1993). They believe that God not only approves of their actions, but that God also demands their actions. Their cause is sacred, consisting of a combined sense of hope for the future and vengeance for the past. Of these two components, the backward-looking desire for vengeance may be the more important trigger for terrorism because the forward-looking component (called apocalyptic thinking or eschatology) produces wild-eyed fanatics who are more a danger to themselves and their own people. The trick to successful use of terrorism in the name of religion rests upon convincing believers that a "neglected duty" exists in the fundamental, mainstream part of the religion. Religious terrorism is therefore not about extremism, fanaticism, sects, or cults, but is instead all about a fundamentalist or militant interpretation of the basic tenets. Most religious traditions are filled with plenty of violent images or implied violence in the core documentaries, and destruction or self-destruction is often a central part of the logic behind religion-based terrorism (Juergensmeyer, 2001). Evil is frequently defined as malignant narcissism from a theological point of view, so a psychopathic leader good at hiding their defects can easily use religion as a moral cover for self-centered purposes (Stitt, 2003). Religions exist to serve the function of absorbing or absolving evil, or at least assuaging guilt in what theologians call theodicy, or the study of how the existence of evil can be reconciled with a good and benevolent God. Most religions theodicize away evil as (1) a test of faith, (2) a product of free will, (3) part of God's plan, or (4) a lesson to let people learn right from wrong. The use and misuse of these theodicies are the most common pathways that religious terrorists follow in the early stages of their behavior (Kraemer, 2004).

To be sure, another usual pattern in religious-based terrorism is the rise of a psychopathic, spiritual leader who is regarded as somewhat eccentric at first (a tendency toward messianism). But then, as this leader develops their charisma, they tend to appear more and more mainstream and scholarly. They begin to mingle political issues with religious issues (a tendency toward theocracy), and little-known religious symbols or pieces of sacred text take on new significance. Quite often, these symbols are claimed to be an important part of that religion's history that has somehow been neglected. The stage is then set for blaming somebody for the betrayal of this sacred heritage. First, the politicians in one's own country are blamed, but soon a foreign influence, such as secularization or modernization, is blamed. Militant religions quickly move to blaming a foreign influence for at least three reasons: (1) it doesn't serve the religion's survival interests to blame a homeland; (2) blaming makes use of a long history of competition, animosity, and war between the world's different religions; and (3) any blaming to be done must occur on the symbolic or cosmic level, which is to say that the enemy cannot have a face, but must be some impersonal, evil-like force or influence. Hence, the most specific enemy a militant religion can have is some global trend such as secularization, modernization, or Westernization. The strength of messianic power is its ability to guarantee a radical change without specifying exactly what this change will look like. However, once a semivague enemy has been identified, the religious movement borrows the idea of "sovereignty" from the political realm, and begins to see itself as the legitimate defender of the faith and the only restorer of dignity to a homeland. Most importantly, such "defenders" justify terrorist action by their accountability only to God, for it is God who has chosen them for this sacred mission in history.

Perhaps the most interesting aspect of religion as a theory of terrorism is how a devout believer could come to mix politics and religion in the ways just described. The answer is in the conception of worship. Most people associate worship with fellowship, dressing up, the ringing of church bells, and communication. But worship is not just about the liturgy of ritual. Worship is part of service to God and all humanity in an attempt to receive instructions from God. Politics is also about service where public service can be conceived of as dedicated listening to a higher public interest. So-called "liberation theology," which permeates much of Latin America, has always had a handle on this aspect of worship as service that is intended to not only satisfy God, but also bring about the emancipation of the poor. Antonio Gramsci (1891–1937), a founder of the Italian Communist Party who is best remembered for the concept of hegemony (Bocock, 1986), or the idea of an all-encompassing worldview, once postulated that the true model of worship was opposition. To engage in any sort of enterprise involving service to God, humanity, or social justice, each group of devout worshippers must transmute their religious culture toward political goals. It is not so much using religion to achieve secular ends but rather the transformation of theology to create "free spaces" that permit creative action consistent with that religion's view on the needed transformation of society. The key theological transformation that supports terrorism, then, is the notion that violence, even though despised, is a form of worship that helps discover the true nature of God, the true nature of peoples' wants and needs, and opens up the possibilities for better communication of instructions to be followed.

Religious terrorism can be quite extreme in its tactics. Not only does it strive to avenge a long history of persecution and injustice, but it also frequently carries out preemptive attacks. This is because a high level of paranoia is usually maintained about the actual degree of threat that the enemy poses. Rarely are religious terrorists swayed by secular sources of information about the degree of actual threat; they are instead driven by doctrinal differences of opinion over interpretations of scriptures and symbols. Religious paranoia evolves in two ways: (1) a rather nonselective targeting pattern, lashing out blindly, often harming innocents; and (2) the creation of offshoot, spin-off, or fringe groups who believe they are commanded to follow a somewhat different mission imperative. Add to this the fact that most adherents have already long felt like alienated and marginal members of society, and you've got a recipe for perhaps the most dangerous and prolific kind of terrorism in the world today.

Many religious terrorist groups can trace their origin to key historical events. Institutional memory is long, as the example of Irish terrorism points out, and it is not uncommon for the group to create rituals designed to "never forget" some long-ago grievance. Religious terrorist campaigns are much longer than straight political terrorist campaigns. Some varieties of religious terrorism have their roots in millenarianism, where the key event is a doomsday or apocalyptic date when something important is supposed to happen. It is known from studies of UFO cults that such groups are often more dangerous after an event fails to happen. This is because of cognitive dissonance, which forces a rearrangement of attitudes and beliefs that are frequently more rigid and fantastic than before. However, political events can also serve as the catalyst for religious terrorism, but far more common are events tied into whatever messianic tradition the religion has (e.g., the return of the prophet Mahdi or the second coming of Christ). Religious terrorists often hold remembrance ceremonies for some "day of infamy," as well as typically having "mourning periods" or dates such as "anniversary of the martyrs." These ceremonial activities are ways to recruit new members who have been standing on the sidelines. Recruitment is then followed by a reeducation program that changes the way a person thinks about good and evil. Anything foreign, secular, or modern without question becomes evil, and anything supporting an all-out, uncompromising struggle against the enemy, including the killing of innocents, becomes good.

The only exceptions are when a group has freed up some nonviolent avenues of experimentation, and nonviolent roles are sometimes provided if an adherent cannot kill.

It is important to understand the practice of martyrdom in the terrorist context. Not only does a martyr serve recruitment and other purposes after their death, but a whole mythology develops around them, which might be called a process of martyrology (Ranstorp, 1996). Targets are chosen not for strategic purposes but for symbolic purposes, and the repercussions of an attack are managed as well. The ideal target is one in which the martyr can inflict more damage than is expected for their size. The idea is to produce an impression that the group is larger and more powerful than it actually is. This feeling of power is enhanced by the use of anonymity, whereby the martyr goes through an indoctrination process through which they are stripped of their real identity and provided with a false background history. The process goes much further than establishing a cover story in case of capture. The process involves changing the martyr's family name and hometown so that any repercussions or reactions to the terrorist event can be channeled toward another family or town. In some cases, the cover story is used to direct government counterterrorism toward the wrong target (especially if the martyr's family is well known and the town is small). In other cases, it is used to give the impression that dozens of martyrs are coming from the same town, when in fact they are not.

In all fairness, it should be said that most militant religious groups adopt terrorism only as a tactic of last resort. The doctrine of just war has not been discussed here, but ethics and/or fair play are integral parts of most religions, and there are sometimes unwritten rules for when the "cosmic struggle"—as Juergensmeyer (2001) calls it—spills over into political struggle. Religious terrorists demonstrate marvelous ingenuity in means, methods, and timing, but their targeting is flawed, and one can easily wonder how strategically effective their "symbolic" success is at times. Sometimes the whole reason for their behavior is to bolster their reputation among competing groups. Copycat or competitive terrorism is not beyond them, and it is supported by the fact that some terrorist acts are scheduled on dates specifically designed to desecrate a competitor's religious holidays and sacred moments.

The Economics Theory of Rational Choice as a Theory of Terrorism

The discipline of economics has many concepts that are relevant to an understanding of terrorism: supply and demand, costs and benefits, and so on. However, fully developed economic or econometric models of terrorism are quite rare, and often involve such things as "psychic" costs and benefits (Nyatepe-Coo, 2004). More down-to-earth economic theories can be found in the literature on deterrence. Rational choice theory, in particular, has found a place in criminology. This theory holds that people will engage in crime after weighing the costs and benefits of their actions to arrive at a rational choice about motivation after perceiving that the chances of gain outweigh any possible punishment or loss. Criminals come to believe that their actions will be beneficial—to themselves, their community, or society—and they come to see that crime pays, or is at least a risk-free way to better their situation. Perhaps the best-known version of this idea in criminology is routine activities theory (Cohen & Felson, 1979), which postulates that three conditions must be present in order for a successful crime to occur: (1) suitable targets or victims who put themselves at risk, (2) the absence of capable guardians or police presence, and (3) motivated offenders among a pool of the unemployed and alienated. Other rational choice theories exist that delve further into models of decision making. In a few models of collective violence that have found their way into criminology, the Olson hypothesis suggests that participants in revolutionary violence predicate their behavior on a rational cost-benefit calculus to pursue the best course of action given their social circumstances.

Rational choice theory in political science follows a similar line. This theory holds that people can be collectively rational, even when making what appear to be irrational decisions as individuals, after perceiving that their participation is important and their personal contribution to the public good outweighs any concerns they may have for the "free rider" problem (Muller & Opp, 1986). For those unfamiliar with it, the free rider problem is a classic paradox in social science and economics that asks why anybody should do something for the public good, when most likely someone else will get credit for it and most everybody else will benefit merely by sitting idly by and doing nothing. Perhaps the most eloquent spokesperson for rational choice ideas in the field of terrorism is Martha Crenshaw (1998), whose writings inform the remarks that immediately follow.

Take, for example, a typical terrorist event that involves hostage taking and the all-too-frequent hostage killing. From an individualist rational point of view, the best choice would be to keep at least some of the hostages alive in order to bargain with the government for leniency. Yet, often a collectivist rational mentality sets in, and the group choice (or groupthink) is to kill all the hostages. Is this killing senseless, the product of deranged minds, or an example of mob behavior? The answer is "no" on all counts from a rational choice point of view. It may be a reasonable and calculated response to circumstances. It may involve a collective judgment about the most efficient course of action that has the most lasting impact on observers (for social learning purposes). And, most importantly, the senselessness of it all may be just what the group needs in order to make their ideological point that they are serious terrorists, not ordinary criminals.

Terrorism, from the rational choice point of view, is not a pathological phenomenon. The resort to terrorism is not an aberration. The central focus of study is on why some groups find terrorism useful, and in standard control theory fashion, why other groups do not find terrorism useful (control theory here referring to a criminological approach that studies self-control or the inhibitions brought on by social control). Some groups may continue to work with established patterns of dissident action. Other groups may resort to terrorism because they have tried other alternatives. Still other groups may choose terrorism as an early choice because they have learned from the experiences of others, usually through the news media. Crenshaw (1998) calls this the contagion effect and claims it has distinctive patterns similar to the copycat effect, found in other theories of collective violence (Gurr, 1970). There may be circumstances in which the terrorist group wants to publicize its cause to the world; a process Crenshaw (1995) calls the globalization of civil war.

Factors that influence the rational choice of terrorism include place, size, time, and the climate of international opinion. A terrorist plot in a democratic society may be less likely to involve senseless violence than would a scheme hatched under an authoritarian regime because under the latter, with the expected repercussions, terrorists realize they have nothing to lose. A small, elite group, typical of those found in authoritarian societies, is more likely to carry out terrorism when the population is quite passive. However, senseless acts of violence can occur in stable societies, in unexpected places and ways in that are timed to capitalize on competition with other groups, manage a tit-for-tat strategy with counterterrorism, or influence the climate of international opinion. Low international opinion, or humiliation, of a terrorist group sometimes causes it to take more sensational action in order to force a repressive counterterrorism reaction, and this tactic plays out best in open, democratic societies. In short, rational choice terrorism often attempts to manage the political agenda on a world stage and is perfectly capable of carrying out large-scale, mass-casualty, spectacular attacks.

The Globalization Theory of Terrorism

Nassar (2004) has probably written the most interesting piece on globalization theory as it relates to terrorism, and although his ideas are fairly critical of the Western world for exporting "nightmares" as well as dreams, he does provide a robust introduction to the complex topic of globalization. Globalization contributes to dreams, fantasies, and rising expectations, but at the same time, it leads to dashed hopes, broken dreams, and unfulfilled goals. Terrorism breeds in the gap between expectations and achievements (an idea that also constitutes a central notion in criminological strain theory). The explanation is also very similar to what is sometimes referred to as rising expectations theory (Davies, 1962). The difference is that most other globalization theories usually add a rich-poor dichotomy. Rich people (or nations) are seen as wanting power and wealth, and poor people (or nations) are seen as wanting justice. The rich people are then seen as one of the root causal factors of terrorism because they contribute to conditions that give rise to it. Perpetrators of "terrorism" (always treated as an ill-defined concept in globalization theory) are never seen as born or raised with any specific predispositions, but just as oppressed and disgruntled poor people who are never given the chance to find any peaceful means for achieving justice.

Globalization theory is further tied into ideas about colonialism, imperialism, and neocolonialism. The first two words are often used interchangeably to describe a set of conditions (technically, extensions of sovereignty) where the mores, values, and beliefs of the colonizers are considered superior to those of the colonized. However, when the assumption is made that egregious displays of power are necessary to maintain superiority, this is the usual meaning of imperialism. Neocolonialism is a concept developed by Marxists and holders of certain conspiracy theories to refer to allegations about First World nations, international organizations, and/or multinational entities employing economic, financial, and trade policies to dominate less powerful countries. Onwudiwe (2001) is typical of the criminological approach when globalization theories are incorporated into dialogue about the causes of terrorism, which is that most terrorist attacks are aimed at the Western world's major powers but take place within the Third World. It is safe to say that globalization approaches remain relatively underdeveloped but may very well evolve into more than explanations of stress on less-fortunate societies.

Sociological and Psychological Theories of Terrorism

Many contemporary sociological perspectives are dominated by approaches that focus upon the social constructions (effects) of fear or shock, and how institutions and processes—especially the media, powerful interest groups, politicians, and primary and secondary groups—help to maintain such constructions. Social constructivism is best understood as a way to look at terrorism from a relativistic standpoint (Gibbs, 1989), and such a standpoint often entails more social critique than theoretical explanation. For instance, social constructivism self-critically looks at the way terrorism can be conceived of as mythology, dialogue, and a form of communication. Social constructivism is all about consequences, not causes, and sometimes the consequence can be a cause or have an amplifying effect, such as when putting a delinquent label on a minor makes their behavior worse. Labeling theory in criminology, for example, is a social constructivist approach that goes about connecting consequences with causes in a way that is, arguably, similar but less systematic than the way sociological functionalists did it a long time ago. Traditional functionalism looks at how the consequences of living under terror affect a society's evolution with regard to values such as achievement, competition, and individualism (O'Connor, 1994). Social constructivism, by contrast, does not seem much concerned about values or evolution, which may quite possibly lead to some confusion between the *effects* of terrorism and the *effectiveness* of terrorism. It is clearly observable, nonetheless, that some societies become "softer" targets after significant terrorist events (usually because of disaster fatigue), and other societies become stronger in the long term (either through reticence or resolve). Effects vary on the basis of common sociological factors such as interaction patterns, social traits such as gender and race, and the stability of the social institutions that people form. Sociologically, terrorism is a synergistic phenomenon with causes that interact with its effects (Ross, 1999).

Many contemporary sociological theories contain strong elements of explanation at the psychological, or micro, level. One is likely to encounter the following, or some variation of them, as the five main sociological theories of terrorism:

- frustration-aggression hypothesis
- relative deprivation hypothesis
- negative identity hypothesis
- narcissistic rage hypothesis
- moral disengagement hypothesis

The frustration-aggression hypothesis is the idea that almost every frustration leads to some form of aggression and that every aggressive act relieves that frustration to some extent. The basic notion is that stress and hassles build up until they reach a point that "breaks the camel's back," and the displacement of released energy provides some benefit in terms of catharsis or ventilation. There are different variants of this model to be found, and many forms of it exist in a variety of criminological thought.

The relative deprivation hypothesis is the idea that as a person goes about choosing their values and interests, they compare what they have and don't have, as well as what they want or don't want, with real or imaginary others. The person then perceives a discrepancy between what is possible for them and what is possible for others, reacting to this discrepancy with anger or an inflamed sense of injustice. Debates exist within criminology regarding relative deprivation and terrorism, on the one hand, with the anomie or strain tradition, which finds causal influence in such objective factors as gross domestic product, and on the other hand, with the left realist tradition, which finds causal influence in subjective experiences of deprivation or discomfort.

The negative identity hypothesis is the idea that, for whatever reason, a person develops a vindictive and covert rejection of the roles and statuses laid out for them by their family, community, or society. For example, a child raised in a well-to-do family may secretly sabotage every effort made to hand them the good life on a "silver platter," deliberately screwing up in school, at work, and everyplace else until the day comes, with some apparent life-altering experience (for example, engaging in terrorism), that the long-nurtured negative identity comes out, and the subject can then make it feel more like a total identity transformation. There are many varieties of this idea that exist in a number of theories across many fields of study.

The narcissistic rage hypothesis is an umbrella idea for all the numerous things that can go wrong in child-rearing, such as too much smothering, too little smothering, ineffective discipline, overly stringent discipline, psychological trauma, coming from a broken home, and so on—all of which leads to the same effect of a "What about me?" reaction in the child. It is actually a two-way process, with the child contributing as much as the parents and other role models. This results in a damaged self-concept, a tendency to blame others for one's inadequacies, and the well-known "splitting" of self into a "good me" and a "bad me," which often forms the basis for personality disorders involving a lack of empathy for the suffering of others. There is not all that much consensus on the primal importance of narcissism, and the literature on child-rearing is full of mixed empirical results.

The moral disengagement hypothesis is the idea that encompasses all the ways a person neutralizes or removes any inhibitions they have about committing acts of horrific violence. Some common patterns include imagining oneself as a hero, portraying oneself as a functionary, minimizing the harm done, dehumanizing the victim, or insulating oneself in routine activities. Organized crime figures, for example, usually hide behind family activities with their wives and children. In the study of terrorism, there are numerous other ways that violence is rationalized that go far beyond denigrating one's enemies and beefing up oneself as a crusader (see Hacker, 1996). Terrorist rationalizations usually involve a complete shift in the way governments and civil society are perceived.

Psychological approaches, with few exceptions (Ross, 1996, 1999), are decidedly clinical in what are often attempts to find something pathological in the terrorist personality. Merari (1990) provides a good overview of psychological approaches, but one of the major names in this area is David Long, former assistant director of the U.S. State Department's Office of the Coordinator for Counterterrorism, who has gone on record saying there's no such thing as a terrorist personality, but then has said they typically suffer from low self-esteem, are attracted to groups with charismatic leaders, and enjoy risk-taking (Long, 1990). A sampling of psychological factors that have been investigated includes ineffective parenting or rebellion against one's parents, a pathological need for absolutism, and a variety of other "syndromes" and hypotheses (see Margolin, 1977), but study after study for the past 30 years has yielded very little valid and reliable information about the abnormal psychology of terrorists other than the following generalizations. As far as we know, most terrorists feel that they are doing nothing wrong when they kill and injure people. They seem to share a feature of the psychological condition known as antisocial personality disorder or psychopathic personality disorder, which is reflected by an absence of empathy for the suffering of others. However, they do not appear unstable or mentally ill for this. A common feature is a type of thinking such as "I am good and right. You are bad and wrong." Their very polarized thinking allows them to distance themselves from opponents and makes it easier for them to kill people. It is not the same kind of simplistic thinking one would expect from someone with low intelligence or moral development. Most terrorists are of above average intelligence and have sophisticated ethical and moral development. A closed-minded certainty is a common feature of terrorist thinking (Merari, 1990).

Although what is not known about the psychology of terrorism exceeds what is known, there have been several promising attempts to merge or combine psychology with sociology (and criminal justice) into what might be called terrorist profiling (Russell & Miller, 1977; Bell, 1982; Galvin, 1983; Strentz, 1988; Hudson, 1999). This line of inquiry has a long history and includes a few rare studies of female terrorists. An early study (Russell & Miller, 1977) found that people who join terrorist organizations tend to have the following characteristics and attributes:

- 22–25 years of age
- 80% male, with women in support roles
- 75% to 80% single
- 66% middle- or upper-class background
- 66% some college or graduate work
- 42% previous participation in working-class advocacy groups
- 17% unemployed
- 18% strong religious beliefs

These data, as well as other known characteristics and attributes of terrorists, have found their way into both public and private databases. One of the best-known databases used by researchers is *The RAND—St. Andrews Chronology of International Terrorism*—but there are also the *International Terrorism: Attributes of Terrorist Events* (*ITERATE*) and *Data on Terrorist Subjects* (*DOTS*) datasets from Vinyard Software and the *Global Terrorism Database (GTD)* at the START Center at the University of Maryland. Theoretical frameworks and/or typologies can be easily developed using any of these databases, although they tend to be heavy on official reports of locational and fatality information. Far less common are interview data, but Merari (1990) represents one of the rare cases of that, having found that most terrorists are between the ages of 16 and 28, male (but 15% female), and often have university degrees and wealthy families. Databases do not normally provide enough information about items like strength of religious belief, so like with other indicators a profiler would be interested in, biographical or anecdotal information is relied upon.

Criminology is heavily informed by sociology and psychology. What sociological and psychological approaches basically tell us is that individuals join terrorist organizations in order to commit acts of terrorism and that this process is the same as when individuals come to belong to criminal subcultures in committing acts of crime. There appears to be no unique terrorist personality, and there are a multitude of pathways. There does appear to be unique socio-psychological phenomena that develop, support, and/or enhance a penchant for cold-blooded, calculated violence that, if not satisfied within a terrorist organization, might be fulfilled someplace else. Terrorism is a social activity. Individuals join a terrorist group usually after they have tried other forms of involvement and activities. It may be that what separates them from ordinary criminals is their higher level of willingness to engage in risk-taking. Their cognitive and emotional commitments to their ideology appear to become stronger when living underground and when facing adversity in the form of counterterrorism. Socialization in an underground context is interesting as it may be far more common than the presumed self-radicalization that goes on with lone wolves. The criminologist Ferracuti (1982) has documented the "fantasy wars" that go on in the terrorist underground. An individual's identity may become tied to the group's identity, but it is just as likely that emotional relationships become as important as (if not more important than) the group's purpose. This means that the distribution of beliefs among members in a terrorist group may be uneven. There may be major differences between individual and group ideology. Ideology may not necessarily be the main component of motivation. From profiling terrorists for many years, it is believed that most of them are action-hungry practitioners, not theoreticians. This knowledge may provide new counterterrorism strategies that attempt to change individual beliefs and weaken group cohesion.

Psychiatric Theories of Mental Illness as a Theory of Terrorism

The leading exponent of the terrorist-as-mentally-ill approach is Jerrold Post (1984, 1990), who has gone on record saying that the most dangerous terrorist is likely to be a religious terrorist, but all terrorists suffer from negative childhood experiences and a damaged sense of self. His analysis of the terrorist "mind-set" (a word that substitutes for terrorist personality, but technically means a fixed attitude or inclination) draws upon a view of mental illness that compels, or forces, people to commit horrible acts. It should be noted that the field of criminal justice holds that this is not the only possible view on mental illness. More "crazy" people come into contact with the law through sheer folly and foolishness than because of a compulsion. Post (1990) makes a somewhat neo-Freudian distinction between terrorists who desire to "destroy the world of their fathers" and those who desire to "carry on the world of their fathers." In short, it boils down to an Oedipus complex, which includes hating your father, or at least the "world" he represents. There is actually some empirical support for this viewpoint. For example, when lone wolf offenders are studied, such as skyjackers, mail bombers, and school shooters, a severely dysfunctional relationship with their father is frequently found (Eskey, O'Connor, Rush & Schmalleger, 2015). The "anarchic-ideologue" terrorist, according to Post (1984), is the one who rebels most against their father, and according to Kaplan (1981), has a pathological need to pursue absolute ends because of their damaged sense of self-worth. For a review of this line of thinking, see Ruby (2002), but it should be pointed out that unbearable depression due to a diminished self-worth is not by itself a cause of terrorism. Nor are anger and hate mental illnesses, and one needs to be careful not to stigmatize the mentally ill with any terrorism label.

A different kind of analysis is provided by Jessica Stern (1999), who attempted to gain psychological insight into the distinction between "doomsday" terrorists, who would use WMD that might end all life on earth, and "dangerous" terrorists, who would limit themselves to the conventional arsenal of terrorism. Stern's concern is primarily with the proliferation of WMD, and cases studies of groups such as Aum Shinrikyo, the Tamil Tigers, Al-Qaeda, and Hezbollah show that terrorists most likely to use WMD tend to be afflicted with paranoia and megalomania. Of these two illnesses, megalomania is more severe, and paranoia is at such a moderate level that it enhances intelligence and keeps people from developing full-blown schizophrenia or sociopathy. Stern (1999) takes exception with arguments that terrorists suffer from any antisocial, psychopathic, or sociopathic disorder. Likewise, Victoroff (2005) says that even though there is no way to measure a terrorist's mental health, it might be promising to measure their sense of oppression and feeling of subjugation, but one would have to account for the deep levels of fervor, hatred, bravado, and other psychodynamic pressures at work.

Walter Laqueur (1999) has offered the idea that the need exists to distinguish between terrorists who are "fanatics" and those who are "extremists." The standard meaning of these terms is that fanatics are religious zealots and extremists are political zealots, but Laqueur (1999) strips away any religious connotation and says that most terrorists are fanatics. The concept of fanaticism carries some implications of mental illness but is not in itself a diagnostic category. Laqueur (1999) claims that fanaticism is characterized by excessive cruelty and sadism, and Taylor (1991) has pointed out that fanaticism is characterized by the following:

- prejudice toward out-groups
- authoritarianism
- an unwillingness to compromise
- a disdain for other alternative views
- a tendency to see things in black and white
- a rigidity of belief
- a perception of the world that reflects a closed mind

To this, one might add the concept of Machiavellianism (Oots & Wiegele, 1985), which refers to an extreme form of the psychological trait of manipulativeness. Terrorists are disposed to manipulate not only their victims, but also their audience. Both the timing of an event and the aftermath of an event are manipulated by terrorists. For example, the counterterrorism reaction by authorities is manipulated. The press and public are manipulated, with terrorists doing everything they can to work the media and obtain liberal press coverage. The fact that terrorism is aimed more at the audience than at the victim has provided numerous points of conjecture for criminologists. It has been the starting point for labeling and constructivist approaches. It has been the source of many theoretical models of terrorist contagion, whereby different terrorist groups compete with one another for media attention, as well as many theoretical models of copycat behavior, whereby different terrorist groups try to outdo a previous group with the harm inflicted. What is not widely known is that the almost addictive, or at least cyclic, quality of a need to manipulate audience reaction tends to go hand-in-hand with biological or physiological cycles for attention-seeking.

Biological and Physiological Theories of Terrorism

David Hubbard (1983) was one of the first biological researchers of terrorism, and his line of work is similar to the familiar cycle of violence hypothesis in criminal justice. In this view, people who commit repetitive and cyclical acts of violence (which would include wife beaters, rapists, and serial killers) are driven by hormonal or neurochemical fluctuations in their body or brain chemistry. Three compounds, in particular, have been singled out as having abnormal levels among terrorists: norepinephrine, acetylcholine, and endorphins. Of these, norepinephrine is suspected as being the most influential because it is associated with the so-called "flight or fight" mechanism in human biology. The theory of fight or flight was developed by W. B. Cannon back in 1929, and refers to a state of arousal under stress in which the heart, lungs, and muscles operate more efficiently. As it applies to terrorism and crime, the behavioral requirements of such activities (fighting exhilaration before an event or fleeing poorly done manipulation of an audience) produce a syndrome of physiological need for arousal at fairly regular intervals. Motives for terrorism appear and reappear when the biological viewpoint is considered, and it is somewhat easy to link a variety of psychological aspects in a terrorist profile with biological factors. For example, xenophobia may be biologically induced because the fear of strangers tends to be discernible even at infantile stages of development. Other explanations might involve insights from sociobiology (Wilson, 1975) or kin selection theory in evolutionary psychology (Daly & Wilson, 1994). Year after year, more and more criminological books are beginning to cover biological factors, but this approach remains nascent for the most part.

Traditional Criminological Theories Applied to Terrorism

It's not easy to apply traditional criminological theories to terrorism. Most of the theories were designed to explain ordinary street crime such as robbery or burglary and have a certain hardiness to their perspectives that makes them difficult to extend. Ruggiero (2005) is typical of those who have attempted to apply or extend such theories, starting with Durkheim's functionalism by asking whether Durkheim would see terrorism as part of the "normality of crime" or as an unacceptable, dysfunctional form of crime. On the one hand, Durkheim said that all crime serves positive functions (of innovation and evolution), but on the other hand, the organic metaphor that Durkheim used seems to suggest that some forms of crime only cause disintegration and are cancerous. The Chicago school of disorganization in criminology would presumably focus on the distinctiveness of different social worlds between terrorists and nonterrorists, analyzing the fractures or blockages in communication of symbolically important language, for example. Strain theorists would likely argue that terrorism is inevitable as a manifestation of the broken promise that everybody can rise from rags to riches, and they would study the adaptations Merton described as innovation or rebellion. Learning theorists would likely emphasize the importance of role models, friends, acquaintances, or the "techniques of neutralization" involved with the drift into a terrorist lifestyle. Labeling theorists would probably say, cynically but truly, that terrorism is "what the other person does." Control theorists would likely focus on terrorists being unattached, unloved, uncommitted to education or business, uninvolved in conventional tasks, and having their hands so idle that time becomes the "devil's playground" for them. Conflict theorists would probably focus on the presence or absence of associations that provide room for collective action and permanent confrontation, although more radical versions of conflict theory might glamorize terrorism as proto-revolutionary action. Integrated theories would likely focus on the influences of aggressive proneness, provocation, and the support of third parties. If one were forced to name the one, single, "master concept" in all of criminology, it might be best to go with general theory's idea of impulsivity (Gottfredson & Hirschi, 1990) as the many formulations of this trait explain all kinds of crime at all times.

Theories Unique to Domestic Terrorism

Freilich (2003) does a good job of reviewing the theories in this category, which is a relatively small area of research that tends to be studied within a field called the sociology of social movements. There are mainly three groups of theories. The first, called economic/ social integration theory, holds that high concentrations of farming, economic depression, and social disorganization are all related to high levels of domestic terrorist activity, militia movements in particular. In some varieties, it tends to be a kind of "farm crisis" or "agrarian reform" theory frequently used by those who study underdeveloped nations or rural crime. The second theory is called resource mobilization theory, which suggests that states that are more prosperous and socially integrated tend to develop more domestic terrorist activity, on the basis that group competition for power and resources is more intense. Cultural theories, the third group of theories, propose that experiences of greater cultural diversity and female empowerment, along with increasing paramilitarism, are likely to develop greater levels of domestic terrorist activity. In terms of research findings, more empirical support seems to exist for the third group of theories, at least according to Freilich (2003), although resource mobilization theory tends to dominate the theoretical literature. See Jenkins (1983) for the many resources studied, including money, organizational facilities, manpower, means of communication, legitimacy, loyalty, authority, moral commitment, and solidarity. In general, there is more empirical support for the idea that domestic terrorism more often plagues richer and affluent nations than it does poor ones.

Briefly, resource mobilization theory describes the process by which a group assembles material or nonmaterial resources and places them under control for the explicit purpose of pursuing a group's interests through collective action. Collecting resources must be accompanied by mobilization of resources. A group may prosper, yet still not contend for power. Four central factors condition the process of mobilization: organization, leadership, political opportunity, and the nature of political institutions. Strong horizontal links between members of a group provide the best organizational structure. Leaders who make themselves available to members and take an interest in members' grievances tend to make the best leaders. Political opportunities refer to moments when the "time is ripe" for action, and groups that seize upon such opportunities tend to succeed. Political institutions refer to moments when dominant political parties are weak or fractured, and these are the times when domestic terrorist groups will succeed by taking action.

Cultural theories are less about cultural conflict (e.g., they hate us for our values and ideas) and more about emotional reactions to the practical problem of finding a meaningful identity in a diverse world that seems too relativistic, diffuse, and aimless. Both terrorism and reactions to terrorism are studied, but the methods are narrative, not empirical. A central concept is power, presumably to bring about or restore a feeling of timelessness and normality such as how people took things for granted back in the "good old days." McAllister & Schmid (2011) categorize cultural theories among the causes of insurgent terrorism, which are multi-layered movements designed to overwhelm a ruling order via a variety of subversive means besides terrorist attacks.

Conclusion

Although the theoretical landscape explored by criminologists may seem vast and extensive, the fact of the matter is that much of it is speculative and only in the beginning stages of model development. Clearly, there are difficulties in pinpointing the key causal variables, and much of this is due to the nature of criminology itself borrowing from different disciplines, so much so that competitive explanations run the risk of canceling one another out. For example, it may be that labeling and constructivist explanations that focus upon identity salience (Arena & Arrigo, 2006) offer a better way to address the cyclic nature of terrorist behavior than do psychological or biological explanations. Sociological theories that avoid psychological reductionism tend to be heavily favored, and there are those (Horgan, 2003) who strongly protest the absurdity of searching for the so-called terrorist personality. One may at least take comfort in criminology's provision of multiple frameworks enabling researchers room to explore and triangulate their efforts. Theory-driven research is better than dredging around in the data, hoping for an idea to pop up. The criminology of terrorism may also provide tentative implications and applications for the law enforcement, military, and intelligence communities. Theoretical work can contribute not only to a more informed accounting and understanding of terrorism, but it can also assist in policy formation by forestalling a tendency to reinvent the wheel whenever the next disastrous and perplexing incident takes place.

REFERENCES

Arena, M. & Arrigo, B. (2006). *The terrorist identity*. New York: New York University Press.

Bell, B. (1982). "Psychology of leaders of terrorist groups." *International Journal of Group Tensions* 12: 84–104.

Bocock, R. (1986). *Hegemony*. London: Tavistock.

Cohen, L. & Felson, M. (1979). "Social change and crime rate trends: A routine activities approach." *American Sociological Review* 44: 588–608.

Crenshaw, M. (Ed.) (1995). *Terrorism in context*. University Park: Pennsylvania State University Press.

Crenshaw, M. (1998). "The logic of terrorism: Terrorist behavior as a product of strategic choice." In W. Reich (Ed.), *Origins of terrorism*. New York: Woodrow Wilson Center Press.

Daly, M. & Wilson, M. (1994). "The evolutionary psychology of male violence." In J. Archer (Ed.), *Male violence* (pp. 253–288). London: Routledge Kegan Paul.

Davies, J. (1962). "Towards a theory of revolution." *American Sociological Review* 27: 5–18.

Eskey, M., O'Connor, T., Rush, J. & Schmalleger, F. (2015). "Mass killings: What we know and where do we go." *Journal of Social Sciences and Humanities* 1(5): 528–539.

Ferracuti, F. (1982). "A sociopsychiatric interpretation of terrorism." *Annals of the American Academy of Political and Social Science* 463: 129–141.

Ferrell, J. (1997). "Against the law: Anarchist criminology." In B. MacLean & D. Milovanovic (Eds.), *Thinking critically about crime*. Richmond, BC: Collective Press.

Ferrell, J. (1999). "Anarchist criminology and social justice." In B. Arrigo (Ed.), *Social justice/criminal justice* (pp. 91–108). Belmont, CA: Wadsworth.

Freilich, J. (2003). *American militias: State-level variations in militia activities*. New York: LFB Press.

Galvin, D. (1983). "The female terrorist: A socio-psychological perspective." *Behavioral Sciences and the Law* 1: 19–32.

Georges-Abeyie, D. & Hass, L. (1982). "Propaganda by deed: Defining terrorism." *Justice Reporter* 2: 1–7.

Gibbs, J. (1989). "Conceptualizations of terrorism." *American Sociological Review* 53(4): 329–340.

Gottfredson, M. & Hirschi, T. (1990). *A general theory of crime.* Stanford: Stanford University Press.

Gurr, T. (1970). *Why men rebel.* Princeton, NJ: Princeton University Press.

Hacker, F. (1996). *Crusaders, criminals, crazies: Terror and terrorists in our time.* New York: Norton.

Hoffman, B. (1993). *Holy terror.* Santa Monica, CA: Rand.

Horgan, J. (2003). "The search for the terrorist personality." In A. Silke (Ed.), *Terrorists, victims, and society* (pp. 3–27). West Sussex, UK: Wiley.

Hubbard, D. (1983). "The psychodynamics of terrorism." In Y. Alexander et al. (Eds.), *International violence* (pp. 45–53). New York: Praeger.

Hudson, R. (1999). *Who becomes a terrorist and why.* Guilford, CT: Lyons Press.

Jenkins, J. (1983). "Resource mobilization theory and the study of social movements." *Annual Review of Sociology* 9: 527–553.

Juergensmeyer, M. (2001). *Terror in the mind of God: The global rise of religious violence.* Berkeley: University of California Press.

Kaplan, A. (1981). "The psychodynamics of terrorism." In Y. Alexander & J. Gleason (Eds.), *Behavioral and quantitative perspectives on terrorism* (pp. 35–50). New York: Pergamon.

Kraemer, E. (2004). "A philosopher looks at terrorism." In A. Nyatepe-Coo & D. Zeisler-Vralsted (Eds.), *Understanding terrorism* (pp. 113–131). Upper Saddle River, NJ: Prentice Hall.

Kushner, H. (2003). *Encyclopedia of terrorism.* Thousand Oaks, CA: Sage.

Laqueur, W. (1999). *The new terrorism.* New York: Oxford University Press.

Long, D. (1990). *The anatomy of terrorism.* New York: Free Press.

Margolin, J. (1977). "Psychological perspectives in terrorism." In Y. Alexander & S. Finger (Eds.), *Terrorism: Interdisciplinary perspectives.* New York: John Jay Press.

McAllister, B. & Schmid, A. (2011). "Theories of terrorism." In A. Schmid (Ed.), *The Routledge handbook of terrorism research* (pp. 201–271). New York: Routledge.

Merari, A. (1990). "The readiness to kill and die: Suicidal terrorism in the Middle East." In W. Reich (Ed.), *Origins of terrorism.* Cambridge, UK: Cambridge University Press.

Muller, E. & Opp, K. (1986). "Rational choice and rebellious collective action." *American Political Science Review* 80: 471–487.

Nassar, J. (2004). *Globalization and terrorism.* Lanham, MD: Rowman & Littlefield.

Nyatepe-Coo, A. (2004). "Economic implications of terrorism." In A. Nyatepe-Coo & D. Zeisler-Vralsted (Eds.), *Understanding terrorism* (pp. 77–89). Upper Saddle River, NJ: Prentice Hall.

O'Connor, T. (1994). "A neofunctional model of crime and crime control." In G. Barak (Ed.), *Varieties of criminology* (pp. 143–158). Westport, CT: Greenwood Press.

Onwudiwe, I. (2001). *The globalization of terrorism.* Andershort, Hampshire: Ashgate Press. The location is Hampshire.

Oots, K. & Wiegele, T. (1985). "Terrorist and victim: Psychiatric and physiological approaches." *Terrorism: An International Journal* 8(1): 1–32.

Passmore, K. (2002). *Fascism: A very short introduction.* New York: Oxford University Press.

Post, J. (1984). "Notes on a psychodynamic theory of terrorist behavior." *Terrorism: An International Journal* 7: 241–256.

Post, J. (1990). "Terrorist psycho-logic: Terrorist behavior as a product of psychological forces." In W. Reich (Ed.), *Origins of terrorism* (pp. 25–40). Cambridge, UK: Cambridge University Press.

Purkis, J. & Bowen, J. (Eds.) (1997). *Twenty-first century anarchism*. London: Cassell.

Ranstorp, M. (1996). "Terrorism in the name of religion." In R. Howard & R. Sawyer (Eds.), *Terrorism and Counterterrorism* (pp. 121–136). Guilford, CT: McGraw-Hill.

Ross, J. (1996). "A model of the psychological causes of oppositional political terrorism." *Peace and Conflict: Journal of Peace Psychology* 2: 2–11. It's volume 2. My search brought us Vol. 2(2), pp. 129–141.

Ross, J. (1999). "Beyond the conceptualization of terrorism: A psychological-structural model." In C. Summers & E. Mardusen (Eds.), *Collective violence*. New York: Rowen & Littlefield.

Ruby, C. (2002). "Are terrorists mentally deranged?" *Analyses of Social Issues and Public Policy* 2(1): 15–26.

Ruggiero, V. (2005). "Political violence: A criminological analysis." In M. Natarajan (Ed.), *Introduction to international criminal justice* (pp. 35–41). New York: McGraw-Hill.

Russell, C. & Miller, B. (1977). "Profile of a terrorist." *Terrorism: An International Journal* 1(1): 17–34.

Smith, B. (1994). *Pipe bombs and pipe dreams: Terrorism in America*. Albany: State University of New York Press.

Smith, B., Damphousse, K., Jackson, F. & Karlson, A. (2002). "The prosecution and punishment of international terrorists in federal court: 1980–1999." *Criminology and Public Policy* 1(3): 311–338.

Stern, J. (1999). *The ultimate terrorists*. Cambridge, MA: Harvard University Press.

Stitt, G. (2003). "The understanding of evil: A joint quest for criminology and theology." In R. Chairs & B. Chilton (Eds.), *Star Trek visions of law & justice* (pp. 203–218). Dallas, TX: Adios Press.

Strentz, T. (1988). "A terrorist psychological profile." *FBI Law Enforcement Bulletin* 57: 11–18.

Taylor, M. (1991). *The fanatics*. London: Brassey's.

Tifft, L. (1979). "The coming redefinition of crime: An anarchist perspective." *Social Problems* 26: 392–402.

Victoroff, J. (2005). "The mind of a terrorist: A review and critique of psychological approaches." *Journal of Conflict Resolution* 49(1): 3–43.

Wilson, E. (1975). *Sociobiology: The new synthesis*. Cambridge, MA: Harvard University Press.

Chapter 2

Right-Wing Domestic Terrorism

Kevin Borgeson

Overview

- Socioeconomics
- Age
- Gender
- Geography
- Social influences

Past research on right-wing domestic terrorists has focused on the violent nature of the group (Flynn & Gerhardt, 1989; Hamm, 2001; Ridgeway, 1995) without providing an in-depth look at the characteristics of members who make up such groups. For example, sociologist Mark Hamm (2001) studied the Aryan Republican Army, a splinter group of the Aryan Nations, and discussed how this group committed bank robberies in order to finance domestic terrorist acts for future groups of the radical right-wing movement known as Christian Identity (see chapter 4 on Christian Identity for further insight). Most of Hamm's (2001) analysis framed members as domestic terrorists, focusing on the violent nature of these individuals, without placing them into a larger framework of all Aryan Nations members.

James Ridgeway's (1995) book, *Blood in the Face*, examined the historical beginnings of the Aryan Nations in Idaho. However, the main focus of his analysis centers on a string of Brink's truck robberies, committed by a group who called themselves The Order. The Order was founded by Robert Mathews and consisted of white supremacists that believed that the Northwest section of the United States should secede from the nation and become a territory for only whites. Although the individuals who committed the crimes met in Idaho at the compound of Richard Butler, the founder of the Aryan Nations and a prominent member in Christian Identity, most did not share the beliefs of Christian Identity. Although these acts of violence occurred, they were committed by splinter offshoots from the main group of Aryan Nations, and as such, may not accurately reflect the beliefs and practices of the parent group.

Aho (1990), in the *Politics of Righteousness*, focused on cultural elements of Christian Identity members and discussed the demographic characteristics that were influential in bringing people to Christian Identity. These beliefs are based on the writings and teaching of Richard Butler. Aho's

TABLE 2.1 | General Demographics of Right-Wing Domestic Terrorists, 1994–2016

	1994	2006	2016
Age	39	39.3	38
Gender	93% Male	87% Male	87% Male
	7% Female	13% Female	13% Female
Race	97% White	100% White	100% White
	3% Native American		
Occupation	Unemployed	Manual Labor	Manual Labor
Residence	Rural	Rural	Rural
Ideology	Christian Identity	Odinism	Christianity
		Christian Identity	Anti-Muslim

Source: Smith (1994), Borgeson and Valeri (2006), and Valeri and Borgeson (2018)

(1990) book—because of its focus on the social correlates that may influence people to become part of this movement and its discussion of the political movements of those who join—makes significant contributions to understanding cultural elements of the group. However, the focus of his book is on Christian Identity, and he does not explore the demographic characteristics of the larger membership of those who would be attracted to such a group.

Hamm (2001), Ridgeway (1995), and Aho (1990) each present a partial view of those who join hate groups. Hamm and Ridgeway, by focusing on the violent individuals and violent acts, paint a picture of all hate group members as domestic terrorists who support an explicitly violent ideology. Aho, although he explores cultural elements, focuses specifically on the elements of religion rather than hate groups as a whole. Because of the limited perspective, each author presents a picture of right-wing domestic terrorists as a homogenous group whose members have similar backgrounds and motivations (see Table 2.1).

The purpose of this chapter is not to deny the social construct of hate group members as domestic terrorists—there is, after all, an element of truth to this. Some people join hate groups for the purpose of engaging in violence. However, there are several other reasons why people join such groups. This chapter explores the variability of backgrounds and beliefs of those people. Using interviews with Aryan Nations and militia members, the demographic characteristics of these groups are examined in an effort to better understand and predict why people join them.

Past and Current Demographic Characteristics

SOCIOECONOMICS

As shown in Table 2.2, the social class in which right-wing hate groups were raised has stayed roughly the same. In 2006, approximately 78.3% of those came from a working class background, and in 2016, the percentage went down slightly to 75%. There was a bit of a shift in those raised

TABLE 2.2 | Social Class of Right-Wing Domestic Terrorists, 2006–2016

	2006	2016
Working	78.3%	75%
Middle	17.4%	25%
Upper	4.3%	0%

Source: Borgeson and Valeri (2006) and Valeri and Borgeson (2018)

TABLE 2.3 | Occupation of Right-Wing Domestic Terrorists, 2006–2016

	2006	2016
White Collar	9%	15%
Manual Labor	52%	50%
Unemployed	26%	20%
Own Business	4%	15%
Social Security Disability Insurance	9%	0%

Source: Borgeson and Valeri (2006) and Valeri and Borgeson (2018)

in middle and upper class backgrounds. In 2006, 17.4% came from a middle class upbringing, and in 2016, the percentage rose 8 points to 25% from this section. Upper class changed with 4.3% claiming to come from this class, and in 2016, it dropped to 0%.

According to Borgeson and Valeri (2006), a surprising 30% of those in their sample came from the military. However, none of those interviewed by them were career military. Similar results were found in Valeri and Borgeson's (2018) study. It is during military service time that the majority of those interviewed stated that they began to develop distrust for the government. This eventually led some members to join radical right-wing groups. Roughly the same percentage in 2016 claimed to have some military background. This percentage did not go up much over the 10-year span even though more militia members were part of the participants in the interviews than in 2006. What did change was the attitude of those they "see as the enemy." More members in 2016 see Islam as a threat to society than in 2006, and therefore, their experience not only "taught them" that Jews "were the enemy," but also that "Islam is a threat" since most of them were deployed at some point in the Middle East.

Specifically, it was in the military that other members "saw that the government was run by Jews." Some of those interviewed reported that it was because of their belief in a "Jewish conspiracy" or "Jewish control of the government" that they began their quest for the answer to the question, "Why are there so many Jews in high places?" Eventually, they found their answers by joining such groups as the KKK, Aryan Nations, and the militia.

As shown in Table 2.3, the occupational demographics of the group members are similar to those of their parents for the decade spanning 2006 to 2016. Half of those who joined in 2006 tended to have manual labor jobs. In comparison, in 2016, there was a decrease of 2%, which can be accounted for by the increase of those who started their own business. Less than 10% in 2006 reported working in a white collar profession. In 2016, those in white collar professions increased by 6% to constitute 15% of those involved in the study. Part of this increase is probably due to those who are sympathizers to those in the alt-right movement; these members generally have higher computer and educational skills and would come from this occupational category. Having a high percentage of members in both 2006 and 2016 coming from a working class background is consistent with membership in other movements (e.g., skinheads; see Borgeson & Valeri, 2017) and is also consistent with Smith's (1994) findings that only 12% of right-wing terrorists had college or university degrees and one-third had not completed high school.

One major change in the statistics from 2006 to 2016 was the shift in those who were unemployed, owned a business, or were on Social Security Disability Insurance (SSDI). As Table 2.3 shows, in 2006, 26% of members were unemployed. In 2016, this statistic dropped 6 points to 20%. Also, the table shows that in the comparison of these characteristics over 10 years, those on SSDI went from 9% in 2006 to 0% in 2016. This high rate of unemployment and collecting unemployment contradicts the work ethic that is part of the movement and runs counter to the philosophy of some of the past and former leaders of the white supremacy movement, particularly those of Richard Butler, the founder of the Aryan Nations. Butler stated that—because the Aryan Nations does not support the way the government is run—the group members should not be reliant on the government for assistance (Alibrandi & Wassmuth, 1999; Ezekiel, 1996). Given that some hate group members believe that "the Jews run the government," then, by taking money from the government, these members are essentially being supported by the people they vilify.

In 2006, only 4% owned their own business compared to 2016, where 15% owned a business.

AGE

In the data by Valeri and Borgeson (2018), the age distribution has a slant toward members being relatively middle aged (see Table 2.4). Valeri and Borgeson's data (2018) show that only 10% fall within the ages 18–24, 60% within the 25–40 cohort, and 30% over the age of 40. This research shows that most members (90%) are middle aged and that the group does not attract those of younger age cohorts.

Previous research has suggested that some hate groups appeal predominately to young males (cf. Blee, 1996; Blee, 2002; Hamm, 1995; Smith, 1994; Borgeson & Valeri, 2006). Whereas past research has been correct in surmising that youths are attracted to the violence, symbols, and hate rock of such groups as skinheads (Valeri & Borgeson, 2018), these findings do not apply to individuals who are attracted to such hate groups as the KKK, Aryan Nations, and militia. Ideology and recruitment for these groups are not based on hate rock, which, as Mark Hamm (1995) has shown, is the strongest predictor for youth joining this subculture. Instead, the members in both the 2006 and 2016 cohort place emphasis on justifying hatred through religion, specifically the biblical teachings of a radical religion called Christian Identity (see chapter 4 in this book for further analysis). Christian Identity teaches its followers that Jews are offspring of the devil, and that their sole purpose on the earth is to destroy Judeo-Christianity and take over the world by controlling the major social institutions in the United States (see Barkum, 1996). More recently, they assert, a greater threat to the existence of Judeo-Christianity has been the rise of Islam in America and the protection of Islamic religious rights by advocacy groups. Adherents to this line of thinking believe that Islam will eventually have more rights than Judeo-Christianity in the United States and

TABLE 2.4 | Age of Right-Wing Domestic Terrorists, 2006–2016

	2006	2016
18–24	NA	10%
25–40	NA	60%
40+	NA	30%

Source: Borgeson and Valeri (2006) and Valeri and Borgeson (2018)

that they need to react violently to this threat to "wipe out the evil hordes" of Muslims who they believe want to make Islam the dominant religion in America. Recent events, such as advocacy groups trying to get a mosque built near the World Trade Center, have only strengthened their anti-Muslim attitudes by reinforcing the belief that the government is plotting against Christian Americans and giving more rights to the religion that they believe "sparked the war on America" during the September 11th terrorist attacks in 2001.

Religion in the general public is practiced more by older generations of adults than those of younger cohorts. Thus, it would make sense that older members of hate groups would use religious justification for their hatred. Younger generations have been shown to have a loose structure with religious beliefs (Valeri & Borgeson, 2018), and they do not adhere to a religious doctrine as their justification for hatred. Some of the younger members are attracted to violence and enjoy the increased sense of worth they get from joining movements such as the skinheads. Some of this youth cohort also uses ideology like Odinism—a religion based on Norse gods—to justify their hatred toward blacks and other minority groups. Since religion is a large part of the movement and it is attractive to older adults, it is not surprising that the average age of 39 has stayed the same over the years.

GENDER

Past research suggests that hate group members are predominately male (see Blee, 2002; Hamm, 1995; Smith, 1994; Borgeson & Valeri, 2006). Consistent with this research, 87% of the individuals who were a part of this 2016 cohort were male, and 13% female. This figure is higher than reported by Smith (1994) but the same as those reported by Borgeson and Valeri in 2006 (see Table 2.5). However, the difference in the 2016 and 2006 cohorts may result from the fact that Smith's sample was limited to individuals who had been indicted, whereas the 2006 and 2016 data were based on individuals who had current involvement in the radical right movement. The small percentage in Smith's (1994) study, Borgeson and Valeri (2006), and the 2016 data used for this chapter is due to the patriarchal nature of the groups. Women play a small role within the movement and are sometimes excluded from attending meetings. As Borgeson and Valeri (2006) demonstrated, Aryan Nations members believe that women should dress in traditional, conservative fashions. Women who have an active role within the organization had a tendency to fulfill stereotypical, supportive functions such as cooking or running women's groups, which Borgeson and Valeri (2006) show was symbolic since these groups had no members. Most members, both in

TABLE 2.5 | Gender of Right-Wing Domestic Terrorists, 2006–2016

	2006	2016
Male	87%	87%
Female	13%	13%

Source: Borgeson and Valeri (2006) and Valeri and Borgeson (2018)

2006 and in 2016, feel that a women's role is to stay home, care for the children, and tend to her "husband" or "boyfriend." One participant in the Borgeson and Valeri (2006: 7) study stated: "I don't believe that women should be in the work force. The Bible states that women are the caretakers of the family. I think that women should concentrate on having as many babies as possible so the white race does not become extinct."

Another reason that women play a small role in radical right groups is correlated with the groups' focus on weapons and violence. Valeri and Borgeson (2018) show that in both organized groups like the KKK and Aryan Nations and loose-structured groups like skinheads, roughly 85% of each group is comprised of males and 15% of females. This figure is not that far off from Borgeson and Valeri (2006) and Valeri and Borgeson's (2018) studies on hate groups. Valeri and Borgeson (2018) point out that one of the reasons women are not attracted to joining the ranks of these groups is that they spend a large amount of time preparing for the racial holy war (RAHOWA). This claim is not a draw for women. This is also true of the general population. Currently, only 70% of men and 30% of women are among the military ranks (Statista Brain, 2017; Valeri & Borgeson, 2018). Valeri and Borgeson (2018) point out that women in the general population (as well as women in the radical right movement) do not join the movement for "patriotic or nationalistic" reasons. Borgeson and Valeri also point out that women in the general population join the ranks of the military for financial and health benefits. None of these benefits that women strive for are provided for by the "war" looking to "secure racial dominance."

Very many in the radical right are not married, nor do they have a partner with whom to share their daily life. It has been shown by some researchers that this lack of connection with a significant other can lead to isolation, depression, and frustration (Valeri & Borgeson, 2018). This frustration that people feel in society needs a safety valve to release the tension. When no normal safety valve is available, some turn to the "guidance" of radical right groups to find out "the real causes to why the world, and their life" is such a mess. While most do not turn to hate groups for answers, those who do usually have authoritarian-type personalities, or they join because this type of group increases their self-worth, allowing them to finally feel accepted and successful at something.

GEOGRAPHY

Whereas most past research on hate groups such as the Aryan Nations, KKK, and skinheads focuses on the psychology and sociology of these groups, little research has examined the geography or the geographic location of why they locate in a specific spot. In the past, hate groups were

TABLE 2.6 | Geography of Right-Wing Domestic Terrorists, 2006–2016

	2006	2016
Rural	54%	20%
Suburban	33%	60%
Urban	13%	20%

Source: Borgeson and Valeri (2006) and Valeri and Borgeson (2018)

concentrated in the South, and for that reason, these groups tended to be viewed as a Southern issue. However, during the past several decades, hate groups have spread across the United States and are present in all 50 states, comprising a total of 917 groups (Southern Poverty Law Center, 2017) Although 54% of hate groups in 2006 lived in rural areas, this decreased to 20% in 2016. As shown in Table 2.6, those living in suburban areas went from 33% in 2006 to 60% in 2016.

One important goal of hate groups located in urban and suburban areas is what Borgeson (2003) referred to as confronting the enemy. Typically, hate groups are located in cities with a high percentage of minorities to either drive the minority groups out of the area or to convince other whites that minorities are physically, mentally, and biologically different from whites. This was proven accurate when Donald Trump won the presidential election in 2016. Trump focused on the recent influx of minorities and immigrants to suburban and urban areas and played on people's fears that this influx was going to change the normal day-to-day life to which people had grown accustomed. Some saw the increased threats of Muslims as a threat to their Christian values and began to commit hate acts against those who were, or who they perceived to be, Muslim.

One interesting statistic is the decrease of hate groups in rural areas. In 2006, 54% of hate group members resided in rural areas, and in 2016, that statistic dropped to 20%. According to Borgeson (2003), most hate group members who resided in these areas had a tendency to want to make the area a pure white area. When a hate group moves in, minorities want to get out. For instance, in the late 1990s, an Aryan Nations compound was opened in Ulysses, Pennsylvania. When the author asked the head of the Aryan Nations why he chose such a spot, he replied, "[T]his place is almost 100% white. When I move in who is going to move out? The blacks—that's who." There are two explanations for this. First, a change is taking place where individuals joining these groups would rather use the 'in your face' approach of confronting the enemy than drive them out. This can be seen in the recent examples of hate rallies that have been held in places like Charlottesville, Virginia. Another explanation is the rise of the Internet. Roughly, only 13% of individuals in the United States do not use the Internet; this is a dramatic increase in users from 2000, when 48% of American adults did not use the Internet. In 2016, only 1% of those between the ages of 18 and 29, 4% of those between 30 and 49, and 16% of those between 50 and 64 did not use the Internet (Anderson & Perrin, 2016).

More hate mongers are turning to the Internet to vocalize their views. With this vocalization has also come a change in the expression of those views—enter the alt-right. With the emergence of the alt-right, there has come a change in the way that members project their hateful views. Hate mongers have traded in their robes and their shaved heads for a clean look where people wear suits, not robes and pointed hats. With a new generation of tech-savvy youth and adults, the alt-right has taken to the Internet and cleaned up their representation of bigoted views—and it worked. This was shown in a study done by Borgeson and Valeri (2004) to see if individuals could detect hate on the Internet when they came in contact with it. Subjects were presented with three types of representation of hate: in your face, subtle, and outright lie. What they found was that when the hate was an 'in your face' style (i.e., using derogatory language against Jews and minorities), participants recognized it as hate and did not consider it a reliable source or fact that could be used in research. But when given a representation of subtle or outright lie, they rated the web page as a reliable source of information that could be used for research. While this study was done over a decade ago, the results today would probably show an increase for participants in the subtle and outright lie categories because hate has become savvy, and more people believe in the "demising decline of white heritage" in society, creating a backlash against minorities, Jews, immigrants, and the GLBT (lesbian, gay, bisexual, and transgender) community.

SOCIAL INFLUENCES

Table 2.7 shows the influences that right-wing, hate group members say were most important to their joining the group. There were five main influences that surfaced in interviews with members: friends, environment, violent image, prison, and Internet.

As Table 2.7 shows, there have been dramatic changes in members' claims for joining. In 2006, 39% of hate group members claimed that friends were the most influential reason for joining. In comparison, 2016 has shown a downward shift of 9% to 30%. Environment saw the biggest increase, with 30% in 2006 claiming this category compared with 40% in 2016. The reason this occurred is that more members have seen dramatic shifts in the immigrant population moving into their areas, making hate mongers believe that the government is passing legislation that "favors Muslims over Christians and undocumented workers over Americans who are legally here." This relative deprivation has led to a backlash against minority groups and is fueled even more by the recent legislation passed by the Trump administration.

The influence of a violent image has stayed the same at 18% for both 2006 and 2016. Violence is only going to be attractive to a small cohort of people, and the statistics staying the same shows that this claim is still true. Also, since the loss of Richard Butler's Aryan Nations compound to the Southern Poverty Law Center in the early 2000s, hate groups have been toning down their rhetoric

TABLE 2.7 | Influences for Joining of Right-Wing Domestic Terrorists, 2006–2016

	2006	2016
Friends	39%	30%
Environment	30%	40%
Violent Image	18%	18%
Prison	9%	0%
Internet	4%	12%

Source: Borgeson and Valeri (2006) and Valeri and Borgeson (2018)

of violence on the Internet and in propaganda they put out for fear of being a victim of a lawsuit by watchdog organizations. Prison also saw a dramatic shift among those members who joined. In 2006, prison accounted for 9% of the claimed influences for joining; in comparison, 2016 saw 0% claiming this was an influence for joining. This is because hate groups like the KKK and Aryan Nations have not been doing as much recruitment in prisons—cleaning up their image to appeal to those who are joining the likes of the alt-right and fueling a new face of hate that is resonating with Americans. This "new face" has a cleaner image and disguised rhetoric that demeans minorities and others who are not Christians.

The last category found in the research was the Internet. In 2006, it accounted for 4% of those who joined. In 2016, 12% claimed that the Internet was influential in their joining the ranks of hate groups. Contrary to what other researchers and watchdog organizations claim, the Internet is not as big of an influence on joining. What they use the Internet for is spreading the word among those who are interested in reading about their beliefs. It is more of a research tool than a recruiting mechanism. Groups know that the face of hate is only going to influence a few people to join, but as one member said to me, "I know we aren't going to get many people to join. But if I can change the mind of at least one person, I have done a good thing." Therefore, those in hate groups know that the Internet is a tool, but one used to disseminate information to the masses, not to get others to become card-carrying members of their groups.

Conclusion

In summary, this chapter suggests that members of right-wing domestic terrorist groups tend to be males in their late 30s. As stated previously, it is typical of hate groups to have predominantly male membership. The average age of those who join an organized hate group is higher than that in other hate groups (Valeri & Borgeson, 2018). One possible explanation for this is that the religious focus of some of these groups might be less appealing to adolescents and young adults than are the hate music or violence associated with other hate groups. The majority of the hate group members in this chapter reported coming from a working class background, and as a source of employment, engaging in manual labor.

The stereotypical image of a hate group member is that of a violent criminal. In 2006, slightly less than half of the members in Borgeson and Valeri's (2006) research claimed to have committed a crime. In 2016, none of the members claimed to have committed a crime or have a criminal record. This decline in criminal activity may be due to members having a distrust of social scientists, fearing that they may be working for the government and trying to pull a sting on them. This may, in turn, result in members not revealing whether they have had previous criminal involvement. Future research needs to look into the motivations for members to engage in crime.

Finally, just as Borgeson and Valeri (2006) demonstrated with their research, none of the people interviewed in 2016 claim to have been reared as racists. Consistent with research by Kathleen Blee (1996, 2002), the current research demonstrates that others introduce individuals to the hate movement; thus, they learn to hate minorities and Jews through their social networks. The majority of individuals who join hate groups are lifers in the movement and will often be members of more than one group. Most of the individuals in the 2006 and 2016 cohort show that they are not just dabblers of hate but lifetime members who are shopping for the organization that best matches their beliefs. Although these individuals may become disenchanted by the message of one hate group, rather than abandoning such groups altogether, they will look for another hate group that can justify their hate with a different, more acceptable message.

REFERENCES

Aho, J. (1990). *The politics of righteousness*. Seattle: University of Washington Press.

Alibrandi, T. & Wassmuth, W. (1999). *Hate is my neighbor*. Ellensburg, WA: Stand Together Publishers.

Anderson, M. & Perrin, A. (September 7, 2016). 13% of American's don't use the internet. Who are they? *Pew Research Center*. Available: www.pewresearch.org/fact-tank/2016/09/07/some-americans-dont-use-the-internet-who-are-they/. Retrieved August 30, 2017.

Barkum, M. (1996). *Evil: Inside human violence and cruelty*. New York: Freeman.

Blee, K. (1996). Becoming a racist: Women in contemporary Ku Klux Klan and neo-Nazi groups. *Gender and Society* 10: 680–702.

Blee, K. (2002). *Inside organized racism: Women in the hate movement*. Berkeley: University of California Press.

Borgeson, K. (January 25, 2003). Selling hate in WNY: Today's KKK and similar hate groups are skilled and stealthy marketers of hate who must be confronted by the communities where they operate. *Buffalo News*. Available: http://buffalonews.com/2003/01/25/selling-hate-in-wny-todays-kkk-and-similar-groups-are-skilled-and-stealthy-marketers-of-hate-whomust-be-confronted-by-the-communities-where-they-operate/. Retrieved August 30, 2017.

Borgeson, K. & Valeri, R. M. (2004). Faces of hate. *Journal of Applied Sociology* 21(2): 99–111.

Borgeson, K. & Valeri, R. M. (2006). *Terrorism in America*. Sudbury: Jones and Bartlett Press.

Borgeson, K. & Valeri, R. M. (2017). *Skinhead history, identity, and culture*. New York: Routledge.

Ezekiel, R. (1996). *The racist mind: Portrait of American neo-Nazis and Klansmen*. New York: Viking.

Flynn, K. & Gerhardt, G. (1989). *The silent brotherhood: Inside America's racist underground*. New York: Free Press.

Hamm, M. (1995). *American skinheads: The criminology and control of hate crime*. New York: Free Press.

Hamm, M. (2001). *In bad company*. Boston: Northeastern University Press.

Ridgeway, J. (1995). *Blood in the face*. New York: Thunder Mountain Press.

Smith, B. (1994). *Terrorism in America: Pipe bombs and pipe dreams*. Albany: University of New York Press.

Southern Poverty Law Center (SPLC). (2017). Active hate groups 2016. *Intelligence Report*. Available at www.splcenter.org/fighting-hate/intelligence-report/2017/active-hate-groups-2016. Retrieved April 28, 2017.

Statista. (2017). Demographics of active duty U.S. military. *Statista Brain*. Available at www.statisticbrain.com/demographics-of-active-duty-u-s-military/. Retrieved September 30, 2017.

Valeri, R. & Borgeson, K. (2018). *Hate crimes: Motivations, typologies and victims*. Durham: Carolina Academic Press.

Chapter 3

Leftist Political Violence

From Terrorism to Social Protest

Michael Loadenthal

Overview

- Terrorism is a difficult to define label, with its application controlled by state authorities (e.g. Executive, courts, legislature, police, military). It is typically used to denote forms of political contestation that challenge the government in symbolic, rhetorical, and practical terms. Because of this patterned application, *terrorism* fails to adequately describe acts and, instead, is a means of defaming a particular tactic, strategy, organization, ideology, or individual.
- The labeling of leftist violence and rightist violence is done irregularly with leftists frequently labeled and prosecuted as *terrorists* and rightists typically described and framed through other discourses such as *extremism*.
- The first wave of global terrorism is often associated with the rise of individual anarchists targeting heads of state in the 19th century, and while this era saw kings and presidents slain by leftists, its promotion of *propaganda of the deed* declined by World War II.
- The 1960s saw a landmark rise in Marxist-Leninist networks and organizations and other leftists adopting violent means (e.g. bombing, armed robbery)—frequently labeled as terrorism—in their opposition to the war in Vietnam, national liberation (e.g. Puerto Rico), and the larger socio-political environment framed as US-led imperialism.
- In the 1980s, when the Marxist-Leninist vanguards declined, they were replaced by a rising tide of clandestine animal liberation networks, and by the 1990s, the addition of environmental campaigns of sabotage, vandalism, and arson—labeled by the government as "eco-terrorism." Though these networks did not employ *lethal* means, due to the frequency of their attacks and their large financial cost, they were quickly cast as domestic terrorists and a premier target for further criminalization through the rhetoric of terrorism.
- Around the millennium, the left engaged in a series of large-scale, counter-summit street protests. Following the attacks of 9/11, these leftist tactics were further criminalized through a rhetorical association with terrorism, and thus a movement on the rise was quickly curtailed.

- Following the discursive shift equating civil disobedience and disruptive protestors as "terrorists" occurring after 9/11, in the early months of 2017, legislative and policing practices have demonstrated a renewed desire to recast demonstrators as an existential danger to state and national security—this time by framing "demonstrators" as "rioters" if property destruction occurs within the demonstration.

The Problem of Defining Leftist *Terrorism*

This discussion of "leftist terrorism" in the United States must begin with a few key disclaimers the reader should keep in mind throughout. First, the discourse on which acts of political violence receive the distinction of *terrorism* is a political question, not a question of tactics, casualties, or legality. Instead, it is a question of rhetoric, discourse, and ideology, and how these coalesce to form laws and other state policies. Since the state (i.e. government, police, military, civil and municipal bureaucracy) determines this rhetoric and writes and enforces the laws, what is termed terrorism amounts to violence enacted by a non-state actor that is *perceived* to challenge the state.[1] These non-state actors do not typically represent an *existential* threat to the state—a threat that would call into question its fundamental nature or existence—and as such, the treatment of militant social protest as a potentially destabilizing force often appears bombastic. Noted terrorism scholar Paul Wilkinson, in his discussion of how democracies respond to non-state violence, describes these "new Marxist and anarchist far left" groups as "more analogous to tiny gangs of bandits than to serious political movements."[2] If we accept Wilkinson's claim, then one must call into question the state's tendency to paint leftist networks as *terroristic* threats that must be confronted in order to maintain the functioning of the republic.

In a 1919 lecture, Max Weber famously argued that states must maintain a 'monopoly on violence' in order to remain a sovereign power.[3] For Weber, if an entity that was not the state was able to produce its own violence, this detracted from the legitimacy of the state (as well as statist violence) and can call into question the centrality of the nation's sovereignty. Weber goes on to describe the state as "a human community that (successfully) claims the monopoly of the legitimate use of force within a given territory."[4] If we accept Weber's framework, then any manner of social protest that violates the law *and* interferes with the state's ability to claim a monopoly on violence can be understood as a threat, and is thus more likely to receive a defamatory label and additional repression. While such a framework does not serve to *define* terrorism, it does serve as a conceptual litmus test in evaluating the definitions offered by various entities constituting the state. While nearly every agency and institution (e.g. the Department of State, the Department of Justice (DOJ)) maintains its own definition of terrorism, for its part, the Federal Bureau of Investigation (FBI) defines domestic terrorism as:

> The unlawful use, or threatened use, of violence by a group or individual based and operating entirely within the United States (or its territories) without foreign direction committed against persons or property to intimidate or coerce a government, the civilian population, or any segment thereof, in furtherance of political or social objectives.[5]

In examining this definition, it is important to note that it includes *only* illegal acts not directed by a foreign agent (thus excluding attacks linked to Foreign Terrorist Organizations such as al-Qaeda), and *includes* attacks on both persons and property, the latter being a hallmark of leftist targeting.

In other statements, the FBI has simplified this notion of *"domestic* terrorism," explaining it as "Americans attacking Americans based on U.S.-based extremist ideologies."[6] Certainly other definitions of *terrorism* exist, and many of which, when compared to the actions of domestic leftists, simply do not make analytical sense. For example, Bard E. O'Neil, a professor at the National War College in Washington, D.C., and the director of the college's study of the Middle East, insurgency, and revolution, authored a book entitled *Insurgency & Terrorism,* which is considered required reading for many studying terrorism. In this book, O'Neil defines terrorism as a "form of warfare in which violence is directed primarily against noncombatants (usually unarmed civilians), rather than operational military or police forces or economic assets (public or private)."[7] As this history will demonstrate, leftist violence when compared to other ideological forms tends to *avoid* targeting noncombatants, and instead, directs its destructive force at military, police, and economic targets, typically through the damaging of symbolic *property.* Based on O'Neil's definition, much of what is determined to be "leftist domestic terrorism" could better be described under a different label.

From a state perspective, terrorist violence is different from criminal violence[8] because it engages in illegal forms of socio-political change through means that the state would like to reserve for itself. Therefore, the academic and historical study of *terrorism* is precisely those acts that the *state* determines to be terroristic. Consequently, when the subject is *leftist* political violence, this is especially important as the label is used to denote a loosely defined milieu, most centrally based around the rejection of capitalism and/or the state. Therefore, in discussing leftist political violence, we are often faced with the state defining its own opponents, including anarchists, anarcho-syndicalists, Marxists, Leninists, Maoists and other Communists, Black Liberationists, anti-fascists, Animal/Earth Liberationists, and a variety of other identity-based or issue-based struggles.

To provide a bit more of a substantive background to this classification, we can examine scholarly works commonly included in the study of terrorism. One such work, Walter Laqueur's *Voices of Terror,* approaches the task of curating the "manifestos, writings and manuals of Al Qaeda, Hamas, and other terrorists from around the world and throughout the ages."[9] By examining whom Laqueur includes as foundational to the "voices of the [leftist] terror," one can observe how these labels are derived. For Laqueur, he includes both a "Socialism and the Armed Struggle" and a "Guerrilla Doctrine Today" chapter, based around the work of anarchists Johann Most and Abraham Guillen, as well as a host of Communist/Socialists, including Auguste Blanqui, Karl Marx, Friedrich Engels, James Connolly, Vladimir Lenin, Mao Tse-tung, Lin Piao, Che Guevara, Regis Debray, and Carlos Marighella. While these men will not appear in the historical account that makes up this chapter, their ideas of 'propaganda of the deed' (*Most*); revolution through clandestine, small group conspiracy (*Blanqui*); and strategies of non-traditional and guerrilla warfare (*Guevara, Debray, Tse-tung, Guillen, Marighella*) are recurrent themes throughout the genealogy of leftist militancy.

As a historical project, reconstructing a subject-driven history for a reader is inherently a subjective task of deciding what to include and what to exclude. The historical account that is to follow takes a liberal approach to the important questions of taxonomy and the power of labels. In other words, for nearly all cases presented, an argument could be made why that particular act of political violence should be included or excluded from a historical account of terrorism. For example, in a society embroiled in poverty, racial injustice and police brutality, are the actions of the Black Liberation Army (BLA) robbing armored cars a crime, terrorism, or something defensive? What about Animal Liberation Front (ALF) cells who use arson to burn down a facility used to slaughter wild horses? Are these actions terrorism, crime, political crime, or strategic, valid social protest? What about Puerto Rican Liberationists trying to gain self-determination and national sovereignty through militant means? Are their actions social protest, secessionist terrorism, or something more difficult to define?

This growing ambiguity has not escaped the attention of those who construct the discourse on terrorism, namely federal authorities and law enforcement. In its 1999 annual report on terrorism, the FBI has a one-page aside tilted "Vandalism or Terrorism?" that features an image of ALF graffiti and states:

> In recent years, it has become increasingly difficult to differentiate acts of terrorism from acts of vandalism, especially as the level of activity undertaken by animal rights and environmental extremists has grown in intensity and scope.[10]

The FBI report goes on to note that several actions by activists "did not meet the FBI's threshold for designation as acts of terrorism, but [were carried out by] . . . individual domestic extremists or extremist movements such as the ALF, [Earth Liberation Front] ELF." In these cases, as the report states, the FBI "provides support and assistance to the primary investigating agencies."[11] Therefore, it seems that even the FBI has difficulty distinguishing militant protest from coercive political violence, and though their questioning of this taxonomy is far from critical, these questions remain unanswered.

This short discussion is meant to raise important questions that exist beyond the scope of this chapter. These questions of ambiguity and asymmetric labeling require individual consideration, historical background, and measured investigation. While it may be easy for us to understand and judge an animal liberationist arson in the 21st century, it is far more difficult to contextualize and understand the drivers that led the anarchist bombers of the 19th century to kill world leaders, bankers, industrialists, and police.

This author does not agree with how these groups, methods, ideologies, and individuals are labeled as "terrorists"; however, for the sake of producing a descriptive account of the subject, the discussion that proceeds is based upon those entities that are ***commonly included in a discussion of leftist terrorism in the United States*** within the academic and historical study of terrorism. This investigation begins from this state-defined and derogatory label, despite the fact that this distinction is more often than not a mark of defamation rather than description.

Distinguishing Leftist and Rightist Political Violence

The discourse and history concerning 'leftist political terrorism' is fraught with value judgments, misleading nomenclatures, and uneven comparisons that attempt to equate its actions to that of rightist networks. The classical rhetorical question—'Terrorist or freedom fighter?'—exemplifies this chasm. Labels such as "extremist," "revolutionary," "militant," and "terrorist" each embody certain conclusions contained within the nuance of the term. To begin differentiating these histories, it is helpful to first make two generalizations. First, leftist violence is decidedly less lethal than other forms (e.g. right-wing, ethno-nationalist) of violence, and furthermore, the means and targeting patterns employed by leftists tend to prioritize avoiding civilian casualties.[12] As noted terrorism studies scholar Bruce Hoffman explains in his classic text, *Inside Terrorism*:

> Whereas left-wing terrorists like the German [Red Army Faction] RAF and Italian [Red Brigade] RB have selectively kidnapped and assassinated persons whom they blamed for economic exploitation or political repression, terrorists motivated by a religious imperative have engaged in more indiscriminate acts of violence, directed against a far wider category of targets encompassing not merely their declared enemies, but anyone who does not share their religious faith.[13]

This desire to avoid alienating the masses is reflective of the manner through which the left in general understands social change. While many of the Marxist-Leninist cadres were decidedly vanguardist, they still envisioned a manner of popular revolt that involved the working class (i.e. international proletariat) taking power. For this to occur, the armed units that constitute the vanguard must be loved and cherished by the people, something difficult to achieve if the population is made to feel unsafe due to frequent explosions in sites of leisure, business, and transport. It is for this reason that leftist violence tends to target *property* or *individual*s, while avoiding more indiscriminate forms of mass violence common in rightist, ethno-nationalist, separatist, and other manners of violent politics. Therefore, while ethno-nationalist violence aims to inspire fear, uncertainty, and a feeling of insecurity amongst a target group (e.g. English Protestants in Northern Ireland, Russians in Chechnya), leftist violence is designed primarily as a propaganda tool, and secondarily as a manner through which one can attack the state and capital. Leftists prioritize an ethical and strategic connection between the means through which one struggles and the revolutionary vision one seeks to foster—something anarchists refer to as prefiguration.[14]

In this manner, leftist political violence, while designed with the same spectacular, highly dramatic intent as other forms of political violence, is more tailored to avoid injuring the wider population. Hoffman argues that this represents the left's desire to produce violent protest and resistance that "appeal[s] to their perceived 'constituencies'," as according to one RAF militant, "the deliberate involvement of innocent civilians in [a] terrorist operation was not only counterproductive, but wrong."[15] Furthermore, the wider populations—if we were to divide them into the binaries of 'conservative' and 'liberal'—follow similar patterns for the interpretation of violent acts. Liberals tend to accept the notion that political violence may "reflect authentic social grievances that need to be remedied by reforms, and perhaps social change."[16] This differs from the more conservative interpretation of non-state political violence, which views such actors as an external *threat* with international connections, and *not* the result of legitimate or potentially legitimate social, political, and economic grievances.

These discursive and rhetorical patterns help to explain not only how those sympathetic to the plight of the marginalized may interpret violent acts, but also how the violent actor understands its own position vis-à-vis the wider civilian population. In distinguishing leftist attacks from other forms, neo-Nazi, jihadist, and nationalist-separatist movements have frequently deployed lethal violence more indiscriminately and with less regard for civilian casualties. Hoffman describes such rightist violence as "sporadic and uncoordinated, seemingly mindless [and] fueled as much by beer and bravado as by a discernible political agenda."[17] He also notes that ethno-nationalist violence tends to involve violence and destructive campaigns, but that this targeting "has largely been restricted to a specially defined 'target set': namely, the members of a specific rival or dominant ethno-nationalist group."[18]

Second, the 'violence' enacted by leftists, tends to be both symbolic and targeting inanimate property, not humans. For example, a leftist group angry at police is far more likely to use an incendiary device to burn a police car (symbolic attack on property) than they are to open fire inside a police station (direct attack on people). According to empirical research, and as reported by the Department of Homeland Security (DHS), attacks by left-wing groups, individuals, and networks tend to avoid human casualties, and rely on means such as "property destruction, vandalism, arson and fire bombings [sic], sabotage, and violent protests."[19] This framing confirms that leftists are not employing murder and attacks on civilians designed to intimidate a target community. Instead, leftist groups in the modern era are focused on damaging property and economically sabotaging the properties of state and corporate entities. Furthermore, leftist targeting patterns tend to favor the symbolic rather than the instrumental. For example, while one could envision leftists vandalizing or destroying a military monument, it would be unheard of in the modern context to hear of leftist attacking a military facility as Nidal Hasan did in 2009, or holding an armed occupation and standoff with federal law enforcement as Ammon Bundy did in 2016 and as his father Cliven Bundy helped to organize in 2014.

One exception to this pattern of symbolic targeting are the actions of the ALF, which tend to target food and clothing retailers, as well as fur farm facilitates, which have often impacted the industry's ability to profit. Anarchist and Marxist attacks on the state and capital have tended to identify large social strife (e.g. poverty) in identifiable, yet symbolic targets (e.g. a bank branch), while so-called "eco-terrorists" have interrupted supply chains, canceled contracts between multinational corporations and affiliates, and bankrupted a variety of animal breeding facilities, fur stores, and other businesses. The ALF specifically has been able to force companies to change policies to avoid further financial loss. In one small example, S.C. Johnson & Sons announced in 2013 that it was ceasing its use of mink oil and removing all products from stores that contain the ingredient following reports of activists tampering with products and placing them back on shelves.[20] These patterns distinguish leftist political violence from that emanating from the right, as the latter tends toward non-symbolic, and lethal attacks on individuals and institutions defined by religion, race, ethnicity, and 'religiously legislated' practices such as abortion and homosexuality.

With these key patterned distinctions in mind, the subsequent sections explore the history of leftist domestic terrorism in the US through four key eras: the late 19th century, the 1960s, 1980s, and 1990s.

"Long Live Dynamite!": The "Anarchist Wave" of Terrorism

The history of leftist political violence in the US is often grounded in the so-called anarchist wave of terrorism. According to political scientist David Rapoport, the history of terrorism since the 19th century can be divided into four waves, beginning with the anarchist wave.[21] During this time, beginning in the 1880s and ending in the 1920s, anarchists carried out direct and often lethal attacks targeting heads of state, members of the industrialist and capitalist class, and sites of opulence and wealth in cities. This is, of course, not the first act of violent socio-political contestation in the US. As Rapoport notes, "secular rebel terrorists" prior to the anarchist rise in the 1880s included the Sons of Liberty's opposition to the Stamp Act and the Ku Klux Klan's campaign against federal Reconstruction. The late 19th century rise of the anarchist militant coincided with similar movements in Europe, such as the secretive network Narodnaya Vola [The People's Will] in Russia who was responsible for the assassination of Tsar Alexander II in 1881, calling the act "self-defense" in the form of "capital punishment."[22]

Around the turn of the century, anarchists became most known for their promotion of 'propaganda of the deed'—a form of political action that sought to demonstrate political critique through direct attacks. The famed anarchist Peter Kropotkin spoke of *propaganda of the deed*, arguing:

> By actions which compel general attention, the new idea seeps into people's minds and wins converts. One such act may, in a few days, make more propaganda than thousands of pamphlets. Above all, it awakens the spirit of revolt.[23]

In these acts of armed propaganda, anarchists carried out small group attacks against the state and capital, differentiating written propaganda from demonstrative acts. This strategy carried with it the belief that "the population bearing witness to these acts would see both the fallibility of power AND would rise up to fill this void."[24] These attacks tended to target symbolic figureheads, often framing attacks as a reaction to forms of systemic and structural violence—[25]such as poverty or social exclusion—highlighted in the anarchist critique of the state. Notable events of the era include the 1892 attempted assassination of US industrialist Henry Clay Frick—accused of anti-union activity—by anarchist Alexander Berkman, and the Haymarket bombing, which occurred in Chicago in 1886. These attacks would most infamously be remembered by recalling the assassination of US President William McKinley in 1901. McKinley was killed inside the Temple of Music at the Pan-American Exposition in Buffalo, New York, by anarchist Leon Czolgosz who shot the President twice in the abdomen.

These sorts of attacks were given a further advancement when noted Italian anarchist militant Luigi Galleani arrived in the US in 1905 and published a pamphlet titled *"Salute è in Voi"* ["The Health Is Within You"], which instructed readers in the manufacturing of explosives. This pamphlet was used by anarchists who placed bombs at the home of John D. Rockefeller on 4 July 1914, in retaliation for the industrialist's role in the repression of striking miners in Colorado.[26] "The Health Is Within You" was also found in the home of an anarchist cell who attempted to place a bomb at St. Patrick's Cathedral in New York; the cell was arrested by an undercover officer embedded in the group. In 1916, Alfonso Fagotti stabbed a police officer at a demonstration in Boston, and the following day, bombed a police station. Later that year on 22 July, a suspected anarchist militant placed a bomb hidden in a suitcase at the Preparedness Day parade in San Francisco. The device detonated and killed ten individuals, injuring an additional 40. Similar bombings targeted a Milwaukee police station in 1917, various state-centric targets in Philadelphia in 1918, and the American Woolen Company in 1919. In April 1919, 36 dynamite-fashioned explosive devices were mailed to US government officials, servants of the court, and businessmen, and on 2 June 1919, nine pipe bombs packed with shrapnel exploded almost simultaneously in New York; Boston; Pittsburgh; Cleveland; Patterson, New Jersey; Philadelphia; and Washington, D.C.[27]

These bombings, shootings, and stabbings were carried out for a variety of political and idio-syncratic reasons, and were positioned within a larger era of anti-state and anti-capitalist social upheaval, often intersecting with popular social movements such as those in support of labor rights or birth control, or those opposing war. This surge in attacks would eventually decline, spurred on by unpopular strikes such as the Wall Street bombing of 1920 in which anarchist bombs killed 40 people and injured more than 140. Through anti-immigrant and anti-leftist legislation and police actions such as the Palmer Raids and the focused attention of J. Edgar Hoover's newly formed FBI, by World War II, anarchist attacks against the state in the US had nearly vanished, opening the door for what followed.

"Bring the War Home!": Marxist-Leninist Cades Resisting the War in Vietnam

Beginning in the early 1960s, the US began to experience a newly invigorated movement of militant attack associated with what was commonly termed the "New Left," with obvious influ-ence from the swell of international Sovietism. In this time period, while anarchist means and critique remained a key background, on the surface it became overshadowed by the growth of Marxist-Leninist groups, many of which grew out of the anti-colonial movements of the early 20th century. The FBI, in its characterization of the revolutionary left, distinguished it as those who "generally profess a revolutionary socialist doctrine and view themselves as protectors of the people against the 'dehumanizing effects' of capitalism and imperialism."[28] According to the FBI, these groups "aim to bring about change in the United States and believe that this change can be realized through revolution rather than through the established political process."[29] Following the rise and decline of previous anti-colonial movements embodied in the Irish Republican Army's fight against Britain and Palestinian resistance to Zionism (as well as the anti-British attacks by Zionists such as Fighters for the Freedom of Israel/Lehi), the US-led war in Vietnam provided the requisite background for a new period of violence.

Many leftists interpreted the Vietnam War as a battle between the forces of imperialism and those of the Third World. This frame meant that US and European revolutionaries developed an analysis and practice that sought to "bring the war [in Vietnam] home [to the US]," and to exploit the seeming vulnerability of the US, which was fighting a losing war. The strides made by the Viet Cong against US forces inspired a generation of revolutionaries who saw the failing war effort as the harbinger for wider change. This led to the development of a variety of armed groups in the "First World" in support of so-called "Third World" revolutions, including those raging in Southeast Asia. Internationally, this included the development of the Red Army Faction in West Germany, the Red Brigades in Italy, Action Directe in France, and the Red Army in Japan. In the US, the group most well known in this regard is the Weather Underground Organization (WUO). It is during this time that the FBI operated its counter-intelligence program, aptly named COINTELPRO. Within this program, the FBI has admitted to conducting 2,218 separate "actions," along side at least 2,305 warrantless phone taps, 697 electronic listening devices, and 57,846 intercepted correspondences.[30]

In constructing this history, it is important to note that in the mainstream study of terrorism large, these 1960s-era vanguards represented an apex for "domestic leftist terrorism," and their decline brought about a decrease in the left's domestic use of lethal violence. To cite only one such framing, in Gus Martin's widely used textbook *Essentials of Terrorism* (now in its fourth edition), the author writes that "the modern American left is characterized by several movements that grew out of the political fervor of the 1960s."[31] Martin is quick to point out the separation between "extremists" such as Students for a Democratic Society (SDS) and the Black Panther Party for Self-Defense, noting that *extremist* movements were not "fundamentally violent . . . [and the groups] not terrorist movements."[32] Martin goes on to explain, "extremist trends within [extremist groups] led to factions that sometimes espoused violent confrontation, and a few engaged in terrorism."[33] Martin is also the author of *Understanding Terrorism* (now in its fifth edition), which maintains a similar approach, further drawing a distinction between "fringe-left ideology," defined as "usually an extreme interpretation of Marxist ideology, using theories of class warfare or ethnonational liberation to justify political violence," and "far-left ideology," defined as "apply[ing] Marxist theory to promote class or ethnonational rights . . . [but] not necessarily engag[ing] in political violence . . . often participat[ing] in democratic processes."[34] Martin focuses his analysis on Marxism and anarchism for his investigation of the left and fascism for the right.

Additionally, it is worth reviewing a second standard terrorism text frequently adopted. Brigitte Nacos' *Terrorism and Counterterrorism* (in its fifth edition) is a battle-tested favorite as its consistent revision and republication demonstrates. In Nacos' work focusing on leftist terrorism in the US, she mirrors the historical account of Martin, beginning with the anarchists of the early 1900s, before moving onto the Marxist-Leninist vanguards of the 1960s such as the WUO, Black Panther Party for Self-Defense, and Symbionese Liberation Army (SLA). Interestingly, Nacos' framing relies on a causal connection between the war in Vietnam and the rise of "extreme left" terrorism, explaining:

> The left-wing groups in the United States that turned to terrorism in the 1960s and 1970s as a result of the Vietnam War and the civil rights struggles were inspired by Marxist ideology, but at the beginning of the twenty-first century, these kinds of "extreme-left" terrorist groups did not exist in the United States.[35]

This portrayal is notable as it describes leftist political violence as a relatively modern import to the US, implying that while it had operated elsewhere in the century prior, it took the anti-Vietnam countercultural reality to open up a space for its entry into an American context.

Using Martin and Nacos' nomenclatures, 1960s- and 1970s-era *terrorism* from the left is typified by the WUO, SLA, BLA, Fuerzas Armadas de Liberación [the Armed Forces for National Liberation] (FALN), the May 19 Communist Organization (M19CO), and the United Freedom Front (UFF). These are briefly profiled as follows:

- **WUO:** Active from 1969 to 1977 and originating as an outgrowth of SDS. The group was based around opposing the war in Vietnam, supporting the movement for Black Power, and generally opposing US militarism and imperialism. The WUO engaged in jailbreaks, militant street demonstrations (e.g. The Days of Rage), expropriations (i.e. armed robberies), small arms attacks, and at least 40 bombings, typically targeting government property.

- **BLA:** Active from 1970 to 1981 and formed by former members of the Black Panther Party for Self-Defense. The Fraternal Order of Police claim that BLA members are responsible for killing up to 13 officers, while the Department of Justice links them to more than 70 attacks, including bombings, bank robberies, murders (e.g. ambushes and assassinations of police), and a 1972 airplane hijacking.
- **SLA:** Active from 1973 to 1975 and self-described as a symbiosis and unification of diverse leftist struggles, including those against racism, patriarchy, colonialism, imperialism, and capitalism. The SLA carried out expropriations, kidnappings, and assassination.
- **FALN:** Active from 1974 to 1983 and focused on furthering independence for Puerto Rico through a campaign of bombing. Called the "most prolific terrorist organization in U.S. history,"[36] the FALN carried out up to 130 bombings in the US during their period of activity, as well as numerous armed robberies. Most bombings targeted property, but FALN attacks did manage to kill at least five individuals and injure more than 60.
- **UFF:** Active from 1975 to 1984 and responsible for at least 20 bombings and nine bank robberies in the US. The UFF spoke out against US foreign policy in Central America and the struggle against apartheid in South Africa. Although UFF bombs were not designed to kill (as the bombers issued warnings), a 1976 courthouse bombing injured 22 people. The FBI stated, "the demise of the UFF . . . was emblematic of the left's declining fortunes [in the mid-1980s]."[37]
- **M19CO:** Active from 1978 to 1985 and formed from members of BLA, WUO, the Black Panther Party, and the Republic of New Africa. The organization sought to free political prisoners (including members of the BLA and FALN), expropriate capital from banks and other institutions, and engage in warfare against the state through a bombing campaign. M19CO focused on confronting US imperialism and racism, and while their bombings did not kill, three officers were killed in an armored car robbery in 1981.

It should be noted that both Nacos' and Martin's listings are incomplete, excluding notable militants of the era such as the George Jackson Brigade (1975–1977) and MOVE (b. 1972), both founded in the 1970s. The George Jackson Brigade was a Washington-based urban guerrilla group that carried out an estimated 20 bombings and seven bank robberies in their short 2-year period of activity. Their attacks targeted governmental sites (e.g. Department of Corrections), infrastructure (e.g. City Light Substation), and local businesses accused of racist practices and seen to be acting against the interest of proletarian labor (e.g. Safeway Market).[38] The Brigade was unique in its membership, as its ranks were made up of former prisoners and students, half of which were women and many of which were Queer.[39] The group known as MOVE, is a Philadelphia-based militant Black liberation and eco-consciousness movement best known for their standoff with the Philadelphia police in 1985 that ended in the death of 11 members, including five children. In this incident, police attempted to force MOVE members from their home by setting fire to the building via an air-dropped explosive device. The bomb set fire to the building and destroyed more than 65 homes, as well as killed many MOVE members. The siege of the MOVE building marks an important milestone in the use of militarized means for the policing of political dissidents.[40] In the arrest warrant that led to the deadly confrontation, MOVE members were charged with multiple counts, including "making terrorist threats," and the mayor and police commissioner similarly classified MOVE as a "terrorist organization."[41]

Overall, these domestic revolutionary groups declined in the late 1970s and into the 1980s. When the Soviet Union collapsed around 1989, some networks were further pushed into irrelevance and instability as they lost both an ideological stalwart and a national sponsor. In its historical accounting, contained within the FBI's 1999 annual report on terrorism, the agency explains:

> From the 1960s to the 1980s, leftist-oriented extremist groups posed the most serious domestic terrorist threat to the United States. In the 1980s, however, the fortunes of the leftist movement declined dramatically as law enforcement dismantled the infrastructure of many of these groups, and as the fall of Communism in Eastern Europe deprived the movement of its ideological foundation and patronage.[42]

It is important to note that while many leftist groups had ideological, rhetorical, and symbolic backing from the Soviet Union (e.g. Cuba's perceived support for the BLA), this does not imply that Soviet forces or their affiliated intelligence agencies directed these networks. For example, while the Central Intelligence Agency had contact with segments of the Algerians fighting French colonialism or the Afghanis fighting Russian take over in their country, the agency did not create or *direct* these movements.[43] This decline in Marxist-aligned and state-supported groups that coincided with the 1980s would soon open up new spaces for militant action, focused in new ways and through new means.

"No Compromise in Defense of Mother Earth!": The Importing of Animal Liberation and Environmental Networks

As the Marxist-Leninist cadres were declining and their campaign of bombings and armored car robberies ending, militant struggle among leftists took a decidedly distinct turn as networks formed in defense of animal lives and the environment. Though the networks embodied in the Animal Liberation Front (ALF) and its later incarnation, the Earth Liberation Front (ELF), have their roots in the UK, they quickly internationalized. Their history can be most clearly dated to 1971,[44] when the Hunt Saboteurs Association was formed to interfere in animal hunts in the UK by scaring off prey with horns and animal scents. This was followed by the founding of the Band of Mercy in 1972, which introduced the tactics of vandalism, sabotage, and arson in defense of animals. Band of Mercy activists vandalized the vehicles of hunters—rather than interfering in active hunts—and deployed arson as a form of sabotage to destroy property belonging to animal testing laboratories and seal culling boats. The Band also introduced the tactic of "animal liberation," wherein live animals are released or removed from sites of captivity before being rehabilitated and placed in new homes.

After 4 years as the Band of Mercy, activists in England factionalized and formed the ALF as a clandestine, moniker-driven network dedicated to "inflicting economic damage on those who profit from the misery and exploitation of animals."[45] The ALF further stated that it was focused on liberating animals from "places of abuse" and to "reveal the horror and atrocities committed against animals behind locked doors."[46] In 1976, the ALF carried out its first animal liberation,

TABLE 3.1 | "Eco-Terrorism" Tactical Trends, United States, 1972–2010

Tactic category	% of Dataset
Vandalism	61.3
Sabotage	14.3
Arson	11.0
Animal liberations	10.1
Anti-personnel tactics (APTs)	1.8
Total	**100 (2,911 incidents)**

targeting a fur farm in Scotland, and by 1977, it had seen its first international claim, with the ALF moniker being used to sign a communiqué in the Netherlands. It took 2 more years for the ALF name to reach the US; in 1979, self-identified ALF activists carried out a raid of the New York University Medical Center, and in 1981, the moniker was used to claim responsibility for a raid targeting an animal research laboratory in Silver Spring, Maryland.

Between 1979 and 2010, the ALF and its allies (including the ELF) carried out at least 2,900 actions in the US.[47] Typically, these acts are carried out by small groups of individuals, at night, through illegal, accessible means. In a typical incident, an ALF/ELF activist may throw a brick through the window of a fur retailer and graffiti a slogan on the storefront. In the more infamous incidents, activists have used improvised incendiary devices (e.g. a bottle filled with gasoline and affixed with a road flare) to damage property, once again, avoiding injury to humans and non-human animal life. In attempting to characterize this 'attack' history, this author located, triangulated, and coded more than 27,000 strikes occurring globally, and analyzed the incident-based data for descriptive patterns.[48] These findings are displayed in Table 3.1, limited to only those strikes that occurred in the US.

From this analysis, it is obvious that "eco-terrorists" at large, and the ALF/ELF specifically, are largely engaged in vandalism and sabotage (nearly 76%), and in less than 2% of cases, adopt tactics designated to injure or kill (i.e. APTs)—such as the detonation of improvised explosive devices (12 incidents) or the mailing of small yield explosive packages (11 incidents).

Typical methods of vandalism include graffiti, glass etching, smashing windows, placing glue into locks, and slashing tires. In these incidents, attacks have tended to target fur and leather retailers and restaurants, particularly fast-food restaurants such as McDonald's and KFC. Typical methods of sabotage involve the intentional destruction of machinery such as construction equipment or laboratory instruments, or the damaging of retail items. It should be noted that these tactical trend figures represent the "eco-terrorist" activity in the US generally, not the ALF/ELF specifically. When non-ALF/ELF "eco-terrorists" (or those termed as such by the government) are removed from the sample, the use of lethal tactics drops significantly. For example, since the US government considers the "Unabomber" Ted Kaczynski an "eco-terrorist," his 16 actions make up a significant part of this 1.8% APT figure, despite him having little in common with ALF/ELF politics and no affiliation whatsoever with its activists.

Despite avoiding casualties, this history of frequent attacks and infrequent arrests quickly garnered the attention of the FBI, who began labeling "eco-terrorists" as "one of the most active extremist elements in the United States" and calling their arsons "terrorist incidents."[49] The day after nearly 3,000 people lost their lives in the attacks of 9/11, US Congressman Greg Walden of Oregon stated to Congress that the ELF was a threat "no less heinous than what we saw occur yesterday in Washington and New York."[50] In 2005, the US Senate Committee on Environmental and Public Works hosted a session entitled "Oversight on Eco-Terrorism Specifically Examining the Earth Liberation Front ("ELF") and the Animal Liberation Front ("ALF")," wherein they claimed that the ALF and ELF constituted the "number one domestic terrorist threat."[51] Similar claims were made by congressmen,[52] governors,[53] FBI leadership,[54] and senators running for president,[55] as well as within testimony in the Senate Judiciary Committee.[56] This claim was not simply a rhetorical one either. Throughout the arrest and prosecution of ALF/ELF members, individuals were charged as *terrorists*, including through the use of "Terrorism Enhancements"[57]; incarcerated in prisons designed to house terrorists (termed Communications Management Units); and charged with violating the Animal Enterprise Terrorism Act (AETA),[58] federal legislation that classifies economic damage to animal industries as domestic terrorism. If the reader thinks that such claims are in the past, they are wrong.

[handwritten margin note: This accusation is based on the scope of the Committee]

This rhetorical frame has filtered down to nearly every level from state legislatures to district judges. In December 2016, Nicole Kissane pled guilty in a plea deal to charges of conspiring to violate the AETA by releasing minks from fur farms, vandalizing a fur store, and vandalizing the home of the store's owner. At the sentencing phase of the trial, District Judge Larry Burns called the crimes a "campaign of terror against an industry"[59] and Acting U.S. Attorney Alana W. Robinson stated, "vandalizing homes and businesses with acid, glue and chemicals in the dark of night is a form of domestic terrorism."[60] Two additional activists, Tyler Lang and Kevin Olliff, were convicted for violating the AETA earlier in 2016 for the releasing of minks.[61] Certainly, the absurdity of charging animal liberation vandals releasing minks as terrorists has not escaped legal advocates such as Rachel Meeropol, an attorney who helped to challenge the law. In her argument, Meeropol stated, "These [AETA] charges demean the definition of terrorism. They not only violate the defendants' individual rights, but also serve to chill the first amendment rights of an entire movement."[62] As their challenge to the court states, the law is unjustly applied, as in this case, "it punishes as an act of 'terrorism' non-violent theft of private property."[63]

The designation of the ALF/ELF as domestic terrorists, and infamously as the "number one domestic terrorist threat," is based on the frequency of their activity, *not* their lethality. While the networks have routinely used vandalism, sabotage, arson, and occasionally explosives to target *property*, these attacks have never killed a single individual![64] In fact, the ALF guidelines, which define the ability for an individual to claim their action as being on behalf of ALF, task individuals with "tak[ing] all necessary precautions against harming any animal, human and non-human."[65] However, when data on their activity are compiled and reported, it is often misleading. For example, in compiled FBI and Department of Justice figures spanning from 2001 to 2011, the ELF and the ALF are listed as the number one and number two most frequently attacking groups, respectively, with 84 attacks attributed to them in this period. These 84 attacks resulted in zero fatalities. The third most active group listed is al-Qaeda, with only four attacks, but 2,996 fatalities. Thus, while it is accurate to say that the ALF/ELF are quite active, to place them above a transnational terrorist network that has killed thousands appears misleading. As the ALF/ELF typically engages in misdemeanor criminal acts targeting property, many have challenged their inclusion in domestic terrorism taxonomies alongside networks such as al-Qaeda.

It is important to note that while the ALF and ELF exemplify this newly visible form of leftist activity, they are far from the only monikers used within this strategic and tactical historical array. In 1987, individuals in Arizona motivated by an environmental concern sabotaged a ski lift, claiming the action for the Evan Mecham Eco-Terrorist International Conspiracy (EMETIC). The small group would go on to carry out at least two other acts of sabotage, targeting the Fairfield Sun Bowl and power lines emanating from a nuclear power plant. This four-person cell, responsible for only three acts of sabotage, was the subject of intense investigation and infiltration by the FBI involving at least 50 agents,[66] providing a preview for how the FBI would deal with similar actions in the years to come. Additional monikers created by individuals to represent their actions as part of a larger network were also common. For example, the moniker Coalition to Save the Preserves (CSP) was used to claim responsibility for eight arsons between 2000 and 2001[67] to halt development of lands in Arizona for new housing. These arsons appear to have been the work of a lone individual, Mark Sands, but are often discussed alongside those of the ELF as they shared its method and analysis.

In these cases, the actions of an individual—often presenting themselves as a group of individuals—are often represented as a coordinated campaign, rather than a few connected incidents by a lone perpetrator. In 2003, a single individual was responsible for detonating three explosive devices targeting businesses financially connected to Huntingdon Life Sciences, an animal breeding and testing company, claiming the attacks for the Revolutionary Cells–Animal Liberation Brigade. These small explosive devices were detonated at night, on separate dates, and damaged the exterior of the buildings, presenting little risk to life. The FBI subsequently linked the attacks to Daniel Andreas San Diego who has been considered a Most Wanted Terrorist by the FBI ever since.[68] It is worth noting that of the 28 people listed as Most Wanted Terrorists, San Diego is one of only two[69] American citizens who are non-Muslim and responsible for crimes in the US. The other 26 individuals on the Most Wanted Terrorist list (including two US citizens[70]) are responsible for *lethal* attacks on US citizens coordinated in conjunction with foreign-based jihadist networks such as al-Qaeda. San Diego is the *only* individual on the list *not* accused or convicted of a lethal attack, nor an attack targeting living beings.

While incidents of so-called "eco-terrorism" were seemingly on the rise throughout the 1980s and 1990s, a quantitative analysis demonstrates that they experienced a precipitous decline in 1998 and would continue to decline annually.[71] Interestingly, the movement cycle for these networks appears to function independently of what were once thought to be primary driving factors. Some have argued that Operation Backfire—a 2005 multi-agency operation that involved the arrest and conviction of the largest ELF/ALF cell on record—and the 2006 passage of the AETA led to a rapid decline in movement activity, as the threat of federal prosecution and aggressive sentencing served to de-incentivize would-be activists. However, while there was a decline between 2005 and 2006, this is quite insignificant when compared to the decline beginning in 1998. The Operation Backfire report authored by the National Consortium for the Study of Terrorism and Responses to Terrorism reached this conclusion as well after an incident-driven analysis,[72] noting that while Operation Backfire did likely diminish the network, it had begun to decline independently in the years preceding.

The case of the 1990–2000 "eco-terrorists" presents a challenging historical puzzle in terms of applying labels. While these groups did not deploy lethal violence or target animate objects with any regularity, the activists and their networks remain classified as "terrorists" due to the effectiveness and frequency of their strikes. Therefore, when the FBI/DOJ describes these networks as "the most active criminal extremist element in the US" and that "eco-terrorism matters [are] a domestic terrorism investigation priority,"[73] one should take pause and question whether this is truly justified.

"Whose Streets? Our Streets?": Summit Hopping and the Terrorization of Dissent

The late 1990s saw the decline of aggressive animal liberation and eco-justice direct actions movements (i.e. "eco-terrorists"), but this militant vacuum was soon filled, and the actions of the past decades eclipsed with the rise of the so-called anti-globalization movement (AGM) and the notion of 'summit hopping.' From 1999 to 2002, a variety of international trade and financial summits were rallying points for large gatherings of the left, and frequently involved demonstrators engaging in illegal street marches, and direct actions (e.g. street blockades). Individual activists and affinity groups—small groups of activists structurally equivalent to a protest cell— 'hopped' from summit to summit, crisscrossing the country and cross-pollinating communities along the way, while solidifying kinship networks and developing and practicing new skill sets. This era is best known for the 1999 mass demonstrations that forced the premature shut down of the World Trade Organization (WTO) ministerial in Seattle; demonstrations opposing the International Monetary Fund and World Bank in Washington, DC; and broad-based marches and blockades surrounding the 2000 Republican National Convention in Philadelphia, ending in more than 400 arrests.

The AGM, while far more akin to a broad-based, popular movement of large-scale marches and assemblies, was quickly recast by the state in terms of terrorism in what could be termed the *terrorization* of dissent. This was largely done through linking the AGM to the tactics, strategies, and organizational methods of anarchists, and framing anarchism through a terroristic or extremist framework. As early as 1999, the FBI began to cast anarchists and leftist allies within the rhetoric of terrorism. In their discussion of "left-wing terrorism" contained within its 1999 report, the FBI notes:

> Anarchists and extremist socialist groups—many of which have an international presence— also represent a latent but potential terrorist threat in the United States. Anarchists, operating individually and in groups, caused much of the damage during the November 30-December 3, 1999 World Trade Organization (WTO) ministerial meeting in Seattle, Washington.[74]

Before exploring this past history, it is helpful to begin in the present. At the time of this writing, the FBI maintains a website focused on "countering violent extremists"[75] domestically. The site begins by reminding the reader:

> The First Amendment to the U.S. Constitution guarantees free speech and religious liberty. People living in American are free to disagree with each other and with the government, but no one has the right to resort to violence as a means of expressing disagreement.[76]

The state repeats this logic in other venues, such as a 2012 report from the Congressional Research Service entitled "The Domestic Terrorist Threat: Background and Issues for Congress," which clarifies that while "anarchism" is an ideology, an "anarchist extremist" is one who embraces such an ideological position *and* "adopts criminal tactics."[77] To the critical reader, this should be very telling. The preamble states that while ideological positions cannot be criminalized, 'disagreeing with the government' must be done through legal means—the implication being that to "resort to violence as a means of expressing disagreement"[78] is what *extremists* or *domestic terrorists* do.

While such statements are not surprising, without defining what is "violence" for the FBI, we find that the taxonomic distinctions that follow serve to criminalize oppositional politics while presenting material seeking to classify and describe. Further into the site is a list exploring "Domestic Extremist Ideologies,"[79] where one can clearly observe the FBI's domestic terrorism categorizations:

- Sovereign citizen extremists
- Animal rights and environmental extremists
- Anarchist extremists
- Abortion extremists
- Militia extremists
- White supremacy extremists[80]

In the details that follow, the FBI notes that "[anarchist extremists] damage property, cause riots and set off firebombs. In some cases, they have injured police officers."[81] This is consistent with the DOJ and FBI's policy to not list domestic terrorist *organizations* but instead delineate domestic terrorist "threats," which according to a DOJ white paper include "animal rights extremists, eco-terrorists, anarchists, anti-government extremists such as 'sovereign citizens' and unauthorized militias, [b]lack separatists, [w]hite supremacists, and anti-abortion extremists."[82] In this phrasing, 'anarchists' are listed without the requisite 'extremist' descriptor, which by the FBI's labeling logic, would imply that law-abiding anarchists were also included in this generalized understanding of the domestic terrorist threat.

This criminalized frame through which anarchism is presented exemplifies the manner through which leftists employing militant means are commonly recast as terrorists in the modern era. In the years since 9/11, it has become routine to see headiness such as "Men in black with a violent agenda"—an article dealing with anarchist protest tactics—which begins with the sentence, "They're not Al-Qaeda, but they are a type of home-grown terrorism group [sic]."[83] This unwieldy use of the terrorism label has extended beyond anarchists as well to include those employing disruptive or attention-grabbing methods, such as two activists charged with a "terrorism hoax" after displaying a large "Hunger Games"-themed banner inside the headquarters of Devon Energy as part of a demonstration against hydraulic fracturing, mining, and pipeline expansion.[84] Once again, what is remarkable in this case is the ability for the state to both rhetorically and legally present such charges, invoking the fear present in accusations of terrorism, for what would otherwise be dealt with as a symbolic act of (albeit disruptive) civil disobedience.

While the FBI does not claim that anarchism is a terroristic ideology (as long as it remains legal), it does infer this by discussing "anarchists and extremist social groups" within a report on domestic terrorism. In his 2002 report to the Senate Select Committee on Intelligence, Executive Assistant Director for Counterterrorism/Counterintelligence, Dale Watson states:

> Anarchists and extremist socialist groups . . . at times also represent a potential threat in the United States. For example, anarchists, operating individually and in groups, caused much of the damage during the 1999 WTO ministerial meeting in Seattle.[85]

The language used here is important. While Watson does not call the "anarchist and extremist socialist" activists *terrorists*, he does call them a "potential threat" and rhetorically links the destruction of corporate property carried out as part of the WTO demonstrations to a historical record of domestic *terrorism*. Similarly, in a 2006 US Department of Justice report focused on the "activities . . . [of] potential protesters at the 2004 Democratic and Republican National political conventions," it notes: "In addition to the threats posed by international terrorists, the FBI was especially concerned about the threats posed by anarchist groups."[86] The report goes on to link anarchists to "violent acts" carried out in protest of the WTO (Seattle, 1999), national political conventions (Philadelphia and Los Angeles, 2000), and the Free Trade Area of the Americas summit (Miami, 2003). Though not *explicitly* calling protestors terrorists, by speaking of them in the same breath as "international terrorists" (e.g. al-Qaeda), the rhetorical linkage is quite clear. For rhetoricians, the smashing of a Starbucks window becomes akin to the lethal conspiracies of Aryan Nations or the assassin's bullets fired by an anti-abortionist. In this rhetorical reality, the term *terrorism* appears even more malleable and asymmetrically applied than originally imagined. It is in this new legal reality that one can explore a few cases, occurring in the 2010s, in the American Midwest.

Between 20–21 May 2012, in Chicago, Illinois, the North Atlantic Treaty Organization (NATO) held its summit in the US for the first time. As a result, a sizable number of protestors assembled in the city to show their dissent. Several days before the summit was set to begin, local police, in conjunction with the FBI and Secret Service,[87] preemptively arrested Brian Church, Jared Chase, and Brent Vincent Betterly, charging them with an Illinois anti-terrorism statute that had never before been used. In the 19 May 2012 court papers,[88] the defendants are charged with three felonies: 1) Material Support for Terrorism, 2) Conspiracy to Commit Terrorism, and 3) Possession of Explosives or Explosive or Incendiary Devices. These charges carried a prison sentence of 17 to 85 years. The evidence, gained through "covert investigation,"[89] claims that the defendants conspired to attack police facilities with Molotov cocktails and to use the police's distracted response to target further sites. The report details their preparations, ensuring to present the defendants as highly organized, well-armed domestic terrorists. Despite recurrent descriptions of "destructive devices" and "improvised explosive-incendiary devices,"[90] when it comes to a descriptive account of these preparations, the court papers describe the "devices" as "empty beer bottles that were filled with gasoline and fitted with fusing."[91] The "fusing" described is later said to be a bandana cut into pieces.[92] This reflects a trend in state-centric descriptions of political violence that tend to call incendiary devices "fire *bombs*,"[93] which needlessly muddies important distinctions between devices designed to destroy property via fire (e.g. time-delayed incendiary device) and those designed to injure and kill through lethal force (e.g. a time-delayed explosive device).

Beyond the description of their actionable offenses, the court papers describe the NATO defendants as "self-proclaimed anarchists, and members of the 'Black Bloc' group, who traveled together . . . in preparation for committing terrorist acts of violence and destruction."[94] While the three defendants certainly planned disruptive and violent actions, is it accurate to label the construction of four accelerant-filled beer bottles as conspiring to commit terrorism? The subsequent grand jury indictment[95] lists 11 counts for which the three have been indicted. These charges include the previous charges, as well as conspiracy to commit arson, solicitation to commit arson, attempted arson, and unlawful use of a weapon. Such a judicial strategy is plain to interpret as the overcharging of defendants is done to:

> Give prosecutors more leverage in negotiating a plea deal later or in boosting their chances of securing at least some convictions if the case does eventually go to trial . . . prosecutors frequently use additional charges in an indictment as bargaining chips in later stages of the case, sometimes offering to drop the most serious charges if a defendant pleads guilty to lesser crimes.[96]

The public framing of three activists, aged 22–27, within a language of conspiracy and terrorism has a public disciplinary effect. The fear-inducing language served to detract media coverage of the anti-NATO protests, delegitimize the political motivations of the defendants, and rhetorically link those opposing the summit to those seeking to undermine democratic means through violence. The state was able to frame the urgency of their police actions and the threat of the attackers because of the preparatory steps taken toward violent ends. Yet, despite these preparations, in reality the defendants posed little risk to life or property as the subjects were under police surveillance constantly. Undercover police were present during the construction of the Molotov cocktails, and according to the defendants' legal council, other undercover agents had "befriended" the defendants and "egged [them] on."[97]

In the second Midwest case, five defendants were arrested in Cleveland, Ohio, and indicted for conspiracy to destroy a bridge via explosives. The defendants were arrested when they attempted to detonate ready-made, yet inert explosive devices they believed to be active, having purchased them from an undercover federal agent. Despite the FBI's assertion that the public was never in danger due to the defendants' constant surveillance, US attorney Steven Dettelbach discussed the case stating, "These defendants were found to have engaged on terrorist activities and will spend nearly a decade in prison."[98] After their arrest, it was revealed that the police investigation was built around information provided by a confidential informant, Shaquille Azir, who was a convicted felon being paid by police. Azir had also been arrested twice for passing bad checks while under FBI direction during the Cleveland case![99] According to the indictment, Azir, as the "confidential human source," began working for the FBI on 20 July 2011,[100] and Azir was first arrested on 25 July 2011 and then again 22 December 2011, according to documents released by the Cuyahoga County Court of Common Pleas Criminal Court Division. Azir also has previous convictions for possession of cocaine, robbery, possession of stolen property, grand theft, and four additional counts of passing bad checks.[101]

Having been arrested himself during his cooperation with police, Azir had a clear motivation in providing his cooperation to the FBI. In the end, for their role in the bridge conspiracy, Douglas Wright received 11.5 years, Brandon Baxter received 9 years and 9 months, Connor Stevens received 8 years and 1 month, and Joshua Stafford received 10 years. In the end, District Court Judge David Dowd concludes that since the men's actions were designed to "intimidate the

United States government,"[102] they were thus planned as acts of *terrorism*. Additionally, while the FBI press release[103] quotes Attorney Dettelbach as stating, "These defendants were found to have engaged in terrorist activities," none of those convicted were convicted of terroristic crimes.[104]

Such cases are increasingly common and reminiscent of the prosecution of eight organizers (known as the "RNC 8") who organized opposition to the 2008 Republican National Convention and were charged with "conspiracy to riot in furtherance of terrorism." Social movement journalist Will Potter writes that the NATO, Cleveland, and RNC 8 cases all share four key elements in the state's criminalization of dissent:

- FBI infiltration and reliance on government informants to manufacture the 'plot'
- Terrorism charges
- Labeling the defendants "self-proclaimed anarchists"
- Unveiling the 'domestic terrorism' arrests days before key protests[105]

Certainly, combined with the larger measures designed to chill dissent and emboldened by the newfound counter-terrorism focus post-9/11, the movements of the 2000s declined rapidly.

It is unclear what would have happened with the AGM if larger historical forces did not alter its course. In September 2001, when organizers were preparing large-scale disruptions targeting the Fall meetings of the International Monetary Fund and World Bank, the terrorist attacks of September 11 caused many protest organizers to cancel their planned marches to be held later that month, isolating those who decided to still march, such as the anarchist Anti-Capitalist Convergence. Following the smaller-than-expected showing at the anti-summit marches in late September 2001, the AGM precipitously declined within a new rhetorical and corporeal reality that sought to associate any oppositional political militancy as an element in the Global War on Terror. During the years after 9/11, leftist social movements witnessed the use of militarized police raids; increased surveillance and infiltration[106]; mass arrests; malicious prosecution; incarceration in Communication Management Units[107]; and the prosecutorial use of terrorism enhancements,[108] federal grand juries, and statues such as the AETA and conspiracy laws, which served to chill dissent and further marginalize so-called militants, leading to a generalized decline in the use of disruptive tactics in the years that followed.

"Make America Great Again": The Riot-ization of Dissent

The intentional conflation of militant protest, civil disobedience, and anarchist politics with that of extremism, domestic terrorism, and threats to national security was part of an intentional strategy to isolate, label, and defame a rising mood of collective resistance in the years around the millennium. While this may have reached an apex in the early 2000s, the 2016 elections promoted a wave of reactionary protests that is still unfolding, and that triggered a shift back toward a federal effort to criminalize dissent and chill political speech and disruptive, effective protest.

According to a review by *The Washington Post*, in less than 2 months of the new administration, "Republican lawmakers in at least 18 states have introduced or voted on legislation to curb mass protests in what civil liberties experts are calling 'an attack on protest rights throughout the states.'"[109] Though these laws vary in form, function, and scope, they share an overriding logic and spirit. It appears in many of the laws that a new rhetorical and discursive reality is being crafted, one wherein militant and disruptive protest is termed "rioting" and the demonstrators thus become "rioters." In Missouri, anti-masking laws would ban the concealing of one's identity "while committing the crime of unlawful assembly or rioting,"[110] including the use of gas masks and ventilators designed to aid demonstrators' breathing when confronted with tear gas and pepper spray used by police. In Tennessee, a newly introduced law would indemnify drivers who hit a demonstrator with their car if the demonstrator is blocking traffic. Republican State Representative Matthew Hill, who advocates for the bill, said:

> If you want to protest, fine, I am for peaceful protesting, not lawless rioters. . . . We don't want anyone to be hurt, but people should not knowingly put themselves in harm's way when you've got moms and dads trying to get their kids to school.[111]

Hill's comments show the subtle manner through which those blocking roadways in protest are quickly recast as "lawless rioters." In Arizona, the state senate voted to expand current racketeering laws designed to prosecute organized crime to include political demonstrations. The bill redefines "rioting" as being actions that result in the damage of property and allows the government to prosecute and seize the assets of everyone who planned or participated in a protest. In his defense of the law, Senator John Kavanagh stated, "You now have a situation where you have full-time, almost professional agent-provocateurs that attempt to create public disorder. . . . A lot of them are ideologues, some of them are anarchists."[112] Not only does this framing again draw the connection between anarchists and violence, but also by including *rioting* within the racketeering law, police are able to arrest protest organizers *before* a demonstration if they have reason to believe property will be damaged.

The introduction of these bills appears timed to coincide with demonstrations opposing the newly elected administration of Donald Trump as president of the United States, though the active, broad-based, and disruptive campaigns simultaneously occurring under the Movement for Black Lives (i.e. #BlackLivesMatter) and anti-Dakota Access Pipeline (i.e. #NoDAPL) movement should not be discounted. Other bills introduced or voted on in the first month of the Trump presidency include similar legislation in Florida, Georgia, Iowa, Indiana, Michigan, Minnesota, Mississippi, North Carolina, North Dakota, Oklahoma, Oregon, South Dakota, Virginia, and Washington.[113] The Oregon law requires public colleges and universities to expel a student convicted of participating in a riot, while a Virginia bill increases penalties for those who refuse to leave an unlawful assembly. In nearly all cases, the use of "rioting" replaces language such as *demonstrator*, *protestor*, or *activist*.

These legislative steps have functioned in tandem with reports of police's increasing employment of aggressive surveillance technologies—typically reserved for national security and counter-terrorism cases. According to a report authored by *The Intercept*, surveillance technologies designed for military and intelligence purposes are increasingly being purchased by police departments, further blurring the line between policing and national security/counter-terrorism. Critics of these technologies note that they have been used to monitor citizens without search warrants and that warrants, when issued, have been overly broad.[114] Some of these technologies appear to have wide usage already. *The Intercept* report states, "nearly 60 law enforcement agencies in 23 states are known to possess a Stingray [a cell site simulator designed to mimic cellular towers and track and/or monitor phone activity]."[115] The American Civil Liberties Union (ACLU) has identified 71 agencies in 24 states with this technology.[116] According to *The Intercept* investigation, in one jurisdiction, Baltimore, Maryland, Stingray devices were used more than 4,300 times from 2007 to 2015. Further investigations have also demonstrated that despite claims to the contrary, these technologies are *not* being used to investigate terrorism, as according to the ACLU, in 128 cases documents in Tacoma, Washington, none of these usages involved the purported task of preventing terrorism.[117] Nationally, at least 13 federal agencies are known to have used technologies that masquerade as a legitimate cell tower to collect cellular traffic wholesale, including the FBI; Drug Enforcement Administration; Secret Service; Immigration and Customs Enforcement; Marshals Service; Bureau of Alcohol Tobacco, Firearms, and Explosives; Internal Revenue Service; National Security Agency; and various branches of the military.[118]

Beyond laws that further criminalize some manners of protest and communications technologies that facilitate mass surveillance, there appears to be a resurgent discourse equating oppositional politics with terrorism—especially anarchism. In one example, a 2017 report co-authored with the Department of Homeland Security and a North Carolina intelligence contractor focuses on a few incidents of property destruction in the run up to the election. These incidents, which include the use of arson to damage a political office, are subtly discussed as "domestic terrorism":

> DHS assesses that anger over the results of the 2016 Presidential election continues to be a driver of domestic terrorist violence throughout the United States—as evidenced by rioting in Portland, Oregon, following the election and violence and destruction of property in Washington during the inauguration.[119]

This framing, one which comingles undefined "domestic terrorism" with anti-Trump marches involving property destruction is troubling to say the least. This is far more than a rhetorical frame as the previous legislative histories demonstrate. In one alarming example, more than 220 individuals arrested during a counter-inaugural march in Washington, D.C. (20 January 2017) have been charged *federally* with felonies such as rioting, conspiracy, and incitement, in an unprecedented *collective* prosecution that challenges firmly established jurisprudence based in the presumption of innocence and the need for the state to present evidence against an individual defendant.[120] In this case, the rhetorical leap from *march* to *riot* takes a literal and juridical turn and becomes prosecutorial policy.

The securitized framing and counter-security measures deployed by law enforcement during public protests reflects a desire to understand a growing wave of popular protest as some manner of existential threat to the state; a national security issue undermining the democratic discourse of social change. This frame is repeated in security briefings and reports, including the previously mentioned North Carolina assessment. It is worth noting that the DHS report does *not* note the rapid rise in Islamaphobic violence or the never before seen series of bomb threats and vandalism targeting Jewish institutions in North Carolina and elsewhere.[121] While such a framing of militant protest generally and anarchists specifically is on the accession, it is not a creation of the Trump administration. Following are some notable government releases that serve to equate anarchists and animal and earth liberationists (e.g. ALF and ELF) with terrorists and terrorism:

- **2008:** A report by the Missouri Information Analysis Center and the Missouri State Highway Patrol on the "anarchist movement" provides a history of anarchism and concludes "we believe the [anarchist] groups discussed pose a significant domestic terrorist threat at this time . . . anarchists operate either as lone wolves, in small cells (3–4 members), or can, at times, rally as anonymous mobs."[122]

- **2009:** In a "terrorist, insurgent and militant group logo recognition guide" prepared by the US Army for its Training and Doctrine Command and Intelligence Support Activity, the ALF is listed as a terrorist network in the UK, and in the US, the report lists the ALF, ELF, Earth First!, Animal Rights Militia, BLA, SLA, WUO, and Puerto Rican separatists as "terrorists/extremists,"[123] preceded by white supremacist, skinhead, neo-Nazi, and anti-abortion networks[124] known to routinely deploy lethal violence.

- **~2011:** In an FBI training document unclassified prior to 2011, the agency describes "animal rights/environmental extremism" within policies and laws dealing with domestic terrorism.[125] In a similarly styled presentation published by the agency's Domestic Terrorism Operations Unit profiles "anarchist extremists" in a 25-slide presentation. The heavily redacted materials describe anarchists engaging in legal, non-terroristic, mass convergences common in the anti-globalization era, noting that these networks have goals such as to "Create a political statement [,] Generate media coverage for their cause [, and] Disrupt law enforcement activity."[126] The fact that the Domestic Terrorism Operations Unit is briefing agents on anarchist protest methods, most of which is legal protected speech, is in itself troubling, and shows the blurring of the FBI's policing and national security/counter-terrorism focus.[127]

- **2012:** In a report authored by the Congressional Research Service and dealing with "The Domestic Terrorist Threat," the words "anarchist" and "anarchism" appear a combined total of 60 times in 66 pages. The report notes that the federal government "has used broad conceptualizations to describe domestic terrorism," noting that this "may lead to inconsistencies in the development and application of the law in the domestic terrorism arena."[128] This statement seems to acknowledge the subjective nature of legally determining the distinction between protest, civil disobedience, extremism, and terrorism.

- **2013:** In a DHS report detailing "homeland security threat[s]" 2008–2013, the author notes "animal-rights and environmental extremists are the most active domestic extremist groups, but white supremacists and militias are more violent."[129] The report notes that "leftwing extremists" include anti-capitalist, anti-globalization, and anarchist philosophies.[130] This framing clearly draws comparisons between a legal protest movement (i.e. the anti-globalization movement) employing common methods of civil disobedience and 'extremism.' The report later notes that "violent anarchists, animal-rights, and environmental groups, promote leaderless resistance tactics including operating in small, autonomous cells or individually to elude detection and complicate law enforcement operations."[131] This framing serves to cast affinity groups and individual actions as akin to terrorist cells

In the contemporary movement, it is still unclear what effect these frames, rhetorics, and legal maneuverings will have on the waves of anti-Trump protests sweeping parts of the nation. From a review of these cases, it appears that while the state is moving to restrict the actions of the right that meet a definition of terrorism, the opposite is occurring when the left is the subject. For example, in the prosecution of Adam Purinton, charged with shooting three individuals and killing one inside a restaurant in Kansas, Purinton reportedly shouted "get out of my country" before shooting the men he believed were "middle eastern" but were in fact Indian. In this case, it is being argued that despite the shooter's obvious ethnic bias, since his actions were primarily motivated by a disagreement and not a more generalized hatred of the ethnic group, the act is more akin to a hate crime than an act of domestic, anti-Arab/Indian/Asian terrorism.[132] Therefore, in this single example, there appears to be an effort to further tailor the application of the terrorist label, while for the left, the trend appears to be heading in the opposite direction toward a wider, more generalized application.

A Documentary History: Domestic Leftist Terrorism Read Through the FBI

Finally, in developing a historical understanding of how leftist groups, networks, and methods are described, criminalized, and added to the lexicon of terrorism, it is helpful to examine the annual reports produced by the nation's premier domestic terrorism tracking agency, the FBI. Through a brief review of a series FBI reports (1996–2005),[133] we can see how the left has been described over time. The following account focuses on what attacks are highlighted nationally, as well as how the actions of leftists are described in these reports—and their centrality or marginality in the overall narratives.

1996 (FBI): This report focuses on three terrorist attacks by right-wing networks (i.e. Eric Robert Rudolph's attack of the Centennial Olympic Park and a robbery and bombing by Phineas Priesthood) and notes:

> Threats from domestic terrorism continue to build as militia extremists . . . gain new adherents, stockpile weapons, and prepare for armed conflict with the federal government. The potential for domestic right-wing terrorism remains a threat.[134]

In their section dealing with "left-wing terrorism," the report highlights "Puerto Rican terrorist groups." The discussion concludes by stating: "Over the last three decades, leftist-oriented extremist groups posed the predominant domestic terrorist threat to the United States. In the 1980s the FBI dismantled many of these groups . . . and the threat has diminished."[135]

1997 (FBI): This report focuses on two incidents of terrorism and two suspected incidents, none of which resulted in injury. The "suspected incidents" are bombings later attributed to Eric Rudolph, the anti-abortion, anti-LGBT, right-wing militant. The report also details a raid targeting the Ku Klux Klan, which had conspired to carry out an armed robbery of a drug dealer. Similar plots by right-wing militias were also uncovered and disrupted. While leftist actions were not the focus of the previous year's report, in 1997 they are entirely excluded. To this end, not even the word "leftist" or "left-wing" is included in the report.[136]

1998 (FBI): This reports represents a shift from the previous 2 years. To begin with, the report's cover displays an iconic image of an arson carried out in Vail, Colorado, by the ELF. The report details five terrorist incidents occurring in US territories, including three in Puerto Rico. The fourth incident is an anti-abortion bombing attributed to Eric Rudolph, and the fifth, the arson in Vail. According to the report, the arson "caused 12 million dollars in damage, but resulted in no deaths or injuries."[137] The report plainly calls the arson an "act of domestic terrorism" and notes that two federal agencies and two police agencies were engaged in a joint investigation. The report also details numerous plots disrupted involving right-wing and militia movements such as The Order.

1999 (FBI): This report notes in the opening page:

> Despite fears of international plots in the United States, 1999 was, in fact, characterized by a sharp increase in domestic terrorism, driven by a troubling upswing in activity carried out by animal rights and environmental extremists. These special interest or single issue terrorists committed eight of the ten terrorist incidents recorded.[138]

The report details six ALF attacks and two ELF attacks, being careful to note that two of the ALF attacks "led to the deaths of lab animals."[139] Though the frequency of these attacks garner attention, their *terrorizing* role rings hollow when read in context. Directly after describing the ALF/ELF annual trend, the report states, "By contrast, the two-state shooting rampage of Benjamin Nathaniel Smith, a right-wing extremist . . . left two individuals dead and eight others wounded."[140] The sentence directly after reads, "A firearms attacks on a Jewish Community Center . . . [by a known Aryan Nations member] wounded three children, a camp counselor and a receptionist."[141] When placed side by side, the actions of those fighting in the name of animals and environment seems ill matched with those advocating white supremacy through shooting children on the basis of ethnicity and religion.

The remainder of the report details attacks that include an ALF arson targeting circus vehicles in New Jersey, the theft of research animals from the University of Minnesota, the arson of a meat company in Oregon, the theft of "55 dogs implanted with pacemakers" from a laboratory in California, the theft of animals from a laboratory at the Western Washington University, the vandalism of laboratory equipment at Washington State University, the arson of a logging company in Oregon, and the arson of a facility at Michigan State University conducting experiments on genetically modified organisms. To underscore the point again, while the arson of property and theft of laboratory animals is illegal, it appears to differ wildly from the attacks the FBI reports to have prevented that year, including an Aryan Nations bombing in Cincinnati, the smuggling of 35 weapons to the Irish Republican Army, a financially motivated plot to bomb a pipeline in Canada, the bombing of a propane storage facility in California, a conspiracy to steal weapons and ambush police by a militia member in Tampa, and a bombing by a known jihadist captured while trying to enter the country illegally.

2000–2001 (FBI): As one would expect, the 2001 report was focused around the attacks of September 11, 2001, and the ongoing threat posed by al-Qaeda and its allies. What is most notable about this report, is that despite the loss of nearly 3,000 human lives and numerous additional attacks on US forces abroad (e.g. *USS Cole*), the "In Focus" section of the report does not detail this threat but instead is explicitly focused on "Trends in

Animal Rights and Environmental Extremism."[142] It seems odd that immediately following the largest terrorist attack to ever occur on US soil—an attack that "claimed more lives than all previous acts of terrorism in the United States combined"[143]—the FBI remains focused on disrupting the campaign of property destruction being carried out by the ALF/ELF. In the chronology of the report, the FBI notes that all eight of the "terrorist incidents" recorded in 2000 were the work of ALF/ELF or its allies (e.g. Revenge of the Trees, Coalition to Save the Preserves). Of the 14 terrorist incidents occurring in 2001, ten were carried out by "eco-terrorists"; two were bank robberies carried out by Clayton Wagner, an anti-abortion militant associated with the Army of God; and the last incident was the al-Qaeda attacks of September 11. Therefore, while the FBI does note that none of the attacks by leftists led to injury or death, the fact that all successful attacks in 2000 and the majority of attacks in 2001 were the work of "eco-terrorists," this frequency seems to motivate the agency's sustained focus on the left's activities.

2002–2005 (FBI): This report, which spans 4 years, continues the trend witnessed in previous years. As the report states:

> In keeping with a longstanding trend, domestic extremists carried out the majority of terrorist incidents during this period [2002–2005]. Twenty three of the 24 recorded terrorist incidents were perpetuated by domestic terrorists. With the exception of a white supremacist's firebombing of a synagogue in Oklahoma City, Oklahoma, all of the domestic terrorist incidents were committed by social interest extremists active in the animal rights and environmental movements.[144]

Interestingly, in another recurring trend, the majority of the *prevented* acts of domestic terrorism was carried out by right-wing groups and would have likely involved civilian fatalities. In this report, eight of the 14 failed attacks are from right-wing groups based in a pro-militia, white supremacist, or anti-abortion politics. These plots involved shootings; the use of cyanide; and assassination attempts targeting government facilities, healthcare clinics, religious sites, and individual ethnic, religious, and racial groups.

Homeland Security Threat Assessment: Evaluating Threats 2008–2013: The final report under review was published by the Department of Homeland Security (DHS). While originally envisioned as an umbrella agency including the FBI, final implementation of the DHS allowed the FBI to remain an independent agency. Therefore, the DHS report represents a somewhat independent (from the FBI) view on homeland security and domestic terrorism worth exploring.

In this report, the author notes that "far left" extremists are typically linked to "single issues" such as animal rights and the environment. This is a continuation of the FBI's taxonomy that separates "single issue extremists" (e.g. ALF, ELF) from "leftwing extremists" (e.g. anarchists, anti-capitalists).[145] Sometimes these are maintained as distinct categories and sometimes that are flattened into a single label, displaying the flexibility through which this label is applied. For example, in the same report that distinguishes "single issue" and "left wing" extremists, the very next page states, "Leftwing extremists, such as violent anarchists, animal-rights, and environmental groups, promote leaderless resistance tactics including operating in small, autonomous cells or individually to elude detection and complicate law enforcement operations."[146]

During this time, other DHS and FBI reports focus on the perceived threat of "leftist"[147] or "eco-terrorist"[148] networks, specially mentioning "animal rights and environmental extremists" and "anarchist extremists," naming the ALF, ELF, Stop Huntingdon Animal Cruelty, the Animal Defense League, Earth First!, CrimethInc., the Ruckus Society, and Recreate 68 specifically.[149] This is similar to the 2011 "Domestic Terrorism and Homegrown Violent Extremism Lexicon," which maintains entries for "anarchist extremists," "animal rights extremists," and "environmental rights extremists."[150]

Conclusion

The history of leftist terrorism in the United States is largely a record of the changing discourse surrounding social protest and the use of militant and illegal means within campaigns of political contestation. The assassination of heads of state, common in the 19th and 20th centuries, likely fits a standard definition of terrorism for many. However, when these political movements target *property* and actively avoid human causalities while still earning a defamatory label from state authorities, this demonstrates a deliberate reframing that serves the purpose of repression far more than it serves as an apt descriptor of the actors themselves. The usage of the label of *terrorism* to describe animal liberation and environmental protest most clearly demonstrates this shift, as does the FBI's description of these networks of vandals as the 'number one domestic terrorism threat.'

From this history, the decision to label a particular individual, organization, network, or ideology as *terroristic* appears more reflective of the wider political context and the implications this has for federal policy. Acts of political violence once thought of in criminal terms have thus changed discursive form from remaining in the realm of policing to now constituting existential threats to national security. Therefore, the history of domestic leftist terrorism cannot be divorced from the genealogy of the discourse used to label these movements, and it is through a careful examination of this historical record that one can observe the power of language and the inherent authority of the state as a site of legalistic, rhetorical, and discursive construction.

NOTES

1   I have made this point in some detail in numerous publications, for example, see: Michael Loadenthal, "Deconstructing 'Eco-Terrorism': Rhetoric, Framing and Statecraft as Seen through the Insight Approach," *Critical Studies on Terrorism* 6, no. 1 (April 2013): 92–117; Michael Loadenthal, "Activism, Terrorism, and Social Movements: The 'Green Scare' as Monarchical Power," *Research in Social Movements, Conflicts and Change, Narratives of Identity in Social Movements, Kent State University* 40, no. 1 (August 16, 2016): 189–226.

2   Paul Wilkinson, *Terrorism versus Democracy: The Liberal State Response*, 1st ed., CASS Series on Political Violence (London, UK: Frank Cass, 2000), 26.

3   Max Weber, "Politik als Beruf (Politics as a Vocation)" (Lecture, Free Students Union, Munich University, January 1919), www.ne.jp/asahi/moriyuki/abukuma/weber/lecture/politics_vocation.html.

4   Ibid., 1–2.

5   Dale L. Watson, "The Terrorist Threat Confronting the United States," Testimony before the Senate Select Committee on Intelligence (Washington, DC: Federal Bureau of Investigation, February 6, 2002), www.fbi.gov/news/testimony/the-terrorist-threat-confronting-the-united-states.

6   Michelle Ye Hee Lee, "The Viral Claim That 'Not One' Refugee Resettled since 9/11 Has Been 'Arrested on Domestic Terrorism Charges'," *Washington Post*, November 19, 2015, Online edition, sec. News: Fact Checker, www.washingtonpost.com/news/fact-checker/wp/2015/11/19/the-viral-claim-that-not-one-refugee-resettled-since-911-has-been-arrested-on-domestic-terrorism-charges/.

7   Bard E. O'Neill, *Insurgency & Terrorism* (Dulles, VA: Potomac Books, 2001), 24.

8   It is interesting to note that in 2011, the FBI stated, "In accordance with U.S. counterterrorism policy, the FBI considers terrorists to be criminals." U.S. Department of Justice, Federal Bureau of Investigation, "Terrorism 2000/2001" (Washington, DC: U.S. Department of Justice, 2001), iii, www.fbi.gov/stats-services/publications/terror/terrorism-2000-2001. Thus for the FBI, while all terrorists are criminals, not all forms of crime are terroristic.

9   Walter Laqueur, ed., *Voices of Terror: Manifestos, Writings and Manuals of Al Qaeda, Hamas, and Other Terrorists from around the World and Throughout the Ages* (New York, NY: Sourcebooks, Inc., 2004) [Quote taken from book cover].

10 Federal Bureau of Investigation, "Terrorism in the United States 1999," Annual Report (Washington, DC: U.S. Department of Justice, Federal Bureau of Investigation, Counterterrorism Threat Assessment and Warning Unit, Counterterrorism Division, 1999), 21, www.fbi.gov/file-repository/stats-services-publications-terror_99.pdf/view.

11 Ibid.

12 Bruce Hoffman, *Inside Terrorism* (New York, NY: Columbia University Press, 2006), 157–158; R. Hrair Dekmejian, *Spectrum of Terror* (Washington, DC: CQ Press, 2007), 10.

13 Hoffman, *Inside Terrorism*, 157–158.

14 Cindy Milstein, *Anarchism and Its Aspirations*, 1st ed., vol. 1, Anarchist Interventions (Oakland, CA: AK Press & The Institute for Anarchist Studies, 2010), 68–70; Anna Feigenbaum, Fabian Frenzel, and Patrick McCurdy, *Protest Camps* (London, UK: Zed Books, 2013), 153; Timothy Luchies, "Towards an Insurrectionary Power/ Knowledge: Movement-Relevance, Anti-Oppression, Prefiguration," *Social Movement Studies* 14, no. 3 (2015): 1–16.

15 This is taken from an interview with Michael "Bommi" Baumann in 1978, contained in: Hoffman, *Inside Terrorism*, 158.

16 Philip Jenkins, *Images of Terror: What We Can and Can't Know about Terrorism* (New York, NY: Aldine Transaction, 2003), 37.

17 Hoffman, *Inside Terrorism*, 158.

18 Ibid.

19 U.S. Department of Homeland Security, Homeland Security Intelligence Council, Under Secretary for Intelligence and Analysis, "Homeland Security Threat Assessment: Evaluating Threats 2008–2013," Assessment (Washington, DC: Strategic Analysis Group, Homeland Environment Threat Analysis Division, Office of Intelligence and Analysis, 2008), 27, http://info.publicintelligence.net/DHS-Threats2008-2013.pdf.

20 Serena Ng and Christina Binkley, "S.C. Johnson Pulls Kiwi Mink Oil after Animal Rights Threat," *Wall Street Journal*, November 22, 2013, Online edition, sec. Business, http://online.wsj.com/news/articles/SB10001424052702303653004579214373428064280.

21 David C. Rapoport, "The Four Waves of Rebel Terror and September 11," *Anthropoetics* 8, no. 1 (Spring/Summer 2002), www.anthropoetics.ucla.edu/apo801/terror.htm.

22 Derek Offord, *The Russian Revolutionary Movement in the 1880s* (Cambridge, UK: Cambridge University Press, 2004), 24.

23 Peter Kropotkin, "The Spirit of Revolt" (Commonweal (Republished by Anarchy Archives), 1892), http://dwardmac.pitzer.edu/anarchist_archives/kropotkin/spiritofrevolt.html.

24 Aragorn!, "Nihilism Anarchy and the 21st Century" (Self Published (Republished by the Anarchist Library), 2009), 25, http://theanarchistlibrary.org/library/aragorn-nihilism-anarchy-and-the-21st-century.

25 Johan Galtung, "Violence, Peace, and Peace Research," *Journal of Peace Research* 6, no. 3 (January 1, 1969): 167–191.

26 Susan Tejada, *In Search of Sacco & Vanzetti: Double Lives, Troubled Times, & the Massachusetts Murder Case That Shook the World* (Boston, MA: Northeastern University Press, 2012), 103.

27 Steve J. Shone, *American Anarchism* (Leiden, Netherlands: Brill, 2013), 203.

28 Watson, "The Terrorist Threat Confronting the United States."

29 Ibid.

30 Ward Churchill and Jim Vander Wall, *The COINTELPRO Papers* (Cambridge, MA: South End Press, 2002), 303.

31 Gus Martin, *Essentials of Terrorism: Concepts and Controversies*, 4th ed. (Los Angeles, CA: Sage Publications, 2016), 171.

32 Gus Martin, *Understanding Terrorism: Challenges, Perspectives, and Issues*, 5th ed. (Los Angeles, CA: Sage Publications, 2015), 172.

33 Martin, *Essentials of Terrorism*, 172.

34 Martin, *Understanding Terrorism*, 166.

35 Brigitte L. Nacos, *Terrorism and Counterterrorism*, 5th ed. (New York, NY: Routledge, 2016), 87.

36 Martin, *Essentials of Terrorism*, 180.

37 Federal Bureau of Investigation, "Terrorism in the United States 1999," 29.

38 Federal Bureau of Investigation, "Subject: George Jackson Bridade [Sic]," Freedom of Information/Privacy Acts Section (Washington, DC & Seattle, WA: Federal Bureau of Investigation, 1977, 1976), https://vault.fbi.gov/George%20Jackson%20Brigade%20/George%20Jackson%20Brigade%20Part%2001%20of%2005.

39 Daniel Burton-Rose, ed., *Creating a Movement with Teeth a Documentary History of the George Jackson Brigade* (Oakland, CA: PM Press, 2010).

40 Michael J. Shapiro, *The Time of the City: Politics, Philosophy and Genre* (New York, NY: Routledge, 2010), 109.

41 Ibid., 108.

42 Federal Bureau of Investigation, "Terrorism in the United States 1999," 19.

43 Jenkins, *Images of Terror*, 38–39.

44 This history is described in great detail in a series of publications I have authored including Michael Loadenthal, "Superglue, Bolt Cutters & Homemade Incendiaries: A Targeting, Tactical & Communication Methods Analysis of the Earth Liberation Front's Attack History 1996–2009" (Centre for the Study of Terrorism and Political Violence, University of St Andrews, St Andrews, Scotland, 2010); Michael Loadenthal, "Nor Hostages, Assassinations, or Hijackings, but Sabotage, Vandalism & Fire: 'Eco-Terrorism' as Political Violence Challenging the State and Capital" (MLitt Dissertation, Centre for the Study of Terrorism and Political Violence, University of St Andrews, St Andrews, Scotland, 2010); Michael Loadenthal, "The Earth Liberation Front: A Social Movement Analysis," *Radical Criminology, Critical Criminology Working Group* 0, no. 2 (September 21, 2013): 15–46; Loadenthal, "Deconstructing 'Eco-Terrorism': Rhetoric, Framing, and Statecraft, Seen through the Insight Approach"; Michael Loadenthal, "Eco-Terrorism? Countering Dominant Narratives of Securitisation: A Critical, Quantitative History of the Earth Liberation Front (1996–2009)," *Perspectives on Terrorism, (Center for Terrorism and Security Studies, Terrorism Research Initiative)* 8, no. 3 (June 25, 2014): 16–50; Michael Loadenthal, "'The Green Scare' & 'Eco-Terrorism': The Development of US Counter-Terrorism Strategy Targeting Direct Action Activists," in *The Terrorization of Dissent: Corporate Repression, Legal Corruption and the Animal Enterprise Terrorism Act*, ed. Jason Del Gandio and Anthony Nocella (New York, NY: Lantern Books, 2014); Loadenthal, "Activism, Terrorism, and Social Movements"; "'Eco-Terrorism': An Incident-Driven History of Attack (1973–2010)." *Journal for the Study of Radicalism* 11, no. 2 (Fall 2017): 1–33.

45 Animalliberationfront.com, "The ALF Credo and Guidelines" (Animalliberationfront.com, n.d.), www.animal-liberationfront.com/ALFront/alf_credo.htm.

46 Ibid.

47 Loadenthal, "Nor Hostages, Assassinations, or Hijackings, but Sabotage, Vandalism & Fire: 'Eco-Terrorism' as Political Violence Challenging the State and Capital," 94.

48 Ibid; Additional quantitative analysis of "eco-terrorism" is included in: Loadenthal, "Superglue, Bolt Cutters & Homemade Incendiaries: A Targeting, Tactical & Communication Methods Analysis of the Earth Liberation Front's Attack History 1996–2009"; Loadenthal, "Eco-Terrorism? Countering Dominant Narratives of Securitisation: A Critical, Quantitative History of the Earth Liberation Front (1996–2009)."

49 Watson, "The Terrorist Threat Confronting the United States."

50 Tim Jensen, "The Rhetoric of Eco-Terrorism," Online Journal, *Harlot: A Revealing Look at the Arts of Persuasion* (March 11, 2012), http://harlotofthearts.org/blog/2012/03/11/the-rhetoric-of-eco-terrorism/.

51 109th Congress, "Oversight on Eco-Terrorism Specifically Examining the Earth Liberation Front ('ELF') and the Animal Liberation Front ('ALF')" (United States Senate Committee on Environmental and Public Works, May 18, 2005), 17, http://epw.senate.gov/hearing_statements.cfm?id=237836; Will Potter, *Green Is the New Red: An Insider's Account of a Social Movement Under Siege* (San Francisco, CA: City Lights Publishers, 2011), 44–45.

52 Jensen, "The Rhetoric of Eco-Terrorism."

53 Jerry Spangler, "Animal Activists Still a Top Threat," *Deseret News*, November 19, 2001, www.deseretnews.com/article/875166/Animal-activists-still-a-top-threat.html?pg=all.

54 109th Congress, "Oversight on Eco-Terrorism Specifically Examining the Earth Liberation Front ('ELF') and the Animal Liberation Front ('ALF')"; James Jarboe, "The Threat of Eco-Terrorism" (FBI/House Resources Committee, Subcommittee on Forests and Forest Health, February 12, 2002), www.fbi.gov/news/testimony/the-threat-of-eco-terrorism.

55 Alex Guillen and Juana Summers, "Rick Santorum Slams 'Reign of Environmental Terror': Alex Guillen and Juana Summers," *Politico*, February 9, 2012, Politico Pro Online edition, www.politico.com/news/stories/0212/72681.html.

56 John Lewis, "Animal Rights Extremism and Ecoterrorism" (FBI/Senate Judiciary Committee, May 18, 2004), www.fbi.gov/news/testimony/animal-rights-extremism-and-ecoterrorism.

57 See for example: Karin J. Immergut et al., "Government's Sentencing Memorandum in the United States District Court for the District of Oregon [Case Numbers CR 06–60069-AA, CR 06–60070-AA, CR 06–60071-AA, CR 06–60078-AA, CR 06–60079-AA, CR 06–60080-AA, CR 06–60120-AA, 06–60122-AA, 06–60123-AA, 06–60124-AA, 06–60125-AA, 06–60126-AA]" (United States District Court for the District of Oregon, May 4, 2007).

58 109th Congress, "Animal Enterprise Terrorism Act—S. 3880" (2006), www.govtrack.us/congress/bills/109/s3880/text.

59 Kristina Davis, "Woman Who Freed Minks from Farms across the Country Gets Plea Deal," *Los Angeles Times*, December 28, 2016, Online edition, sec. Local: LA Now, www.latimes.com/local/lanow/la-me-fur-rampage-20161228-story.html.

60 The United States Attorney's Office Southern District of California, John Parmley, and Michael Kaplan, "Animal Rights Activist Sentenced to 21 Months for Cross-Country Crime Spree Targeting Fur Industry," News Release Summary (Southern District of California: United States Department of Justice, January 17, 2017), www.justice.gov/usao-sdca/pr/animal-rights-activist-sentenced-21-months-cross-country-crime-spree-targeting-fur.

61 Chicagoist, "Activist Who Freed 2,000 Minks From Illinois Farm Sentenced Under Obscure Terrorism Law," News, Chicagoist (March 23, 2016), http://chicagoist.com/2016/03/23/second_animal_rights_activist_sente.php.

62 Ed Pilkington, "Animal Rights 'Terrorists'? Legality of Industry-Friendly Law to Be Challenged," *The Guardian*, February 19, 2015, Online edition, sec. US News, www.theguardian.com/us-news/2015/feb/19/animal-rights-activists-challenge-federal-terrorism-charges.

63 United States of America v. Kevin Johnson, Tyler Lang, No. No. 14 CR 390, accessed January 1, 2017.

64 Loadenthal, "Nor Hostages, Assassinations, or Hijackings, but Sabotage, Vandalism & Fire: 'Eco-Terrorism' as Political Violence Challenging the State and Capital," 36, 97–99; Randy Borum and Chuck Tilby, "Anarchist Direct Actions: A Challenge for Law Enforcement," *Studies in Conflict & Terrorism* 28, no. 3 (2005): 212, doi:10.1080/10576100590928106; Stefan H. Leader and Peter Probst, "The Earth Liberation Front And Environmental Terrorism," *Terrorism and Political Violence* 15, no. 4 (2003): 44, doi:10.1080/09546550390449872; Bron Taylor, "Religion, Violence and Radical Environmentalism: From Earth First! To the Unabomber to the Earth Liberation Front," *Terrorism and Political Violence* 10, no. 4 (1998): 3, 8, doi:10.1080/09546559808427480.

65 Animalliberationfront.com, "The ALF Credo and Guidelines."

66 Laura Lambert, "Evan Mecham Eco-Terrorist International Conspiracy," in *The SAGE Encyclopedia of Terrorism*, 2nd ed., ed. Gus Martin (Thousand Oaks, CA: Sage Publications, 2011), 190.

67 This is according to data collected by the National Consortium for the Study of Terrorism and Responses to Terrorism, www.start.umd.edu/gtd/search/Results.aspx?chart=overtime&casualties_type=&casualties_max=&perpetrator=10056.

68 See San Diego listing at www.fbi.gov/wanted/wanted_terrorists/daniel-andreas-san-diego/@@download.pdf and the complete Most Wanted Terrorist list hosted at www.fbi.gov/wanted/wanted_terrorists

69 The other individual being Joanne Chesimard, better known as Assata Shakur, convicted for the murder of a police officer linked to BLA.

70 Jehad Serwan Mostafa, Abdul Rahman Yasin.

71 Loadenthal, "'The Green Scare' & 'Eco-Terrorism': The Development of US Counter-Terrorism Strategy Targeting Direct Action Activists," 95.

72 Nick Deshpande, Howard Ernst, and National Consortium for the Study of Terrorism and Responses to Terrorism, "Countering Eco-Terrorism in the United States: The Case of 'Operation Backfire,'" Final Report to the Science & Technology Directorate, U.S. Department of Homeland Security (College Park, MD: National Consortium for the Study of Terrorism and Responses to Terrorism (START), September 2012), 26–27, www.start.umd.edu/sites/default/files/files/publications/Countermeasures_OperationBackfire.pdf.

73 Lewis, "Animal Rights Extremism and Ecoterrorism."

74 Federal Bureau of Investigation, "Terrorism in the United States 1999," 19.

75 The site is hosted at https://cve.fbi.gov/, as of 12 March 2017.

76 Federal Bureau of Investigation, "What Are Known Violent Extremist Groups? Domestic Extremist Ideologies: 'Enter the Website'" (FBI, 2017), https://cve.fbi.gov.

77 Jerome P. Bjelopera, "The Domestic Terrorist Threat: Background and Issues for Congress," CRS Report for Congress (Washington, DC: Congressional Research Service, May 15, 2012), 8.

78 Federal Bureau of Investigation, "What Are Known Violent Extremist Groups? Domestic Extremist Ideologies: 'Enter the Website'."

79 Federal Bureau of Investigation, "What Are Known Violent Extremist Groups?: Domestic Extremist Ideologies" (FBI, 2016), https://cve.fbi.gov/whatare/?state=domestic.

80 Ibid.

81 Federal Bureau of Investigation, "What Are Known Violent Extremist Groups? Domestic Extremist Ideologies: Anarchist Extremists" (FBI, 2016), https://cve.fbi.gov/whatare/?state=domestic.

82 DOJ, "Counterterrorism White Paper", 2006 as qtd. in Bjelopera, "The Domestic Terrorist Threat: Background and Issues for Congress."

83 "Men in Black with a Violent Agenda," FOX Tampa Bay, May 24, 2012, Online edition, sec. News, www.myfoxtampabay.com/story/18599070/the-men-in-black-with-a-violent-agenda.

84 Molly Redden, "Tar Sands Protesters Arrested on Terrorism-Related Charges for . . . Glittery Banner," *Mother Jones*, December 17, 2013, Online edition, sec. Politics, www.motherjones.com/politics/2013/12/tar-sands-keystone-protesters-arrested-terrorism-glitter.

85 Watson, "The Terrorist Threat Confronting the United States."

86 U.S. Department of Justice, Office of Inspector General, Oversight and Review Division, "A Review of the FBI's Investigative Activities Concerning Potential Protesters at the 2004 Democratic and Republican National Political Conventions" (Washington, DC: U.S. Department of Justice, April 27, 2006), 10, https://oig.justice.gov/special/s0604/final.pdf.

87 Frank Main, Mark Konkol, and Michael Lansu, "'NATO 3' Plotted Attacks on Obama Election HQ, Rahm's House, Police Stations, Prosecutors Say: Chicago Sun-Times," *Chicago Sun-Times*, May 19, 2012, www.suntimes.com/12635179-761/3-protesters-charged-with-conspiracy-to-commit-terrorism.html.

88 "The People of the State of Illinois vs. Brian Church, Jared Chase, Brent Betterly [12MC1–15344, 12MC1–15345, 12MC1–15347]" (Circuit Court of Cook County, IL: County Department, Criminal Division, May 19, 2012).

89 Ibid., 2.

90 Ibid.

91 Ibid.

92 Ibid.

93 Loadenthal, "Eco-Terrorism? Countering Dominant Narratives of Securitisation: A Critical, Quantitative History of the Earth Liberation Front (1996–2009)."

94 State of Illinois County of Cook, "The People of the State of Illinois vs. Brian Church, Jared Chase, Brent Betterly [12MC1–15344, 12MC1–15345, 12MC1–15347]."

95 "The June 2012 Grand Jury of the Circuit Court of Cook County (Brian Church, Jared Chase, Brent Betterly)" (Circuit Court of Cook County, IL: County Department, Criminal Division, June 13, 2012).

96 Michael Tarm, "NATO Protesters Indicted on 11 Counts in Chicago," *Associated Press*, June 27, 2012, www.foxnews.com/us/2012/06/20/apnewsbreak-nato-protesters-indicted-on-11-counts/.

97 Main, Konkol, and Lansu, "'NATO 3' Plotted Attacks on Obama Election HQ, Rahm's House, Police Stations, Prosecutors Say: Chicago Sun-Times."

98 Mark Rockwell, "Men Who Targeted Ohio Bridge with C-4 Plot Sentenced" (Government Security News, November 21, 2012), www.gsnmagazine.com/node/27872?c=federal_agencies_legislative.

99 The Smoking Gun, "Unmasked: Meet The FBI's Bridge Bomb Plot Snitch," *The Smoking Gun*, May 2, 2012, www.thesmokinggun.com/documents/fbi-informant-shaquille-azir-756123.

100 "United States of America v. Douglas L. Wright [Criminal Complaint]" (United States District Court for the Northern District of Ohio, April 30, 2012), 2.

101 The Smoking Gun, "Unmasked."

102 Robert Rozboril, "Brecksville Bridge Bomb Plotters Sentenced, Mayor Shares Thoughts about FBI, Suspects," *Sun News—Cleveland.com*, November 30, 2012, www.cleveland.com/brecksville/index.ssf/2012/11/brecksville_bridge_bomb_plotte.html.

103 "Three Men Sentenced to Prison for Roles in Plot to Bomb Ohio Bridge," FBI, November 20, 2012, www.fbi.gov/cleveland/press-releases/2012/three-men-sentenced-to-prison-for-roles-in-plot-to-bomb-ohio-bridge.

104 According to the FBI press release, as of 20 November 2012, the three convicted defendants had, "pleaded guilty . . . to conspiracy to use weapons of mass destruction, attempted use of weapons of mass destruction, and malicious use of an explosive device to destroy property used in interstate commerce" Ibid.

105 Will Potter, "3 NATO Protesters Charged with 'Terrorism' in Chicago: Identical to Other FBI Plots" (Green Is The New Red, May 21, 2012), www.greenisthenewred.com/blog/three-nato-protesters-terrorists/6119/.

106 See for example: Denny Walsh, "'Anna' the Informant: Student's Path to FBI Informant," *Sacramento Bee*, September 12, 2007, Online edition, www.sacbee.com/101/story/374324.html; Michael Loadenthal, "When Cops 'Go Native': Policing Revolution Through Sexual Infiltration and Panopticonism," *Critical Studies on Terrorism* 7, no. 1 (April 2014): 24–42, doi:10.1080/17539153.2013.877670; Ed Pilkington in New York, "Role of FBI Informant in Eco-Terrorism Case Probed after Documents Hint at Entrapment," *The Guardian*, January 13, 2015, www.theguardian.com/us-news/2015/jan/13/fbi-informant-anna-eric-mcdavid-eco-terrorism.

107 Daniel McGowan, "Tales from Inside the U.S. Gitmo," *The Huffington Post*, July 9, 2009, www.huffing-tonpost.com/daniel-mcgowan/tales-from-inside-the-us_b_212632.html; Will Potter, "The Secret US Prisons You've Never Heard of before," TED Talk, TED Fellows Retreat 2015, 2015, www.ted.com/talks/will_potter_the_secret_us_prisons_you_ve_never_heard_of_before.

108 Immergut et al., "Government's Sentencing Memorandum."

109 Christopher Ingraham, "Republican Lawmakers Introduce Bills to Curb Protesting in at Least 18 States," *Washington Post*, February 24, 2017, Online edition, sec. News: Wonkblog, www.washingtonpost.com/news/wonk/wp/2017/02/24/republican-lawmakers-introduce-bills-to-curb-protesting-in-at-least-17-states/.

110 CNN Wire, "Missouri Lawmaker Wants to Ban Masks at Protests," Q13 FOX News, February 2, 2017, Online edition, sec. National & World News: Politics, http://q13fox.com/2017/02/02/missouri-lawmaker-wants-to-ban-masks-at-protests/.

111 CNN Wire, "Tennessee Bill Would Make Drivers Immune from Civil Liability If They Hit Protesters in Street," FOX31 Denver, February 14, 2017, Online edition, sec. National/World News, http://kdvr.com/2017/02/13/tennessee-bill-would-make-drivers-immune-from-civil-liability-if-they-hit-protesters-blocking-street/.

112 Howard Fischer, "Arizona Senate Votes to Seize Assets of Those Who Plan, Participate in Protests That Turn Violent," *Arizona Capitol Times*, February 23, 2017, Online edition, sec. Featured News, http://azcapitoltimes.com/news/2017/02/22/arizona-senate-crackdown-on-protests/.

113 Ingraham, "Republican Lawmakers Introduce Bills to Curb Protesting in at Least 18 States."

114 Jeremy Scahill and Margot Williams, "A Secret Catalogue of Government Gear for Spying on Your Cellphone," *The Intercept*, December 17, 2015, Online edition, https://theintercept.com/2015/12/17/a-secret-catalogue-of-government-gear-for-spying-on-your-cellphone/.

115 Ibid.

116 American Civil Liberties Union, "Stingray Tracking Devices: Who's Got Them?," *American Civil Liberties Union*, 2017, www.aclu.org/map/stingray-tracking-devices-whos-got-them.

117 Scahill and Williams, "A Secret Catalogue of Government Gear for Spying on Your Cellphone."

118 American Civil Liberties Union, "Stingray Tracking Devices."

119 North Carolina Information Sharing and Analysis Center and Department of Homeland Security Office of Intelligence & Analysis, "North Carolina: Recent Spike in Election-Related Physical and Cyber Incidents against Political Institutions Likely to Decrease in the Short Term, but Threat Environment Remain Unpredictable," Unclassified/For Official Use Only (February 21, 2017).

120 For the sake of transparency, this author is one of the named defendants—"United States vs. Michael Loadenthal (Case No: 2017 CF2 1246)"—which at the time of writing (March 2017), is still ongoing. At this stage, all defendants have been indicted, but only a few have been individually accused of specific, identified, criminal acts. The police and prosecution have retained all cellphones, cameras and other devices upon arrest, and have offered hundreds of hours of video (e.g. traffic cameras, officer body cameras, CCTV located on businesses, social media postings, etc.) as evidence. Some defendants, including this author, have also had their social media accounts, cloud storage, and phone records subpoenaed during the Grand Jury phase.

121 Ryan Devereaux, "Homeland Security Sees Anger at Trump as a Driver of 'Domestic Terrorist Violence'," *The Intercept*, March 2, 2017, Online edition, https://theintercept.com/2017/03/02/homeland-security-sees-anger-at-trump-as-a-driver-of-domestic-terrorist-violence/.

122 Missouri Information Analysis Center, Division of Drug & Crime Control, "MIAC Strategic Report: Anarchist Movement," Strategic Report (Jefferson City, MO: Missouri Information Analysis Center & Missouri State Highway Patrol, November 28, 2008), 5.

123 US Army Training And Doctrine Command and Intelligence Support Activity, "Terrorist, Insurgent & Militant Group Logo Recognition Guide" (Leavenworth, KS: Intelligence Support Activity, February 15, 2009), 76–77.

124 Ibid., 73–75.

125   Federal Bureau of Investigation, "Animal Rights/Environmental Extremism" (PowerPoint, FBI026408, Washington, DC, December 8, 2011), 10, 12, 13.

126   Federal Bureau of Investigation, Domestic Terrorism Operations Unit, "Anarchist Extremism" (PowerPoint, FBI026192, Washington, DC, December 8, 2011), 18.

127   John Hudson, "FBI Drops Law Enforcement as 'Primary' Mission," *Foreign Policy*, January 5, 2014.

128   Bjelopera, "The Domestic Terrorist Threat: Background and Issues for Congress," 67.

129   U.S. Department of Homeland Security, Homeland Security Intelligence Council, Under Secretary for Intelligence and Analysis, "Homeland Security Threat Assessment: Evaluating Threats 2008–2013," 25.

130   Ibid.

131   Ibid., 26.

132   Judy L. Thomas, "Olathe Attack Is a Hate Crime, but Not Likely Domestic Terrorism, Expert Says," *The Kansas City Star*, February 28, 2017, Online edition, sec. Crime, www.kansascity.com/news/local/crime/article135556933.html.

133   After the 2005 report, the FBI appears to have discontinued the publishing of *annual* reports on terrorism.

134   Federal Bureau of Investigation, "Terrorism in the United States 1997," Annual Report (Washington, DC: Federal Bureau of Investigation, Counterterrorism Threat Assessment and Warning Unit, National Security Division, 1997), ii, www.fbi.gov/file-repository/stats-services-publications-terror_97.pdf/view.

135   Ibid., 17–18.

136   Ibid.

137   Federal Bureau of Investigation, "Terrorism in the United States 1998," Annual Report (Washington, DC: Federal Bureau of Investigation, Counterterrorism Threat Assessment and Warning Unit, National Security Division, 1998), 1, www.fbi.gov/file-repository/stats-services-publications-terror_98.pdf/view.

138   Federal Bureau of Investigation, "Terrorism in the United States 1999," 1.

139   Ibid.

140   Ibid., 1–2.

141   Ibid., 2.

142   U.S. Department of Justice, Federal Bureau of Investigation, "Terrorism 2000/2001," 26–29.

143   Ibid., 1.

144   U.S. Department of Justice, Federal Bureau of Investigation, "Terrorism 2002–2005" (Washington, DC: Federal Bureau of Investigation, Counterterrorism Division, 2005), 1, www.fbi.gov/file-repository/stats-services-publications-terrorism-2002-2005-terror02_05.pdf/view.

145   U.S. Department of Homeland Security, Homeland Security Intelligence Council, Under Secretary for Intelligence and Analysis, "Homeland Security Threat Assessment: Evaluating Threats 2008–2013," 25.

146   Ibid., 26.

147   U.S. Department of Homeland Security, "Leftwing Extremists Likely to Increase Use of Cyber Attacks over the Coming Decade," Assessment (Washington, DC: Strategic Analysis Group, Homeland Environment and Threat Analysis Division, Office of Intelligence and Analysis, US Department of Homeland Security, January 26, 2009).

148   E.g. FBI Counterterrorism and Cyber Divisions, "Tactics Used by Eco-Terrorists to Detect and Thwart Law Enforcement Operations" (Washington, DC: FBI/Investigation Intelligence Assessment, 2004).

149   U.S. Department of Homeland Security, "Leftwing Extremists Likely to Increase Use of Cyber Attacks over the Coming Decade," 9.

150   U.S. Department of Homeland Security, "Domestic Terrorism and Homegrown Violent Extremism Lexicon" (Washington, DC: Office of Intelligence and Analysis, Homeland Counterterrorism Division, Homegrown Violent Extremism Branch, November 10, 2011).

REFERENCES

109th Congress. "Animal Enterprise Terrorism Act—S. 3880" 2006. www.govtrack.us/congress/bills/109/s3880/text.
———. "Oversight on Eco-Terrorism Specifically Examining the Earth Liberation Front ('ELF') and the Animal Liberation Front ('ALF')." United States Senate Committee on Environmental and Public Works, May 18, 2005. http://epw.senate.gov/hearing_statements.cfm?id=237836.

American Civil Liberties Union. "Stingray Tracking Devices: Who's Got Them?" American Civil Liberties Union, 2017. www.aclu.org/map/stingray-tracking-devices-whos-got-them.

Animalliberationfront.com. "The ALF Credo and Guidelines." Animalliberationfront.com, n.d. www.animalliberationfront.com/ALFront/alf_credo.htm.

Aragorn! "Nihilism Anarchy and the 21st Century." Self Published (Republished by the Anarchist Library), 2009. http://theanarchistlibrary.org/library/aragorn-nihilism-anarchy-and-the-21st-century.

Bjelopera, Jerome P. "The Domestic Terrorist Threat: Background and Issues for Congress." CRS Report for Congress. Washington, DC: Congressional Research Service, May 15, 2012.

Borum, Randy, and Chuck Tilby. "Anarchist Direct Actions: A Challenge for Law Enforcement." *Studies in Conflict & Terrorism* 28, no. 3 (2005): 201–223. doi:10.1080/10576100590928106.

Burton-Rose, Daniel, ed. *Creating a Movement with Teeth a Documentary History of the George Jackson Brigade.* Oakland, CA: PM Press, 2010.

Chicagoist. "Activist Who Freed 2,000 Minks from Illinois Farm Sentenced Under Obscure Terrorism Law." News. Chicagoist, March 23, 2016. http://chicagoist.com/2016/03/23/second_animal_rights_activist_sente.php.

Churchill, Ward, and Jim Vander Wall. *The COINTELPRO Papers.* Cambridge, MA: South End Press, 2002.

CNN Wire. "Missouri Lawmaker Wants to Ban Masks at Protests." Q13 FOX News, February 2, 2017, Online edition, sec. National & World News: Politics. http://q13fox.com/2017/02/02/missouri-lawmaker-wants-to-ban-masks-at-protests/.
———. "Tennessee Bill Would Make Drivers Immune from Civil Liability If They Hit Protesters in Street." FOX31 Denver, February 14, 2017, Online edition, sec. National/World News. http://kdvr.com/2017/02/13/tennessee-bill-would-make-drivers-immune-from-civil-liability-if-they-hit-protesters-blocking-street/.

Davis, Kristina. "Woman Who Freed Minks from Farms across the Country Gets Plea Deal." *Los Angeles Times,* December 28, 2016, Online edition, sec. Local: LA Now. www.latimes.com/local/lanow/la-me-fur-rampage-20161228-story.html.

Dekmejian, R. Hrair. *Spectrum of Terror.* Washington, DC: CQ Press, 2007.

Deshpande, Nick, Howard Ernst, and National Consortium for the Study of Terrorism and Responses to Terrorism. "Countering Eco-Terrorism in the United States: The Case of 'Operation Backfire'." Final Report to the Science & Technology Directorate, U.S. Department of Homeland Security. College Park, MD: National Consortium for the Study of Terrorism and Responses to Terrorism (START), September 2012. www.start.umd.edu/sites/default/files/files/publications/Countermeasures_OperationBackfire.pdf.

Devereaux, Ryan. "Homeland Security Sees Anger at Trump as a Driver of 'Domestic Terrorist Violence'." The Intercept. March 2, 2017, Online edition. https://theintercept.com/2017/03/02/homeland-security-sees-anger-at-trump-as-a-driver-of-domestic-terrorist-violence/.

FBI Cleveland Division/US Attorney's Office Northern District of Ohio. "Three Men Sentenced to Prison for Roles in Plot to Bomb Ohio Bridge." FBI, November 20, 2012. www.fbi.gov/cleveland/press-releases/2012/three-men-sentenced-to-prison-for-roles-in-plot-to-bomb-ohio-bridge.

FBI Counterterrorism and Cyber Divisions. "Tactics Used by Eco-Terrorists to Detect and Thwart Law Enforcement Operations." Washington, DC: FBI/Investigation Intelligence Assessment, 2004.

Federal Bureau of Investigation. "Animal Rights/Environmental Extremism." PowerPoint presented at the FBI026408, Washington, DC, December 8, 2011.

———. "Subject: George Jackson Bridade [Sic]." Freedom of Information/Privacy Acts Section. Washington, DC & Seattle, WA: Federal Bureau of Investigation, 1977, 1976. https://vault.fbi.gov/George%20Jackson%20 Brigade%20/George%20Jackson%20Brigade%20Part%2001%20of%2005.

———. "Terrorism in the United States 1997." Annual Report. Washington, DC: Federal Bureau of Investigation, Counterterrorism Threat Assessment and Warning Unit, National Security Division, 1997. www.fbi.gov/ file-repository/stats-services-publications-terror_97.pdf/view.

———. "Terrorism in the United States 1998." Annual Report. Washington, DC: Federal Bureau of Investigation, Counterterrorism Threat Assessment and Warning Unit, National Security Division, 1998. www.fbi.gov/ file-repository/stats-services-publications-terror_98.pdf/view.

———. "Terrorism in the United States 1999." Annual Report. Washington, DC: U.S. Department of Justice, Federal Bureau of Investigation, Counterterrorism Threat Assessment and Warning Unit, Counterterrorism Division, 1999. www.fbi.gov/file-repository/stats-services-publications-terror_99.pdf/view.

———. "What Are Known Violent Extremist Groups? Domestic Extremist Ideologies." FBI, 2016. https://cve.fbi.gov/ whatare/?state=domestic.

———. "What Are Known Violent Extremist Groups? Domestic Extremist Ideologies: Anarchist Extremists." FBI, 2016. https://cve.fbi.gov/whatare/?state=domestic.

———. "What Are Known Violent Extremist Groups? Domestic Extremist Ideologies: 'Enter the Website'." FBI, 2017. https://cve.fbi.gov.

Federal Bureau of Investigation, Domestic Terrorism Operations Unit. "Anarchist Extremism." PowerPoint presented at the FBI026192, Washington, DC, December 8, 2011.

Feigenbaum, Anna, Fabian Frenzel, and Patrick McCurdy. *Protest Camps*. London, UK: Zed Books, 2013.

Fischer, Howard. "Arizona Senate Votes to Seize Assets of Those Who Plan, Participate in Protests That Turn Violent." *Arizona Capitol Times*, February 23, 2017, Online edition, sec. Featured News. http://azcapitoltimes.com/ news/2017/02/22/arizona-senate-crackdown-on-protests/.

Galtung, Johan. "Violence, Peace, and Peace Research." *Journal of Peace Research* 6, no. 3 (January 1, 1969): 167–191.

Guillen, Alex, and Juana Summers. "Rick Santorum Slams 'Reign of Environmental Terror': Alex Guillen and Juana Summers." Politico, February 9, 2012, Politico Pro Online edition. www.politico.com/news/stories/0212/72681. html.

Hoffman, Bruce. *Inside Terrorism*. New York, NY: Columbia University Press, 2006.

Hudson, John. "FBI Drops Law Enforcement as 'Primary' Mission." *Foreign Policy*, January 5, 2014.

Immergut, Karin J., Kirk A. Engdall, Stephen F. Peifer, and John C. Ray. "Government's Sentencing Memorandum in the United States District Court for the District of Oregon [Case Numbers CR 06–60069-AA, CR 06–60070-AA, CR 06–60071-AA, CR 06–60078-AA, CR 06–60079-AA, CR 06–60080-AA, CR 06–60120-AA, 06–60122-AA, 06–60123-AA, 06–60124-AA, 06–60125-AA, 06–60126-AA]." United States District Court for the District of Oregon, May 4, 2007.

Ingraham, Christopher. "Republican Lawmakers Introduce Bills to Curb Protesting in at Least 18 States." *Washington Post*, February 24, 2017, Online edition, sec. News: Wonkblog. www.washingtonpost.com/news/wonk/ wp/2017/02/24/republican-lawmakers-introduce-bills-to-curb-protesting-in-at-least-17-states/.

Jarboe, James. "The Threat of Eco-Terrorism." FBI/House Resources Committee, Subcommittee on Forests and Forest Health, February 12, 2002. www.fbi.gov/news/testimony/the-threat-of-eco-terrorism.

Jenkins, Philip. *Images of Terror: What We Can and Can't Know about Terrorism*. New York, NY: Aldine Transaction, 2003.

Jensen, Tim. "The Rhetoric of Eco-Terrorism." Online Journal. *Harlot: A Revealing Look at the Arts of Persuasion*, March 11, 2012. http://harlotofthearts.org/blog/2012/03/11/the-rhetoric-of-eco-terrorism/.

Kropotkin, Peter. "The Spirit of Revolt." Commonweal (Republished by Anarchy Archives), 1892. http://dwardmac.pitzer.edu/anarchist_archives/kropotkin/spiritofrevolt.html.

Lambert, Laura. "Evan Mecham Eco-Terrorist International Conspiracy." In *The Sage Encyclopedia of Terrorism*. 2nd edition, edited by Gus Martin, 190. Thousand Oaks, CA: Sage Publications, 2011.

Laqueur, Walter, ed. *Voices of Terror: Manifestos, Writings and Manuals of Al Qaeda, Hamas, and Other Terrorists from around the World and Throughout the Ages*. New York, NY: Sourcebooks, Inc., 2004.

Leader, Stefan H., and Peter Probst. "The Earth Liberation Front And Environmental Terrorism." *Terrorism and Political Violence* 15, no. 4 (2003): 37–58. doi:10.1080/09546550390449872.

Lee, Michelle Ye Hee. "The Viral Claim That 'Not One' Refugee Resettled since 9/11 Has Been 'Arrested on Domestic Terrorism Charges'." *Washington Post*, November 19, 2015, Online edition, sec. News: Fact Checker. www.washingtonpost.com/news/fact-checker/wp/2015/11/19/the-viral-claim-that-not-one-refugee-resettled-since-911-has-been-arrested-on-domestic-terrorism-charges/.

Lewis, John. "Animal Rights Extremism and Ecoterrorism." FBI/Senate Judiciary Committee, May 18, 2004. www.fbi.gov/news/testimony/animal-rights-extremism-and-ecoterrorism.

Loadenthal, Michael. "Activism, Terrorism, and Social Movements: The 'Green Scare' as Monarchical Power." *Research in Social Movements, Conflicts and Change, Narratives of Identity in Social Movements, Kent State University* 40, no. 1 (August 16, 2016): 189–226.

———. "Deconstructing 'Eco-Terrorism': Rhetoric, Framing and Statecraft as Seen through the Insight Approach." *Critical Studies on Terrorism* 6, no. 1 (April 2013): 92–117.

———. "The Earth Liberation Front: A Social Movement Analysis." *Radical Criminology, Critical Criminology Working Group* 0, no. 2 (September 21, 2013): 15–46.

———. "'Eco-Terrorism': An Incident-Driven History of Attack (1973–2010)." *Journal for the Study of Radicalism* 11, no. 2 (Fall 2017): 1–33.

———. "Eco-Terrorism? Countering Dominant Narratives of Securitisation: A Critical, Quantitative History of the Earth Liberation Front (1996–2009)." *Perspectives on Terrorism (Center for Terrorism and Security Studies, Terrorism Research Initiative)* 8, no. 3 (June 25, 2014): 16–50.

———. "'The Green Scare' & 'Eco-Terrorism': The Development of US Counter-Terrorism Strategy Targeting Direct Action Activists." In *The Terrorization of Dissent: Corporate Repression, Legal Corruption and the Animal Enterprise Terrorism Act*, edited by Jason Del Gandio and Anthony Nocella. New York, NY: Lantern Books, 2014.

———. "Nor Hostages, Assassinations, or Hijackings, but Sabotage, Vandalism & Fire: 'Eco-Terrorism' as Political Violence Challenging the State and Capital." MLitt Dissertation, Centre for the Study of Terrorism and Political Violence, University of St Andrews, St Andrews, Scotland, 2010.

———. "Superglue, Bolt Cutters & Homemade Incendiaries: A Targeting, Tactical & Communication Methods Analysis of the Earth Liberation Front's Attack History 1996–2009." Centre for the Study of Terrorism and Political Violence, University of St Andrews, St Andrews, Scotland, 2010.

———. "When Cops 'Go Native': Policing Revolution through Sexual Infiltration and Panopticonism." *Critical Studies on Terrorism* 7, no. 1 (April 2014): 24–42. doi:10.1080/17539153.2013.877670.

Luchies, Timothy. "Towards an Insurrectionary Power/ Knowledge: Movement-Relevance, Anti-Oppression, Prefiguration." *Social Movement Studies* 14, no. 3 (2015): 1–16.

Main, Frank, Mark Konkol, and Michael Lansu. "'NATO 3' Plotted Attacks on Obama Election HQ, Rahm's House, Police Stations, Prosecutors Say: Chicago Sun-Times." *Chicago Sun-Times*, May 19, 2012. www.suntimes.com/12635179-761/3-protesters-charged-with-conspiracy-to-commit-terrorism.html.

Martin, Gus. *Essentials of Terrorism: Concepts and Controversies*. 4th edition. Los Angeles, CA: Sage Publications, 2016.

————. *Understanding Terrorism: Challenges, Perspectives, and Issues*. 5th edition. Los Angeles, CA: Sage Publications, 2015.

McGowan, Daniel. "Tales from Inside the U.S. Gitmo." *The Huffington Post*, July 9, 2009. www.huffingtonpost.com/ daniel-mcgowan/tales-from-inside-the-us_b_212632.html.

"Men in Black with a Violent Agenda." FOX Tampa Bay, May 24, 2012, Online edition, sec. News. www. myfoxtampabay.com/story/18599070/the-men-in-black-with-a-violent-agenda.

Milstein, Cindy. *Anarchism and Its Aspirations*. 1st edition, Vol. 1. Anarchist Interventions. Oakland, CA: AK Press & The Institute for Anarchist Studies, 2010.

Missouri Information Analysis Center, Division of Drug & Crime Control. "MIAC Strategic Report: Anarchist Movement." Strategic Report. Jefferson City, MO: Missouri Information Analysis Center & Missouri State Highway Patrol, November 28, 2008.

Nacos, Brigitte L. *Terrorism and Counterterrorism*. 5th edition. New York, NY: Routledge, 2016.

Ng, Serena, and Christina Binkley. "S.C. Johnson Pulls Kiwi Mink Oil after Animal Rights Threat." *Wall Street Journal*, November 22, 2013, Online edition, sec. Business. http://online.wsj.com/news/articles/SB1000142405270230 3653004579214373428064280.

North Carolina Information Sharing and Analysis Center, and Department of Homeland Security Office of Intelligence & Analysis. "North Carolina: Recent Spike in Election-Related Physical and Cyber Incidents against Political Institutions Likely to Decrease in the Short Term, but Threat Environment Remain Unpredictable." Unclassified/ For Official Use Only, February 21, 2017.

Offord, Derek. *The Russian Revolutionary Movement in the 1880s*. Cambridge, UK: Cambridge University Press, 2004.

O'Neill, Bard E. *Insurgency & Terrorism*. Dulles, VA: Potomac Books, 2001.

Pilkington, Ed. "Animal Rights 'Terrorists'? Legality of Industry-Friendly Law to Be Challenged." *The Guardian*, February 19, 2015, Online edition, sec. US news. www.theguardian.com/us-news/2015/feb/19/animal-rights-activists-challenge-federal-terrorism-charges.

Potter, Will. "3 NATO Protesters Charged with 'Terrorism' in Chicago: Identical to Other FBI Plots." Green Is the New Red, May 21, 2012. www.greenisthenewred.com/blog/three-nato-protesters-terrorists/6119/.

————. *Green Is the New Red: An Insider's Account of a Social Movement under Siege*. San Francisco, CA: City Lights Publishers, 2011.

————. "The Secret US Prisons You've Never Heard of before." TED Talk. TED Fellows Retreat 2015, 2015. www.ted. com/talks/will_potter_the_secret_us_prisons_you_ve_never_heard_of_before.

Rapoport, David C. "The Four Waves of Rebel Terror and September 11." *Anthropoetics* 8, no. 1 (Spring/Summer 2002). www.anthropoetics.ucla.edu/apo801/terror.htm.

Redden, Molly. "Tar Sands Protesters Arrested on Terrorism-Related Charges for . . . Glittery Banner." *Mother Jones*, December 17, 2013, Online edition, sec. Politics. www.motherjones.com/politics/2013/12/ tar-sands-keystone-protesters-arrested-terrorism-glitter.

Rockwell, Mark. "Men Who Targeted Ohio Bridge with C-4 Plot Sentenced." Government Security News, November 21, 2012. www.gsnmagazine.com/node/27872?c=federal_agencies_legislative.

Rozboril, Robert. "Brecksville Bridge Bomb Plotters Sentenced, Mayor Shares Thoughts about FBI, Suspects." Sun News—Cleveland.com, November 30, 2012. www.cleveland.com/brecksville/index.ssf/2012/11/brecksville_ bridge_bomb_plotte.html.

Scahill, Jeremy, and Margot Williams. "A Secret Catalogue of Government Gear for Spying on Your Cellphone." *The Intercept*, December 17, 2015, Online edition. https://theintercept.com/2015/12/17/a-secret-catalogue-of-government-gear-for-spying-on-your-cellphone/.

Shapiro, Michael J. *The Time of the City: Politics, Philosophy and Genre*. New York, NY: Routledge, 2010.

Shone, Steve J. *American Anarchism*. Leiden, Netherlands: Brill, 2013.

The Smoking Gun. "Unmasked: Meet the FBI's Bridge Bomb Plot Snitch." *The Smoking Gun*, May 2, 2012. www.thesmokinggun.com/documents/fbi-informant-shaquille-azir-756123.

Spangler, Jerry. "Animal Activists Still a Top Threat." *Deseret News*, November 19, 2001. www.deseretnews.com/article/875166/Animal-activists-still-a-top-threat.html?pg=all.

State of Illinois County of Cook. "The June 2012 Grand Jury of the Circuit Court of Cook County (Brian Church, Jared Chase, Brent Betterly)." Circuit Court of Cook County, IL: County Department, Criminal Division, June 13, 2012.

———. "The People of the State of Illinois vs. Brian Church, Jared Chase, Brent Betterly [12MC1–15344, 12MC1–15345, 12MC1–15347]." Circuit Court of Cook County, IL: County Department, Criminal Division, May 19, 2012.

Tarm, Michael. "NATO Protesters Indicted on 11 Counts in Chicago." *Associated Press*, June 27, 2012. www.foxnews.com/us/2012/06/20/apnewsbreak-nato-protesters-indicted-on-11-counts/.

Taylor, Bron. "Religion, Violence and Radical Environmentalism: From Earth First! To the Unabomber to the Earth Liberation Front." *Terrorism and Political Violence* 10, no. 4 (1998): 1–42. doi:10.1080/09546559808427480.

Tejada, Susan. *In Search of Sacco & Vanzetti: Double Lives, Troubled Times, & the Massachusetts Murder Case That Shook the World*. Boston, MA: Northeastern University Press, 2012.

Thomas, Judy L. "Olathe Attack Is a Hate Crime, but Not Likely Domestic Terrorism, Expert Says." *The Kansas City Star*, February 28, 2017, Online edition, sec. Crime. www.kansascity.com/news/local/crime/article135556933.html.

The United States Attorney's Office Southern District of California, John Parmley, and Michael Kaplan. "Animal Rights Activist Sentenced to 21 Months for Cross-Country Crime Spree Targeting Fur Industry." News Release Summary. Southern District of California: United States Department of Justice, January 17, 2017. www.justice.gov/usao-sdca/pr/animal-rights-activist-sentenced-21-months-cross-country-crime-spree-targeting-fur.

United States of America v. Kevin Johnson, Tyler Lang, No. No. 14 CR 390. Accessed January 1, 2017.

US Army Training And Doctrine Command, and Intelligence Support Activity. "Terrorist, Insurgent & Militant Group Logo Recognition Guide." Leavenworth, KS: Intelligence Support Activity, February 15, 2009.

U.S. Department of Homeland Security. "Domestic Terrorism and Homegrown Violent Extremism Lexicon." Washington, DC: Office of Intelligence and Analysis, Homeland Counterterrorism Division, Homegrown Violent Extremism Branch, November 10, 2011.

———. "Leftwing Extremists Likely to Increase Use of Cyber Attacks over the Coming Decade." Assessment. Washington, DC: Strategic Analysis Group, Homeland Environment and Threat Analysis Division, Office of Intelligence and Analysis, US Department of Homeland Security, January 26, 2009.

U.S. Department of Homeland Security, Homeland Security Intelligence Council, Under Secretary for Intelligence and Analysis. "Homeland Security Threat Assessment: Evaluating Threats 2008–2013." Assessment. Washington, DC: Strategic Analysis Group, Homeland Environment Threat Analysis Division, Office of Intelligence and Analysis, 2008. http://info.publicintelligence.net/DHS-Threats2008-2013.pdf.

U.S. Department of Justice, Federal Bureau of Investigation. "Terrorism 2000/2001." Washington, DC: U.S. Department of Justice, 2001. www.fbi.gov/stats-services/publications/terror/terrorism-2000-2001.

———. "Terrorism 2002–2005." Washington, DC: Federal Bureau of Investigation, Counterterrorism Division, 2005. www.fbi.gov/file-repository/stats-services-publications-terrorism-2002-2005-terror02_05.pdf/view.

U.S. Department of Justice, Office of Inspector General, Oversight and Review Division. "A Review of the FBI's Investigative Activities Concerning Potential Protesters at the 2004 Democratic and Republican National Political Conventions." Washington, DC: U.S. Department of Justice, April 27, 2006. https://oig.justice.gov/special/s0604/final.pdf.

Walsh, Denny. "'Anna' the Informant: Student's Path to FBI Informant." *Sacramento Bee*, September 12, 2007, online edition. Retrieved from www.sacbee.com/101/story/374324.html.

Watson, Dale L. "The Terrorist Threat Confronting the United States." Testimony before the Senate Select Committee on Intelligence. Washington, DC: Federal Bureau of Investigation, February 6, 2002. www.fbi.gov/news/testimony/the-terrorist-threat-confronting-the-united-states.

Weber, Max. "Politik als Beruf (Politics as a Vocation)." Lecture presented at the Free Students Union, Munich University, January 1919. www.ne.jp/asahi/moriyuki/abukuma/weber/lecture/politics_vocation.html.

White, Gregory A., and US Magistrate Judge. "United States of America v. Douglas L. Wright [Criminal Complaint]." United States District Court for the Northern District of Ohio, April 30, 2012.

Wilkinson, Paul. *Terrorism versus Democracy: The Liberal State Response*. 1st edition. CASS Series on Political Violence. London, UK: Frank Cass, 2000.

York, Ed Pilkington in New. "Role of FBI Informant in Eco-Terrorism Case Probed after Documents Hint at Entrapment." *The Guardian*, January 13, 2015. www.theguardian.com/us-news/2015/jan/13/fbi-informant-anna-eric-mcdavid-eco-terrorism.

Part II

Terrorist Beliefs and Ideologies

Chapter 4

Christian Identity

Kevin Borgeson

Overview

- Intro
- Pre-Adamic Man
- Serpent Seed
- Noah
- Preventive Measures
- Abraham
- House of Israel
- Lost Tribes
- Jesus
- Armageddon

Some social scientists (Post, 1984, 1990) see religious-based terrorism as one of the biggest threats to society due to justifications based on a "higher power." On August 10, 1999, Aryan Nations member Buford Furrow did just this as he walked into a Jewish day care center in Granada Hill, Los Angeles, California, and began shooting randomly at workers and children based on his belief in the Christian Identity (CI) faith. In the end, his act wounded three children, a camp counselor, and one receptionist. From the day care center, Furrow fled away in his van. After several minutes, Furrow knew that they would be looking for his van, so he stole a Toyota. Furrow eventually made it to Chatsworth in the car he had stolen, where he saw postal worker Joseph Santos Illeto. Furrow approached Illeto and asked if he could mail a letter for him. When Illeto stopped, he pulled out a gun and shot him point blank (Murr, 1999). Eventually, Furrow was apprehended in Las Vegas, Nevada, where he turned himself in, confessing to the murder. When asked about why he committed the murder, he said that Illeto was chosen because he was of Latino or Asian descent and the day care center was picked because he was "hunting for Jews" (Murr, 1999). For those in the Aryan Nations and the Ku Klux Klan, hate acts like those performed by Buford Furrows are done with religious justification from a religious doctrine they refer to as "Two Seed Line Christian Identity," which is outlined in this chapter. Christian Identity does not use a historical analysis of the Bible; instead, the Bible must be read as a revisionist interpretation that proves their racist and anti-Semitic dogma.

In James Aho's *The Politics of Righteousness*, he points out that Christian Identity adherents "see the world through three specific doctrines: 'dualism, conspiracy, and the coming apocalypse'" (Aho, 1990, p. 220). Christian Identity inherited these features from another religious phenomenon dating back to the late 1880s, British Israelism. "British Israelism (BI), in the most general terms, refers to the belief that the British are lineal descendants of the 'ten lost tribes' of Israel" (Barkun, 1997, p. 4). British Israelism had its earliest advocate in the late 1700s in Richard Brothers. According to Michael Barkun, the author of *Religion and the Racist Right: The Origins of the Christian Identity Movement*, Brothers began having visions in 1791 that he was to help the Jews. Around 1793,

> . . . he concluded that he had a divine mission to lead the Jews back to Palestine. He decided that he himself was a descendant of the house of David, and that most Jews were hidden between Existing European, and particularly British Peoples, unaware of their exalted biblical lineage. This idea of "hidden Israel" that believed itself Gentile, ignorant of its true biological origins, marks the initial appearance of what is to become British—Israleism's "central motif."
>
> (Barkun, 1997, p. 6)

Brothers did not garner much support and was eventually institutionalized.

One of the earliest leaders to gain support for British Israelism was John Wilson. Unlike Brothers, Wilson believed that the Jews did not have a special covenant with God. Wilson did not believe that there was such a place as Israel, and the biblical Scriptures told him that Israel was a people, not a place. Wilson was crucial in today's Christian Identity movement because he introduced the idea that the Anglo-Saxon, Caucasian race was the true house of Israel. He believed that the special ordinances given to Israel were not given to the Jews but to the white Caucasian race. Unlike preceding BI believers—such as Richard Brothers, who felt Jews were equal and had a place in the New Jerusalem—Wilson felt that Jews did not hold a "religious status equal to their newly discovered Northern European Brethren" (Barkun, 1997, p. 7). Wilson believed that the Caucasian race could be traced back to the English throne and that England would be the place for the "new Jerusalem."

Probably the best-known British Israelism preacher of his time was Edward Hines, who taught BI in the late 1880s. Hines was influenced by Wilson but took a different look at the emphasis of Britain in biblical prophecy. The Hines philosophy of BI played on nationalistic and patriotic themes that Wilson's type of British Israeliem excluded. Michael Barkun contends that the Hines BI style played into the sentiments of England at that time (1870s). Germany was seen as a rival among the Brits, and a xenophobic philosophy permeated the larger social system in relation to the Germanic people. The British began seeing the Germans as a threat and did not want to share the special covenant of biblical prophecy with them. Like most religions, BI developed several denominations and belief systems in regard to Jews, Jerusalem, the lost tribes, and the oncoming apocalyptic end to society.

One of the early denominations was pyramidology, the belief that the truth to the end of the world is locked in the structure of the pyramids. This eventually extended to beliefs in numerology—in which most answers could be found (lost tribes, etc.) in significant dates and their sequencing. For instance, Aho (1990, p. 11) points out the triangulation method used by various BI in order to discover the locations of the lost tribe:

> The five planets visible to the naked eye plus the sun and the moon multiplied by 360=2,520 years. This we are told is seven prophetic cycles. But 2,520 years added onto 576 B.C., the year when Benjamin was captured Babylonia, is exactly 1945, the year when Iceland became independent from Denmark. This is "conclusive evidence" that Iceland was the final stopping place of Benjamin.

Although this phenomenon did gather support, it had one element that would eventually become its undoing—predictions. Because BI members felt that all social events could be predicted by using the "power of the pyramids," including the oncoming apocalypse, they gave exact dates of the end of the world. When the end did not happen, leaders had to explain away what happened. Most followers became disillusioned by these inaccurate predictions, turning to CI, which did not rely on specific dates but just that "the end times are near."

It wasn't just inaccurate predictions that led to the acceptance of CI into the American society. In the early 1920s, BI started to make a stance that would resonate with CI adherents in America—anti-Semitism. The most famous case was that of William J. Cameron, the editor of *The Dearborn Independent*, owned by Henry Ford. From 1920 to 1927, Cameron ran a series of articles titled the "Jewish Problem" (Ridgeway, 1995). Also, at this time, the Ku Klux Klan had a premier status in the United States. The KKK influenced the larger social order, and BI began to incorporate tenets that would become CI.

As BI died down, CI began to emerge in its place. The most popular denomination among CI adherents is the "two seed theory." Adherents of this denomination believe that the Old Testament and the New Testament need to be looked at together. The remainder of this chapter outlines the eight most important elements of CI: pre-Adamite, Serpent seed, Noah, Babel, Abraham, Jacob/Esau, Jesus, and Armageddon. The biblical Scriptures that CI uses to justify their hatred toward those of the Jewish faith are also addressed.

Pre-Adamic Man

> God blessed them, and God said unto them, be fruitful, and multiply, and replenish the earth, and subdue it: and have dominion over the fish of the sea, and over the fowl of the air, and over every living thing that moveth upon the earth.
>
> (Gen. 1:28)

According to CI believers, you have to believe that not all men and women are created equal. This is exemplified by the following quote by an Aryan Nations leader:

> This is what I tell people when they ask me if all people were created equal. I say no. In Genesis 1:31 God said that everything that he created was very good. Well if he says that it is

very good who am I to say that it is not? But, they were created differently. You can't make a dog meow or a cat bark, you simply can't make something out of somebody that they weren't created to be. There is no way on God's green earth that any other race will be equal to the white race. This is not said to be mean, this is a statistical fact that the white race is the most intelligent race on the planet. All you have to do is look around you. Everywhere you see a high rate of civilization you find the white man.

To proponents of this religion, God chose the Caucasian people of the world as his chosen people, not the Jews. They believe the Bible was written for whites, and for no one else. Whites are the true house of Israel, and all of God's prophecies are for those of Anglo-Saxon, Germanic, and Scandinavian heritage. Most Identity believers feel that the world was created in eons, not days. Over this long period of time (millions of years), God produced a series of creations in succession to provide the living components needed for each phase. In order to understand Christian Identity, we have to begin with what they believe was the separate creation of minorities—what some Identity supporters refer to as "mud people," or what is called "pre-Adamic" man by some Identity evangelists.

Minorities, according to Identity, are to have a subservient presence on the Earth to the "Adamic pure white race." In Genesis 1:26, it states: "Let us make man in our image, after our image and let them have dominion over the fish of the sea and the fowl over the air, and over the cattle and over every creeping thing that creepeth upon the earth." Therefore, in Genesis 1:27, CI adherents believe that minorities were created—not as equals—but to be used by whites. Identity believers call this "the sixth day." This is the time that all subservient beings were made. One Aryan Nations member described it this way: "Those pre Adam and Eve creations are placed here for some purpose, and that purpose is to serve the white Adamic race." For most CI advocates, God justifies the term "white supremacy." According to this member, they have been wrongly accused by society, they are not racists, and they are doing the work of God:

> If a black holds up his fist and says black power, nobody says anything. If a Mexican holds up his fist and says viva la rosé, nobody says anything. But let a white man be proud of his race, or be concerned about it, now he's a racist. They call us white supremacists; well I can show you several places where God said we are a special people, a peculiar people, to be above all the other peoples of the earth. If that sounds like white supremacy to you, take it up with God he said it, I didn't.

In the Identity ministry, the semantic distinction of male and female becomes important. For Identity enthusiasts, male and female refers to the creations (pre-Adamites), and man and woman refer to Adam and Eve. This is important because in Genesis 3:15, God refers to the damnation of the satanic seed line and places "enmity" between the seed of the serpent and the seed of the woman.

How Identity members know that pre-Adamites existed is in the content of the passage of Genesis 1:28, where it was stated that "God blessed them, and God said unto them, Be fruitful, and multiply, and replenish the earth, and subdue it: and have dominion over the fish of the sea, and over the fowl of the air, and over every living thing that moveth upon the earth." To Identity adherents, this is the proof that all humans are not equal and were not created at the same time because, according to one Aryan Nations member, "in order to replenish something, there needs to be an existence prior to the replenishing." Since Identity believers advocate white supremacy, it is only logical that the next step for them would be to claim that whites are given a special existence, through Adam, and that they have a special quality. That quality is a soul.

This is seen in the verse where God breathed life only into Adam and his offspring. In other words, what this means to CI believers is that minorities (pre-Adamites) do not have a soul. Only the true Adamic (white) race was given a soul.

> And the LORD God formed man [of] the dust of the ground, and breathed into his nostrils the breath of life; and man became a living soul.
>
> (Gen. 2:7)

One of the most important passages in understanding CI white supremacy is that of the creation of Adam and Eve and what CI adherents refer to as "the breath of life." Most Identity believers accept as the truth that God gave the whites a spiritual uniqueness (i.e., a soul) that is destined upon them after conception. If God believes that there is "even one ounce of bad blood (i.e., race mixing), then that individual will not have a place in heaven."

The creation of Adam came on the "eighth day" after God had all the right sequences in place. In all the days preceding, "[God] brought the herbs, the grass, the trees, the fish, and cattle to prepare for [Adam and Eve] because he was supplanting life giving standards" (Wickstrom, n.d.). Adam was created "to live in innocence, and with full, unimpaired, responsibility because there was no evil nature within him. Both were created with a bias toward good and were given freedom of the will" (Gayman, n.d., p. 58). According to Identity members, minorities cannot have a soul because they "genetically are not human they are beasts of the field." Only true white Aryans, those who come from the seed of Adam, are considered to have a soul because they (Adamites) are the only race that can blush. "Aw Dawm" (Adam) means one who blushes and shows color in the face.

The Serpent Seed

> And I will put enmity between thee and thy woman, and between thy seed and her seed; it shall bruise thy head, and thou shalt bruise his heel.
>
> (Gen. 3:15)

Genetic difference plays an important part in understanding Christian Identity's interpretation of the Bible. The serpent seed is portrayed as an apocalyptic battle between good and evil, and in the end (Armageddon), Yahweh (the Hebrew writing of God) will come down and ask the true white Aryan race to pick up arms and become his "battleaxe," laying the evil seed and redeeming the true white seed line on Israel soil (i.e., United States of America).

CI believers think that "the seduction of Eve was purely sexual in nature" (11th Hour Remnant Messenger). For Identity believers, "Israel is not a land, it is a people" (Wickstrom, n.d.), and those people are the Adamic white race. According to most Identity members, "The most important verse in the Bible is Genesis 3:15: 'And I will put enmity between thee and the woman, and between thy seed and her seed; it shall bruise thy head, and thou shalt bruise his heel.'" This is seen as the fight between good and evil, whites and Jews, and God and the devil. Proof of two seeds, according to members, is in Genesis 3:13, which states: "And the LORD God said unto the woman, what [is] this [that] thou hast done? And the woman said, the serpent beguiled me, and I did eat." According to the 11th Hour Remnant Messenger, an anti-Jewish resource center, "The references thereafter to the covering of the genitals (Genesis 3:7) and the punishment of pain in childbirth (Genesis 3:16) could hardly be due the literal consumption of fruit from a tree."

As one Aryan Nations member stated:

> She did not eat a literal piece of fruit. You take two key words beguiled and eat and put them back in the Hebrew. You find that one of the words for beguiled is to morally seduce. What it means for the word eat is to lay with. When you put this back into context it says that the serpent seduced me and I lay with him. You can verify this in the par Abel of the wheat and the tare in Mathew 13. There were two seeds planted in the same field at the same planting time. When the blades sprung forth, so did also the tares. Cain and Abel were twins, but they had two different fathers.

Dan Gayman, the author of *The Two Seeds of Genesis 3:15*, states that the possibility of one birth producing twins by two different fathers is not far-fetched. In Gayman's book, he cites the example of Grete Bardaum, who in 1987 gave birth to fraternal twins—one black, the other white. The example is taken from a *Newsweek* article that stated that a black American G.I. was the father of the black child and a German white man was the father of the white child.

Eve gave birth to two sons, Cain and Abel. The Bible depicts that Cain slew his brother Abel, and God declared that Cain was bred from a satanic seed line:

> Not of Cain who was of that wicked one (Satan his father), and slew his brother. And wherefore slew he him? Because his own works were evil, and his brothers righteous. (11th Hour Remnant Messenger, I John 3:12 KJV)
>
> And Adam knew his wife again; and she bare a son, and called his name Seth: For God, [said she], hath appointed me another seed instead of Abel, whom Cain slew.

Seth, the replacement, was "to establish a true bloodline through which Messiah, Jesus the Christ, is to redeem mankind from the fall of Adam. Without this true, untainted blood line, His chosen cannot receive promise of redemption by the propitiation of Christ on the cross" (11th Hour Remnant Messenger). Cain becomes upset because God did not bless him, and he is asked to leave the kingdom of God. This is important to CI adherents because CI people see this as the introduction of the satanic seed line (Jewish) into the Adamic world. After God banished Cain to the Land of Nod, Cain started his own seed line with pre-Adamites.

It was at this point that God wanted to establish a true white seed line by placing Seth into the seed line to keep the true white Christian identity going. Due to Cain's jealousy, God took on names that resembled those of the true blessed Adamic seed line (i.e., Seth's) "to confuse the bloodline and lineage with that of Cain. It would be easy to confuse this fact in the beginning, and there was much intermingling of race and bloodline as a result of this deception" (11th Hour Remnant Messenger).

Seth Seed Line	**Cain Seed Line**
Enos	Enoch
Cainan	Irad
Mahalaleel	Mehujael
Jared	Methusael
Enoch	Lamech
Methesulah	
Lamech	
Noah	
Shem Japeph Ham	

Due to the extreme amount of race mixing that went on for generations, God became angry at his children because he preaches "Kind after their Kind," meaning that each creation is to stay among themselves: birds with birds, cattle with cattle, male with female (pre-Adamites), and man and woman (true Aryan Adamites). In order to rid the world of this evil, God established the Flood to wipe out the genetic improprieties on Earth.

Noah

And the LORD said, I will destroy man whom I have created from the face of the earth; both man, and beast, and the creeping thing, and the fowls of the air; for it repenteth me that I have made them. But Noah found grace in the eyes of the LORD.

(Gen. 6:7–9)

Among Identity supporters, there are two opposing lines of thinking regarding the Flood: that it was universal, and that it was local. Most members of the Aryan Nations believe that the Flood was not universal, but that it was restricted to the Tarim Basin, north of what is today Tibet.

The Egyptians wrote about Noah's flood, the Chinese wrote it, and even call him Noah. How could they have written about it if they were destroyed in the flood? This is the verse that no one can get over, around, under, or through: Genesis: 9 is the last chapter regarding the flood. 10:1 they are getting off the boat and having babies. Ham had Cush, Cush had Nimrod. Verse 10 of chapter ten says Nimrod became the mighty ruler of four cities and the land of shiner. How in the world were there enough people to populate four cities? In less than two hundred years, unless there were people already there.

Because the Flood was localized, non-Adamic people outside the region were saved from this catastrophe. God was punishing only those who had had sexual relations with "six-day creation" beings and were their offspring. God was not mad at those who were "sixth day" creations and did not intermingle with those of Adamic descent. Most philosophical interpretation of CI religion is an offshoot of a biological approach, as stated by this believer:

> They say that the flood drowned everyone upon the face of the earth. Everybody that survived is a descendant of the three sons of Noah. Noah and his wife and sons Hamm, Shem, and Jacob begotten all the people on the face of the earth. That means that they were the common parents within a period of 2,400 years before Christ, of all the Asiatics, of all the Negroes, and all the white men on the face of the earth. It is biologically unsound, unscientific, it is not genetic, and there is no proof in it.

For the supporters of this ideology, God was trying to create a pure bloodline:

> To accomplish this purpose in redeeming Adamic man through the virgin birth through in his incarnation in Jesus Christ. The Bible tells us that all living perished except for Noah and his family. It can only reference to those that who lived in the proximity of the floods, those who are the offspring of man. No others are possible the Bible is written to and for his chosen Adamic man.
>
> (11th Hour Remnant Messenger)

Noah was chosen because he resided in the Tarim Basin area and was of pure Adamic stock. Noah and his family were saved from the Flood and its wrath because of their strict adherence to the structural laws of kind after kind. God wished to create a pure bloodline for the redemption of the Adamic race and for the resurrection of God in the flesh form of Jesus Christ. "Several million of Adamic mankind and their mixed blood offspring that lived there, all that had turned from God, would perish as well as all the animals that were indigenous to the area that were not taken on the ark" (11th Hour Remnant Messenger). Noah and his family stayed on the Ark for more than 7 months. It wasn't until an earthquake created a crack in the basin, allowing the water that had built up during the Flood to dissipate, that Noah and his family left the Ark.

The 11th Hour Remnant Messenger gives four main reasons for why they feel the Flood happened. The purpose of the Flood was to destroy:

- The offspring from Satan's fallen angels who seduced Adamic women and produced Giant/Nephalim
- Adamic man/women who have race mixed
- Adamic man/women who have mixed with the offspring of Cain
- Evil and violence of the Tarim Basin

CI advocates claim that because pre-Adamites still exist to this day, the Flood upon the earth was restricted to the basin, and because minorities exist today, they must have lived outside the area. After the Flood, Noah's sons, Ham and Japheth, were dispersed "to what is now North Africa and Eastern Russia respectively" (11th Hour Remnant Messenger).

Preventive Measures

> Therefore is the name of it called Babel; because the LORD did there confound the language of all the earth: and from thence did the LORD scatter them abroad upon the face of all the earth. (Gen. 11:9)

In the story of Babel, the Bible describes how Nimrod is the builder of Babel. At this time, there was only one language in the world. God saw the making of Babel as idolatry, seeing man slip back into violating his divine laws. Because there were descendants of Ham, Noah's son, God felt that he could not destroy the city. In order to add confusion to the world, God gave different languages according to their "family, tribe, or group of people" (11th Hour Remnant Messenger). Some Aryan Nations members described this to me as a preventive measure on God's part in order to prevent any future race mixing.

> Other religions (meaning main-stream Judea Christian) will say well Ham married a Black and Japheth married an oriental; another will say Hamm turned Black and Japheth became oriental. In Genesis 1 it says about ten times that kind goes with kind. He confused the language to create confusion among those there to prevent people from temptation.

> "The earth was all one land mass at this time. It was easy for all peoples to walk or ride beasts of burden or horses all over the land mass" (11th Hour Remnant Messenger). Because there were other minority groups—blacks and Orientals—God broke apart the landmass, making what today are our continents. According to CI believers, God did this in order to make it more difficult for people to unite to do future evil deeds. For most CI supporters, Genesis 11:7 proves that God planned this separation. Some believers see it as a sign that God wished to keep the races separate. It is a rationale still used today by some Identity supporters. By using Babel, they rationalize that minorities should live on the planet, but only in separate areas, isolating themselves from the true Adamic seed line. Babel has also become a justification by non-CI adherents; most state that God separated the races for a reason and that most of today's blacks should be returned to Africa, where God sent them. To most CI supporters, this is not being racist; this is abiding by the laws of God.

Because the Bible was written for those of Anglo-Saxon, Germanic, and Scandinavian heritage, Identity members purport that those who are of non-Adamic races will not understand the Bible because they are not true Hebrews. This can be seen in the following translation of Romans 9:3 by a CI believer:

> To my kinsmen according to the flesh who are Israelites. He is telling you in this that his kinsmen are Israelites. To whom pertained the adoption and the glory covenants and the giving of the law and the service of God and the promises. That's everything that the Bible has to offer. Adoption, covenants, and promises and he says right there that it only belongs to Israel.

Believers feel that teachings that exist in the pulpits of today's churches are misled because they are not the entire chosen race of God. Therefore, when someone says that the Bible is being misread by Christian Identity adherents, they state that it is the pagan religions that exist in today's society that do not understand the Bible because it was never written for them. Until the pagans wish to open their eyes and see the true words of God, they will not be Christians. According to Identity, Noah's sons departed to the land of North Africa and Eastern Russia, and the Adamic true bloodline is established through the Shem lineage.

Abraham

> Now the LORD has said unto Abram, Get thee out of thy country, and from thy kindred, and from thy father's house, unto a land I will show thee. And I will make of thee a great nation, and I will bless thee, and make thy name great shall be a blessing.
>
> (Gen. 12:1–2)

According to the 11th Hour Remnant Messenger, this is the "the first covenant with Adamic man, now Hebrew man since the flood in the man of Abram/Abraham, God the father is fulfilling his plan to redeem his chosen children from the bondage of Satan and his followers" (11th Hour Remnant Messenger). Abraham and his wife gave birth to Isaac, whom God also blessed. It would be Isaac's son Jacob on whom the CI movement based the true race of Israel. "Jacob was the second born to Isaac and Rebecca, a fraternal twin having Isaac as his father. The Adamic/Hebrew seed line will remain intact through this union" (11th Hour Remnant Messenger).

The other fraternal twin born to Rebekah was Esau, Satan's child. According to some Aryan Nations members, "It is this union that is at battle to this day. And due to this union of the bad seed, God blesses Jacob and changes his name to Israel." To these believers, Israel is not a land but a race. To CI adherents, the covenants of God would go to Abraham and to his seed.

This battle is for the rights to the true name of who is the house of Israel. According to CI adherents, the Jews have falsely misled the general public into believing that they are

> The chosen people of God . . . the Jews have done this by interpreting the bible wrong, as well as telling the big Jewish Lie, that six million people died in WWII. Six million didn't die. That whole thing is just a way for the Jews to get sympathy and get the thing they want. Which in the end is world domination. We (meaning white Adamic race) are in a battle that we are going to lose if we don't wake up people real soon. The Jews control our schools, media, police, laws, you name it. This isn't a battle that the Jews are going to win. Shortly, the white Adamic race will wake up to the real agenda of the Jews and help us overthrow them.

The apocalyptic battle that CI adherents believe in originated in the Bible in the passage of Jacob and Esau. Jacob and Esau were twins, with Esau being the firstborn of the two. Esau—an "Adamite, Semite, and a Hebrew," as well as the firstborn—felt that he was heir to the birthright of his lineage (Weisman, 1991, p. 5). Normally, this would be the case, but according to Charles Weisman (1991, p. 5), the author of *Who Is Esau-Edom?*, God said that

> Esau married daughters of Canaan or Canaanites (Gen. 28:6; 36:2), the daughters of Heth or Hittites (Gen. 26:34; 27:46; 36:2), the daughters of Ishmael (Gen. 28:9; 36:3), the daughters of

the Hivites (Gen. 36:2), and had intermarried with the Horites (Gen. 36:19–21; Jasher 30:28) . . . the descendants of Esau from these marriages became known as "Edomites" or "Edom."

(Gen. 36:1, 9)

Because Esau "race-mixed" with what CI adherents believe are today's Jews, he fell into displeasure with his parents, as well as with God, and this is why God favored Jacob over Esau. A hostile relationship developed between the two brothers. The "antagonistic relationship between Esau and Jacob was magnified and intensified when Esau 'sold his birthright to Jacob' for a mere bowl of pottage" (Gen. 25:33). According to Bertrand Comparet, a well-known CI preacher in the 1950s and 1960s, the story of Esau selling his birthright is more symbolic than most preachers want you to believe:

What the bible tells you about Esau selling his birthright for a bowl of stew: that isn't when he lost it. That was merely a formal ceremony by which he gave up any claim to it; but he lost it when he did the thing that rendered it impossible for him to continue as the head of the clan. His descendants from then on would be mongrelized, half satanic. So recognizing that he was already out of the line for leadership, he sold it for a bowl of stew.

(Comparet, n.d. a, *The Cain-Satanic Seedline*, p. 20)

Jacob then had the legal right to receive the blessings of the inheritance that he had received from Isaac by pretending he was Esau. When Esau realized what had happened and that Jacob now possessed the blessings that could have been his, "Esau hated Jacob because of the blessing" (Weisman, 1991, p. 58).

Like earlier interpretations, a biological approach is applied to the Bible. Like early positivist theorists of criminology, CI believers state that the bad traits that a Jew inherits can be passed on to other Jews. Wesley Swift, a leading CI proponent who wrote several books, pamphlets, and tracts, stated in a sermon:

Laws of heredity are well established. Christ recognized the laws of heredity even in the patterns of thought and conduct and he turned to that were his adversaries. I expect you to be this way you are going to be just like your father. He was a liar, a devil, and a murderer and his offspring will be like him. So, you have a perpetual Juke family among certain people.

What Swift is referring to is the study done in 1877 by Richard Dugdale, who looked to "infer that criminal (and anti-social) behavior is inherited. He (Dugdale) was able to trace a number of criminals, prostitutes, and paupers in the family line, all derived from the original criminal father" (Dugdale, as cited in Williams & McShane, 1999, p. 37).

Charles Weisman points out that "this contrasting and conflicting ways and thinking between Jews and the white European is not artificial or a result of their environment, but is based on the nature of their physical conditions. The conflicting differences that exist between Jews and those of the white race are primarily a result of their genetic differences, or their 'nature and constitution.' Jews act and think differently from white people because there is a difference in their brains" (Weisman, 1991, pp. 55–56). CI adherents believe that all of today's Jews still have this jealousy and are deliberately passing a Jewish agenda, to take over the world and "kill Israel (White Christians) for it is the only way to get the revenge for Esau" (Weisman, 1991, p. 98). According to CI adherents, the inheritance was to be the domination, or ruler, of the earth.

According to Charles Weisman, "Jacob-Israel birthright and blessings include a status of dominion in the earth with God as their head. This dominion conflicts with the Edomite Jew's plan of one-world dominion" (Weisman, 1991, p. 98). In order to get the Edomite (i.e., Jewish) plan enacted, they must destroy all the white Israelites on earth to negate Jacob-Israel's special status, therefore inheriting the title of being God's chosen people. The fight is seen as that of good (Aryan) and evil (Jewish). The battle is over the genetic lineage of the true house of Israel. That true genetic lineage is the true inheritor of the earth.

CI believers do not see the Jews as having a "special covenant" with the Lord. They see the battle as that of Jews (evil seed) trying to taint the Aryan (good seed) line, and they believe that the Jews confuse the masses into believing that the Jews are God's chosen people. They will do this through taking over the major institutions in the world (schools, media, government, financial, etc.).

According to CI adherents, evidence of this struggle has been seen throughout history and is shown in the writings of the Bible and the Talmud. According to CI believers, the two religions are diametrically opposed to each other and, therefore, cannot exist together because Judaism "rejects the commandments of God" (Weisman, 1991, p. 54). This leads to the apocalyptic outlook that the war is between the Jews and the white race. Richard Butler states that "it is a contest of who is going to win" (Butler, 2001).

House of Israel

Israel, to CI believers, is not a land but a people. For Aryan Nations members, nationality defines who is Israel, the chosen people of God. For CI proponents, this nationality is the

> Anglo-Saxon, Germanic, and Scandinavian Nations. . . . God first made His great promises to Abraham and repeated them to Abraham's son Isaac, and Grandson; Jacob (Whose name God changed to ISRAEL, "A Prince, Ruling With God"). ISRAEL had 12 sons. The descendants of each son became a tribe, so that all the descendants of Dan became the Tribe of Dan, the descendants of Judah, the tribe of Judah and so on. After their long captivity in Egypt, they became one nation of 12 Tribes (Like the one United States of 50 States), which continued until Solomon's death.
>
> Then the 10 Northern Tribes revolted and set up their own kingdom, keeping the name ISRAEL, while the old, southern, two-tribe nation was called JUDAH. Thereafter, their histories are recorded separately, in the Books of Kings and of Chronicles, which, like the prophets, carefully distinguish between them. About 715 B.C., ISRAEL was captured by Assyria and deported to the lands around the south end of the Caspian Sea and they never returned to Palestine.
>
> (Comparet, n.d. b *Israel's Fingerprints*)

According to CI believers, the house of Israel is the recipient of all the promises from the Bible. To them, Israel is the Scandinavian, Germanic people. How adherents know that Israel is the white race is seen in the promises that are made in the Bible. These promises are the following:

THE ISRAELITES. THEREFORE, WE MUST LOOK FOR ISRAELITES AMONG THE CHRISTIANS. THE PROPHECIES AND PROMISES TO ISRAEL HAVE BEEN FULFILLED TO THE ANGLO-SAXON AND SCANDINAVIAN NATIONS!

FIRST they are Christians and have been from early times.

SECOND THEY ARE A GREAT NATION AND A COMPANY OF NATIONS: The United States is the largest civilized nation in the world; the British Commonwealth of Nations is legally "a company of nations." The Scandinavian nations, all of the same blood, can be identified by their history and their heraldry as the Tribes of Dan, Benjamin and Issachar.

THIRD THEY ARE VERY NUMEROUS: In the last two centuries, the United States increased from a mere handful to about 200,000,000 people; in the last 3 centuries, the British Empire increased from 5,000,000 to over 70,000,000 Anglo-Saxons.

FOURTH THEY EXPANDED IN COLONIES IN ALL DIRECTIONS, as God prophesied in Genesis 28:14, Deut. 32:8, Isaiah 54:2–3, etc. Their lands are on every continent and in every sea. No other nations had such colonies.

FIFTH THEY "POSSESS THE DESOLATE HERITAGES" OF THE EARTH, AS GOD PROPHESIED. In Isaiah 49:8, "thus saith the Lord: in an acceptable time have I heard thee and give thee for a covenant of the people, to establish the earth, to cause to inherit the desolate heritages." Who else has so successfully developed the waste places, which were desolate when they first occupied them? Compare our own Southwestern States with what any other nation has done with similar deserts; compare the British colonies with those of nations of other races.

SIXTH THEY ARE A SEAGOING PEOPLE: God said of ISRAEL, "His seed shall be in many waters." Numbers 24:7 and "I will set his hand also in the sea and his right hand in the rivers." Psalm 89:25. The two greatest navies belong to the United States and Great Britain; the three greatest Merchant Marines to these two and Norway. [Note: This was written before the U. S. destroyed their Merchant Marine.]

SEVENTH THEY "POSSESS THE GATES OF THEIR ENEMIES." Clearly, Genesis 22:17, refers to the "gateways" of hostile nations, the great waterways of the world. The two great Anglo-Saxon nations alone have power to close every important "gate" in the world and have done it in two World Wars.

EIGHTH THEY MAINTAINED THE CONTINUITY OF THE THRONE OF DAVID: It has been proved that all the Kings of England, Ireland and Scotland are descendants of King David of ISRAEL, fulfilling the prophecy that "David shall never lack a man to reign over the House of Israel." Time allows me to give only a very few of the many prophecies about ISRAEL which have been fulfilled by the ANGLO-SAXON-SCANDINAVIAN people and by no others. At least 100 of them have been found. When you consider that there are more than 100 recognized nations, the mathematical odds against all of these being fulfilled by just one small group of nations, all of the same blood is billions to one. Do you think this happened by mere accident?

(Comparet, n.d. b, *Israel's Fingerprints*)

According to this philosophy, then, Christianity did not descend from Jews. According to CI believers, Jews are against Christianity and want to have it wiped off the face of the earth. Where they get this anti-Christian stance is from one of the two major books of their religion: the Talmud. Here is an explanation of this by one CI minister:

> Judea Christianity is an oxymoron. There is nothing, no way that anyone can say that we got our religion from them. That's why I tell people to go read the Talmud and tell me that we got our religion from them. Because we don't. The Talmud is the sickest excuse for a religion on the face of the earth.

According to most CI adherents:

> The Talmud use to be oral tradition. Eventually someone wrote these things down, compiled it into a book, and called it the Talmud. Ever since that time it has been used by the Jews.

According to CI believers, the Talmud is written laws, or norms, of what Jews should do to wipe Christians and Christianity off the face of the planet. Here is an example of a few of the things that the Talmud permits, according to CI believers (11th Hour Remnant Messenger):

- Raping of Christian Women Because Christians are seen as Inferior
- Have Sex With A Girl Under Three Years of Age
- Blasphemy against Jesus Christ

According to CI adherents, the Talmud allows "crimes against nature," such as sodomy, rape, and oral sex. One believer went on to give further proof that the Talmud is anti-Christian, describing a blood ritual by Jews against Christians:

> They (Jews) actually take blood [from Christian children] and mix it into their bread for their feast of purum. If you go back and look at the majority of children who disappear in this country [United States] disappear during that period of time [Passover].

This "proof" further supports their anti-Semitism toward Jews. Some CI believers do not refer to what they are doing as anti-Semitic, however, because they believe that that is a term (Semite) that is reserved for those that are the true Hebrews of the Bible, as explained by one CI believer:

> I am not an anti-Semite. I am anti-Jew. Those people that call themselves Jews do not have one ounce of Hebrew blood in them. In order to call yourself a Semite you have to have descended from the Hebrew race; and they have not.

Because of this battle going on between Jews and Christians, some followers do not recognize any truth in what Jews have to say. The believe that there is an apocalyptic battle taking place on the soil of earth today and that the Jews will lie to win back what should have been theirs—the covenants and promises that God outlined in the Bible to the people of Israel.

Not all enthusiasts think this way. Some feel that the Jews are saying some truth, but that they are just trying to fool the public into believing that the Jews are the chosen people:

> They have made the statement themselves that they will tell you 90% truth to get you to believe the 10% lie. I am a Jew and I own a clothing store. I have a Pendleton shirt, it is 100% wool. Now is that a lie, because I am a Jew and I said it? No. They talk about it, does that mean we should disregard it? NO anyone who studies the scripture, I mean studies the scripture, I don't see how they can study the scripture and come up with anything else.

The Lost Tribes

As the preceding section demonstrates, adherents of Christian Identity believe that the Bible describes those who are to be the "Anglo-Saxon, Scandinavian and Germanic people" (American Institute of Theology, n.d., p. 112) as the descendants of the lost 12 tribes of Israel and that they deserve all the privileges that come with this distinction. Believers contend that the 12 tribes of Israel can be further divided into two kingdoms, the North and the South. After the passing away of King Solomon in about 925 B.C., the Northern Kingdom was composed of 10 of the lost tribes descended from Jacob. Approximately 150 years before the first temple fell in 585 B.C., the Northern Kingdom was completely conquered by the Assyrians. As was custom at that time, the victorious army carried the newly subject people off and recolonized the area. The 10 tribes were then "lost." Leonard Zeskind (1986, p. 13), in *The Christian Identity Movement*, gives a quote from the British Israelite magazine *Destiny* describing this:

> When the people of the Northern Kingdom went into Assyrian captivity, they did not remain there. During the subsequent dissolution of the Assyrian power through its involvement in foreign wars, the people of Israel escaped in successive independent waves, leaving the land of their captures when the opportunity came to do so. Under different names (Scutai, SakGoths, Massageate, Khumri, Cimmerans, Goths, Ostrogoths, Visigoths, etc.), they moved westward into the wilderness, across Asia Minor, then into Europe and eventually into the Scandinavian countries and the British Isle.

The 10 Northern tribes were nomadic in nature; they were used by the Assyrians as slave warrior labor and sent out to conquer empires. The remaining two tribes—Benjamin and Judah— became encapsulated into the tribe of Judah and were stationary. This would change starting in 705 B.C. with the death of King Sargon II. After his passing away, rival tribes began to attack Assyria in order to gain its wealth and landholdings. The king of Judah, King Hezekiah, ran one of the armies. According to the interpretation of CI theology, they were successful (AIT, n.d., p. 113). In 701 B.C.,

> the new King of Assyria, Sennacherib, set about recovering his empire; one rebellious city after another was conquered, with the hideous cruelty characteristic of Assyria; and in 701 B.C., Sennacherib's huge army invaded the kingdom of Judah . . . none of the smaller cities of Judah were able to resist.

> (AIT, n.d., p. 113)

TABLE 4.1 | The 12 Lost Tribes of Israel

Country	Tribe
Denmark	Dan
Norway	Naphtali
Finland	Issachar
Germany	Judah
France	Zebulun
Italy	Gad
Holland	Reuben
Spain	Simeon
Iceland	Benjamin
Great Britain	Ephraim
USA	Manasseh
Sweden	Asher

At this point, the Assyrian pilgrimage began to include the 10 tribes of the North, as well as most of the people of the two Southern tribes of Judah. As the tribes moved, they began to expand along both sides of what is now known as the Caspian Sea. Along this pilgrimage, according to CI texts, groups from the tribes began to settle in areas, and these people would be the ancestors of the white race. Table 4.1 shows the names of the tribes and where their descendants are today.

To CI believers, the importance of the "Caucasian" race being the true lost tribe is crucial to their understanding of self. Most adherents refer to this as the unlocking of "one's true identity": "Once you understand your true identity everything changes. Your view of the world is never the same. You have to understand that the Jews are trying to suppress who the true lost sheep are."

Jesus

In mainstream religions, Jesus is considered the king of the Jews. According to CI adherents, this is not the case. The reason Jews claim this, according to CI believers, is so that they get special privilege in society as being the true house of God. For CI's anti-Jewish belief, there must be a removal of Jesus as a Jew. There are several beliefs among CI adherents that allow this; most of their justification is outlined via passages in the Bible. One of the most used passages is John 10:26, when "Christ said to the Jews, But ye believe me not, because ye are not my sheep!" After Jesus told the Jews they were not of his people (race), he described how his true Israel "sheep" would react: "My sheep hear my voice, and I know them and they follow me."

According to CI believers, Jesus was put on the earth in order to convince those who obeyed the Jewish laws that they were following the orders of Satan and that the true house of Israel was that of the white Anglo-Saxon Caucasian race:

God's instructions were to keep his family tree [line] pure. There was to be no race mixing! It was intended by God that his family, put on Earth in flesh bodies but born of the spirit would through purity of spirit and obedience to Divine Law, bring order and righteousness to a world laboring under the rule of Satan (the Jews). John 8:23, "I am from above ye are from beneath." John 8:41, "Ye do the deeds of your father." John 8:44, "you have the devil for your father and the lust (desires) of your father will ye do." Jesus was not speaking to people, of his own race, when he made these accusations; for Jesus is not a Jew.

Jerome Walters (2001, pp. 24–25) points out in *One Aryan Nation Under God* that the word "Jew" has several different meanings for Christian Identity members:

- Jew "can a be label for someone who is from the country of Judea."
- The term Jew can designate a distinct race of people as long as it is not applied to Jesus or his disciples.
- Identity doctrine uses the term "Jew" to refer to a specific ungodly religion.

The first meaning implies a specific geographic area. This is important because some adherents of CI also believe that they can use geographic descriptions to prove that Jesus was not a Jew. For instance, Wesley Swift, in *Was Jesus Christ a Jew?* states "that Galileans were not Jews [*sic*]" (Swift, n.d., p. 12). Swift goes on to show biblical proof of this by citing John 6:

Jesus Christ had twelve disciples. One of them was a Jew [sic]; that was Judas Iscariot. All the rest came out of the Galilee, out of the household of His section. He asked them a question concerning His identity, and Simon Peter said: "Master, where shall we go? Thou hast the words of eternal life. We believe and are sure that though art the Christ." That means the Embodiment of Yahweh, the Very Son, the Embodiment of the Most High.

Swift goes on to prove his point. "Jesus said: 'Have not I chosen you twelve, and one of you is a devil?' While that may be just a name you call somebody, to Christ it is a generation of Lucifer." Swift finishes up his geographic proof of Galilee not being a locality for Jews by citing John 7:1: "After these things Jesus walked in Galilee: For he would not walk in Jewry [sic], because the Jews sought to kill him" (Swift, n.d., p. 12).

The implication of race, in the second meaning, hints that there must be distinguishable characteristics among those who claim to call themselves Jews. Several interviews with prominent Aryan Nations leaders suggested this:

I have no problem telling who is a Jew and who isn't. That is because I have been awoken to my true Identity, that I am the true Israel. Israel as we see it is not that sand pit across the ocean. Those are the devil. The true Israel is the true race of Adam.

CI believers see the Bible as a prophetic canon and view prophecy as a dualistic battle between good and evil. They believe that the Jews, as a race, are born with a disposition to lie, cheat, and feed off the true house of Israel (Adamic white race). It is because of this belief that The Turner Diaries and The International Jew play such an important part in their understanding of how the Jewish race is trying to take over the world. Jews supposedly will accomplish this by taking over all institutions of society to control the mind-set of true Israel (whites). This is summed up best by the 11th Hour Remnant Messenger:

These Jews or Jewry were and still are the evil offspring of Satan from Cain, again through Esau and through those mixed blooded house of Judah which returned from Babylon 400 years before.

Several Aryan Nations members said to me: "How can Jesus be a Jew? Jews don't believe in Jesus and they are fighting to destroy the house of real Christianity today." Most see Judaism as the equivalent of Satanism. Equating Judaism with the devil constructs an evil seed on the planet, and that seed wishes to destroy the Christian faith. Playing on this factor throughout the Bible causes fear among adherents. This fear gets tapped into in order to convince others that something needs to be done about the demonic seed that is walking the planet.

"Proving that Jesus wasn't a Jew" allows for the entrance of conspiracy (covered in the next chapter), as well as the rationale for Jesus's real reason to be here. The 11th Hour Remnant Messenger sums it up into four possible reasons:

God the father, sent his only begotten son, Jesus Christ incarnate, to die on the cross and accomplish the following missions:

1. Kingsman redeemer—To enter into the Adamic/Hebrew Race and "purchase mankind" from the power of Satan
2. Forgive the sin of Adamic/Hebrew man—Die a sinless death, shedding his blood and water on the cross in obedience to God, His father [Blood=remission of sin. Water= Life/Agape/ way of salvation]
3. The resurrection of Jesus Christ by God his father to reveal and demonstrate the power of God and the deity of Jesus Christ
4. The only hope for the Adamic/Hebrew/mankind eternal salvation

The second function of this biblical interpretation is to allow a cognitive rational for their hatred. One prominent Aryan Nations leader told me: "I could never hate for the sake of hating. A lot of the Klan is like that. To me I hate the Jews because that is what Yahweh (God) wants. It says so in the Bible." This revisionist interpretation of the Bible allows for the white Adamic race to see Jesus as "the segregationist supreme, calling the white race to pursue racial purity and 'build an Ark of Safety' for the race" (Walters, 2001, pp. 26–27). Claiming that a superior power believes that the white race is superior and should rule minorities provides a rationale to be adopted by bigots, allowing them to justify their actions. Because God and his incarnate son made this law, how can hate mongers doing something wrong? They do not hate because they are doing the work of God. What they are really doing is showing their love for the white race. As we show later in the book, this cognitive dissonance allows for the objectification of what they see as another. Once this is done, it allows for the possibility of carrying out God's plan, becoming "the battleaxe and the sword to wipe the evil Jew off the face of the earth"

Armageddon

According to Pastor Don Campbell, the word "Armageddon" is of Hebrew origin:

"It comes from two Hebrew words Har Megedon. Literally translated this means land of the gathering."

Most CI adherents believe that the gathering for Armageddon will be the United States of America:

> So where this land of the gathering? The land for the re-gathering of the house of Israel is the US. Some say that the Jews going back to Israel is prophecy fulfilled. The only prophecy that it's fulfilling is the fact that they are being gathered back there for the burning. They will be destroyed in the very land where the Esau-Edomites killed Yashua. God told David that he would set his descendants in a new land. One that they would not have to move from again. David was standing in Palestine when he said that in a new land it would have to be different than Palestine. The New Jerusalem is in the United States.

The prediction of America as the New Jerusalem is not based on just hearsay or from a crystal ball; the justification comes from biblical prophecy:

> The bible refers to the New Jerusalem as a nation being born in a day. What nation on this planet was born in a day? This one, July 4th 1776. It also is described as being bordered by two seas and divided by many rivers.

To some CI adherents, the battle of Armageddon is taking place as we speak. Some saw the incidents of September 11 and the constant battles between Israel (the Jewish state) and the Muslims as a sign of beginning of an apocalyptic battle.

REFERENCES

11th Hour Remnant Messenger. (n.d.). Unpublished brochure.

Aho, J. (1990). *The politics of righteousness.* Seattle: University of Washington Press.

American Institute of Theology. (n.d.). *AIT Bible correspondence course.* Harrison, AR: AIT.

Barkun, M. (1997). *Religion and the radical right.* Chapel Hill: University of North Carolina Press.

Butler, R. (Producer). (2001). *My side of the story* [Videotape]. Coeur d'Alene, ID.

Comparet, B. (n.d.a). *The Cain-Satanic Seedline.* Retrieved September 8, 2007, from www.churchoftrueisrael.com/comparet/compcainsatan.html.

Comparet, B. (n.d.b). *Israel's Fingerprints.* Retrieved September 8, 2007, from www.churchoftrueisrael.com/comparet/comp4.html.

Gayman, D. (n.d.). *The two seeds of genesis 3:15.* USA.

Murr, A. (1999). "A visit from the dark side." *Newsweek.* Retrieved October, 1, 2017. Retrieved from www.newsweek.com/visitor-dark-side-16584.

Post, J. (1984). "Notes on a psychodynamic theory of terrorist behavior." *Terrorism: An International Journal* 7: 241–256.

Post, J. (1990). "Terrorist psycho-logic: Terrorist behavior as a product of psychological forces." In W. Reich (Ed.), *Origins of terrorism* (pp. 25–40). Cambridge, UK: Cambridge University Press.

Ridgeway, J. (1995). *Blood in the face.* New York: Thunder Mountain Press.

Swift, W. (n.d.). *Was Jesus Christ a Jew?* Retrieved June 16, 2008, from www.churchoftrueisrael.com/swift/swift1.html.

Walters, J. (2001). *One Aryan nation under God.* Naperville, IL: Sourcebooks.

Weisman, C. (1991). *Who is Esau-Edom?* Burnsville, MN: Weisman.

Wickstrom, J. (n.d.). *Children of Light vs. Children of Darkness.* [Cassette Recording].

Williams, F. & McShane, M. (1999). *Criminological theory.* [third edition]. Englewoods Cliffs, NJ: Prentice Hall.

Zeskind, L. (1986). *The Christian identity movement.* Atlanta, GA: Center for Democratic Renewal.

Chapter 5

Islamist Terror in America

Christopher J. Wright

Overview

- Islam is the world's second largest religion, with much diversity in it
- The *Salaafi jihadi* ideology is responsible for most Islamist terror in the US and abroad, but is opposed by most Muslims
- Most radical Islamists prefer to go abroad than commit terror in the homeland
- Those that return from abroad to the US are less likely to succeed in terror attacks
- Homegrown terrorists represent the vast majority of Islamist terrorists in the US
- Homegrown Islamist terrorists are far more deadly when they act alone

Introduction

In this chapter about Islamist terror in the US, we use several terms that may be unfamiliar to students. This is probably because so few Americans identify as Muslim. Even though Islam is the second largest religion in the world with well over 1 billion adherents, Muslims are a religious minority in the US. Estimates of the number of Muslims here vary, but a 2016 study by Pew Research estimates that about 1% of the US population consider themselves Muslims (Mohammad, 2016). This 1% number is not evenly distributed across the country. In some areas, that number is significantly higher. In Dearborn, Michigan, for instance, four of ten residents are of Arab descent—most of them Muslim (United States Census Bureau, n.d.). Muslims in New Jersey make up two to three times the national average. This uneven distribution of Muslim-Americans means that in many areas of the US, there are virtually no Muslims. Because of this, many students may find that they have never met a Muslim. For others, going to college was the first time they were exposed to someone of the Islamic faith. Islam, for many in the US, is something foreign to their experience, so any notion they have about Muslims is second-hand, most likely through the media.

Even if you are a Muslim or have Muslim friends, just what does it mean to be a Muslim? As the world's second largest religion, Islam has as many divides within it as Christianity. To many, being a Muslim means being a devout follower of the faith as it has been traditionally practiced in various Muslim-majority countries. *Islam* means "surrender" or "submission," implying that those who follow Islam have submitted to the will of God. To others, being a Muslim means picking and choosing some parts of Islamic tradition as "authentic" and rejecting other parts of tradition that violate their sense of modernity. They may think of some traditionalists as old fashioned, uptight, or as mistaking cultural traditions for orthodox religious beliefs.

Still others think of being a Muslim as a cultural affinity with little religious meaning attached to their lives. They may think of themselves as part of a broader Muslim community and may even celebrate religious holidays or choose to not eat pork out of a sense of respect for tradition. This group of self-identifying Muslims might run the gambit from those who may have some faith in central Islamic tenants to agnostics and even atheists. These cultural Muslims have a corollary in cultural Christians in the US and Europe, where it is common to find people who celebrate Easter and Christmas, have their children christened or baptized, or are married in a church by a priest or pastor, but who nevertheless reject some to all of the central tenants of orthodox or traditional Christianity.

In this chapter, we do not treat Islam as a single thing. Islam, like Christianity, has many divisions and means many things to many different people. We also do not pretend that we know what "true Islam" really is or what a "good Muslim" really believes. That is up for Muslims to decide for themselves. That is a task for theology, not the social sciences. As this chapter spends considerable time discussing the beliefs of *some* Muslims as the primary motivation for their terrorism, it is important for the reader to understand that when we speak of those beliefs, they may in no way reflect the beliefs of *other* Muslims.

The main sectarian divisions within Islam are between *Sunni* and *Shia*. Sunni Islam is the larger of the two divisions, with far more Muslims identifying as Sunni than Shia. Only in a few Islamic countries are there Shia majorities: Iran, Iraq, Azerbaijan, and Bahrain. In Lebanon, they are the largest religious group, but by no means a majority. And in Yemen, Pakistan, Turkey, and elsewhere, there are large Shia minorities. To many Muslims, the Sunni/Shia divide is a relatively minor distinction and irrelevant to their daily lives. To other Muslims, though, the Sunni or Shia identity is centrally important. This distinction tends to be stressed in countries where one or the other group controls political power at the expense of the other. How bad can such sectarian divisions get? The current civil wars in Syria and Iraq are outgrowths of this Sunni/Shia political divide. In Iraq, the Sunni minority perceived the Shia majority government as oppressive. In Syria, the Sunni majority saw itself at odds with a government dominated by the minority Alawites—an offshoot of Shiite Islam. Once these civil wars were in full swing, Shia Iran came to the aid of the Shia-dominated Iraqi and Syrian governments while rich Sunni states in the Gulf—like Saudi Arabia and the UAE—sent large sums of money and aid to Sunni rebels.

Another important distinction is between those Muslims who believe that Islam is a religion to be practiced by individuals, families, and voluntary communities in a secular state and those who believe that *sharia*—or Islamic law—ought to be the law of the land. *Islamism* is the belief that *sharia* ought to replace man-made law. *Islamists* are those who advocate *sharia* as a way to govern a society in the formal, legal sense. *Islamists* do not believe in the separation of church and state—or in this case, the separation of mosque and state. They want the government to enforce Islamic law like governments enforce any law with mechanisms such as fines, prison sentences, and in some cases even the death penalty. Many Muslims reject Islamism and the Islamist vision of the unification of mosque and state.

Even among Islamists there are competing versions of sharia, of what an Islamic state should look like in practice, and how to achieve their end goals. Many Islamists reject violence as the way to achieving their dreams of a theocratic state. Groups like the Muslim Brotherhood in Egypt have officially rejected violence as a means to achieving political victory and have worked to get Islamist candidates elected to office in order to change the system of government. In fact, this group of Islamists won Egypt's first elections following the 2011 Arab Spring movement, which overthrew the 30-year secular dictatorship of Hosni Mubarak. Turkey's ruling Justice and Development Party is considered Islamist, but it is moderate as far as Islamist parties go. Turkey is a member of NATO and has actively participated in military operations against the Islamic State of Iraq and Syria (ISIS).

Islamism has both violent and non-violent strains within it, but it is from within Islamism that nearly all modern terrorism in the name of Islam arises. Al Qaeda and the Muslim Brotherhood may differ on what an Islamic government might look like, and they might disagree on what methods are legitimate for getting such a government, but they do agree that the only legitimate form of government is one in which *sharia* dictates legally acceptable behavior. A government in which Islamic law trumps the laws passed by democratically elected institutions.

Nearly all Muslim terrorists and terror organizations are motivated by Islamism—political Islam. It is for this reason that we use the term *Islamist terror* rather than *Islamic terror* here. Not only is the term less offensive to practicing Muslims who reject Islamism, violence, or both, but it is also the accurate term.

The vast majority of terrorism in the world today is committed by Islamist groups and their adherents. In 2016, there were 60 groups listed by the US State Department as Foreign Terrorist Organizations (FTOs). Of these, 43—or 69%—are Islamist in orientation. The vast majority of Islamist terror organizations on the list were Sunni. Sunni Islamist groups on the list include al Qaeda and its regional affiliates, ISIS and its affiliates, and other groups such as Hamas. These groups often follow a particular strain of Sunni Islam that believes that Muslims ought to follow the example of the earliest generations after Islam's founder Muhammad, called the *Salaf*. *Salafism* is an extremely conservative view of Sunni Islam whose followers seek a more "pure" Islam, an Islam that they believe is more like the one practiced by those in the religion's foundational period of the 7th century. Many of these *Salafi* also believe that *jihad*—a word that means "struggle" in Arabic and that can be applied in many contexts—is best understood as a mandatory obligation to fight for Islam. Thus, organizations like al Qaeda and ISIS are *Salafi jihadi* groups in a wider movement of *Salafi jihadism*.

Maher (2016) distinguishes *Salafi jihadism* from other conservative strains of Sunni Islam by five defining characteristics, only one of which is adherence to violent *jihad* as an obligation on individual Muslims. In this chapter, we only mention one other doctrine—*takfir*. *Takfir* is something akin to excommunication, and it encapsulates the idea that some people have strayed so far from "proper" Islamic teachings that they have, in effect, become non-Muslims. The idea is controversial even within conservative Sunni circles because a widely held Islamic belief is that all who have declared the oneness of God and Muhammad as God's final prophet are Muslim. When *Salafis* declare that another group of Muslims are *takfir*, they are saying that they are non-Muslims. "As such . . . ," says Maher (2016, p. 71), "the concept is used to license intra-Muslim violence, particularly in highly sectarian environments." In practice, this means that wars that pit Sunnis against Shia, any on the opposing side (Shia) are considered "non-believers" and therefore legitimate targets of violence. The same is applied to Sunni regimes allied with the United States. For instance, much of Osama bin Laden's ire in the 1990s was directed toward the Saudi royal family for being overly friendly with the US, and regime change in Saudi Arabia remains a primary goal of al Qaeda. Even though it is a conservative society that already uses *sharia* as the basis for its laws, declaring the ruling powers of Saudi Arabia *takfir* (i.e., apostates) justifies attacks against them.

Shia Islamists are also represented on the State Department's 2016 Foreign Terrorist Organization list. They include Hezbollah in Lebanon and *Kitai'b Hizbollah* in Iraq. Both groups are funded and sponsored by the Shia Islamist government of Iran. Both groups have been involved in the sectarian conflicts between Sunni and Shia in Syria and Iraq. Both groups have also targeted Americans in Iraq, Lebanon, and elsewhere. However, Shia Islamists have rarely targeted the American homeland. This is probably due to the fact that their sponsors in Iran fear US retribution should they attack America directly. This state sponsorship is a double-edge sword for terrorist organizations that receive it. On the one hand, they have a ready supply of cash and material, making them much less like terrorist organizations as classically conceived and more like regular armies with uniforms. This is the case with Hezbollah, which functions as a quasi-state in southern Lebanon and has large armaments such as anti-tank and anti-aircraft weapons. On the other hand, they are less free to use these weapons against their enemies because doing so might have negative repercussions to the state supplying them—in this case, Iran. Because these Shia Islamist terror groups have rarely ventured to attack the US at home, the following mostly deals with *Salafi jihadists* and their presence in the US.

9/11 and the Study of Islamist Terror in the US

When asked what a typical Islamist terrorist is like, students have often answered by offering Saudi-born Osama bin Laden as the archetype of a terrorist and al Qaeda as the typical terrorist organization. Sometimes the name Mohammad Atta, the Egyptian born ringleader of the 19 hijackers that carried out the 9/11 attacks, is offered. Occasionally, students cannot name anyone specifically but instead describe a hypothetical Islamic radical living in a cave somewhere plotting with others to do harm to the US or its interests in a spectacular attack that kills many people. Invariably, the prototype for what an Islamic terrorist is like is based on the notion that they are foreigners, mostly living abroad, mostly part of a large organized force, and mostly wanting to come to the US for the purpose of doing maximum harm.

It is easy to see why many would hold this to be the typical Islamist terrorist. 9/11 looms large in the collective psyche of Americans and for arguably good reasons: al Qaeda's actions on that day killed nearly 3,000 people and account for nearly 99% of all deaths in the US at the hands of violent Islamists in the past 30 years. The 9/11 attacks were carried out by foreign Islamists who specifically came to the US to do us harm. Fifteen of the 19 hijackers were Saudi while the others were from Egypt, Lebanon, and the UAE. The attack was well planned, complex, high impact, and high casualty. Fifteen years after declaring a "war on terrorism" and despite Osama bin Laden being killed, al Qaeda remains a threat to the US and its interests.

But was 9/11 typical in any way? Authors such as LaFree (2011) have argued that 9/11 represents a "black swan" event. Actual real life black swans do exist, but they are not nearly as common as white swans. In fact, Europeans thought all swans were white until explorers noted that swans with darker plumage lived in Australia. Black swan events are those events that fall outside the realm of regular expectations, have high impact, and defy prediction. As a black swan event, 9/11 can be understood to have warped perception as to the nature of terrorist organizations and attacks. We see it as typical, when in fact it was very much atypical. For instance, quantitative studies show that most terrorist groups are short lived and that most attacks either fail or are low casualty events (LaFree, 2011). So, while 9/11 was spectacularly destructive and it is therefore easy to see why it would immediately come to mind when thinking about Islamist terror, it was very unusual. It does not represent the typical terror attack in the US, or even the typical terror plot, most of which fail to graduate from idea to reality.

The sheer magnitude of 9/11 causes many in the public to misperceive the Islamist terror threat because it was not representative of what the typical attack looks like. Because of this, the temptation arises, especially in the academic world, to dismiss 9/11 and keep it out of the various statistics used in tracking terror. It can be easy to mistakenly conflate how *typical* an attack is to how *relevant* or *important* it is. This is a problem on many fronts, and one in which researchers, journalists, and students reading their reports ought to be cautiously aware. For instance, Zuckerman, Bucci, and Carafano's (2013) report on domestic Islamist terror for the conservative Heritage Foundation was entitled "60 Terrorist Plots *Since* 9/11: Continued Lessons in Domestic Counterterrorism." A study by Bergen et al. (2017) for the more liberal-leaning New America Foundation is titled "Terrorism in America *After* 9/11" (emphasis mine in both cases). Both are excellent reports, but the fact that they exclude 9/11 may have the unintended consequence of impressing on the reader that Islamist terror attacks on the homeland are something so rare as to be hardly worthy of serious concern.

The rarity of a terrorist attack cannot be dismissed so easily when its actual *impact* is so great. To exclude 9/11 from statistical analysis of terrorism in the most recent decades is to overlook the vast majority of the victims of terrorism. Whether intentional or not, it has the effect of downplaying and minimizing the actual risk of Islamist terror. To think about this problem by way of analogy, imagine a study on the impact of hurricanes that only counted property damage and death starting a few days *after* Katrina devastated New Orleans. One could rightfully make the argument that since the Katrina hurricane was so much more devastating than most that it teaches us little about how to prepare or respond to hurricanes. Katrina, as a black swan event, doesn't represent hurricanes in general. In fact, hurricanes rarely kill any one. All of this is true, yet misleading about the potential danger of hurricanes.

Since hurricanes are naturally occurring phenomena without human choice as an element of causation, perhaps the analogy has its limitations. Let us conclude our discussion of 9/11's importance with another analogy, one that includes human choice and action. This time let us imagine a hypothetical study on the dangers of atomic weapons. This hypothetical study only looks at data beginning on August 10, 1945—the day *after* the bomb was dropped on Nagasaki and 4 days after Hiroshima. The statistically valid and robust conclusions of which would show precisely zero uses of a nuclear weapon since then and zero people killed as a result of their use. Using these statistics alone, would one then go on to minimize the dangers of nuclear weapons simply because their use has been atypical? No, of course not! The very real danger of nuclear weapons has little to do with how typical their use has historically been.

It is quite likely that well-organized terrorist groups such as al Qaeda or ISIS would have committed more attacks on the scale of 9/11 had they had the means to do so. That is to say, at least *some* of the security measures and counterterror actions pursued after 9/11 are partially responsible for the fact that another attack of the scale of 9/11 has not happened.

The broader point is that there are two potential problems when analyzing data on Islamist or other terror in the US. The first is drawing broader conclusions based on rare or atypical events. 9/11 was a black swan event. It was unusual. Most Islamist terror attacks do not follow the pattern established on 9/11. The second problem is to dismiss 9/11 altogether as an outlier and therefore of little importance to the broader study of Islamist terror in the US. To exclude it from the data so it does not skew findings would be a mistake because, despite being rare, 9/11 was important and impactful on multiple levels. Moreover, it shows us the devastation organized, large-scale attacks by transnational terror organizations can have.

TRANSNATIONAL AND DOMESTIC TERROR

When researchers and analysts think about terrorism, they often put different groups, individuals, or attacks into distinct categories. The 9/11 attack is often thought of and labeled as either *transnational or international terror* that happened to take place on US soil. These labels are placed on groups like al Qaeda and attacks like 9/11 because they represent a kind of terror that transcends national boundaries. Osama bin Laden was the son of a wealthy Saudi businessman who spent time in the late 1980s fighting the Soviets in Afghanistan. The group of Arab and other foreign fighters he led there would later form the core of al Qaeda. His number two, Ayman al-Zawahiri—now the leader of al Qaeda after bin Laden's death—is from Egypt and had spent time in jail there for his involvement in the terrorist activities of the Egyptian Islamic Jihad organization. Khalid Shiekh Muhammad, the operational planner of 9/11, was born in Pakistan but spent time in the US, where he graduated from the North Carolina Agricultural and Technical State University in Greensboro. Prior to 9/11, al Qaeda carried out attacks against the US embassies in Kenya and Tanzania and against the *USS Cole* as it was anchored in Aden, Yemen. Transnational terror, as typified by al Qaeda and the 9/11 attacks, is the type of terrorism that students and the public at large often find archetypal. International or transnational terrorism is thought of as a problem of *foreign* radicals seeking to inflict harm against the West—including the US.

A second category many have used is that of *domestic terrorism*. Domestic terrorism was and often continues to be thought of as somehow separate from the phenomenon of international terrorism. Groups such as the KKK, the Aryan Nations, or the Weather Underground Organization are said to be domestic because the perpetrators and victims of violence are normally confined to single countries. Further, the underlying ideologies that inspired violence from these groups are often seen as fringe elements of larger domestic movements. They are considered the violent wings of political movements within the US.

This type of violence has a long history in the US and can be understood using terms normally applied to political movements or ideologies—that of "right-wing" or "left-wing." These terms are used nearly every day in our political discourse. The ideas represented by such "domestic" terror groups may not be ones in which the reader may agree, but they are ideas that are familiar to us. A "domestic terror" attack might be typified by Dylann Roof, who opened fire on a historically black church in Charleston, South Carolina, killing nine congregants. This was the case of an American killing other Americans in the name of a racist ideology that is very familiar to most American readers.

HOMEGROWN TERROR AND RADICALIZATION

A third category that some analysts use is *homegrown terrorists*, or alternatively *homegrown jihadis*, for those who were born and raised outside Muslim majority countries but who carry out domestic attacks in the name of Islam. As formally defined,

> homegrown *jihadi*[s] [are] those who have been raised in the West, become naturalized citizens of Western countries, or who have spent substantial time and who have substantial ties to a Western country but who have adopted the *Salafi-jihadi* ideology and are [at the very least] would-be *jihadis*.

(Wright, 2016)

The term first gained traction after the July 7, 2005, London bombings (7/7) when a group of four suicide bombers killed 52 in a series of bombings. Three of the 7/7 bombers had been born in the UK, and the fourth was a convert to Islam from Jamaica who had been raised in England. While all the attackers had deep ties to the UK, there was still a perception that the form of violent Islamism embraced by them was somehow foreign (Gartenstein-Ross & Grossman, 2009).

In the US, the term "homegrown *jihadi*" has been used to describe hundreds of people and plots involving Americans or long-time US residents who have plotted or killed in the name of al Qaeda, ISIS, al Shabaab, or other *Salafi jihadi* groups. For example, the 2009 shooting at Fort Hood, Texas, killed 13 and was carried out by an American named Nidal Hasan, who is said to have been *radicalized* to the point where he believed it was his duty to kill his fellow soldiers. By "radicalization," we mean the process by which seemingly ordinary citizens transform into militant and violent Islamists and thus become homegrown terrorists (Dalfaard-Nielson, 2010). In hindsight, it seems like it should have been easy to see that the Virginia native was undergoing this transformation. Born to immigrant parents, Hasan was raised in suburban Washington, D.C., where he joined the Army immediately after high school. Hasan earned both his bachelor's degree and medical degree on the Army's dime, specializing in psychiatry. The son of immigrants who joins the Army and becomes a doctor could be the hero in any number of stories focusing on the American dream. What had go so wrong?

It is not clear when Nidal Hasan's radicalization began. His parents were Palestinian refugees, and Hasan had relatives, including a brother, who lived in what he would have certainly considered the illegitimately occupied territory of the West Bank. Resentment against a US foreign policy generally supportive of Israel surely would have been part and parcel to his daily life. Despite this, Hasan reportedly joined the Army over the objections of his parents (McKinley & Dao, 2009). After his mother died in 2001, he began to attend mosque at the Dar al-Hijrah Islamic Center in Falls Church, Virginia, much more regularly than had been his previous custom.

The imam at the mosque at the time of Hasan's Islamic reawakening was Anwar al-Awlaki, a New Mexico native who had publicly condemned 9/11 shortly after the attacks. However, Awlaki's condemnations may have been for public show: several of the 9/11 attackers had worshipped in at least two mosques where Awlaki preached, and later he would flee the US and become a leader of al Qaeda in the Arabian Peninsula (AQAP). Awlaki was killed in 2011 in a US drone strike in

Yemen that also killed his 16-year-old American-born son. Another American named Samir Khan was also killed in the strike. We return to Awlaki and Khan later in this chapter.

It is also probable that the 2003 US invasion of Iraq played some part in Hasan's transformation. The first signs of disgruntlement came a year later when relatives report that he sought legal advice about getting out of the Army (McKinley & Dao, 2009). However, since the military had paid for his recently finished medical degree, his obligatory terms of service had been extended in order to "pay back" the Army for the extensive training they had invested in him. Hasan would not be discharged as he wished.

Sometime before Hasan was transferred to Fort Hood, fellow soldiers recall that he became more and more agitated about US military involvement in the Middle East. In June 2007, he presented a lecture to fellow military graduate students entitled, "Why the War on Terror Is a War on Islam." In it, he claimed, "It's getting harder and harder for Muslims in the service to morally justify being in a military that seems constantly engaged against fellow Muslims" (McKinley & Dao, 2009). Another lecture was titled, "The Koranic World View as It Relates to Muslims in the U.S. Military." The "Conclusions" slide on the PowerPoint presentation read,

> Fighting to establish an Islamic State to please God, even by force, is condoned by Islam. . . . Muslim Soldiers should not serve in any capacity that renders them at risk to hurting/killing believers unjustly . . .
>
> (Priest, 2009)

In 2008, Hasan began an e-mail correspondence with his former imam, Anwar al-Awlaki. By this time, Awlaki was in Yemen and was regularly appearing in propaganda videos produced by al Qaeda in the Arabian Peninsula. He also had created his own website, where he held question-and-answer sessions about Islamic jurisprudence and practices and where he justified attacks by Muslims in the West against their home countries. Awlaki also condemned fellow clerics who supported the presence of US troops in the Middle East and who said it was permissible for Muslims to serve in Western armies. In a comment on Awlaki's website, Hasan is believed to be the author of a post in which suicide bombers were compared to soldiers who throw themselves on a grenade to save others (Ddrogin & Fiore, 2009). In one of the emails to Awlaki, Hasan asked whether it was permissible to kill non-combatants in a suicide attack.

The emails came to the attention of counterterrorism analysts in at least two units led by the FBI, and they were passed on to the military's Defense Criminal Investigative Services. The investigators tasked with looking into the matter claimed the emails were "fairly benign," assumed they were part of research Hasan was doing for a master's degree, and concluded Hasan "was not involved in terrorist activity" (Blake, 2013). The matter was dropped, and later efforts to investigate Hasan went nowhere. Meanwhile, Hasan had new business cards printed that noted he was an Army medical doctor specializing in psychiatry. Printed on the cards was the acronym "SoA (SWT)," which was a well-established code in *jihadist* circles that stands for "Soldier of Allah," followed by Arabic shorthand for "Glory to God" (Fox News, 2009). A few months later, Hasan went on the shooting spree that killed 13 fellow soldiers and wounded dozens more before he was shot and neutralized. Hasan had gone from all-American success story to *Salafi jihadi* terrorist. He had been radicalized and was now a homegrown terrorist.

The American Foreign Fighter Phenomenon

The three commonly used categories discussed in the preceding section paint three pictures of the terrorist threat to the US homeland. *Transnational* or *international terror* poses a threat to the US when foreigners enter to the US to carry out attacks. 9/11 is an example of this type of Islamist terror. *Domestic terror* is normally conceived of as groups whose ideological roots are American or are the violent offshoots of political disagreements within the US. The KKK or The Weather Underground are examples of this type of terror. Islamist inspired acts of terror are normally excluded from this category because Islam is often thought of as somehow foreign. *Homegrown terror* is used to describe Islamist attacks on US soil in which the participants themselves are American citizens or have deep connections to the US as their own homeland. These terrorists go from ordinary citizens to Islamist militants in a process called *radicalization*. The Fort Hood attack by Virginia native Nidal Hasan is typical of this type of attack.

These distinct categories may be useful for some analyses, but they do not paint a complete picture of Islamist terror in the US or the contribution Americans make to Islamist insurgencies around the world. What do we make of a growing number radicalized Muslims who travel from their homes in the West to commit acts of violence abroad? Normally, transnational Islamist terror conceives of foreign *jihadis* coming to the US. A growing number of studies show that the opposite is also true: homegrown American radicals are leaving the US to go abroad to commit acts of violence (Wright, 2014).

A number of high-profile cases illustrate the point that this phenomenon is widespread. The Alabama born and raised Omar Hammami became radicalized online and was killed in Somalia in 2013 while fighting with a faction of al Shabaab (Brown & Straw, 2013). Born to upper middle class parents, Hammami was popular growing up and was class president of his high school in the rural Southern town in which he was raised. In contrast, the Michigan born Colleen LaRose grew up in poverty, was allegedly sexually abused by her father, and ran away to become an underage prostitute. At the time of her secret conversion to Islam, when she began calling herself "Fatima" and took on the online persona of "Jihad Jane," she was living in a trailer with her boyfriend. Soon thereafter, she went to Ireland to meet up with another American woman from Colorado named Jamie Paulin-Ramirez. In Ireland, the two Americans met up with a cell of Muslims of Arab descent, and the group plotted to use stolen US passports to travel to Sweden and assassinate the cartoonist Lars Vilks for his alleged "blasphemy" for drawing the Islamic prophet Muhammad (Hurdle, 2014). Washington, D.C., native David Headley has been convicted of helping the Pakistani Lashkar-i-Taiba terrorist organization plot the Mumbai, India, attacks that killed over 150 (Yaccino, 2013).

In each of these cases, Americans went abroad to commit acts of terror or to join organizations on the State Department's Foreign Terrorist Organization list. The rise of the Islamic State of Iraq and Syria (ISIS) further reinforces this picture as numerous media reports and credible statements from law enforcement and intelligence agencies suggest that thousands of young men and women have left their homes in the West to join the terrorist organization (Stern & Berger, 2015).

But Americans are not just the foot soldiers of foreign terrorist groups, they are sometimes leaders. As previously noted, New Mexico native Anwar al-Awlaki was a leader in the al Qaeda in the Arabian Peninsula (AQAP) organization until he was killed in a drone strike in 2011. He may have been involved in the initial radicalization of Nidal Hasan and was definitely instrumental in giving Hasan the intellectual and theological justifications he needed to go from passive supporter of *Salafi jihad* to mass murderer. As a leader in AQAP, Awlaki was also involved in the plot by Nigerian Umar Farouk Abdulmutallab, who failed to detonate an "underwear bomb" as his flight from Amsterdam was on approach to Detroit (Temple-Raston, 2010). The same drone strike that killed Awlaki also killed North Carolinian Samir Khan, who had gone to Yemen to join AQAP. There, he became editor in chief of AQAP's English language *Inspire* magazine. In the magazine's second issue, Khan explained his path to radicalization in an article he titled, "I am proud to be a traitor to America." In other issues, the magazine described "How to make a bomb in the kitchen of your mom" and followed up with more precise instructions on how to make a pressure cooker bomb. These instructions would later be used by two Russians who had immigrated to the US as children, Tamerlan and Dzhokar Tsarnaev, to build the bombs used in the 2013 attack on the Boston Marathon (Serrano, Mason, & Dilanian, 2013).

Americans going abroad to fight in Islamist insurgencies is not new. According to J.M. Berger (2011), the phenomenon was observed as far back as the mid-1980s as VHS tapes of radical clerics began to circulate in the US calling on the faithful to join the *jihad* against the Soviets in Afghanistan. At least 30 Americans have been documented going to Afghanistan to fight with the US-backed *mujahideen*. However, that number represents only known cases and does not take into account those who went to fight in Afghanistan undetected. Conservative estimates suggest that the actual number of American fighters is closer to 150 (Berger, 2011, p. 8). What has changed since the Afghan civil war is that the US is no longer supporting these insurgencies, but fighting them. At the time, the Cold War was in its final stages, and the greater threat perceived to be from expansionist Soviet communism than the nascent *Salafi jihadi* movement. Another important factor is that with the elevation of *jihadi* groups to the State Department's Foreign Terrorist Organization list, support of these groups in any way became a crime. Under US law, it is unlawful if a person "knowingly provides material support or resources to a foreign terrorist organization, or attempts or conspires to do so" (18 US § 2339B).

This ambiguously worded statute has been defined broadly enough so that nearly any act in support of a group on the FTO list could be considered "material support." For instance, in the suburbs of Boston, a pharmacist named Tarek Mehanna was convicted of "material support" for translating documents from Arabic to English on behalf of al Qaeda in Iraq—the group which would later become ISIS. Mehanna's lawyers argued that what their client had done was protected speech under the First Amendment. Mehanna's 17-year sentence to federal prison was upheld by the First Circuit Court of Appeals, and the matter was settled when the Supreme Court declined to hear the case (Anderson, 2013). Many civil libertarians continue to be troubled by the case, arguing that while Mehanna's actions advocating al Qaeda and the *Salafi jihadi* worldview is certainly troubling, it should nevertheless be protected in much the same way as the speech of neo-Nazis is protected (Akbar, 2013).

Mehanna's case probably marks the outer edge of how far prosecuting attorneys are willing to stretch the term "material support." Far more common is the phenomenon of would-be *jihadis* prosecuted for attempting to go abroad to join groups such as al Qaeda or ISIS. In most cases, they have been arrested prior to ever leaving the US and are typically in transit—for instance, at an airport—when initially detained. This is even the case with Mehanna as he was first arrested at Boston's Logan International Airport in transit to Saudi Arabia. In these more common cases, the act of attempting to join a FTO is construed as "conspiracy to provide material support"—with communications and plans with known terrorist operatives abroad laying the groundwork for a "conspiracy" charge, and "material support" meaning the physical presence of the would-be *jihadi* in the ranks of the organization. By attempting to join a terrorist group abroad, the suspect is attempting to give his or her labor to that organization—"material support."

The exact number of Americans who have traveled overseas in order to provide material support to terrorist organizations is not known. Berger (2011) estimates that between 1980 and 2010, "at least 1,400 Americans have taken part in some form of military jihad" overseas (p. xi). As already pointed out, though, this number includes those who legally went abroad during the Afghanistan war. For the year's 1990–2010, which marks the years after the Cold War, Hegghammer (2013) looked at a range of estimates for Americans traveling abroad given by experts in the field. He found vast variations in the numbers—with some estimating as few as 188 traveling abroad to participate in foreign *jihad* and others estimating the number to be as high as 2,169.

This author adopted Hegghammer's conservative estimate of 161 *jihadis* leaving the US during this time frame, and then compared that number with those known to have come from abroad to the US (Wright, 2014). In that time, only 39 *jihadis* were known to come to the US from abroad. This includes the 19 9/11 hijackers, which was by far the terror plot with the largest number of foreign conspirators. The numbers show that the impulse for American *jihadis* to leave the US to fight far exceeds the impulse to stay in the US. They show that for every foreign transnational terrorist coming to the US, there are five Americans leaving or attempting to leave. If the estimates of net *jihadi* migration in and out of the US are correct, the policy implications are substantial. The threat of terrorism in the US from abroad is substantially overshadowed by the threat of Americans leaving the US to commit acts of violence somewhere else. If our post-9/11 Homeland Security strategy has largely focused on intercepting those that would do us harm at the border as they try to get into to the US, then we are focusing on the wrong thing. The threat is far more likely to be a US citizen trying to leave the US. The rest of the world should fear American *jihadis* committing violence in their countries more so than Americans need fear what foreigners may do when they come here.

These numbers seem to be verified by other studies. For instance, a March 2017 report by the George Washington University's "Extremism Tracker: ISIS in America" claims that of the 117 individuals that have been charged in the US with ISIS-related offenses in the 3-year period from March 2014 to March 2017, 45% of them were "accused of attempting to travel or successfully traveled abroad" (The George Washington University Program on Extremism, 2017). A similar study by the Center on National Security at Fordham Law School claims that in the same time period, 62 individuals—or 48% of the total cases—were those arrested or convicted of attempting to travel abroad. Another 17% were arrested or convicted as "facilitators"—either helping others travel abroad or attempting to send money to proscribed terrorist organization. A total of 78% of all involved in the time period that these data covered were US citizens (Center on National Security at Fordham Law, 2017). In other words, the vast majority of Islamist terrorists in the US are Americans. The majority (65%) of Americans who are would-be *jihadist*s have no intention of attacking the US here at home.

The numbers from other Western countries also suggest that would-be *jihadis*, in general, prefer to fight abroad rather than at home (Hegghammer, 2013). The rise of ISIS has only made the phenomenon worse, with estimates of the total number of European-born *jihadis* in Syria somewhere between 5,000 and 10,000. Those numbers become more alarming when we keep in mind the fact that they represent not a decade of movement from the West to Syria, but only the 3 years of ISIS existing as a stand-alone organization. Why is this? Why do Americans—and Westerners in general—who have adopted the *Salafi jihadi* ideology tend to want to go abroad rather than stay at home to commit acts of violence?

The first thing to understand is that in the mind of a would-be *jihadi*, he or she is not going abroad to become a *terrorist*. Instead, he or she is going abroad to fight in an ongoing war. As David Mamet (2013) has pointed out, foreign fighters appeared in at least 26% of civil wars over the past 200 years. In the 1930s, for instance, thousands of Americans went to fight in the Spanish Civil War because they were convinced either of the correctness of the cause or in the dangers of the authoritarianism of Franco. They went for ideological reasons. Some also went to fulfill their romantic fantasy of adventure in war. In the case of ongoing civil wars in Syria and Somalia, the children of immigrants from those countries may see one side of the conflict as *their* side. They go for ethno-nationalistic reasons.

However, something more is going on here than political ideology and nationalism. In the case of Syria, for instance, Sunni Muslims are bombarded with images of Sunnis suffering at the hands of the Shia-led governments and militias of the Syrian and Iraqi regimes. While these Sunni Muslims may not be Arabs, the Islamic idea of the *ummah* is important in understanding the phenomenon. *Ummah* is best thought of as "the nation," but in this case it means the body of believers in Islam. For most Muslims, this means all those who have publicly pronounced faith in Islam. However, many S*alafists* consider only practicing Sunnis as part of the broader *ummah*. The war, to them, is not ethno-nationalist—it is ethno-religious. To many *Salafi* and other conservative Islamic sects, when they think of their own nationality, they do not think in terms of American, British, or Moroccan—they would self-identify as Muslim. They would think of Sunnis as Muslim and Shia as either *takfiri*—apostate non-Muslims—or as deviants who have strayed and have left the fold. This group fights to protect Sunni Muslims against their perceived oppressors—the Shia. To the extent that religion plays a role, it plays the role usually filled by nationalism in modern conflicts.

Another important factor is the role religious norms play in the choice to go abroad or stay at home (Hegghammer, 2013). Sunni Islam has a long tradition of just war theory—theories that explain why some wars are just and others are not. While there is considerable variation among these scholars, there is near unanimity in justifying violence when it is in self-defense or when it is in defense of the *ummah* from non-believers. The narrative told by *Salafi jihadists* is that Islamist insurgencies in Somalia, Syria, Iraq, and elsewhere are really cases of Sunnis protecting themselves in defensive wars started by outside forces. These areas are "war zones," and therefore, fighting here is perceived as more legitimate than, say, Minneapolis. To the extent that American soldiers are targets, they are targets because they are on the wrong side in the conflict. Studies show that even among those who have adopted the *Salafi jihadi* ideology in the West, substantial majorities see fighting in Islamist insurgencies abroad as legitimate but attacking civilians in their homeland as unacceptable (Hegghammer, 2013; Bartlett, Birdwell, & King, 2010; Neumann & Rogers, 2007). In other words, these radicals see killing Americans civilians here as wrong but killing American soldiers in conflict zones as morally justifiable.

In over a decade of monitoring what *jihadis* say to each other online, this author has personally witnessed hundreds of debates as to whether attacks such as 9/11 or the Orlando Pulse nighclub shootings were justified. Invariably, for those who believe attacking civilians is unjustified, they explain such attacks away in terms of conspiracy theories: our side (eg, al Qaeda or ISIS) didn't really carry out the attack—it was a "false flag" operation carried out by the CIA or the Mossad. The takeaway here is that even among the most radical supporters of violent Islamism, most believe attacking civilian targets is unjustified. This goes a long way in explaining why the majority of those arrested and convicted of terror-related offenses in the US are accused of "conspiracy to provide material aid to foreign terrorist organizations" in the form of either money sent to these groups or attempts to travel abroad to join them.

Homegrown *Jihadis* and Foreign Fighter Veterans in the US

If the vast majority of Islamist radicals prefer to go abroad, then those who choose to stay at home to commit acts of terror must be the most radical of the radical. A small subset of individuals from a small subset of radicals among Muslims in America who, as pointed out previously, are a small subset of Americans in general—probably about 1% of the population. If not more radical, then at least they believe differently than most of their *Salafi jihadi* allies. That is, something has convinced them of the legitimacy of killing civilians at home.

Even among attacks by homegrown Islamist terrorists, their choice of who to attack reveals that they see themselves as soldiers in a war, more comfortable in attacking military targets than civilians. For instance, Nidal Hasan's targets were active duty servicemen and women at Fort Hood. Further recall that his business cards read SoA—Soldier of Allah. Other cases also illustrate this point. In 2009, Tennessee native Abdulhakim Mujahid Muhammad (born as Carlos Leon Bledsoe) opened fire on a US military recruiting station in North Little Rock, Arkansas, killing one and injuring another. Muhammad justified the attacks on the grounds that he was a "soldier" of al Qaeda in the Arabian Peninsula fighting other soldiers who were waging war against "Islam and Muslims" (Muhammad, 2010). In 2007, six men—all of them either US citizens or long-time permanent residents—unsuccessfully plotted to attack the Army instillation at Fort Dix, New Jersey. Their intention was to kill "as many soldiers as possible" in retaliation for perceived American attacks against Muslims (Parry, 2007). In 2005, four Muslim converts unsuccessfully plotted to bomb military instillations in the Los Angeles area (Murr, 2007), and in 2009, three US citizens and a long-time resident from Haiti plotted to shoot down military airplanes flying out of an Air National Guard base in Newburgh, New York (Hernandez & Chan, 2009). Would-be homegrown terrorists seem to prefer attacking military targets, even when those targets are in the US.

American *Jihadi* Veterans of Foreign Wars: The Returnees

While going to fight abroad in Islamist insurgencies is nothing new, what is new is the scale of those going abroad due to the number of Sunnis killed in the Syrian conflict and the rise of ISIS. There is a fear that, once abroad, the already radical Western foreign fighters will become even more radical. Having joined al Shabaab, al Qaeda, or ISIS originally for the purposes of fighting in a perceived defensive war against enemies in a war zone, the fear is that they will adopt the views of the organizations they join and begin to see the US as the more potent enemy. A related fear is that once in an actual war zone, they will learn new skills—such as bomb building—and therefore become better at the task of killing. Studies show that the vast majority of plots in the US are either foiled before they come to fruition or fail to inflict mass casualties because those carrying them out are ill prepared. These *returnees*—veteran Western foreign fighters who come back to their home countries—are perceived as more dangerous for these two reasons: 1) they are more radical, and 2) they are better trained (Wright, 2016).

The conclusion that these returnees are a bigger threat than other homegrown terrorists has been found by a number of researchers (Hegghammer, 2013; Byman, 2015; Nilson, 2015). Public conclusions drawn by these analyses might be summed up nicely in the title of a Brookings policy paper, "Be Afraid. Be A Little Afraid: The Threat of Terrorism from Western Foreign Fighters in Syria and Iraq" (Byman & Shapiro, 2014). In 2014, President Barack Obama addressed the UN General Assembly and urged member nations to do more to address the growing problem, and in February 2015, fears of radicalized American returnees led the White House to host a 3-day summit on preventing the phenomenon (Wright, 2016). UN Security Council Resolution 2178, adopted in September 2014, "requires states to prevent and suppress recruiting, organizing, transporting, and equipping of [foreign terrorist fighters]." Like the US after 9/11, other nations are beginning to prosecute those attempting to go abroad to fight out of fear for what they might do once they return.

But are these fears justified? In the case of Western Europe, the numbers seem to suggest that, yes, veteran *jihadis* involvement in a terrorist plot makes that plot more likely to go from the planning stages to fruition. Their involvement also makes the likelihood of the plot being more deadly increase (Hegghammer, 2013).

The US case is different. Table 5.1 shows the number of *jihadi* plots in the US between 1990 and 2010, and compares data for plots with these veteran returnees against those without them. These data show that the presence of a veteran foreign fighter returnee *decreases* the likelihood that a plot will come to fruition. The presence of a returnee also *decreases* the likelihood that an executed plot will cause mass casualties. This is the case in the US but not in Europe. Why?

These data suggest that counterterrorism measures taken against returnees and those *jihadis* currently in place in the US are largely effective. Since 9/11, the US has prosecuted many would-be

TABLE 5.1 | Plots and Fatalities Involving Homegrown Terrorists and Returnees to the US

Number of plots in the US with homegrown *jihadis*	Number of plots involving returnees (as % of total)	Total number of deaths in homegrown plots	Number of homegrown plots executed (as % of total)	Number of executed plots with returnees (as % of total)	Number of deaths in plots with returnees (as % of total)	Number of deaths in plots with no returnees
27	9 (33%)	22	5 (19%)	1 (4%)	1 (5%)	21 (95%)

Source: Adapted from Wright, 2016, p. 36.

jihadis before they ever left to go abroad. This has not been the case in Europe. For those who do manage to escape from the US, they are more than likely to be detected once abroad. US intelligence agencies have many fewer restrictions on the kind of information they collect and store when the subject of their surveillance is outside the nation's boundaries than do law enforcement agencies such as the FBI. The fact a US citizen has traveled abroad to a conflict zone will more than likely put them on the radar of intelligence—information that is then passed on to law enforcement.

Some returnees, having experienced the realities of war and observed the strict version of *sharia* as implemented by the factions they go to fight with, may have no desire to commit acts of violence in their home countries in the West. For instance, Brooklyn native Mohimanul Alam Bhuiya quickly became disillusioned with ISIS after joining the group in 2014. From somewhere along the border between Turkey and Syria, he contacted the FBI asking for help returning home, preferring to plead guilty to two terrorism charges than to remain a soldier for ISIS. As part of his plea arrangement, he is now working to deter other young Muslims tempted by the lure of a pure "Islamic state" (Hong, 2017). Efforts by various governments to "deradicalize" those thought most in danger of becoming *jihadis* have, at best, a mixed record. Many such programs have shown little or no impact on actually deterring or reversing radicalization (Poole, 2017). What is clear, though, is that not all of those who go abroad come back more radical.

Others may actually return wanting to commit acts of terror in the US, but they are unable to do so because they are under observation by those tasked with preventing terror plots. If going abroad really does increase their level of commitment to acts of violence at home, it also makes it harder for them to carry out those attacks because it increases their likelihood of being under observation by intelligence and law enforcement agents. For instance, Lyman Faris was an al Qaeda operative who became a US citizen in 1999. While in Pakistan, Faris was tasked with overseeing a plot to attack the Brooklyn Bridge and derail a train in the Washington, DC, area. The detention of the mastermind of the 9/11 plot, Khalid Shiekh Mohammad, led to Faris' name being revealed. Arrested and threatened with a lengthy jail sentence, Faris worked as a double-agent sending messages back and forth to al Qaeda. Faris also led the FBI to Nuradin Abdi, a resident of Ohio who had come to the US as a refugee from Somalia. Along with an American convert to Islam, Christopher Paul, Abdi plotted to blow up a mall in Columbus. Paul was also implicated in plots to attack European tourist spots (The New America Foundation, n.d.). The detection of one trained foreign fighter led to the conviction of several others. In all cases, their plots never evolved past the planning stages.

The role of geography also cannot be overlooked. Simply put, Europe is geographically closer to the conflict zones than the US. Would-be *jihadis* from the US must get on an airplane to reach these conflict zones and must board an airplane to come back. While this does not pose an impossible barrier for veterans of Islamist conflicts, the security measures put on those flying to or from the US are a substantial barrier nonetheless. Geography means returning to Europe from the conflict in Syria requires none of the security checks now standard at most airports. Trains, buses, and ships that might transport veteran foreign fighters back to their country of origin are generally reported to have far fewer security precautions than airlines.

A recent example of this is Ayoub el Khazzani, who is reported to have been known by authorities as a *jihadi* sympathizer and was on the French equivalent of the terror watch list. The fact that he decided to attack on a train from Amsterdam to Paris meant that he was not subject to the scrutiny that would have followed him had he taken an airplane. It is sheer happenstance that two off-duty members of the US military were sitting near Khazzani on the train and were able to wrestle him to the ground before he was able to kill anyone. The same is probably true of the November 2015 Paris attackers who killed 130. All seven of those directly involved in the attacks were citizens of EU countries and were either known by authorities as *jihadi* sympathizers or known to have traveled to Syria to fight with ISIS but were able to return undetected and undeterred. This proximity to Syria and North Africa also means that the availability of weapons to returnees is probably much higher than in the past. The same routes that funnel *jihadis* back and forth from Europe to conflict zones like Syria are also being used to smuggle weapons to be used in domestic terror attacks in the West. It explains why in both attacks, those involved were able to use automatic weapons generally prohibited throughout Europe (Wright, 2016).

Tighter border restrictions are another reason why some plots in the US have failed. For instance, the plot to attack the Los Angeles International Airport on New Year's Eve 1999 was foiled as Ahmed Ressam—a veteran of al Qaeda training camps in Pakistan—was arrested while crossing the border from Canada to the US. His arrest not only put the plot on hold, it also led to a nation-wide sweep of al Qaeda sympathizers who were also implicated and later jailed. None of the plots linked to any of the suspects ever came to fruition (*United States v. Ressam*, 2008). Under present EU rules, once a foreign national crosses into any European country, he is free to travel unrestricted through most countries. Crossing the border from France to Germany is no more difficult than crossing from Tennessee into Kentucky. The border is marked by a sign post, and nothing more.

Successful Homegrown *Jihadi* Plots in the US

As noted previously, the vast majority of Islamist terrorists in the US are arrested and prosecuted for crimes unrelated to plots to kill Americans on US soil. Moreover, among those who do plot to commit acts of terror in the homeland, the vast majority are detected and foiled, and therefore, the plots never go beyond the planning stages. But some do succeed. As more than one counter-terror observer has noted, "We have to succeed 100% of the time. The terrorists only have to succeed once." What, if anything, do these plots that succeeded have in common, and what can they teach us?

Here, 9/11 does serve as a good place to begin looking at successful terror attacks—not because it is irrelevant, but because the counter-terror policies enacted after 9/11 are so much more robust than those enacted before it. When a terror plot comes to fruition now, it does so in spite of 15 years of enhanced counter-terrorism policies.

Tables 5.2 and 5.3 use data provided by the New America Foundation (2017) on successful *jihadi* attacks in the US. Here, the term "successful" is defined as an attack in which at least one person was killed. Other *jihadi* attacks that may have wounded victims but did not kill them are not included. Also excluded were attacks that were carried out in which the only people killed were the perpetrators themselves. This last category would include the 2016 Ohio State University attack by Somali refugee Abdul Razak Ali Artan who rammed his vehicle into a crowd of fellow students and then stabbed several of them before being shot by the police. Although 13 victims were wounded in this attack, some of them seriously, the only casualty was the *jihadist*-inspired terrorist himself (*The Columbus Dispatch*, 2016). Another example of an excluded attack would be the 2015 Garland, Texas, shooting where the participants in the "Muhammad Art Exhibit and Contest" were targeted by two ISIS supporters, Elton Simpson and Nadir Hamid Soofi. The only victim was a wounded security guard, but the two ISIS supporters were killed in the shoot-out by SWAT team members who were on the scene (Golgowski, 2015). I note these excluded attacks because the actual number of *jihadist* attacks in which victims were wounded but not killed is much higher than this. If we include plots that were planned but never came to fruition, then the number of would-be *jihadi* attacks are several orders of magnitude higher. The data in Tables 5.2 and 5.3 only represent a small minority of *jihadist* plots in the US—those that were deadly.

TABLE 5.2 | Deadly *Jihadist*-Inspired Attacks in the US, Post-9/11—January 2017

Year	Attack	Perpetrator(s)	Homegrown?	Foreign Fighter?	Number of Victims	
					Killed	Wounded
2002	Los Angeles Airport Shooting	Hesham Hadayet	No	No	2	4
2006	Seattle Jewish Federation Shooting	Naveed Haq	Yes	No	1	5
2009	Little Rock Shooting	Abdulhakim Muhammad	Yes	Yes	1	1
2009	Ft. Hood	Nidal Hasan	Yes	No	13	32
2013	Boston Marathon	Tamerlan Tsarnaev Dzhokhar Tsarnaev	Yes	No	4	170
2014	WA & NJ Killing Spree	Ali Muhammad Brown	Yes	No	4	0
2014	Oklahoma Beheading	Alton Nolen	Yes	No	1	0
2015	Chatanooga, TN Military Shooting	Mohammad Abdulazeez	Yes	No	5	2
2015	San Bernardino, CA Shooting	Syed Rizwan Farook Tashfeen Malik (Farook)	Yes	No	14	21
2016	Pulse Nightclub Shooting	Omar Mateen	Yes	No	49	53
2017	Colorado Security Guard Shooting	Joshua Cummings	Yes	No	1	0

TABLE 5.3 | Summary Data on Deadly *Jihadi* Plots in the US, Post-9/11–January 2017

Total deadly *jihadi* plots	11
Average cell size	1.2
Homegrown *jihadis*?	10/11 (91)
Foreign fighter returnees involved?	1/11 (9)
Total wounded in deadly *jihadi* plots	288
Total killed in *jihadi* plots	95
Average number of fatal casualties per attack	8.6

From these data, we can make several inferences about gaps in intelligence and law enforcement prevention efforts. First, what does the fact that 11 *jihadist* plots were able to inflict 95 fatal casualties post-9/11 tell us? Are these numbers high? Or are these numbers low? In order to make comparisons, let us look at right-wing–inspired terrorist attacks. Using the same dataset from the New America Foundation (2017), we can see that in that same time period there were 19 right-wing–inspired attacks in the US that killed 51 people—an average of 2.7 killed per attack. Even though there were fewer successful *jihadi* attacks (11 vs 19), both the total number killed (95 vs 51) and the average number killed per attack (8.6 vs 2.7) were greater than right-wing attacks. *Jihadi attacks were less frequently carried out than right-wing attacks, but they were more deadly.*

THE SMALLER THE CELL SIZE, THE MORE LIKELY IT IS THAT IT WILL SUCCEED AND BE DEADLY

The average cell size of those involved in these attacks is 1.2, with the most frequent number involved in the attack being 1. As mentioned previously, the vast majority of *jihadi* plots in the US are disrupted prior to the actual attack. Detection nearly always involves communications, and communications, by definition, means that more than one person is involved. Communications can be between the would-be *jihadi* and his real world friends, between him and his online acquaintances (including those who may be known members of a terrorist group abroad), or between him and his family or religious community. The more the would-be *jihadi* talks to other people about his plans, the more chances he will be discovered. A substantial number of these plots are disrupted by FBI informants (48%), tips from family members or members of the community—including members of the mosque where the suspects attend (26%), or tips from the general public (8%) (New America Foundation, 2017). The problems associated with detecting and preventing single-cell or "lone wolf" terrorism is dealt with elsewhere in this book.

At least post-9/11, *multi-cell* jihadi *terrorist attacks are no more deadly, on average, than single-cell attacks.* In only two of the 11 successful post-9/11 *jihadi* attacks were there more than one person involved in the actual attack. Those two cases involved the Boston Marathon bombings by the Tsarnaev brothers and the San Bernardino shootings by Syed Farook and his wife Tashfeen. The Boston Marathon bombings killed four, and the San Bernardino shootings killed 14. So, in the former case, fewer people were killed than the average of 8.6 in the typical *jihadi* attack, and in the latter case, more were killed. The small number (2) of multi-cell attacks makes the inference weak, but the inference nonetheless is that adding more cell members does not necessarily lead to more casualties—even when the plot goes undetected.

TERRORIST CELLS CONSISTING OF CLOSE FAMILY MEMBERS DO NOT FOLLOW THE GENERAL PATTERN, AND ARE LESS LIKELY TO BE DETECTED AND PREVENTED

Both multi-cell attacks during this time frame consisted of close relatives—a husband and wife team and two brothers. This is probably due to the fact that family members, such as a husband

and wife or brothers with a close relationship, are better equipped to safeguard secrets. Additionally, their physical proximity also means that in the process of plotting an attack, they will rely less on digital communications platforms, which can be detected. In other words, when they plot, they can plot face-to-face in the privacy of their own home—communications far less likely to be intercepted than cell phone calls, Internet chats, or messages on social media.

THE VAST MAJORITY OF SUCCESSFUL PLOTS ARE BY HOMEGROWN *JIHADIS*, NOT FOREIGNERS

Ten of the 11 successful plots were carried out by those who either were born in the US or who were long-time residents and whose radicalization clearly happened domestically. The one case involving no clear homegrown *jihadi* was that of Hesham Hadayet's (2002) attack on the El Al ticket counter at the Los Angeles International Airport. Despite Hadayet being in the US for nearly a decade prior to the attack—a time frame normally long enough to qualify as "homegrown"—his asylum application was rejected by the Immigration and Naturalization Service (INS) due to his association with a known *jihadi* group in his native Egypt (Ramirez, 2002). In other words, he had been in the US a long time, but he is known to have been radicalized before coming here. While he may not be a homegrown *jihadi*, he certainly was not sent to the US as part of an international terrorist plot. The failure to prevent this attack was a failure of the INS to find and deport him in a timely manner, the kind of thing the post-9/11 security enhancements were supposed to have ensured.

PLOTS BY FOREIGN FIGHTER RETURNEES ARE NO MORE DEADLY THAN THOSE WITHOUT THEM

This comports with other studies (Wright, 2016) and the data in Table 5.1.

Conclusion

This chapter introduced you into a world that may seem strange. Islam may have been unfamiliar, but the world of *Salafi jihadism* was completely alien. A key point is that Islam is something big enough to mean different things to different people. These differences of opinion on just what it means to be Muslim is at the core of many of the world's conflicts today. Many Muslims are comfortable with the modern world and the secular state. Others, especially *Salafi jihadis*, are not. So much so that they are willing to fight for their vision of an "Islamic state" and "defend" fellow Sunni Muslims in what are essentially civil wars around the world. While it is true that the now 15-year-old "war on terror" is largely a war against certain Islamist groups, it is also the case that our allies in this war are also mostly Muslims. In Afghanistan, our troops fight side-by-side with Muslim Afghanis against a common enemy. In Iraq, our forces are helping Muslim Kurds fight ISIS. In the Horn of Africa, they are assisting the government of Muslim Somalia to keep al Shabaab at bay. The vast majority of terror in the world today is committed in the name of Islam, but it is also true that the vast majority of the victims of this terror are Muslims. Muslims are far more likely to be killed in Islamist attacks than are non-Muslims. Of the ten countries most impacted by terrorist attacks in 2016, nine of them were majority Muslim (Global Terrorism Index, 2016).

While Sunni *Salafi jihadis* see the conflicts that produce most of the world's terror as pitting Muslims against non-Muslims, these conflicts are overwhelmingly between Muslims. The doctrine of *takfir* allows them to see the world in this way. This doctrine allows them to believe that both the Shia Islamist government in Iran and the Sunni Kingdom of Saudi Arabia are really "non-believers" and justifies attacks on them. The vast majority of homegrown *jihadis* see themselves as potential warriors in this conflict, not as terrorists. They prefer to go abroad and fight than stay at home and commit acts of terror. Because of this, the majority of Islamist terrorism related prosecutions in the US are for "conspiracy to give material support" in the form of money sent to foreign terrorist organizations, attempts to travel abroad to join them, or aiding those traveling abroad. Far more Americans have left to fight in Islamist insurgencies around the world than would-be terrorists have come here to commit acts of terror. This is partially because of the impetus to fight in these wars and partially because post-9/11 border security measures have been successful. The raw statistics imply that Syrians have more to fear from American *jihadis* than Americans from Syrian *jihadis*.

Among those who stay, there is a preference for military over non-military targets. They believe themselves warriors and military targets as more legitimate than civilian, despite the fact that groups like al Qaeda and ISIS encourage sympathizers to stay in the US and hit civilian soft targets. Those homegrown *jihadis* that plot to harm the US at home are mostly detected prior to actually carrying out an attack. This is because their communications are often intercepted by intelligence, law enforcement, friends, family, or other Muslims in the community. When they are able to attack, they often fail to kill anyone. In many cases, the only person killed is the would-be *jihadist*. The presence of a foreign fighter returnee does not increase the deadliness of an attack. In fact, the presence of a returnee decreases the likelihood that the attack will ever get past the planning stages.

Lone wolf *jihadi* attacks are much more likely to be carried to fruition and actually kill intended targets. In some cases, these *jihadis* were on the radar of law enforcement but were cleared as being non-threats. Intelligence and law enforcement should reevaluate the standards by which they determine which *jihadi* sympathizers are deemed "dangerous" and which are not. When a plot does involve multiple people, it is far more likely to succeed when those involved are close family members. Since 9/11, there have been fewer successful *jihadi* inspired attacks than right-wing inspired attacks, but these attacks are more deadly. The 9/11 attacks remind us that although the typical successful attack kills very few people, they have the *potential* to kill many more. Events like Category 5 hurricanes, nuclear war, or terrorist attacks on the scale of 9/11 may be rare, but they are so destructive that they cannot be ignored. The next successful Islamist attack in the US is likely to be a single homegrown *jihadi* who uses a gun and kills very few people before he himself is killed. However, this in no way implies that measures enacted to prevent another 9/11 by well-organized, large cell, transnational terrorist groups should be abandoned. Continued vigilance against such an attack is encouraged, but the real gap in preventing Islamist attacks in the US is in detecting and disrupting homegrown radicals who tell few people of their plans to commit terror on US soil.

REFERENCES

Akbar, A. (2013, December 31). *How Tarek Mehanna Went to Prison for a Thought Crime*. Retrieved January 20, 2017, from The Nation: www.thenation.com/article/how-tarek-mehanna-went-prison-thought-crime/

Anderson, T. (2013, November 13). *Federal Appeals Court Upholds Tarek Mehanna Terror Convictions*. Retrieved January 17, 2017, from The Boston Globe: www.bostonglobe.com/metro/2013/11/13/tarek-mehanna-terror-convictions-upheld-federal-appeals-court/4PlBQdkihh6yQkUV1ETldN/story.html

Bartlett, J., Birdwell, J., & King, M. (2010). *The Edge of Violence*. London: Demos.

Bergen, P., Ford, A., Sims, A., & Sterman, D. (2017, March 2). *Terrorism in America after 9/11*. Retrieved from The New America Foundation: www.newamerica.org/in-depth/terrorism-in-america/

Berger, J. (2011). *GI Joe: Americans Who Go to War in the Name of Islam*. Dulles, VA: Potomac Books.

Blake, M. (2013, August 27). *Internal Documents Reveal How the FBI Blew Fort Hood*. Retrieved March 17, 2017, from Mother Jones: www.motherjones.com/politics/2013/08/nidal-hasan-anwar-awlaki-emails-fbi-fort-hood

Brown, S., & Straw, J. (2013, September 12). Omar Hammami American Jihadi, Killed in Somali Ambush by Militants. *The New York Post*.

Byman, D. (2015). The Homecoming: What Happens When Arab Foreign Fighters in Iraq and Syria Return? *Studies in Conflict & Terrorism, 38*(8), 581–602.

Byman, D., & Shapiro, J. (2014). *Be Afraid: Be Afraid a Little Afraid: The Threat of Terrorism from Western Foreign Fighters in Syria and Iraq*. Washington, DC: The Brookings Institution. Retrieved September 30, 2015, from www.brookings.edu/wp-content/uploads/2016/06/Be-Afraid-web.pdf

Center on National Security at Fordham Law. (2017, March). *Case by Case: ISIS Prosecutions in the United States (Statistical Update 3/1/2014–2/27/2017)*. Retrieved March 29, 2017, from The Center on National Security at Fordham Law: https://static1.squarespace.com/static/55dc76f7e4b013c872183fea/t/58b4e2169f7456f6702fd133/1488249367229/Case+by+Case+-+Feb+2017+update.pdf

The Columbus Dispatch. (2016, November 30). *ISIS Claims Credit for Inspiring Attack at Ohio State That Injured 11*. Retrieved January 15, 2017, from The Columbus Dispatch: www.dispatch.com/news/20161129/isis-claims-credit-for-inspiring-attack-at-ohio-state-that-injured-11

Dalfaard-Nielson, A. (2010). Violent Radicalization in Europe: What We Know and What We Do Not Know. *Studies in Conflict and Terrorism, 33*(9), 797–814.

Ddrogin, B., & Fiore, F. (2009, November 7). *Retracing Steps of Suspected Fort Hood Shooter, Nidal Malik Hasan*. Retrieved March 17, 2017, from The Los Angeles Times: http://articles.latimes.com/2009/nov/07/nation/na-fort-hood-hasan7

Fox News. (2009, November 12). *Hasan Called Himself 'Soldier of Allah' on Business Cards*. Retrieved March 17, 2017, from FoxNews.com: www.foxnews.com/story/2009/11/12/hasan-called-himself-soldier-allah-on-business-cards.html

Gartenstein-Ross, D., & Grossman, L. (2009). *Homegrown Terrorism in the U.S. & U.K.* Washington, DC: Foundation for the Defense of Democracies.

The George Washington University Program on Extremism. (2017, March). *GW Extremism Tracker: ISIS in American—March 2017 Update*. Retrieved March 27, 2017, from https://cchs.gwu.edu/sites/cchs.gwu.edu/files/downloads/March%202017%20Snapshot.pdf

Global Terrorism Index 2016. (2016). Retrieved January 15, 2017, from Institute for Economics and Peace: http://visionofhumanity.org/app/uploads/2017/02/Global-Terrorism-Index-2016.pdf

Golgowski, N. (2015, May 11). *SWAT Team Killed Muhammad Cartoon Contest's Gunmen, Not Lone Officer: Texas Police Chief*. Retrieved January 15, 2017, from The NY Daily News: www.nydailynews.com/news/national/swat-team-killed-muhammad-cartoon-contests-gunmen-police-article-1.2218538

Hegghammer, T. (2013). Should I Stay or Should I Go? Explaining Variation in Western Jihadists' Choice between Domestic and Foreign Fighting. *American Political Science Review, 107*(1), 1–15.

Hernandez, J. C., & Chan, S. (2009, May 21). *N.Y. Bomb Plot Suspects Acted Alone, Police Say*. Retrieved March 28, 2017, from The New York Times: www.nytimes.com/2009/05/22/nyregion/22terror.html?_r=0

Hong, N. (2017, March 7). *Former ISIS Recruit Now a Weapon against Terrorism*. Retrieved March 8, 2017, from The Wall Street Journal: www.wsj.com/articles/former-isis-recruit-becomes-prosecutors-aide-1488898751?mod=e2tw

Hurdle, J. (2014, January 6). 10 Years for Plot to Murder Cartoonist. *The New York Times*.

LaFree, G. (2011). Using Open Source Data to Counter Common Myths about Terrorism. In J. G. Brian Forst (Ed.), *Criminologistics on Terrorism and Homeland Security*. Cambridge: Cambridge University Press.

Maher, S. (2016). *Salafi-Jihadism: The History of an Idea*. Oxford: Oxford University Press.

Mamet, D. (2013). *Foreign Fighters: Transnational Identity in Civil Conflicts*. Oxford: Oxford University Press.

McKinley, J. C., & Dao, J. (2009, November 8). *Fort Hood Gunman Gave Signals before His Rampage*. Retrieved February 17, 2017, from The New York Times: www.nytimes.com/2009/11/09/us/09reconstruct.html

Mohammad, B. (2016, January 6). *A New Estimate of the U.S. Muslim Population*. Retrieved from Pew Research Center Fact Tank: www.pewresearch.org/fact-tank/2016/01/06/a-new-estimate-of-the-u-s-muslim-population/

Muhammad, A. M. (2010, January 10). *Letter from Abdulhakim Mujahid Muhammad to Judge Wright*. Retrieved March 18, 2017, from http://graphics8.nytimes.com/packages/pdf/us/20100210-convert-letter.pdf

Murr, A. (2007, December 14). *Guilty Plea in Terror Case*. Retrieved March 20, 2017, from Newsweek: www.newsweek.com/guilty-plea-terror-case-95253

Neumann, P., & Rogers, B. (2007). *Recruitment and Mobilisation for the Islamist Militant Movement in Europe*. London: International Centre for theStudy of Radicalisation and Political Violence, King's College London.

The New America Foundation. (2017). *2003 Ohio Shopping Mall Plot*. Retrieved March 20, 2017, from The New America Foundation: http://securitydata.newamerica.net/extremists/terror-plot.html?id=1527

Nilson, M. (2015). Foreign Fighters and the Radicalization of Local Jihad: Interview Evidence from Swedish Jihadists. *Studies in Conflict & Terrorism, 38*(5), 343–358.

Parry, W. (2007, May 8). *6 Charged in Plot to Attack Army Post*. Retrieved March 28, 2017, from The Washington Post: www.washingtonpost.com/wp-dyn/content/article/2007/05/08/AR2007050800454.html

Poole, P. (2017, March 10). *Justice Department Enlists 'Reformed' ISIS Fighter in Risky Deradicalization Scheme*. Retrieved March 11, 2017, from PJ Media: https://pjmedia.com/homeland-security/2017/03/10/justice-department-enlists-reformed-isis-fighter-in-risky-deradicalization-scheme/?singlepage=true

Priest, D. (2009, November 10). *Fort Hood Suspect Warned of Threats within the Ranks*. Retrieved February 23, 2017, from The Washington Post: www.washingtonpost.com/wp-dyn/content/story/2009/11/09/ST2009110903704.html

Ramirez, E. (2002, October 10). *Panel Probes LAX Gunman*. Retrieved February 10, 2017, from The Los Angeles Times: http://articles.latimes.com/2002/oct/10/local/me-lax10

Serrano, R. A., Mason, M., & Dilanian, K. (2013, April 23). *Boston Bombing Suspect Describes Plot*. Retrieved March 20, 2017, from The Los Angeles Times: http://articles.latimes.com/2013/apr/23/nation/la-na-boston-bombings-20130424

Stern, J., & Berger, J. (2015). *ISIS: The State of Terror*. New York: Harper Collins.

Temple-Raston, D. (2010, February 19). *Officials: Cleric Had Role In Christmas Bomb Attempt*. Retrieved March 8, 2017, from National Public Radio: www.npr.org/templates/story/story.php?storyId=123894237

United States Census Bureau. (n.d.). Retrieved from American Fact Finder Report: https://factfinder.census.gov/faces/tableservices/jsf/pages/productview.xhtml?pid=ACS_10_1YR_DP02&prodType=table

United States v. Ressam, 553 US 272 (2008).

Wright, C. J. (2014). America as Exporter of Transnational Islamist Terror in the Post 9/11 Era. *Paper presented at the 2014 Annual Meeting of the Louisiana Political Science Association*.

Wright, C. J. (2016). How Dangerous Are Domestic Terror Plotters with Foreign Fighter Experience? The Case of Homegrown Jihadis in the US. *Perspectives on Terrorism, 10*(1), 32–40.

Yaccino, S. (2013, January 24). Planner of Mumbai Attacks Is Given 35 Year Sentence. *The New York Times*.

Zuckerman, J., Bucci, S., & Carafano, J. (2013). *60 Terrorist Plots since 9/11: Continued Lessons in Domestic Counterterrorism*. Washinton, DC: The Heritage Foundation.

Chapter 6

The Sovereign Citizens Movement

Robin Maria Valeri

In the united states of America, every man and every woman has the inherent power to be a King or Queen in their own home, on their own property without government encroachment or interference.

We the People are sovereign American Nationals OR "state" Citizens and there is no superior authority. It is up to us to reclaim our sovereignty and re-establish a lawful, de jure government of the people, by the people and for the people.

The Global Sovereign's Handbook, Johnny Liberty (2004, p. 33)

Overview

- Sovereign citizens is an ideology or movement that is anti-government. Sovereign citizen ideology encourages adherents to take back their sovereign status. The actions involved in taking back one's sovereign status are frequently unlawful and sometimes violent.
- Adherents of sovereign citizen ideology, while they all share anti-government beliefs, are quite diverse in terms of race, ethnicity, religion, age, and education.
- Adherents of sovereign citizen ideology should not be underestimated. However innocuous or far-fetched their beliefs may seem, these beliefs, whether couched in specious historical, legal, or religious rhetoric, can be used to justify any behavior, including murder and "traditional" terrorist actions.
- Sovereign citizens are resourceful! They have developed and continue to develop and used a variety of means, both violent and non-violent, to advance their cause.
- Non-violent actions include the filing of false liens, tax forms, and other forms of "paper terrorism" to stall or bring down the government.
- Violent actions include kidnapping, murder, arson, and other forms of "traditional" terrorism.

Fundamentals of the Sovereign Citizens Movement

The Sovereign Citizens Movement is a leaderless anti-government movement whose followers share certain anti-government beliefs and practices based on "common law" (ADL, 2012; Berger, 2016; Crowell, 2015; FBI, April 13, 2010; Fleishman, n.d.; Theret, 2012). A key belief is that individuals can separate themselves from their state and federal government by declaring their sovereignty. As you are reading this chapter, it is important to keep in mind that the Sovereign Citizens Movement is not an organization. It is an ideology that people choose to believe and follow.

SOVEREIGN CITIZEN GROUPS AND INDIVIDUALS

Adherents of sovereign citizen ideology include sovereign citizens[1] whose origins and history trace back to England and the Magna Carta, as well as members of the Moorish Nation and Washita Nation. While these latter two groups follow some sovereign citizen ideology, they have different origins and histories from sovereign citizens and from each other. The Moorish nation traces its "deep roots" back to the Moorish Empire and more recent roots to the Moorish Science Temple of America, which was founded by B. Timothy Drew (Noble Ali) in 1913. The Washitaw Nation traces its "deep roots" back to America's ancient ones, the "Mound Builders," and to "Empress" Verdiacee "Tiara" Washitaw-Turner Goston El-Bey, who founded the movement in the 1990s. (For a more complete history of these groups, see Valeri, forthcoming.)

Many sovereign citizens operate independently to regain their sovereign status. But some individual sovereign citizens will form groups in order to achieve specific goals, such as creating Common Law Grand Juries. These groups include Common Law Citizens, Constitutionalists, Constitution Rangers, Embassy of Heaven, Freemen, Greater Ministries (based in Florida), Guardians of the Free Republics, Non-Foreign/Non-Resident Aliens, Republic for the United States of America, and We the People (based in Colorado). In addition to these sovereign citizen groups, there are also Moorish and Washita Nation groups such as the Moorish Nation, United Mawshakh Nation of Nuurs, United Nuwaubian Nation of Moors (U.N.N.M.), and the Washitaw Nation.

SOVEREIGN CITIZENS' BELIEFS

The core beliefs of sovereign citizens are that an individual is sovereign or a "state" unto him/herself; cannot be controlled by a government unless he/she gives explicit consent; and can, for the most part, live according to God's laws and do almost anything as long as it does not hurt anyone else.

Sovereign citizens believe that they are governed by common law rather than statutory laws. If a sovereign citizen believes in any form of government, it is the county government, because county governments are the closest to the people. For this reason, sovereign citizens believe that the only constitutionally legal law enforcement is an elected county sheriff whose job is limited to enforcing popular law and, more importantly, protecting the people from any illegal activity carried out by the government or its representatives. It should be noted that sovereign citizens do not believe that a sheriff has the right to enforce statutory laws such as traffic violations. A sheriff's actions are only considered to be legitimate if he/she is acting on a written affidavit filed by a private citizen. According to the sovereign citizens, if the sheriff fails in his/her duties, it is their right to hang the sheriff. This is why common symbols of the Sovereign Citizens Movement are the hangman's noose and a sheriff's badge.

Because sovereign citizens believe that they have not explicitly consented to live under the rule of either the federal government or a state government, they also believe that they are not obligated to follow the laws, pay taxes, or obtain the licenses or certificates mandated by the federal or state governments. Sovereign citizens consider the issuing of and/or requirement for birth certificates, social security numbers, fishing licenses, drivers' licenses, marriage licenses, the use of ZIP codes, etc., as an attempt by the government to "trick" citizens into forming contracts with the government. and thereby not only giving their consent to be ruled by the government, but by doing so also giving up their freedom (Fleishman, n.d.).

Note that sovereign citizens of the Moorish Nation and Washita Nation also believe that individuals can declare their sovereign status and separate themselves from state and federal governments, but their rationale for these beliefs differ from those of Sovereign Citizens. As is discussed, sovereign citizens espouse a variety of practices to personally free themselves from government rule.

SHARED IDENTITY

While the Sovereign Citizens Movement is not an organization, for this chapter it is helpful to think about the movement and its adherents as a "group." Fortunately, psychology offers a fairly loose definition of a group, specifically "a group exists when two or more people define themselves as members of it and when its existence is recognized by at least one other. The 'other' . . . is some person or group of people who do not so define themselves" (Brown, 2006, p. 4). While the fact that the Sovereign Citizens Movement meets the definition of a group because there are two or more individuals who have defined themselves as sovereign citizens and their existence is recognized by at least one other, specifically the government, may not be particularly helpful; what is important is that group members have a shared or common identity. The shared identity of sovereign citizens is based on sovereign citizen ideology, history, and actions. Having a shared identity means that sovereign citizens will hold similar beliefs and behave in similar manners, especially when their sovereign identity is made salient. As noted by Taylor and Louis (2005), the shared identity of terrorist organizations tends to be simple and clear, offering straightforward and uncomplicated explanations for what is wrong and a clear path for remedying the situation. While a remedy suggests hope for a better future, the path provides an individual with instruction on what he/she should do to achieve that remedy.

Recognizing that shared identity can help us understand and perhaps even predict and influence the attitudes and actions of sovereign citizens. First, it reminds us that when sovereign

believe their own propaganda and are perhaps only con artists. In summary, sovereign citizens have adopted the anti-government beliefs of the Posse Comitatus as well as their paper and military/violent tactics.

SOVEREIGN CITIZENS TODAY

It's a plain and simple fact: If you are a human and were born in a State, you are a Sovereign State Citizen and should not be claiming U.S. citizenship. If a public employee tells you otherwise, they've committed a crime! It's actually *fraud* and *treason* to try to trick you! The solution is in Sovereign, State Citizenship! A human cannot be born in, fifty states at the same time. Nor can he be a Citizen of 50 states at the same time. You were born in one state. That makes you a Citizen of that State, not the U.S.

(Sovereign Citizenship Network, n.d.)

To us, being "sovereign" means that the government does not control *any* aspect of your life, so that God and not them are fully in control of your life. Remember, the only authority government has comes from passing laws against crime, and if you don't violate any of God's laws, then the government has no jurisdiction whatsoever over you.

(famguardian.org, n.d. a)

Today, the beliefs of sovereign citizens center around the anti-government rhetoric of the Posse Comitatus, which they have adopted and expanded. The book *The Global Sovereign's Handbook* by Johnny Liberty provides an excellent glimpse into the beliefs of the Sovereign Citizens Movement.

CONSPIRACY THEORY

Sovereign citizens, like Posse members, believe that at one time an idealized and minimalist government, which was based on common law, existed in the early days of America. "The Declaration of Independence established that the people are sovereign under God's Natural Law" (Robinson, 2009, p. 23). According to the sovereign citizens, the original government treated each citizen as "sovereign," and because it did not impose any taxes, regulations, unjust laws, or other burdens, allowed people to live as they wished. However, this original government, which they refer to as the "de jure" government had somehow been subverted and replaced with an illegitimate government that exists today, the "de facto" government (ADL, 2012; Berger, 2016; Crowell, 2015; Fleishman, n.d.; Loeser, 2015; Theret, 2012). Members of the Sovereign Citizens Movement will point to the constitution, specific constitutional amendments, and other acts or laws such as the Federal Reserve Act and the removal of United States currency from the gold standard, to explain how this subversion of the original government took place (see Valeri, forthcoming, for more details). While all sovereign citizens may not agree on the exact cause and players involved in the subversion of the original government, all of them agree that the original government has been subverted and that most people mistakenly believe that today's government is the "real" and legitimate government. They also share the desire to return the government to its original utopian form.

Note that while the arguments put forward by sovereign citizens and discussed next regarding the legitimacy of the government may sound compelling, there are several flaws in their arguments.

Missing Thirteenth Amendment: Titles of Nobility Act

In short, the Titles of Nobility Act, stated that if a citizen accepted or claimed a title of nobility or honor, such as a lawyer using the title "Esquire," that individual's citizenship would be revoked and render them incapable of holding office. For that reason, many sovereign citizens refuse to use lawyers.

Note that on May 1, 1810, Congress passed the Titles of Nobility Amendment. (Silversmith, 1999). But this Amendment never became part of the Constitution because it was not ratified by a sufficient number of states (see Adler, 2010, for a more complete discussion). However, because the Titles of Nobility had been published as the 13th Amendment in the Laws of the United States of America (United States, 1815–1816a, p. 74), with the caveat that it had not yet been ratified (United States, 1815–1816b, p. ix) some sovereign citizens claim that this proves that the Titles of Nobility Act was ratified.

Thirteenth Amendment: Abolishing of Slavery and the Sixteenth Amendment: Income Tax

The Sixteenth Amendment allowed for the creation of an income tax. Sovereign citizens believe that the 16th Amendment was not lawfully ratified and therefore is unconstitutional (ADL, 2012; Crowell, 2015; Fleishman, n.d.; Loeser, 2015; Theret, 2012). They also believe it places the taxpayer in a position of involuntary servitude, which is contrary to the 13th Amendment.

Fourteenth Amendment: Civil Rights

Sovereign Citizens use the Fourteenth Amendment to justify their sovereign status (ADL, 2012; Berger, 2016; Crowell, 2015; Fleishman, n.d.; Loeser, 2015; Theret, 2012). According to them, while the 14th Amendment allows people who were born or naturalized to the United States to become citizens of the United States and the state where they reside, the phrase "subject to the jurisdiction" suggests that becoming a citizen is at the discretion of the individual and would require explicit consent. The sovereign citizens believe that no one would willingly give up their sovereign status. To force people to become citizens, the federal and state governments have tricked individuals into signing contracts, in the form of birth certificates and various licenses, with them. Thus, sovereign citizens believe that by nullifying these contracts, they can free themselves from federal and state government rule. That is why sovereign citizens, including Terry Nichols who was instrumental in the bombing of the Federal Building in Oklahoma City, write to various federal and state officials repudiating their allegiance and revoking their signature on licenses or other contracts.

The Federal Reserve Act

Sovereign citizens believe that the Federal Reserve is not a legitimate government institution and that printing money is against the Constitution (ADL, 2012; Crowell, 2015; Fleishman, n.d.; Loeser, 2015; Theret, 2012).

1933 Removal of United States Currency From Gold Standard

Sovereign citizens believe that when the government removed U.S. currency from the gold standard, it needed to guarantee its value with something (ADL, 2012; Berger, 2016; Crowell, 2015; Fleishman, n.d.; Loeser, 2015; Theret, 2012). The sovereign citizens believe that the United States government decided to pledge its citizen and their future earnings as collateral. Sovereigns believe that when someone is born, the United States Treasury sets up a secret bank account in the individual's name and deposits an unknown but significant amount of money into that account. The sovereign citizens contend that by doing this, the government creates a second identity or "Strawman" for each individual so that there is the true person and the corporate version established by the government. According to the sovereign citizens, evidence of this second, corporate identity is that on birth certificates, social security cards, etc., an individual's name is written in all capital (upper case) letters. The result of this second identity is both good and bad for sovereign citizens.

The down side is that the real person needs to distinguish him/herself from the corporate identity, often referred to as the Strawman, in order to avoid being subjected to the laws of the government. To do this, when speaking with officials, they will often say they are the executor or trustee for the corporation known as and give their name. They will follow similar procedures when signing documents designating that they "Name in Upper and Lower Case" are the trustee or executor for NAME all upper case, or by putting punctuation or symbols in their Name#, or by adding a prefix or suffix to their name. For example, John Doe is the trustee for JOHN DOE or J.oh_n$ Doe# is the executor for JOHN DOE.

On the upside, given their belief in this hidden and vast bank account, the sovereign citizens have created a scheme to benefit from these secret bank accounts, using them as collateral or to pay off depts. This is frequently referred to as Redemption Theory or "Freeing money from the Strawman" (FBI, September, 2011). For example, Richard D. Schwein, Jr., tried to pay off his mortgage with a "bonded promissory note" that he purported to be worth $10 million (FBI, September 30, 2013).

Finally, because sovereign citizens do not think that paper money is a valid form of currency, some of them have created their own bogus but official looking and sounding currency such as "Public Office Money Certificates." Sovereign citizens will try to use these certificates as currency. Whenever someone unknowingly accepts these as legitimate currency, it allows the sovereign citizen to get something for free.

Actions of the Sovereign Citizens

In this section, we examine the broad range of activities carried out by sovereign citizens and discuss how those behaviors are used to establish an individual's sovereign identity and how, once a sovereign identity is established, that identity will shape the individual's actions.

DEVELOPING A SOVEREIGN IDENTITY: RESCINDING LICENSES AND CITIZENSHIP

The easiest way for a person to establish their identity as a sovereign citizen is by rescinding licenses and their citizenship. Doing so allows him/her to act in a manner consistent with sovereign beliefs and thus proclaim their new identity to themselves, "I am a sovereign citizen," and to members of their former group, "I am no longer part of your group." Especially in a leaderless group where there is no official group to join or induction ceremonies, declaring sovereign status to others, especially government officials, is crucial to development of a sovereign identity. First, the action itself, of rejecting licenses, etc., is a means for the sovereign citizen to declare to him/herself, "I did this. This is who I am." This is consistent with self-perception theory (Bem, 1967, 1972), which posits that an individual can come to know themselves and what they believe by looking at their own actions. Second, the distal nature of the communication allows these individuals to safely, with little risk of rejection or negative feedback, declare their identity to individuals outside the group. Thus, the correspondence with an official serves to communicate and establish both their new relationship with the government and their new identity. If the government fails to respond to these actions, this allows the sovereign to believe his/her claim has been accepted and is legitimate. Furthermore, as noted by Taylor and Louis (2005, p. 183), "By ostentatious anticonformity, disaffected individuals express a collective identity derived from the rejection of another group's norms." Rescinding licenses and citizenship are clearly acts of anti-conformity that establish the collective or shared identity of the Sovereign Citizens Movement through their rejection of government laws and regulations.

As discussed previously, people frequently look to their own actions to decide what their attitudes or beliefs are and therefore who they are. In this case, their actions confirm and strengthen their commitment to the Sovereign Citizens Movement through the commitment-initiating process referred to as foot-in-the-door (Cialdini, 2008). While this is a common technique used by social influence practitioners to influence others, it can also be a self-persuasion technique. The foot-in-the-door technique works by getting someone to agree to a small request, and then asking for a larger but related request. Agreeing to the small request impacts an individual's identity because the individual now sees themselves as someone who does or believes in "X." To be consistent with this new identity requires agreement with the second and larger request. Thus, a small initial commitment can morph into a large, life changing one by changing an individual's identity. Most likely for sovereign citizens, the individual, prior to revoking licenses and citizenship, made an initial commitment to learning about the movement, thought "I agree with these beliefs," increasing their commitment to the movement, and may have even expressed their commitment, either in person or via the web, to other sovereign citizens, further increasing their commitment to the movement. Now, they, and perhaps others, identify the individual as a sovereign citizen and expect him/her to act in a manner consistent with sovereign beliefs. Rescinding one's licenses and citizenship are easily implemented actions that confirm their sovereign identity.

Revealing a new identity, a new set of beliefs, risks rejection from others. For that reason, this is often a gradual process and tends to start with individuals or situations that the individual anticipates will be low in risk of rejection. As the individual becomes more comfortable with their new identity, they will share it with a broader audience and take larger risks. An individual who starts revoking licenses and/or renouncing citizenship is proclaiming their new identity, as a sovereign citizen, to people outside the group. Doing these things is relatively "safe" because the communicating occurs at a distance, via mail or computer, and avoids the possibility of a face-to-face confrontation. In the mind of the sovereign citizen, engaging in these actions allows him/her to establish an understanding with the government, specifically an understanding that they are "sovereign" and, therefore, separate from the government and not under its jurisdiction. For example, famguardian.org (n.d. b) provides instructions on how to cancel your social security number using IRS form 966.

Some sovereign citizens have sought to establish or confirm their sovereign identity face-to-face during court appearances or traffic stops. In these situations, the individual's sovereign identity is very salient. Therefore, it makes it more likely that the individual will act in a manner consistent with sovereign identity and behaviors. This is important to note because some of these behaviors include violence.

While sovereign citizens have a history of driving without licenses or license plates or with contrived licenses and license plates, claiming to be the "republic" of a given state or a diplomat, members of the Moorish Nation, or members of the Washitaw Nation, to name a few, and handling resulting encounters with law enforcement in a peaceful manner, there have been several instances of sovereign citizens killing law enforcement during these stops. Similarly, although sovereign citizens have a history of behaving in a non-violent manner during court appearance, there have been instances of sovereign citizens going to a courthouse with the intention of engaging in violence. Examples of these are discussed later in the chapter. But given that some sovereign citizens have engaged in violence, it is essential for law enforcement and other officials, when they encounter a sovereign citizen, to be prepared for violence and to take appropriate precautionary measures. For example, many law enforcement agencies have established a policy requiring an officer to call for and await back-up prior to interacting with someone who is a potential sovereign citizen. Note that transitioning from the more distal and impersonal license/citizenship revocation correspondence to personal encounters represents an increase in commitment to the movement because the individual is making an active, effortful, freely chosen, and now public commitment to someone outside the organization (Cialdini, 2008).

For those sovereign citizens who are driving without license plates or with sovereign citizen type license plates and acting peacefully when they are stopped, traffic stops provide them with the opportunity to further establish their identity as sovereigns; to declare their new relationship to the government; and, if they do not receive a citation, to infer that their claim of sovereign status is legitimate. However, receiving citation bolsters sovereigns' commitment to the group because it confirms to them and to others their membership in the group and their willingness to "suffer for" or stand by their beliefs.

It is important to realize that these sovereign citizens who are driving without license plates *want* to be stopped so that they can proclaim their new identity and establish it with the appropriate authorities. Essentially, these individuals are setting up a situation for an encounter with law enforcement and are prepared for it. The individuals will know what they are going to say, may have an actual script to follow, and may have even rehearsed the encounter. Often times, sovereign citizens will try to record their encounter with law enforcement. When a sovereign citizen is stopped by law enforcement, typically the sovereign citizen will try to gain control of the situation by challenging the officer. Common tactics used by sovereign citizens are to ask for identification from the officer to prove that he/she is a legitimate member of law enforcement; to ask the officer to recite their oath of office; or to ask the officer whether they, the sovereign citizen, is being detained by the officer; and if the officer says no, to then ask if they are free to go. Again, these tactics are meant to rile the officer, with the hope of causing the officer to make a mistake. Therefore, it is essential for departments to have procedures for handling encounters with sovereign citizens, for the officers to know the department's policies and procedures, and for the officer to act in a manner consistent with these policies. Just as the sovereign citizen has practiced how to handle an encounter with law enforcement, law enforcement should be able to identify possible indicators that someone is a sovereign citizen and to know and practice handling encounters with someone who is a potential sovereign citizen.

Common indicators that someone is a sovereign citizen include bumper stickers, contrived license plates, no trespassing signs on the car, or a vehicle for sale sign on the car. Sovereign citizens will typically only open their car window an inch or two to talk with an officer and when asked for their driver's license and registration may contend that they are not driving but traveling in their conveyance and that they have the right to travel freely. They may deny having a driver's license, or they may produce a contrived traveler's card or a contrived driver's license. Typically, a sovereign citizen will not produce a legitimate driver's license until he/she is being arrested for driving without a valid license.

THREATENING COMMUNICATIONS

Sovereign citizens have sent threatening letters to government officials, lawyers, or law enforcement typically in retaliation for lawful actions taken against them. The purpose of the letter is to frighten or intimidate the target. Two examples of people who have sent threatening communications are David Myrland (ADL, 2012; Morlin, 2011) and Cherron Marie Phillips (FBI, October 15, 2014). David Myrland, after being stopped for a traffic violation in Kirkland, Washington, and having his car impounded, sent threatening letters to the mayor of Kirkland and others. He warned the mayor that " . . . '50 armed men and women' would come to arrest her and that she should not resist." (ADL, 2012, p. 34). Cherron Marie Phillips retaliated against a dozen people involved in the investigation and prosecution of her brother by filing false maritime liens against their property (FBI, October 15, 2014).

COMMON LAW COURTS

Another type of threat is the letters sent by Common Law Courts or "de jure Grand Juries," which are set up by sovereign citizens (ADL, 2012, 2014; Theret, 2012). These Common Law Courts, which were established in several states, including Florida, Illinois, Missouri, Ohio, and Oregon, were organized by groups of sovereign citizens, functioned outside the existing judicial system, and operated using common law to resolve disputes. While some of these "courts" might have attempted to resolve real disputes, others served to intimidate public officials through the issuing of indictments, court summonses, arrest warrants, or death threats (ADL, 2012, 2014; Theret, 2012). For example, in 1993, Emilio Ippolito established the "Constitutional Court of We the People" in Tampa, Florida. In addition to granting divorces, this "court" sent threatening letters to and issued arrest warrants against judges and jury members. Ippolito and six others were convicted in 1997 for interfering with trials in Florida and California (ADL, 1998, 2012). More recently, the Guardians of Free Republics, in 2010, issued ultimatums to all 50 governors to vacate their offices. In October 2011, one "grand jury" sent "indictments" to all district attorneys in Oregon charging them with treason, kidnapping, and slave trafficking, and suggesting that in some cases the death penalty might be warranted (ADL, 2012, p. 34; Jonsson, 2010; Webster, 2010). Because these courts were visible and thus relatively easy to identify, law enforcement has been able to take action against them. As a result, their use by sovereign citizens has dwindled.

The extreme actions of these Common Law Courts can best be explained by theories in group dynamics, especially that of group polarization (Burnstein & Vinokur, 1973; Fraser et al., 1971; Myers & Lamm, 1976; Vinokur & Burnstein, 1974). Research on group polarization suggests that groups make more extreme decisions than the decision that would be made, had the decision of each individual member been averaged, and that the more extreme the group is the more extreme that decision will be. Group polarization is driven by persuasion, social comparison, and differentiation. A group discussion sets up a dynamic where each person wants to be viewed favorably by the group so they put forward proposals that the group will favor, ones that are consistent with the group's norms and make them look good. As group members weigh in with their reasons for supporting a proposal, each member will hear arguments that they had not considered. As a result, each individual's own position will be strengthened, thus strengthening the group's rational for its position and its conviction that the position advocated is valid. Additionally, discussion reveals the group's norms. Through a process of social comparison, some members will realize that their beliefs fall short of the group's standard. To rectify this situation, they will bring their views in line with that of the group. Additionally, some group members who wish to differentiate themselves from the crowd, to demonstrate the strength of their convictions or their commitment to the group, will be motivated to take a position that is in the direction of, but more extreme than the group norm. Together, these changes will move the group to a more extreme position. Especially given the extreme views held by sovereign citizens, it is easy to see how one of their courts could decide to issue not only warrants but also death threats.

Note that in each of the previously mentioned examples, the communication was distal, via the mail, and was designed to gain attention or frighten the target. In contrast to these distal communications, other sovereign citizens have confronted their targets directly. For example, in February 2012, Vahe Ohanian entered a sheriff's department in Valencia, California, and threatened the deputies, telling them that he would return with a shotgun (ADL, 2012; Jonas, 2012). On April 1, 2010, retired naval Lt. Commander Walter Fitzpatrick III, who was a leading member of "American Grand Jury" was arrested for disorderly conduct, disrupting a meeting, and resisting arrest when he tried to make a "citizen's arrest" of a grand jury foreman who had refused to convene a grand jury to indict Barack Obama for treason (ADL, n.d.; Gunter, 2011; History Commons, n.d.).

PAPER TERRORISM

Psychologists define aggression as a behavior intended to hurt another. Direct aggression is face-to-face, physically harming someone or verbally insulting them. Indirect aggression does not require contact with the target but is still intended to harm the target. For example, gossiping about the target or isolating the target are both forms of indirect aggression. Finally, aggression can be either emotional or instrumental. Emotional aggression stems from angry feelings, and tends to be unplanned and spontaneous. In contrast, instrumental aggression is goal oriented and involves premeditation or planning. Based on these definitions, the paper terrorism tactics used by sovereign citizens would constitute indirect, instrumental aggression because they do not require contact with the target, are pre-mediated, and are intended to hurt the target. Sovereign citizens are using these tactics not only to intimate, as is the case with their threatening messages, but also to financially hurt the targeted individuals.

Sovereign citizens commonly use paper terrorism in retaliation against individuals who they view as having harmed them or their friends or family. Paper terrorism also hurts the government by stalling judiciary operations or undermining the tax system. These tactics are consistent with the movement's goal to shut down or bring about the collapse of the government. This section provides a few interesting examples of the paper terrorism tactics used by the sovereign citizens that were described by the ADL (n.d.). In May 2009, Marlon T. Moore, who had recently been released from federal prison after serving a 6-year sentence for money laundering charges, was arrested for filing tax forms that claimed a total return of $14 trillion. A fellow prisoner reported that Moore has become a sovereign citizen while in a federal prison in Florida (ADL, n.d.). In February 2008, in Dane County Wisconsin, Bryan D. Hoel was convicted for criminal slander. Hoel had filed a $600,000 bogus lien against the state revenue investigator who was investigating a state tax case against Hoel. Hoel claimed that he had trademarked his name and that the investigator was "violating" the trademark by using his name without his permission. Note that because of Wisconsin's past experiences with the Posse Comitatus and their members filing false liens against public officials, Wisconsin has some of the oldest bogus lien laws in the country (ADL, n.d.). In addition to filing false tax forms and liens on individuals, sovereign citizens also file false tax forms to avoid paying taxes or to collect tax refunds, and encourage others to do so, too. One such example is former Minneapolis police officer Douglas Earl Leiter, who was convicted as the leader of the Common Law Venue, an organization that taught people how to establish bogus trusts and evade taxes (ADL, n.d.).

STANDOFFS WITH LAW ENFORCEMENT

In a previous section of the chapter, we discussed standoffs between sovereign citizens and law enforcement. As was noted in the discussion of shared identity, the history and norms of a group impact the actions of its individual members. From this history, we know that sovereign citizens are willing to engage in standoffs with law enforcement and that they are willing to take violent action against law enforcement. We also know that many sovereign citizens will stockpile weapons so that they are prepared for such a possibility. One example of weapons stockpiling is that of Harold Call (German, 2010; USAO, 2009). Call, in 2009, was arrested in Nevada for possession of an unregistered machine gun. In addition to the machine gun, Call had a cache of weapons that included grenades, firearms, night vision goggles, and other supplies. Obviously, sovereign citizens who are stockpiling weapons are doing so to prepare for the possibility that they may need to resort to violence. Two examples of standoffs between sovereign citizens and law enforcement are that of Ed and Elaine Brown in New Hampshire and members of the Richard McLaren faction of the "Republic of Texas." Both of these examples demonstrate how "paper terrorists" can turn violent.

Calhoun and Weston (2016) in their book *Threat Assessment and Management Strategies* (p. 119) describe a "path to intended violence" that helps to explain why these paper terrorists may take up violence. Calhoun and Weston (p. 127) state

Control Theory

> Some subjects initially announce their grievances in legal, proper ways. They file lawsuits, initiate complaints, or make protests. They feel . . . that they have pursed every legitimate option open to them, but all without success. That continued failure, as well as an ultimate inability to recognize more or different options, moves the subject forward to violence, almost as a last resort. The complete frustration caused by feeling powerless and unheard pushes these subjects onto the path to intended violence.

Once an individual decides to act violently, he/she needs to engage in the research, planning, and preparation necessary for implementing the violence. Note that these steps involve behaviors that can be observed and reported. As part of preparation, if the individual does not plan to escape, he or she may also engage in final acts such as saying goodbye or making a statement about the purpose or justification for the actions and ensuring the distribution of this statement. Once a plan has been developed, the materials acquired, and the preparations complete, the individual is ready to implement the violence. As shown in the following two examples, the sovereign citizens involved moved from pseudo legal tactics to violence. In each case, they indicated to the media that they were willing to resort to violence.

The story of Ed and Elaine Brown is one of sovereign citizen tax protestors (Elliott, 2007). According to a story in the New Hampshire Sunday news, in 1993, Ed Brown became involved in the Constitution Defense Militia. Consistent with the militia's beliefs, the Browns stopped paying their income taxes in 1996. Ten years later, in 2006, the Browns were indicted for federal tax violations. In 2007, each of the Browns was convicted on various charges relating to this case and sentenced to prison. After the trial, the Browns ordered the court clerk to close their case, citing themselves as the "court" and "judge." On their MySpace page, the Browns "vowed to resist arrest violently and die rather than go to prison" (Badkhen, 2007). The Browns refused to surrender to law enforcement, which led to a 9-month standoff. After their arrest by U.S. Deputy Marshals, it was found that they had a cache of weapons that included improvised explosive devices, assault rifles, booby traps, and 60,000 rounds of ammunition (ADL n.d.). Again, the actions of the Browns, from joining the Constitution Defense Militia to the standoff and vow to resist arrest, can all be explained by foot-in-the-door (Cialdini, 2008) and the resulting spiral of increasing commitment that all stems from making a commitment to a cause and then continuing to act in a manner consistent with it.

In Spring 1997, members of Richard McLaren's faction of "Republic of Texas" initiated a standoff between their group and law enforcement when they kidnapped, or in their own terms took as "prisoners of war," Joe and Margaret Ann Rowe, a local couple who lived near the group's compound. At the time of the standoff, the "Republic of Texas" was composed of a number of factions who share the belief that Texas is an independent nation because it was never lawfully annexed by the United States (*McLaren v. US INC.*, 1998). One of those groups was led by McLaren, who was originally from Missouri, moved to Texas in 1977, and tried unsuccessfully to start a vineyard (Babineck, 2007; Foer, 1997). At some point, McLaren stopped paying the subdivision maintenance fees where he lived, became a contentious figure in the community, embraced the idea that Texas was an independent country, and turned his home into an "embassy." Consistent with sovereign citizen's beliefs and practices, McLaren's group began filing false liens against property owners, issued "arrest warrants," "ordered" Governor George W. Bush to leave office, and invited the county sheriffs to work for them. Also, in July 1996, the group tried unsuccessfully to take over the state capitol (CNN, 1997). While the actions of the group led to the filing of state and federal arrest warrants against them, the group was largely ignored until their actions in 1997 (Babineck, 2007). According to a news story (*Chicago Tribune*, 1997), in April 1997, three members of McLaren's group kidnapped the Rowes, with whom they had an ongoing dispute. According to Mrs. Rowe, the kidnappers were serious about killing them and had fired shots into their house before kidnapping the couple. A *New York Times* article (1997) reported that "Mr. McLaren, reached by telephone at the embassy, said tonight: 'We are at war with the United Nations and all foreign entities. We are not at war with the American people, but we are at war with the Federal agencies which have no jurisdiction here'" (Verhovek, 1997). McLaren contends that the purpose of the stand-off was to force Texas to hold a referendum on the independence of Texas. After a week, the standoff ended peacefully on May 3, 1997 (*New York Times*, 1997). As part of the "cease fire agreement," labeled as "International Agreement and Terms of Cease Fire" by McLaren, it was agreed that " . . . the Republic of Texas will 'commence legal actions in the District Court of [sic] The District of Columbia for the rights of the inhabitants on the soil of Texas to by popular vote decide [the] issue of Texas Independence'" (*McLaren v. US INC.*, 1998). Note that while McLaren had committed publicly to be at war and thus suggested that his group would be willing to act violently, his commitment to having a public vote on independence for Texas was used to avert violence.

In each of these instances, the language used in their communications, as well as their actions—threatening violence and/or brandishing weapons suggests that they had come to believe that violence might be their only way forward. If you consider the role that identity played in the actions of each of these groups, you see the impact of the shared identity as well as the role of consistency. First, returning to our previous discussion of shared identity, because the Sovereign Citizens Movement has a history of standoffs with law enforcement, going all the way back to their Posse roots, preparing for and engaging in a standoff is consistent with the norms of sovereign citizens. Therefore, engaging in a standoff would be an easy step for the Browns or the McLaren faction to take. Additionally, the commitment of each group to its cause led to the escalation in behaviors, from statements issued, to legal battles, to the standoffs, and all that transpired during the standoff, with each additional action serving to strengthen their beliefs. Finally, the slow wheels of justice, coupled with the reluctance to take action, played a role in encouraging each of these groups to believe their causes and actions were legitimate.

VIOLENCE AGAINST COUNTY OFFICIALS AND COURT OFFICIALS

While the preceding examples all feature standoffs with law enforcement, there are other examples of violence by sovereign citizens. An example of a group transitioning from threats to intentional physical violence are the actions of the Juris Christian Assembly against the Stanislaus County Recorder Karen Mathews. In 1994, members of Juris Christian Assembly attacked Stanislaus County Recorder Karen Mathews at her home (Fleishman, n.d.). In an interview, Mathews describes how she was first threatened via phone calls, then gunshots, and later a fake pipe bomb because she would not complete the paper work necessary for the sovereign citizens to engage in paper terrorism. An account of the incident follows:

> She refused to remove IRS liens against several common-law-courts activists and also refused to place their bogus liens on property owned by IRS officials, state representatives and a member of Congress. Mathews says she got menacing phone calls at home. There were gunshots aimed at the office window. . . . a fake pipe bomb under her car. She got a death threat with a bullet attached to it. Her elderly parents have been threatened. Then, in January 1994, a man attacked her in her garage at her home in Modesto, beating and slashing her. As she lay on the ground, he pointed an unloaded gun at her head and pulled the trigger. "He let me know I was a messenger to all the recorders in California," said Mathews, 47. "Their intention was to kill if we didn't begin to record these phony documents."
>
> (Cannon, 1996)

This example highlights two important points. First, it shows that the group wants something more than to scare their victim. They wanted Mathews to complete specific paperwork and record their documents. Second, it shows a change in tactics from threats to physical harm. In Mathews' case, the threats became more menacing and more direct—from phone calls, to gunshots outside her office, to a fake pipe bomb under her car, to actual violence against her.

A second such example is that of millionaire Robert Beale. In 2009, in Minneapolis, Minnesota, Beale was convicted of conspiring to threaten and intimidate a federal judge who was overseeing a tax evasion case against him. Beale, working with three other sovereign citizens had planned to show up at the court and "arrest" the judge if she did not dismiss the charges against him (ADL, n.d.). The ADL (n.d.) reported that Beale was recorded in a telephone conversation as saying, "'I want her to be intimidated'. . . . He also said that God 'wants me to destroy the judge. . . . He wants me to get rid of her.'" This statement is important because it suggests that Beale already had his justification in place had he decided to harm the judge. In addition to the "arrest," Beale had also engaged in the placing of liens against individuals. The change in tactics, from liens to arrest and possible greater physical harm, reveals both a change from indirect to direct aggression and an increase in the severity of the harm.

The third example of intended violence, described next, is indicative of the fact that many sovereign citizens possess a cache of weapons. It is also one that had the potential to turn into a standoff had Marx been successful. Dennis Marx, a sovereign citizen and former TSA employee, attacked the Forsyth County Courthouse in Georgia on June 6, 2014, with the intention of entering the courthouse and taking hostages. During the attempted takeover, Marx was killed in a gun battle with law enforcement. When Marx's body and belongings were searched, homemade explosives, ammunition, and smoke grenades were found in his possession (*Atlanta Journal-Constitution*, June 6, 2014; Jonsson, 2014). Note that previous to these actions Marx had been arrested by sheriff's deputies for possession of marijuana and weapons charges, and on June 6, 2014, was supposed to enter a plea at the courthouse regarding these charges. Also note that Marx had then retaliated by suing the sheriff's department for Civil Rights violations and excessive use of force (Botelho et al., 2014; *Dennis Marx v. Forsyth*, 2013; Neiwert, 2014).

These are only a few examples of intended violence by sovereign citizens. Note that in many cases of intended violence, the sovereign citizen is retaliating for actions taken by the target, in the course of their work, that involved the sovereign citizen. Or the sovereign citizen is attempting to prevent actions being taken by the target against the sovereign citizen (see ADL, n.d.; USAO, 2016). Also note the diverse backgrounds of the sovereign citizens, including former military, law enforcement, and a millionaire. This highlights the point that anyone can become a sovereign citizen.

TARGETING LAW ENFORCEMENT

Given that sovereign citizens are operating within the United States and that their goal is to cause the collapse of the government, it is important to consider the methods they would use to accomplish this and who or what they would target. In the United States, it is law enforcement, rather than the military, that ensures the peace and that would be called upon to respond to attacks by sovereign citizens. If you consider that sovereigns believe the only legitimate law is common law; the only legitimate law enforcement is a duly elected county sheriff; and that if the sheriff does something "wrong," it is their right to hang the sheriff, it stands to reason that they do not believe other law enforcement agencies are legitimate and thus do not believe that these officers are serving in any legitimate capacity. Also given the harshness with which they are willing to treat a sheriff, it also stands to reason that they would be as harsh, if not more so, when dealing with law enforcement they believe to be illegitimate. Targeting and attacking the police is not only consistent with their beliefs, it is an attempt to intimidate law enforcement so that they will be reluctant to interfere with sovereign citizens, and it also serves to threaten the confidence of the citizenry that their government can protect them. Next, three examples of sovereign citizens attacking police are discussed. Note that each of these attacks involved some preparation or planning.

This first example highlights how the tactics used by a sovereign citizen can change from non-violent to violent and provides some evidence as to why that might occur. On May 20, 2010, Jerry and Joseph Kane, a father and son, killed two West Memphis, Arkansas, police—Officer Bill Evans and Sergeant Brandon Paudert—during a traffic stop. The Kanes then fled from the scene. When the police located and attempted to apprehend them, the Kanes opened fire on the police, wounding Crittenden County Sheriff Dick Busby and Deputy W. A. Wren. As the Kane's attempted to flee the scene of the second shooting in their vehicle, Arkansas Game and Fish Officer Michael Neal rammed their minivan, forcing the Kanes to stop. The Kane's vehicle was surrounded by police, and the Kanes were killed in a shootout (ADL, n.d.; Bartels, 2010; Harris, 2010).

Prior to this incident, the father Jerry Kane espoused the anti-government views typical of sovereign citizens and, with his son, traveled the country presenting debt elimination "workshops" at $100 to $300 per man, wives and children could attend for free, that purportedly taught people how to end their mortgage and foreclosure problems. These workshops espoused the fake debt elimination schemes advanced by sovereigns (see Kane, May 19, 2014). Prior to this vehicle stop, Jerry Kane had been in other encounters with police, including being cited for driving without a license (MacNab, August 1, 2010). At the time of the stop, there were warrants for Kane's arrest in two states. In previous encounters with law enforcement, the Kanes had acted peacefully, and the vehicle, when impounded and inventoried, did not contain any contraband such as drugs, weapons, or ammunition. However, during this stop, Jerry and Joseph Kane's behaviors changed drastically. After being stopped, Jerry Kane exited the vehicle, began arguing with Officer Evans and pushed him into a ditch. Joe Kane then exited the vehicle with a semi-automatic AK-47 and shot Evans a number of times. He then turned his gun on Sergeant Paudert, who had arrived on scene as backup and had, when the shooting began, taken cover behind a police vehicle and begun firing at Joe Kane. Joe Kane wounded Paudert, and then followed Paudert around the vehicle shooting Paudert several times in the back of the head. Joe then returned to the wounded Evans and shot at him several more times before driving away with his father. A package delivery man who had stopped his truck before the exit, witnessed the shooting and called 911.

What had happened in the lives of the Kanes that caused them to move from non-violence to violence? Calhoun and Weston discuss the *last-straw syndrome*, suggesting that something significant changes in the life of the individual that causes him/her to turn violent. There is evidence that Jerry Kane was experiencing difficulties in his life and that these factors, either alone or in combination, pushed Jerry to turn violent. First, attendance at Kane's workshop was dwindling. Just prior to the shootout, Kane had said in his most recent online radio show that he planned to conduct one more workshop in Florida and then cut his workshop schedule (MacNab, August 1, 2010). According to MacNab (August 1, 2010), at his most recent workshop in Las Vegas, only six people had attended and, prior to that, no one had shown up for a workshop in Denver, Colorado. Considering that Kane would travel extensively to conduct these workshops, the recent low turnouts must have been frustrating and perhaps even caused Kane some financial strain. Second, on April 10, 2010, Jerry was stopped by police at a DUI check point in Lincoln County, New Mexico, and detained for driving without a license. As a result, Jerry Kane spent 2 days in jail prior to making bail. Bob Paudert, Brandon's father and the West Memphis Chief of Police, believes that this was the last straw for Jerry Kane. In his online radio show dated May 6, 2010, Kane (Kane, Jerry, May 6, 2010) referred to the stop as a "Nazi checkpoint," suggested he was going to sue the police department for kidnapping and extortion, and threatened that he had already done a background check on the officer and knew where the officer lived and his wife's name (Noll, 2010; *New York Times*, May 22, 2010). According to Bob Paudert, "After spending two days in jail in New Mexico Jerry bonded out. He then [legally] purchased a [semi-automatic] AK-47, several hundred rounds of ammo and magazines, a 45 caliber five shot pistol, hunting knife and a brick or pound of marijuana [this amount of marijuana would indicate an intent to sell and constitute a felony]" (personal communication, August 7, 2016). Certainly, the purchase of these weapons is a strong indicator that Jerry had decided to resort to violence. Prior to that, in a YouTube video (Noll, 2010; SPLC Video, n.d.), Jerry Kane(May 24, 2010) had discussed that killing should be avoided and only used as a last resort. In the video clip purported to be from August 2, 2009, Kane, in response to a question about a "rogue" IRS agent, states

> So what we're after here is not fighting, it's conquering. I don't want to have to kill anybody. But if they keep messing with me that's what it's going to have to. That's what it's going to come down to is I'm going to have to kill. And if I have to kill one then I'm not going to be able to stop. I just know it. I mean I have an addictive personality.

Apparently, this last traffic stop, either alone or coupled with the arrest warrants and low workshop turnouts was enough "messing" to push Jerry and Joe to "have to kill."

Unfortunately, this was not the first time that members of law enforcement have been killed by sovereign citizens, nor would it be the last. Prior to this instance, in 1993, an Alabama officer was shot and killed by George Sibley and Linda Block (MacNab, 2010). Based upon a report that a boy who was sitting in the back of a vehicle that was parked in a strip mall was asking for help, an officer approached the vehicle and asked the driver, George Sibley, to see his license. After making a few statements typical of sovereign citizens, Sibley shot the officer. The officer then tried to escape back to his car but Linda got out of vehicle, went around it, and shot and killed the officer.

More recently, on July 17, 2016, a sovereign citizen, Gavin Eugene Long, ambushed police in Baton Rouge, Louisiana, killing three officers and wounding three others (Moore, 2017). As indicated by paper work he filed on May 16, 2015, with the Jackson County, Missouri, recorder of deeds in which he changed his name to Cosmo Ausar Setepenra, he also declared that he was a citizen of "United Washitaw de Dugdahmoundyah Mu'ur Nation, Mid-West Washita Tribes," indicating that Long was a member of the Moorish-based sovereign citizens (Moore, 2017).

These examples are a stark reminder of sovereign citizen's willingness to target law enforcement, and to do so with premeditation. The examples below reveal that sovereign citizens are also willing to commit terrorist attacks against government institutions, even those that have the potential to harm civilians.

"TRADITIONAL" TERRORISM

Perhaps the most well-known instance of a terrorist attack associated with the sovereign citizens is the bombing of the Alfred P. Murrah Federal Building in Oklahoma City, Oklahoma, on April 19, 1995. The explosion killed 168 people. Timothy McVeigh, working with Terry Nichols, made a fertilizer bomb that they placed in the back of a Ryder truck. McVeigh then drove to Oklahoma City, parked the truck in front of the Murrah Federal Building, and left the vehicle with a 2-minute fuse burning inside of it. McVeigh claimed the bombing was in revenge for the government sieges at Waco and Ruby Ridge. Although it does not seem that the sovereign citizens claim McVeigh as one of their followers, the actions of Nichols, as describe previously in Fourteenth Amendment Civil Rights, suggest that he considered himself to be a sovereign citizen. Furthermore, his involvement with McVeigh suggests that Nichols progressed from non-violence to violence.

In 1997, the "Constitutional Law Group" set fire to an IRS office in Colorado Springs, Colorado (*USA v. Dowel*, 2005; TIGTA Fact Sheet, 2012). A review of the case notes reveals that Jack

Dowell and James Cleaver devised a plan to set fire to an IRS Office in Colorado Springs, Colorado. With help from other members of their "Constitutional Law Group," including Dowell's cousin, Thomas Dowell, they put the plan into action. Cleaver, along with Thomas Dowell, broke into the IRS building, opened unlocked file cabinets, doused them with gasoline, and then left a 15-minute fuse to ignite everything. Jack Dowell remained sentry outside, using a two-way radio to let the others know when it was clear to act and to alert them to anyone passing by.

In February of 2010, Andrew Joseph Stack, a software engineer and sovereign citizen, after posting an anti-government, anti-tax message/suicide note flew his small plane, a single-engine fixed-wing Piper, into an IRS office in Austin, Texas (Brick, 2010). In the final paragraphs of his suicide note, Stack wrote I know I'm hardly the first one to decide I have had all I can stand. It has always been a myth that people have stopped dying for their freedom in this country, and it isn't limited to the blacks, and poor immigrants. . . . But I also know that by not adding my body to the count, I insure nothing will change. . . . American zombies wake up and revolt; it will take nothing less. . . . Well, Mr. Big Brother IRS man, let's try something different; take my pound of flesh and sleep well.

(Weisenthal, 2010)

In June 2012, Anson Chi, a former software engineer and sovereign citizen, was arrested for trying to blow up a natural gas pipeline in a residential area of Plano, Texas, with explosives (MacNab, 2012). When the bomb went off, Chi was injured and natural gas began leaking out. Fortunately, there was no explosion. According to MacNab, Chi espoused his sovereign citizen beliefs on his blog TruthWorldOrder. Included on the blog was a copy of his resume, in which he referred to his employment as paid slavery and his college education as miseducation. MacNab reported that Chi's outdated MySpace page and YouTube account also included sovereign citizen ideology and evidence, in the form of a video, that he supported the New Hampshire tax protesters Edward and Elaine Brown in their standoff with police. When police searched Chi's bedroom, located in his parents' home where Chi had been living, they found a bomb making lab.

Conclusion

The examples presented in this chapter reveal some of the anti-government beliefs held by sovereign citizens and the extent to which they are willing to act on their beliefs. Their beliefs and actions not only reflect the norms and behaviors of this group but also provide a "play book" for other sovereign citizens uncertain of what to believe or how to act. These individuals, through their actions, are attempting to facilitate a return to an idealized but fanciful world in which an individual is sovereign or a "state" unto him/herself and is free from government regulation or interference.

Because the beliefs of sovereign citizens may seem ludicrous or delusional, the threat they pose is often underrated. However, both their non-violent and violent actions should be considered acts of terrorism because they are designed, at a minimum, to disrupt the functioning of the government and, in the extreme, to lead to its downfall.

While the paper work of sovereign citizens to rescind their citizenship and licenses may seem little more than a nuisance, the implications of these actions are much greater. First, it is a clear indication that an individual has come to identify as a sovereign citizen. Their actions reflect the fact that the individual has moved from considering sovereign ideology and perhaps communicating with members of the movement to adopting sovereign beliefs and a sovereign identity, and they indicate that the individual's beliefs in the movement are strong enough that they are willing to share them with people outside the group. Unfortunately, a lack of response to these activities by officials will be construed by the sovereign citizen to mean that their claim is a legitimate one. Second, filing the claim also serves the purpose of interfering with the functioning of the government.

The paper terrorism tactics of filing liens or tax forms on others constitutes an act of aggression and should also be considered an act of terrorism because engaging in these behaviors not only causes emotional and perhaps financial harm to the targeted individual, but also, similar to a hate crime, invokes fear and sends a message to similar others, whether they are county clerks, court officials, or law enforcement. Garlick notes that "Hate crimes have a special impact on the victim and the victim's community. . . . Members of the target community recognize the crime as a direct attack on their own identity, resulting in . . . anxiety, fear, and intimidation" (Garlick, 2018). Not only will the targeted individual suffer emotionally but he/she will also need to invest time in straightening out any complications resulting from the paper terrorism of the sovereign citizen. Additionally, anyone who, in the course of their duties, interacts with a sovereign citizen will be compelled to invest time and energy ensuring that these tactics are not being used against them. Furthermore, it may cause individuals to ignore the actions of sovereign citizens rather than engage with them and have to deal with the consequences. On a larger level, the paper terrorism tactics are designed to interfere with or shutdown the government. As Johnny Liberty notes, only a small but sufficient number of individuals are needed to overthrow a government.

Just as rescinding one's citizenship and licenses establishes to the individual and to people outside the group that an individual has adopted a sovereign identity and squanders the time of the clerks involved with the paperwork, so too does driving without a license plate or one of the sovereign created license plate help to establish an individual's sovereign identity and squander the time of law enforcement in making a traffic stop and any officials involved in processing the paper work. As with rescinding licenses, a lack of response, in this case, no citation, would also serve to confirm the sovereign citizen's beliefs in the legitimacy of their claim.

Because sovereign citizens are domestic terrorists and law enforcement represents the people or organizations who would be called upon to respond to their actions, any actions against law enforcement should be viewed as terrorism. The reason for this is that by attacking and killing police they are seeking to destabilize local, state, and federal organizations that are involved in ensuring peace in the United States. Their actions may also undermine the confidence of the citizenry in law enforcement's ability to serve and protect them.

Finally, as discussed previously, sovereign citizens have engaged in "traditional" acts of terrorism. While many of their actions have targeted government offices, they have or could have resulted in a large number of deaths.

The difficulty in dealing with sovereign citizens stems from the scope of actions they may engage in. Some of these actions are non-violent, rescinding licenses, sending threatening letters, and filing false liens or tax forms, while others are violent or have the potential for violence, engaging in standoffs, shoot-outs, kidnapping, assault, and murder. All are designed to impede the government with the hope of causing its collapse. The difficulty faced by law enforcement and other officials is trying to determine when a sovereign citizen will become violent. While Calhoun and Weston's last-straw syndrome suggest that people turn from non-violence to violence after something significant has changed in their lives and that these individuals feel hopeless, believe they have pursued all legitimate options, and cannot imagine any other options other than violence. The difficulty faced by officials lies in needing to know this information prior to engaging with them. Without it, one must assume that a sovereign citizen could act violently. In summary, the sovereign citizens should be considered a serious terrorist threat.

NOTE

1 Sovereign Citizen, with capitalized "S" and "C" is used to refer to those members of the movement who trace their roots back to England. While sovereign citizen, with lower case "s" and "c" is used to refer to sovereign citizen ideology.

REFERENCES

ADL (June 29, 1998). Paper terrorism's forgotten victims: The use of bogus liens against private individuals and businesses. Retrieved June 29, 2016, from http://archive.adl.org/mwd/privlien.html

ADL (2012). The lawless ones: The resurgence of the Sovereign citizen movement (2nd Ed.). Retrieved August 6, 2016, from www.adl.org/assets/pdf/combating-hate/Lawless-Ones-2012-Edition-WEB-final.pdf

ADL (February 20, 2014). Sovereign citizens create vigilante "Grand Juries" in latest attempt to flout the law. Retrieved June 24, 2016, from www.adl.org/press-center/press-releases/extremism/adl-sovereign-citizens-create-vigilante-grand-juries-to-flout-law.html?referrer=www.google.com/#.V6hOd_krLIU

ADL (n.d.). The lawless ones: The resurgence of the Sovereign citizen movement list of recent Sovereign citizen incidents, by state 2007–2010. Retrieved August 6, 2016, from www.adl.org/assets/pdf/combating-hate/sovereign-citizen-incidents-by-state-2007-2010.pdf

Adler, J. (July 26, 2010). The move to "restore" the 13th Amendment. *Newsweek*. Retrieved August 6, 2016, from www.newsweek.com/move-restore-13th-amendment-74391

Atlanta Journal-Constitution (June 6, 2014). Forsyth deputy shot, suspect dead. *The Atlanta Journal-Constitution*. Retrieved August 1, 2016, from www.ajc.com/news/news/police-activity-around-forsyth-courthouse/ngFsZ/

Babineck, M. (May 3, 2007). Texas separatist still thinks cause will succeed. *Houston Chronicle*. Retrieved August 9, 2016, from www.chron.com/news/houston-texas/article/Texas-separatist-still-thinks-cause-will-succeed-1604025.php

Badkhen, A. (October 6, 2007). Marshals ploy ended standoff peacefully: Acted like supporters to lure out tax evaders. *Boston Globe*. Retrieved August 2, 2016, from http://archive.boston.com/news/local/articles/2007/10/06/marshals_ploy_ended_standoff_peacefully/

Bartels, C. (May 21, 2010). 2 Officers slain on I-40 drug patrol in Arkansas. *The Dallas Morning News*. Retrieved August 3, 2016, from http://web.archive.org/web/20100524085626/www.dallasnews.com/sharedcontent/dws/news/texassouthwest/stories/DN-copshot_21tex.ART.State.Edition1.edfc2f2.html

Bell, D. (2016). *The Sovereign citizen movement: The shifting ideological winds*. (Unpublished Master's thesis). Naval PostGraduate School, Monterey, CA.

Bem, D. J. (1967). Self-perception: An alternative explanation of cognitive dissonance phenomena. *Psychological Review, 74*, 183–200.

Bem, D. J. (1972). Self-perception theory. In L. Berkowitz (Ed.), *Advances in experimental social psychology* (Vol. 6, Pp. 1–62). New York, NY: Academic Press.

Berger, J. M. (June 2016). *Without prejudice: What Sovereign citizens believe.* Program on Extremism, George Washington University.

Botelho, G., McLaughlin, E. C., & Hanna, J. (June 6, 2014). Authorities: Georgia courthouse attacker prepared to inflict mayhem. *CNN.* Retrieved August 1, 2016, from www.cnn.com/2014/06/06/justice/georgia-courthouse-shooting/

Brick, M. (February 18, 2010). Man crashes plane into Texas I.R.S. office. *NY Times.* Retrieved August 1, 2016, from www.nytimes.com/2010/02/19/us/19crash.html?_r=0

Brown, R. (2006). *Group processes.* Malden, MA: Blackwell Publishing.

Burnstein, E., & Vinokur, A. (1973). Testing two classes of theories about group-induced shifts in individual choice. *Journal of Experimental Social Psychology, 9*, 123–137.

Calhoun, F. S., & Weston, S. W. (2016). *Threat assessment and management strategies: Identifying the howlers and hunters.* Boca Raton, FL: CRC Press & Taylor and Francis Group.

Cannon, A. (May 24, 1996). Rightists now using 'courts' to intimidate public officials: The activists say the current government is illegal: Their weapons include phony liens and threats. *Phill.Com.* Retrieved July 18, 2016, from http://articles.philly.com/1996-05-24/news/25623832_1_judicial-system-legal-system-courts

Chicago Tribune (April 29, 1997). Texas separatists call for help: Negotiators report "some progress" to diffuse standoff. *Chicago Tribune.* Retrieved August 2, 2016, from http://articles.chicagotribune.com/1997-04-29/news/9704290127_1_margaret-ann-rowe-republic-members-standoff-ends

Cialdini, R. B. (2008). *Influence: Science and practice* (5th ed.). Boston: Allyn & Bacon.

CNN (April 27, 1997). One injured in separatist standoff. *CNN.* Retrieved August 2, 2016, from www.cnn.com/US/9704/27/texas.update/index.html?iref=newssearch

Crowell, M. (November, 2015). A quick guide to Sovereign citizens. *Administration of Justice Bulletin, UNC School of Government, 2015/04.* Retrieved August 6, 2016, from http://sogpubs.unc.edu/electronicversions/pdfs/aojb1504.pdf

Dennis Marx v. Forsyth County Sheriff's Office et al. (2013). Case No. 2:13-cv-00175-RWS, U.S. District Court for the Northern District of Georgia (Gainesville Div.).

Elliott, P. (January 18, 2007). Man holed up in home after tax verdict. *The Washington Post.* Retrieved August 2, 2016, from www.washingtonpost.com/wp-dyn/content/article/2007/01/18/AR2007011801138.html

famguardian.org (n.d. a). Instructions: 0.10 Restoring your sovereignty. Retrieved July 10, 2016, from http://famguardian.org/taxfreedom/Instructions/0.10RestoringYourSov.htm

famguardian.org (n.d. b) Instructions: 3.17. Quit Social Security and Rescind the Social Security Number. Retrieved March 3, 2018, from https://famguardian.org/TaxFreedom/Instructions/3.17QuitSocialSecurity.htm

FBI (April 13, 2010). Domestic terrorism: The Sovereign citizen movement. Retrieved August 6, 2016, from https://archives.fbi.gov/archives/news/stories/2010/april/sovereigncitizens_041310

FBI (September, 2011). Sovereign citizens: A growing domestic threat to law enforcement. *FBI Law Enforcement Bulletin.* Retrieved August 6, 2016, from https://leb.fbi.gov/2011/september/sovereign-citizens-a-growing-domestic-threat-to-law-enforcement

FBI (September 13, 2013). Sovereign citizens member sentence to two years in prison for mailing fictitious financial instrument. Press Release. Retrieved July 4, 2016, from www.fbi.gov/birmingham/press-releases/2013/sovereign-citizens-member-sentenced-to-two-years-in-prison-for-mailing-fictitious-financial-instrument

FBI (October 15, 2014). Sovereign citizen who retaliated against federal officials by filing false liens sentence to seven years in prison. Retrieved July 4, 2016, from www.fbi.gov/chicago/press-releases/2014/sovereign-citizen-who-retaliated-against-federal-officials-by-filing-false-liens-sentenced-to-seven-years-in-prison

Fleishman, D. (n.d.). Paper terrorism: The impact of the "Sovereign citizen" on local government. *The Public Law Journal*. Retrieved August 6, 2016, from www.calbar.ca.gov/publiclaw

Foer, F. (May 4, 1997). The Republic of Texas. *Slate.com*. Retrieved August 9, 2016, from www.slate.com/articles/news_and_politics/the_gist/1997/05/the_republic_of_texas.html

Fraser, C., Gouge, C., & Billig, M. (1971). Risky shifts, cautious shifts, and group polarization. *European Journal of Social Psychology, 1*, 7–30.

Garlick, M. (2018). Hate crime laws. In R. M. Valeri & K. Borgesion (Eds.), *Hate crimes*. Durham, NC: Carolina Academic Press.

German, J. (August 24, 2010). Gun charges send man to prison. *Las Vegas Review-Journal*. Retrieved August 8, 2016, from www.reviewjournal.com/news/gun-charge-sends-man-prison

Gunter, B. (October 25, 2011). Oath keeper convicted on weapons charge: Attempted "citizen's arrest". *Southern Poverty Law Center*. Retrieved July 31, 2016, from www.splcenter.org/hatewatch/2011/10/25/oathkeeperconvicte dweaponschargeattempted%E2%80%98citizen%E2%80%99sarrest%E2%80%99

Harris, D. (July 1, 2010). Deadly Arkansas shooting by "Sovereigns" Jerry and Joe Kane who shun U.S. Law. *ABC News*.

History Commons (n.d.). Profile: Walter Fitzpatrick. Retrieved July 31, 2016, from www.historycommons.org/entity.jsp?entity=walter_fitzpatrick_1

Imrie, R. (September 23, 1990). With leaders in jail, Posse Comitatus' fate is uncertain. *Los Angeles Times*. Retrieved June 29, 2006, from http://articles.latimes.com/print/19900923/news/mn1546_1_posseleaderscomitatus

Jonas, K. (February 29, 2012). Valencia man arrested after alleged threats to law enforcement. *SignalsSCV.com: The Santa Clarita Valley Signal*. Retrieved August 8, 2016, from www.signalscv.com/archives/60834/

Jonsson, P. (April 3, 2010). Guardians of the free republics looked to Gandhi, King, and Mandela. *Christian Science Monitor*. Retrieved August 8, 2016, from www.csmonitor.com/USA/2010/0403/Guardians-of-the-free-Republics-looked-to-Gandhi-King-and-Mandela

Jonsson, P. (June 6, 2014). Forsyth county courthouse shooting: Dennis Marx plotted "sovereign citizen" attack. *Christian Science Monitor*. Retrieved August 6, 2016, from www.csmonitor.com/USA/2014/0607/Forsyth-County-Courthouse-shooting-Dennis-Marx-plotted-sovereign-citizen-attack-video

Kane, Jerry. (May 6, 2010). Episode 23 Jerry Kane's once-a-month update. Retrieved August 7, 2010, from www.talkshoe.com/talkshoe/web/audioPop.jsp?episodeId=352556&cmd=apop

Kane, Jerry. (May 24, 2010). West Memphis cop killer preaching violence on government. Retrieved August 8, 2017, from www.youtube.com/watch?v=wfdPIYVdtqs

Kane, Jerry. (May 19, 2014). All day classes. Retrieved August 3, 2016, from www.youtube.com/view_play_list?p=AE395BBD4C81C7A9

Liberty, J. (2004). *The global sovereign handbook*. Panama City, Panama: Institute for Communications Resources, Inc. Retrieved August 6, 2016, from www.spingola.com/GlobalSovereignHandbook.pdf

Loeser, C. E. (2015). From paper terrorists to cop killers: The Sovereign citizens threat. *North Carolina Law Review, 93*, 1106–1139.

MacNab, J. J. (August 1, 2010). "Sovereign" citizen Kane. *Southern Poverty Law Center*. Retrieved August 4, 2016, from www.splcenter.org/fighting-hate/intelligence-report/2010/sovereign-citizen-kane

MacNab, J. J. (July 3, 2012). Sovereign extremist injured in Texas bomb explosion. *Forbes*. Retrieved August 1, 2016, from www.forbes.com/sites/jjmacnab/2012/07/03/sovereign-extremist-injured-in-texas-bomb-explosion/

McLaren v. US INC., 2 F. Supp. 2d 48—Dist. Court, Dist. of Columbia 1998. Retrieved August 2, 2016, from https://scholar.google.com/scholar_case?q=%22Richard+Lance+McLaren%22&hl=en&as_sdt=3,44&case=6167664160081150182&scilh=0

Moore, H. C. (June 30, 2017). IN RE: Gavin Long: The office of the district attorney, for the 19th judicial district, Parish of East Baton Rouge, Louisiana. Retrieved from www.ebrda.org/

Morlin, B. (December 5, 2011). "Sovereign citizen" sentenced for "deadly force" threats. *Southern Poverty Law Center.* Retrieved August 8, 2016, from www.splcenter.org/hatewatch/2011/12/05/%E2%80%98sovere ign-citizen%E2%80%99-sentenced-%E2%80%98deadly-force%E2%80%99-threats

Myers, D. G., & Lamm, H. (1976). The group polarization phenomenon. *Psychological Bulletin, 83,* 602–627.

Neiwert, D. (June 6, 2014). "Sovereign citizen" is suspected in Georgia courthouse shooting. Southern Poverty Law Center. Retrieved August 1, 2016, from www.splcenter.org/hatewatch/2014/06/06/sovereign-citizen-suspected-georgia-courthouse-shooting

New York Times (June 10, 1997). Four Texas separatists indicted in kidnapping. *New York Times.* Retrieved August 2, 2016, from www.nytimes.com/1997/06/10/us/four-texas-separatists-indicted-in-kidnapping.html?ref=topics

New York Times (May 22, 2010). Man who shot police had antigovernment views. *New York Times.* Retrieved August 3, 2016, from www.nytimes.com/2010/05/22/us/22arkansas.html?_r=0&pagewanted=print

Noll, S. (May 21, 2010). West Memphis officers killed: Shooters identified. WREG-TV. Retrieved August 10, 2016, from www.constantinereport.com/west-memphis-suspects-in-murders-of-two-police-officers-linked-to-aryan-nations-sovereign-movement/

Pitcavage, M. (May 6, 1996). "Patriot" profile #3: Every man a king: The rise and fall of the Montana Freemen. *Anti-Defamation League.* Retrieved July 15, 2016, from http://archive.adl.org/mwd/freemen.html

Robinson, D. E. (2009). Reclaim your sovereignty: Take back your Christian name. MAINE-PATRIOT.com, Brunswick, Maine.

Silversmith, J. A. (1999). The missing "thirteenth amendment": Constitutional nonsense and titles of nobility. *Southern California Interdisciplinary Law Journal, 8,* 577–611.

Sovereign Citizenship Network (n.d.). Retrieved July 10, 2016, from http://webcache.googleusercontent.com/search ?q=cache:lcNx3p_2VJAJ:sovereigncitizenship.net/home.html+&cd=4&hl=en&ct=clnk&gl=us

SPLC Video (n.d.). "Sovereign citizens" and law enforcement: Understanding the threat. Southern Poverty Law Center Intelligence Project. Retrieved from www.splcenter.org

Taylor, D. M., & Louis, W. (2005). Terrorism and the quest for identity. In F. M. Moghaddam & A. J. Marsella (Eds.), *Understanding terrorism* (Pp. 169–186). Washington, DC: American Psychological Association.

Theret, M. (2012). Sovereign citizens: A homegrown terrorist threat and its negative impact on South Carolina. *South Carolina Law Review, 63,* 853–886.

TIGTA Factsheet (February 2012). TIGTA, JTTF, and the Sovereign Citizen Movement. Treasury Inspector General for Tax Administration.

United States (1815–1816a). *Laws of the United States of America, from the 4th of March 1789 to the 4th of March 1815: Including the Constitution of the United States, the old act of confederation, treaties, and many other valuable ordinances and documents, with copious notes and references.* Philadelphia: Publishers John Bioren and W. John Duane, Vol. 1, p. 74.

United States (1815–1816b). *Laws of the United States of America, from the 4th of March 1789 to the 4th of March 1815: Including the constitution of the United States, the old act of confederation, treaties, and many other valuable ordinances and documents, with copious notes and references.* Philadelphia: Publishers John Bioren and W. John Duane, Vol. 1, p. ix.

United States v. Dowell (2005). United States of America, Plaintiff-appellee, v. Jack Dowell, Defendant-appellant, 430 F.3d 1100 (10th Cir 2005).

USAO (March 6, 2009). Members of anti-government movement arrested on federal money laundering, tax evasion and weapons charges. United States Attorney's Office: Nevada. Retrieved August 8, 2016, from www.justice.gov/archive/usao/nv/news/2009/03062009.html

USAO (June 24, 2016). Jacksonville man sentenced for assassination attempt on federal judge. United States Attorney's Office: Middle District Florida. Retrieved June 28, 2016, from www.justice.gov/usaomdfl/pr/jacksonvillemansentencedassassinationattemptfederaljudge

Valeri, R. M. (forthcoming). *Sovereign citizens: From ideology to action*.

Verhovek, S. H. (April 28, 1997). Hostages taken in standoff with militant Texas group. *New York Times*. Retrieved August 2, 2016, from www.nytimes.com/1997/04/28/us/hostages-taken-in-standoff-with-militant-texas-group.html

Vinokur, A., & Burnstein, E. (1974). Effects of partially shared persuasive arguments on group-induced shifts: A group problem solving approach. *Journal of Personality and Social Psychology*, *29*, 305–315.

Webster, S. C. (April 3, 2010). FBI, DHS probe "Guardians" who demanded governors resign. *Raw Story*. Retrieved August 8, 2016, from www.rawstory.com/2010/04/fbi-dhs-probe-guardians-demanded-governors-resign/

Weisenthal, M. (February 18, 2010). The insane manifesto of Austin Texas crash pilot Joseph Andrew Stack. *Business Insider*. Retrieved August 6, 2016, from www.businessinsider.com/joseph-andrew-stacks-insane-manifesto-2010-2

Part III

Recruitment and Radicalized

Chapter 7

From Declarations to Deeds

Terrorist Propaganda and the Spread of Hate and Terrorism Through Cyberspace

Robin Maria Valeri

Overview

- The Purpose of Terrorist Propaganda
- Modes of Communication
    - Print Media
    - Interpersonal Communication
    - (Surface) Web Pages and Social Networks
    - Twitter
    - Music, Video, and Computer Games
    - Encryption, the Deep and Dark Web
- Recruitment Strategies
    - The Need to Belong and Be Valued
    - Similarity, Familiarity, and Liking
    - Commitment and Consistency
    - Polarizing Attitudes
    - The Illusion of Consensus
    - Authority
- Should Hate Speech Be Banned?
- Counter-Messaging
- Conclusions

The Purpose of Terrorist Propaganda

Terrorist propaganda is pervasive. The reason for this is that terrorists are resourceful and, as is discussed in this chapter, use all available means (and mediums) to present their message to the public, recruit members, and garner support. Readers should note that while this book focuses on terrorism in America, given the global reach of cyberspace, it would be impossible to discuss only terrorist propaganda generated by Americans that targets Americans. Therefore, this chapter seeks to examine terrorist propaganda as it relates to Americans, including both perpetrators and victims of terrorism. Furthermore, because some of the beliefs that drive terrorism stem from hate and prejudice, this chapter not only examines the propaganda of terrorist organizations but also that of extremist groups, including hate groups. In the first part of the chapter, modes of communication used by hate groups and terrorists are discussed. In the second part of the chapter, terrorist messages and their psychological underpinning are examined. The chapter concludes with a discussion about banning hate speech and counter-messaging tactics.

If we first consider the purpose of terrorism, it quickly becomes evident that terrorists use propaganda to achieve or support the same goals they hope to accomplish through terrorist actions. Weinberg (2008) suggests that acts of terrorism are perpetrated for several reasons: to cause fear and anxiety among the public, to shine a spotlight on their cause, and to provoke authorities into responding to the threat in a manner that is consistent with the terrorist's message, thus confirming the terrorist's accusations against the authorities and winning the terrorist organization new recruits. Terrorist acts are also committed to raise the morale of both the terrorist group and the segment of the population whose cause they are championing, to acquire money or other resources, and to maintain discipline within the organizations. Similarly, terrorists use propaganda to promote their cause, instill fear in the public, gain recruits, raise the morale of their members and the people they are championing, maintain discipline with the organization, and garner resources that can be used to fund the terrorists themselves as well as to help them achieve their social, political, or religious goals.

Modes of Communication

The Internet has proven to be a wonderful resource for terrorists and other purveyors of hate and prejudice because it allows them to quickly, easily, and inexpensively broadcast their message to a worldwide audience. As of June 30, 2017, over half of the world's population (51.7%) was using the Internet, which represented a dramatic increase (a 976.4% growth) since 2000 (Internet World Stats, n.d.). Just over 88% of North America and 80% of Europe access the Internet (Internet World Stats, n.d.). The largest increases in Internet usage have occurred in Africa (an 8,503% increase since 2000, which means that now 31% of Africa is using the Internet), the Middle East (with a 4,374% increase since 2000 and almost 59% of that population using the Internet), Latin American and the Caribbean (2,137 % increase and 62 percent of the population now connected), and Asia (a 1,595% increase and almost 47% of the population accessing the Internet) (Internet World Stats, n.d.). Much of this increase has occurred because people are now able to access the

Internet through mobile devices such as cell phones and tablets. The increases in Internet usage in many of these areas, especially the Middle East and Africa, has also facilitated the use of the Internet by terrorists in these regions.

As discussed later in this chapter, hate groups have a history of using any and all means of communication to spread their message (Becker, Byers, & Jipson, 2000). In 2000, Becker and colleagues noted that

> Since the beginning of the modern American white racialist movement, after the Second World War, racialist have used a variety of communication tools to reach prospective members. . . . From the beginning of the movement, traditional print communication has been used . . . as the dominant form. . . . Today [in 2000] a variety of additional tools are utilized, including computerized mediated communication, radio, music, phone lines/messages, videos, and cable television programs. . . . However it is the internet that provides the most opportunities today.
>
> (Becker, Byers, & Jipson, 2000, p. 34)

Almost 20 years later, the same can be said about extremist groups' and terrorist groups' communication strategies. These groups continue to use a variety of communication tools to promote their message, garner resources, and gain recruits, and the Internet still provides many of those opportunities. Extremist and terrorist groups have clearly adopted the Internet as a tool, but since 2000 have expanded their usage from early newsgroups, listservs, and bulletin boards, to web pages, and now to social media, the deep web, and the dark web. Not only has the Internet expanded the number of tools in their communication tool box, but it has also provided hate groups and terrorist groups with a means of enhancing the reach of older modes of communication. Today, the Internet

> play[s] an important-and, in many ways, unique-role in radicalizing homegrown and domestic terrorists. Supporters of Al Qaeda, Sovereign Citizens, white supremacists and neo-Nazis, environmental and animal liberationists, and other violent extremist groups all have embraced the Internet with great enthusiasm and vigor. They are using it as a platform to spread their ideas, connect with each other, make new recruits, and incite illegal and violent actions.
>
> (Neumann, 2012, p. 45)

PRINT MEDIA

Historically, terrorist groups have relied upon print media or interpersonal communication as a means of disseminating their message, recruiting members, and spreading hate and fear. The Ku Klux Klan, which dates back to 1865 and who the Southern Poverty Law Center refers to as "America's first terrorist organization" (Klan Watch Project, 2011, p. 5), in addition to their many atrocities, which included night rides, cross burnings, and lynchings, would also hold meetings and other gatherings, publish their own newspapers, and distribute flyers, all in an effort to recruit members and spread their message. For example, the Seattle, Washington, Klan newspaper *Watcher on the Tower*, which was published in 1923 and 1924, featured articles consistent with their beliefs in Protestant Christianity, Americanism, and white supremacy (Cook, n.d.). In one article, it was reported that newly inducted members of the Royal Riders of the Red Robe, an auxiliary of the KKK comprised of English speaking Anglo-Saxons who were not native born Americans, promised to "bring another member into the fold by the next meeting" (*Watcher on the Tower*, September 1, 1923). Today, the Klan still distributes flyers to spread their message, inspire fear, and recruit new members. Residents in towns and cities across the United States awake to find KKK flyers in their driveways. For example, on Martin Luther King, Jr. Day, 2017, Santa Ana residents found KKK flyers in their driveways (*Los Angeles Times*, January 19, 2015) that called Martin Luther King, Jr., a communist and a pervert and stated that "RACIAL PURITY IS AMERICA'S SECURITY," while residents in Freeport and Augusta, Maine, found KKK flyers in their driveways (Bouchard, January 30, 2017) stating that "You can sleep tonight knowing the Klan is awake!," and in Riverview, Michigan, on Valentine's Day 2017, many resident found KKK flyers admonishing people to "Love your own race" and "Stop homosexuality and race mixing" (Kasuba, February 15, 2017). In each of these instances, the flyers also included contact information for the Klan.

In addition to these "old-fashioned" and labor intensive flyer distributions, hate groups have also turned to technology to facilitate the distribution of their message. In 2016, computer hackers targeted network printers at several universities and printed hate message "adorned with swastikas and asking whether '[you] white men [are] sick and tired of the Jews destroying your country'" (Speyer, January 18, 2017). While Jared Taylor (Taylor, January 25, 2017), on his website American Renaissance, used Donald Trump's election, which he describe as "a sign of rising white consciousness," and inauguration as an opportunity to encourage "racial activists" to spread the word in one of the "oldest ways," by placing posters urging people to free themselves of White Guilt, in high traffic areas, especially on college campuses, which he described as "bastions of anti-white propaganda that gets more extreme every year." These "eye catching, downloadable posters" were available for free on the American Renaissance website. The website whitegenocideproject.com also has downloadable posters and flyers promoting "the mantra" that anti-racist equals anti-white. Of course, hate groups, including terrorist groups, still rely on books and magazines, as well as posters and flyers to spread their message. But now these materials, which include the Islamic State's (ISIS) *Dabiq* and *Rumiyah* magazines, Al Qaeda's *Inspire Magazine*, as well as sovereign citizens' books and white supremacist racist/nationalist's books, can be either downloaded or purchased online.

INTERPERSONAL COMMUNICATION

In additional to print media, terrorist groups also continue to rely on interpersonal communication as a means of spreading their message and recruiting new members. In some instances, friendship provides the basis for spreading hate. Borgeson and Valeri (2017) suggest that for many women, their entry into racist/nationalist skinhead groups is through their friendships. For example, one female skinhead commented, "One day at a Goth show some Nazis [neo-Nazi skinheads] showed up, I eventually met them, and started hanging with them, after a while I started to see that, that is where I belong" (Borgeson & Valeri, 2017, p. 79). In other instances, racist/nationalist individuals and even groups seek out other like-minded individuals. Organizational meetings, such as those reported in the newspaper *The Bradford Era*, facilitate these individuals or groups coming together. For example, on August 30, 2016, *The Bradford Era* reported that the National Socialist Movement had hosted a meeting in Potter County, Pennsylvania, on August 13, 2016, and planned to hold another meeting on October 8, 2016, in Ulysses, Pennsylvania for "All White Patriots" (Davis, August 30, 2016). The leader of the National Socialist Movement Steve Bowers said, "Our goal is to turn Pennsylvania into a stronghold of white supremacy" (Davis, August 2, 2016). The paper also reported that the Aryan Strikeforce was planning to hold a "White Solidarity Meeting" with the National Socialist Movement (Davis, August 30, 2016). Organizations such as the Hammerskins also rely on "meet and great" session as a means of vetting individuals seeking to join the Hammerskins. So, while the Hammerskins maintain a web presence, the webpage provides only limited information and access to unregistered users. Individuals who wish to attend one of their events or shows, such as the Ian Stuart Memorial Concert in Australia, must contact a member and attend meetings prior to attending the event.

> As with every event put on by both Blood & Honour Australia and the Southern Cross Hammerskins, if we haven't met you previously, you'll need to attend beforehand one of the regularly held meet & greets in your state . . . coming to these events is a great way to get to know both people from your area and from the broader WN [white nationalist] community around the country. As we say every year, you don't have to be a skinhead to come along, many aren't; all White Nationalists are welcome.
>
> (Stormfront Forum, July 4, 2016)

Because many of the webpages and social media pages include forums or other means of sharing ideas and discussing beliefs, these outlets help to forge friendships between like-minded individuals and strengthen their beliefs and commitment to the cause. In some cases, as with Alex, a young woman in Washington State, terrorists make it a point to regularly communicate, one-on-one, with potential recruits as a means of drawing them further into the group (Callimachi, June 27, 2015). In Alex's cases, ISIS representatives communicated with her for several hours each day via Twitter, email, and Skype in order to persuade her to convert to Islam and join ISIS. There tactics were so effective that Alex had planned to travel to Syria.

While hate groups and terrorist organization continue to rely on interpersonal means of recruitment, oftentimes facilitated through the Internet, this chapter focuses on propaganda rather than interpersonal recruitment. To learn more about interpersonal recruitment, readers are directed to Chapter 2 on right wing terrorism, Chapter 5 on Islamic terror in America, and Chapter 9 on prison recruitment for further discussion of interpersonal recruitment tactics used by various groups.

(SURFACE) WEB PAGES AND SOCIAL NETWORKS

Until recently, there were a plethora of hate websites on the surface web. In fact, the history of hate on the web dates back to the early 1990s when the World Wide Web went public. At that time, Stormfront.org, which is considered by many to be the first white supremacist webpage, started an online bulletin board in 1990, went public in 1994, and became the first white nationalist website in 1995 (Coveners League, n.d.; Hankes & Zhang, February 22, 2017; SPLC, August 29, 2017). Approximately 20 years later, in summer 2014, the Southern Poverty Law Center dubbed Stormfront as the "murder capital of the Internet" because "nearly 100 bias-related homicides were attributable to registered members of his [Don Black's] website [Stormfront. org]" (Beirich, Summer 2014). These murderers/terrorists included Buford O'Neil Furrow who, in 1999, shot and wounded people outside a Jewish Community Center in California; Richard Scott Baumhammers, who, in 2000, killed his Jewish neighbor; Ian Andrew Bishop who, in 2002, killed his brother because he thought he was gay; and Richard Andrew Poplawksi, who, in 2009, killed three police officers and wounded a fourth (Beirich, Summer 2014). Other registered members of Stormfront.org who were murderers/terrorists include Anders Behring Breivik, who, in 2011, killed eight people in Oslow and another 69 people on Utoya Island, Norway; Luka Rocco Magnotta (real name Eric Clinton Kirk Newman), who, in 2012, tortured, killed, and dismembered a Chinese immigrant; and Wade Michael Page, who, in 2012, shot and killed six people at a Sikh temple (Beirich, Summer 2014). In August 2017, Stormfront's website ceased operation when its domain name was seized (Crocker, August 26, 2017; SPL Center, August 29, 2017). However, a little more than a month later, Stormfront.org was back online (Schulberg, Liebelson, & Craggs, October 3, 2017).

In addition to Stormfront.org, there have been websites for a number of other hate, racist/ nationalist, or terrorist groups, including Ku Klux Klan organizations, the Aryan Nations, racist/ nationalist skinhead groups, and the sovereign citizens. Some of these webpages, at least at the time of writing this chapter, still exist. There are also websites for the Animal Liberation Front (ALF) and Earth Liberation Front (ELF). With the advent of social networks such as Facebook, many of these organizations started social network pages. In a recent review of skinhead social networks on Facebook and VK, one of the largest European social networks, no racist/nationalist skinheads were found on Facebook but there were several on VK (Valeri, Sweazy, & Borgeson, 2017).

However, since the white supremacist rally in Charlottesville, Virginia, on August 12, 2017, that resulted in the death of one anti-racist protestor, many Internet service providers have cut their ties to racist/nationalist groups (Selk, August 16, 2017). When the Daily Stormer, a neo-Nazi website, published an article mocking the victims of the violence at the rally, Go Daddy, the hosting site, decided to cut ties with them (Astor, Caron, & Victor, August 13, 2017). Almost immediately, other Internet service providers joined the ban against the Daily Stormer as well as against other hate groups (Astor, Caron, & Victor, August 13, 2017). On Tuesday August 15, PayPal, an online payment processor, announced that it would ban groups that promoted hate, violence, or intolerance from using PayPal as a means of accepting donations (Jan, August 16, 2017). While some might assume that these bans will result in the disappearance of hate websites, this is far from likely. In the past, hate groups, such as racist/nationalist skinhead groups have dealt with their websites being taken down by creating new sites using different names (Borgeson & Valeri, 2005). Other hate groups have adopted more banal names and websites such as American Renaissance and Keystone United in an effort to appeal to a more mainstream audience (Valeri & Borgeson, 2016). These websites, at least at the writing of this chapter, continue to have a presence on the web. It is expected that hate groups whose webpages are banned will either seek out a different Internet service provider, as did Stormfront.org, or engage in name changing tactics. This, in fact, has been one tactic used by ISIS. As Nance and Sampson note

After two years of ISIS presence in the jihadist media world, there have been increased demands to remove all content associated with ISIS from the Internet. This has had a direct effect on the recycling nature of ISIS media websites where domain names have begun to cease resembling their media center because of the risk of being detected.

(Nance & Sampson, 2017, p. 37)

As Nance and Sampson further note,

their [al-Qaeda and ISIS] online web forums . . . [were] as much a standard weapon for them as the AK-47 assault rifle. Used to post lectures, graphics, and eventually videos, these sites have served as the backbone of terrorist propaganda for over 20 years . . . used for posting the latest sermons, mission reports, martyrdom celebrations, or the occasional speech by terrorist VIPs.

(p. 45)

What tends to bring these sites down is some high-profile posting that draws attention to the site. This was the case with the Daily Stormer when it mocked the victims of the Charlottesville incident, as well as with the Muntada al Ansar website when it posted the Nick Berg video (Nance & Sampson, 2017). The result for ISIS was that "with the repeated takedowns of materials on WordPress, Tumblr, and other platforms, those efforts have been driven into Telegram feeds, and some remain in Twitter form . . . also Facebook groups that are occasionally identified as originating from ISIS" (p. 46).

TWITTER

Twitter, the online social networking program that allows users to send messages of up to 140 characters, less if a graphic is included, was started in 2006 (Carlson, 2011). ISIS, with its vast media wing successfully adopted Twitter as a means of recruiting new fighters, distributing propaganda and announcing/celebrating its victories (Berger, 2014; Nance & Sampson, 2017). Berger (2014) explains that key to ISIS's Twitter success in 2014 was the widespread use of its own Arab language Twitter app named "The Dawn of Glad Tidings," which allows users to keep up with the latest news about their jihadi fighters. The information posted on Dawn is controlled by ISIS's social media wing, and the same content that is tweeted to an account is also "tweeted by the accounts of everyone else who has signed up for the app, spaced out to avoid triggering Twitter's spam-detection algorithm" (Berger, 2014). Berger (2014) explains how, thanks to organized hashtag campaigns with its users, ISIS is able to get its tweets listed onto an Arabic twitter account's (@ActiveHashtags) daily top trending tags. According to Berger (2014), when this happens, it results in an average of 72 retweets per tweet, thus exposing more users to ISIS's message. Berger and Morgan (2015), in a census of Twitter, estimated that, between October and November 2014, there were at least 46,000 Twitter accounts held by ISIS supporters. Based on a sample of 20,000 ISIS supporters, these researchers determined that the majority of supporters resided in territories held by ISIS, followed by supporters in Saudi Arabia. Of these users, 75% designated Arabic as their primary language, approximately 20% designated English as their primary language, and approximately 5% designated French as their primary language. Berger and Morgan (2015), as well as Nance and Sampson (2017), noted that Twitter's suspension of ISIS-related accounts proved detrimental to ISIS's use of Twitter. However, Berger and Morgan (2015) noted that while suspension of ISIS Twitter accounts may make it more difficult for new people to join its network, it does not make it impossible. Perhaps, more importantly, the suspension of Twitter accounts might result in a "more focused and coherent group dynamic [that] could speed up and intensify the radicalization process" (Berger & Morgan, 2015, p. 58) and could also close down avenues for ISIS members to leave the network.

Because of ISIS's prolific use of Twitter, other researchers have also sought to compare ISIS's use of Twitter with that of opposition networks (Bodine-Baron, Helmus, Magnuson, & Winkelman, 2016) and with that of white nationalists (Berger, September 2016). Bodine-Baron and colleagues (2016), during the 10-month period of July 1, 2014 through April 30, 2015, examined tweets sent by Islamic State supporters, as indicated by their use of Islamic State in their tweets, with that of Islamic State opponents, as indicated by their use of Daesh in their tweets. Consistent with their hypothesis that people who used "Daesh" in their tweets would be opponents of ISIS while users of "Islamic State" would be supporters, these researchers found that Daesh users tended to be critical of ISIS while Islamic State users tended to be highly supportive of ISIS. While the number of ISIS opponents on Twitter tended to be greater than the number of supporters (ten to one, on a daily basis, and averaging six to one during the 10-month period), ISIS supporters out-tweeted opponents, producing 50% more tweets per day than their opponents (Bodine-Baron et al., 2016). In contrast to the conclusion of Berger and Morgan (2015), Bodine-Baron and colleagues (2016) suggest that Twitter should continue to suspend ISIS supporter accounts because it might push them to use less accessible social media channels. Finally, research by Berger (2016) suggests that while American white nationalists may have been slow to embrace Twitter, they have made great strides in their use of it. According to Berger (September 2016), the number of American white nationalists on Twitter grew by 600% between 2012 and 2016. Berger (September 2016) speculates that these groups are learning from ISIS's success on social media and applying what they have learned to their own organizations. But, because the white nationalist movement is composed of several different and competing factions, their message is less consistent than that of ISIS. But the most popular theme in their tweets related to "white genocide" is the idea that diversity and multi-culturalism is endangering the "survival" of the white race. In fact, the webpage whitegenocideproject.com encourages supporters to "Post the STOP WHITE GENOCIDE repeater phrases!" (whitegenocideproject.com, n.d.).

MUSIC, VIDEOS, AND COMPUTER GAMES

Just as white nationalists have learned the value of social media from ISIS, ISIS may have learned the value of music from white supremacists and white nationalists. Given that extremists groups and terrorist groups frequently target youth and young adults, it is not surprising that they would use music and videos to reach this audience. Music has long been used by white supremacists to recruit followers (Borgeson & Valeri, 2017; Pieslak, 2015). An example of this dates back to the 1970s when the National Front in Britain was trying to recruit youth to their organization. To do this they sponsored football (soccer) matches and Rock Against Communism (RAC) concerts as well as helped to establish a record label White Noise Club. Ian Stuart Donaldson (stage name Ian Stuart), who joined the National Front in 1979 and was a fan of Hitler, and his band Skrewdriver, played a pivotal role in the success of this enterprise. Skrewdriver was the headliner for RAC events, and under the leadership of Stuart, their concerts were turned into Hitler style rallies with shouts of "Sieg Heil" accompanied by right arm salutes.

Although Donaldson was killed in a car accident in 1993, his music had already spread to audiences in Europe and the United States. Even today, his music continues to inspire white power rock and white racist/nationalist events. There are annual Ian Stuart Memorial Concerts (see www.bloodandhonourworldwide.co.uk/history/isdmemorial.html). Until recently, the Skrewdriver.com website (the domain name was posted for sale on September 11, 2017) described Donaldson as

> He would become the most popular and loved man in the entire skinhead scene. In 1982 his band, Skrewdriver, sent shockwaves throughout the entire world when it introduced Nationalist and Racial lyrics to it's music. . . . Their concerts were feared by the left wing. . . . Hail the New Dawn was released in 1984, and the band's popularity soared. Skrewdriver became known in every White country around the globe. From England to Italy, America to Germany, Ian Stuart was at the forefront of the White Power Scene.
>
> (Skrewdriver.com)

Christian Picciolini, former neo-Nazi skinhead and leader of the white power band Final Solution, discussed the importance of white power music in recruiting youth to the movement. Picciolini states

> I believe very, very strongly that music is one of the best marketing tools for anybody to influence kids, not just white power groups. . . . With the white power movement, it's probably the most powerful tool they have. It's aggressive, it's informative, it's insightful . . . and it's unifying.
>
> (Ludwig, November 17, 2014)

Because music is such a powerful recruitment tool and can also serve as a revenue source, over the years white power groups have created their own recording companies, such as Panzerfaust Records, Micetrap, Resistance Records, American Defense Records, and Antipathy Records. Today, the Internet facilitates the distribution of hate music. While some hate websites include their own links to music, hate music is or has been available through Amazon, iTunes, Spotify, and YouTube (Hankes, November 21, 2014; SPLC, December 8, 2014; March 9, 2015). For example, jihadi raps such as Dirty Kuffar (see www.youtube.com/watch?v=XMAFN-pwqOw) and jihdi nasheeds, Islamic devotional music, supporting and encouraging terrorism can be found on the Internet (Marshall, November 9, 2014; Mekhennet, August 31, 2011; Smirke, October 10, 2014; Stuster, April 29, 2013). Note that the song Dirty Kuffar references the National Front and includes pictures of skinheads and a swastika. Said, who as part of his doctoral studies examined the importance and impact of nasheeds, in an interview with Euronews discussed the Islamic State's involvement in the production of recent nasheeds. According to Said, the most famous nasheed was "My ummah, Dawn has appeared, so await the expected victory," which was released at the end of 2013 by an ISIS funded media unit Ajnad Media Foundation (Seymat, August 10, 2014).

Al-Tamimi, a Shillman-Ginsburg fellow at the Middle East Forum, who was also interviewed for the article, describes the song as a quasi-official anthem for ISIS. The lyrics of the song, as translated by Al-Tamimi, include "The Islamic State has arisen by the blood of the righteous . . . by the jihad of the pious" (Seymat, August 10, 2014). The white power movement and ISIS are not alone in using music as a recruitment tool. Music is used by both Christian and Islamic extremist groups, environmental groups, and animal rights groups to recruit adherents (see Pieslak, 2015, for a more complete discussion).

In addition to facilitating access to music, the Internet also provides an easy means of posting and accessing videos. The use of movies/videos is not new. For example, the 1915 movie *Birth of a Nation*, based on the novel *The Clansman*, in which the Ku Klux Klan (KKK) is portrayed favorably, is often considered to be the inspiration for the reformation of the KKK. Today, ISIS, because of its horrific videos of beheadings and other atrocities, is probably one of the more well-known terrorist groups posting videos on the Internet. In addition to these, there are also Islamic extremist sermons, such as those of Anwar al Awlaki; recruitment videos; and live videos of terrorist attacks such as those carried out by Al Shabaab at the Westgate Shopping Mall in Nairobi, Kenya (Alexander, September 22, 2013). The sermons of Anwar al Awlaki include "Call to Jihad" and admonish Muslims to never trust a non-Muslim and to kill Americans (Shane, August 27, 2015). Awlaki's videos are considered to have influenced the Boston Marathon bombers and the San Bernardino attackers to engage in terrorism (Eckholm, December 27, 2015; Shane, August 27, 2015). *The Recruitment Manual of Abu Amru Al Qa'idy* (Al Qaeda), which can be found online, suggests several different books, recordings, and videos, also available via the Internet, that can be used to help a new recruit understand "why we have not brought the Islamic Caliphate through peaceful means" and convince the recruit of "the obligation of Jihad and the duty of preparing for it." The list of recommended videos includes the series *Winds of Paradise* produced by As Sahab, the multi-media wing of Al Qaeda. "Winds of Paradise" is described as "[It] takes on a . . . personal approach as you actually get to see these Mujahideen and how they lived their lives as pious warriors. Every series . . . makes the heart of the believers ache for Jihad . . . " (Winds of Paradise, n.d.). Islamic extremists are not the only ones producing videos. WhiteRabbitRadioTV has several cartoons with white supremacist themes, including the reoccurring theme that anti-racist means anti-white. While Jared Taylor, on American Renaissance, an online magazine that bills itself as "race realists" and "advocating for white rights," has videos that, in terms of tone and production quality, resemble those found on the websites of major news organizations. Stormfront had even produced a video *Adolf Hitler: The Greatest Story Never Told!*

In addition to movies and videos, hate groups and terrorist groups use computer games as a means of reaching youth and inculcating their beliefs. In 1999, *The Economist* ("Downloading Hate", 1999) reported that Stormfront had a "Kids' Page" that included a white power version of the computer game "Doom." Other white power/white supremacist groups have also used video games as recruiting tools (Borgeson & Valeri, 2004). Ebdrup (October 10, 2012) reported that right-wing extremists in Germany had made a video game in which the player shoots asylum families. Of course, military style computer games, such as "America's Army," "Modern Warfare," and "Call of Duty," which provide entertainment and can also serve as a recruitment tool, are not new and are often based in actual warfare. In 2003, Hezbollah created their own video game "Special Force" in which players earned points for attacking Israeli military and killing Israel's prime minister (Hall, November 1, 2014; Wakin, May 18, 2003). More recently, ISIS has created their own versions of the computer game "Grand Theft Auto" called "Grand Theft Auto: Salil al-Sawarem [Clang of Swords]" (Hall, November 1, 2014). Movies, videos, and video games, similar to music, provide an entertaining means for extremist groups and terrorist organizations to connect with potential recruits, especially youth, and promote their message while bolstering the morale and reinforcing the beliefs of existing members.

Encryption and the Deep and Dark Web

As discussed previously, many hate and terrorist groups have operated on the surface web and others continue to do so. However, many groups whose websites have been banned, in addition to engaging in the name changing games discussed previously, have also turned to the Deep Web, Dark Web, and other means of encryption that allow them to communicate with each other without detection. One popular encryption application is Telegram. Telegram is a mobile phone application launched in 2013 that allows users to "Encrypt personal and business secrets. Destruct your message with a timer. Connect from most remote locations. [and] Coordinate groups of up to 10000 members" (Telegram, n.d.). Nance and Sampson noted that Telegram is ISIS's preferred communication application and that "In September 2015, ISIS added the ability to create channels, which changed the app from a secret messaging platform to a massive hidden forum platform ripe with content from the world's active terrorist organizations" (p. 50). In addition to Telegram, ISIS has also encouraged its followers to use the encrypted apps Signal, Chatsecure, SilentText, SilentPhone, LinPhone, and Surespot (Calamur, February 5, 2016; Katz, July 14, 2016; Nance & Sampson, 2017; O'Neil, April 13, 2016). ISIS made this recommendation following Twitter's 2016 announcement that it had suspended over 125,000 accounts related to ISIS. But ISIS is not the only group to use encryption. In 2016, three "Crusaders" in the United States who wanted to kill Muslims used the app Zello to encrypt their phone calls in order to avoid detection (Wootson, October 15, 2016).

The preceding examples are not the earliest use of encryption technologies. Terrorist groups have also turned to the Deep Web and Dark Web as a means of concealing their communications. Most Internet users search and find information on the surface web. the surface web is "anything that can be indexed by a typical search engine like Google, Bing, or Yahoo. . . . From a purist's definition . . . the Surface Web is anything that a search engine can find while **the Deep Web is anything that a search engine can't find**" [bold in original] (Bright Planet, March 27, 2014). Thus, mainstream companies operate in the surface web. But the part of the web not indexed by traditional search engines is referred to as the "deep web." "Deep Web content can be found almost anytime you navigate away from Google and do a search directly in a website" (Bright Planet, March 27, 2014). In these instances, you are searching the website's database, that of an organization or business, such as a library, government organization, or other business. "The Dark Web then is classified as a small portion of the Deep Web that has been intentionally hidden and is inaccessible through standard web browsers" (Bright Planet, March 27, 2014). In order to access information on the Dark Web, users must use special browsers such as The Onion Router (Tor). Tor is designed to conceal its users by encrypting information and randomly passing it through a series of network relays before the communication reaches the final user. This method of encryption prevents anyone who is "spying" from knowing both the sender and the received of the message.

The Dark Web can and is used for both legal and illegal business. Many newspapers, such as *The Guardian*, have a Tor hidden service to allow whistle blowers to share information with them anonymously (Hern, August 23, 2017). There is also a Tor version of Facebook for people living under repressive regimes and in places that censor the web such as China and Iran (Hern, August 23, 2017). The Silk Road is probably one of the more well-known Dark Web markets for illegal goods. Many "shoppers" in the Dark Web use Bitcoin, an anonymous currency, to make purchases. Ali Shukri Amin, a 17-year-old from Virginia, who pled guilty to providing material support to terrorists, in addition to recruiting and posting propaganda for ISIS, also encouraged people to financially support ISIS by using Bitcoin. He instructed people to use a "Dark Wallet" when donating Bitcoin to ISIS because it would allow donors' identities to remain anonymous (*United States of America v Ali Shukri Amin*, June 11, 2015).

Terrorists use to operate in all three areas of the web. But many terrorist groups, and at least some white supremacist groups who have been driven off the surface web, use the Deep Web and the Dark Web. The Daily Stormer, when it was forced to leave the surface web, launched a site on the Dark Web (Hern, August 23, 2017). The obvious appeal to these groups is that the sites are hidden and that the users can remain anonymous. Also, Tor, unlike many Internet providers on the surface web, continues to defend free speech. After the Daily Stormer created its hidden site using Tor, Tor argued that

> the same rights that protect the good protect the Daily Stormer too. "We can't build free and open source tools that protect journalists, human rights activists, and ordinary people around the world if we also control who uses those tools. . . . Tor is designed to defend human rights and privacy by preventing anyone from censoring things, even us."
>
> (Hern, August 23, 2017)

Stormfront.org, which is considered to be the first white supremacist website, had discussion about Tor as early as 2004, just after Tor became available to the public (O'Neil, June 23, 2015). But because Tor was developed by the United States military and received funding from the United States government, many extremist groups question whether communication on it is truly anonymous. As a result, some of these groups have attempted to develop their own encryption tools. As early as 2007, al-Qaeda was publishing encryption tools (Nance & Sampson, 2017). In fact, the first edition of AQAP's *Inspire* magazine, in an article entitled "How to use Asrar al-Mujahideen: Sending and receiving encrypted messages," provided directions on exactly that, sending and receiving encrypted messages. The articles warns "spies are actively paying attention to the Emails, especially if you are an individual that is known to be jihādī-minded . . . [so use] an encryption software. One such software is a program created by our brothers called Asrar al-Mujahideen 2.0" (*Inspire Magazine*, Summer, 2010; p. 41). Since then, both al-Qaeda and ISIS continue to release their own encryption tools. Note that, in 2011, "the Global Islamic Media Front had to warn its users against downloading its own encryption program, 'Mujahideen Secrets 2.0,' because it had been compromised" (O'Neil, June 23, 2015). Also, in 2011, "Apartheid" was released, "a security-focused version of the Linux operating system meant 'for proud whites' that came with Tor pre-installed in order to protect users' identity and communications" (O'Neil, June 23, 2015). While use of Apartheid has ceased, white supremacists have switched to other means of protecting their anonymity, including the use of VPNs (virtual private networks), I2p (Invisible Internet Project), Freenet, Debian, Ubuntu, Tails, and full disk encryption (O'Neil, June 23, 2015).

It should be evident to the reader that extremist groups, including terrorist groups, rely on a variety of communication strategies and devices to deliver their message. While they are willing to embrace new technologies, they have not abandoned older communication modalities: in fact, they may use new technologies to facilitate or encourage the delivery of their message in person or in print. Also, extremist groups respond to attempts to keep them from getting their message out; rather than giving up, they find new and creative means for delivering their message.

Recruitment Strategies

While the purpose of Modes of Communication was to draw readers' attention to the breath of communication strategies used by extremist groups and terrorist organizations, the next section explores the psychological factors that underlie the success of their recruitment campaigns. ISIS has received a good deal of media coverage resulting from their ability to recruit supporters from around the globe. Although other extremist groups and terrorist organizations may not be as purposeful in their recruitment efforts, an overview of ISIS's strategies provides a good starting point for this discussion. Berger (2015) outlines four steps in ISIS's recruitment strategy. First, potential recruits are identified and contact is made. Potential recruits may be identified because they have sought out contact with ISIS on their own or ISIS supporters have identified them by monitoring the online communications of mainstream and radical Muslim communities and/or by surfing the web for anti-Western sentiment, pro-Islamic views, or pro-ISIS support. Once a potential recruit is identified, contact is made. If the target seems receptive to communicating with ISIS, the ISIS recruiters and supporters will next begin using recruiting tactics consistent with those employed by cults (Hassan, 2015). They will do this by creating a small community around the target, showering him/her with almost constant attention and positively reinforcing any expression or sentiment from the target that is consistent with the group's beliefs. As part of this stage, they will also begin to encourage the target to separate him/herself from non-supporters and others outside this micro community until the target is isolated. Then they will gradually move communication with the recruit to private and often encrypted communication channels. Finally, the target will be encouraged to take actions that are consistent with ISIS's beliefs. This could be by becoming an online advocate for ISIS, traveling to the Islamic State, or engaging in terrorism. Note that an excellent description of ISIS's use of this strategy to recruit an American woman and persuade her to travel to the Islamic State is described in the *New York Times* article titled *"ISIS and the Lonely Young American"* (Callimachi, June 27, 2015).

Although Hassan (2015) uses different terminology to describe the recruitment process used by cults, the steps are quite similar to those outlined by Berger (2015). Once a recruit is identified, the recruiter works to establish rapport with the recruit, and then works to reshape the recruits understanding of the world by tearing down his/her old values and beliefs and rebuilding them in a manner that is consistent with the ideology and goals of the cult. The reshaping process typically involves isolating the recruit away from his/her family and friends, surrounding them with cult members, and flooding them with new and often emotion laden information. Finally, the recruit is given a new purpose in life and new activities, ones that are consistent with his/her new identity and that of the cult, such as recruiting, raising money, or engaging in other activities on behalf of the cult.

While other terrorist organizations and extremist groups may lack the disciplined and well-orchestrated recruiting efforts of ISIS, the same psychological principles that underlie ISIS's recruitment strategies and success also underlie the recruitment efforts of other groups. So how does an extremist group, whether it is a terrorist group or hate group, shift the beliefs and attitudes of a relatively naïve individual from someone who is "just curious" or seeking information to someone who comes to accept the group's extreme beliefs and is willing to act on those beliefs?

THE NEED TO BELONG AND BE VALUED

As mentioned previously, the recruitment tactics used by these groups, especially Al Qaeda and ISIS, are similar to those of a cult. Hassan (2015) notes, that cults, in which he includes ISIS, Boko Haram, the Unification Church, and Scientology, are successful at recruiting new members because people either do not believe in mind control/undue influence and/or believe that they will be impervious to recruitment attempts by these groups. Furthermore, the majority of people who are recruited into these organizations are lured in during a time of stress or vulnerability by people posing as friends or people who have their "best interest" in mind (Hassan, 2015). This was true of "Alex" the Lonely Young American who, when she was recruited, had recently dropped out of college and was feeling intense loneliness. It is also true of the many young white men who are unable to find a job and suffer from low self-esteem join white supremacist groups because they offer sympathy and an excuse for their lack of employment (Schafer & Navarro, 2003). The attention offered to Alex by her new online "friends" made her feel like she belonged, was part of a group, and was valued. Similarly, the unemployed white male is made to feel a part of a group, his self-worth bolstered, and he is assured that he is not to blame for his predicament. Each of these examples illustrates how our need for self-esteem (Greenberg, Solomon, & Pyszzynski, 1997; Leary & Baumeister, 2000; Maslow 1968; 1970; Valeri & Borgeson, 2016) and our need to belong (Baumeister & Leary, 1995; Borgeson & Valeri, 2017; Leary, 2001; Maslow, 1968, 1970) can drive us to seek out individuals and groups that make us feel valued and feel that we belong. Unfortunately, as is also illustrated by these two examples, sometimes the individuals or groups connected with are ones promoting hate, prejudice, and violence.

Berger (2015) and Hassan (2015) both agree that recruitment starts once contact is initiated. This frequently begins when an individual, in this case the potential recruit, expresses an opinion that is somewhat consistent with the group's beliefs or initiates contact with the group. This opens the door, if only a crack, for recruitment and attitude change to occur. The extremist group or terrorist group uses the initial statement or opinion of the recruit to establish similarity and friendship with him/her and as an anchor for establishing and strengthening commitment to the group's beliefs.

SIMILARITY, FAMILIARITY, AND LIKING

We tend to like people who are similar to us, familiar to us, or with whom we associate positive emotions (Bierley, McSweeney, & Vannieuwkerk, 1985; Cialdini, 2009; Seiter, 2007). We are also more likely to agree with and help people we like (Dovidio, Gaertner, Shnabel, Saguy, &

Johnson, 2010; Levine, Prosser, Evans, & Reicher, 2005). Cults, extremist groups, and terrorist organizations know this and use it as one of their recruitment tactics. According to Hassan (2015), recruiters are instructed in ways to get potential recruits to like them. Recruiters will try to learn as much about a recruit as possible and will use effusive praise and flattery as a means of promoting liking and friendship. In the case of Alex, the recruiter posed as a friend and showered her with attention, lavish praise, and even sent her small gifts. In the Al Qa'idy training manual, once a potential recruit has been identified, the recruiter is instructed to get close to the candidate in two ways, "by getting close through daily work (routines) [and] getting close through weekly work" (Al Qa'idy, n.d.). Suggestions for daily work include starting a job or school with the recruit and sending the recruit a daily religious sms message. Suggestions for weekly work included visiting the recruit at his home and being nice to the recruit even if the recruit does something to offend you. The most effective work is considered to be "Invite him to lunch or breakfast, this . . . removes barriers between you and him and makes you become closer to him . . . give him a gift" (Al Qa'idy, n.d.). Note that these shared activities promote feelings of similarity and familiarity with the recruiter and associate the recruiter with positive emotions. The recruitment manual even includes an 8-item scale to measure the success of your efforts to establish feelings of closeness and friendship with the recruit. Questions include "Is he eager to see you? Does he talk with you about his private affairs and his hobbies? . . . Does he love to spend a lot of time with you?" (Al Qa'idy, n.d.). Based on the score the recruiter earns, the recruiter is advised to take one of three actions. If the score is too low, the recruiter is encouraged to abandon these recruitment efforts and turn his/her energy to finding a new candidate for recruitment, continue his/her recruitment efforts with the current recruit for another month, or to move on to the next stage of recruitment with the caveat that "you should know that your close relationship with him must continue" (Al Qa'idy, n.d.). Obviously, these tactics are meant to facilitate the formation of a friendship between the recruit and recruiter.

Note that this "friendship" is also facilitated through reciprocity in the form of gift giving (Cialdini, 2009; Razran, 1938). Reciprocity is a powerful tool for increasing compliance (Cialdini, 2009; Razran, 1940; Rind & Strohmetz, 2001; Strohmetz, Rind, Fisher, & Lynn, 2002). Research demonstrates that people are more likely to comply with a request from someone to whom they feel indebted. People feel in debt to someone who has done them a favor or given them a gift, even if that favor or gift was unrequested (Regan, 1971). Furthermore, to rid themselves of feeling in debt, people are often willing to not just repay the favor in kind but to give back more than they received (Regan, 1971).

While the formation of this "friendship" was purposeful, with many hate groups there is not an orchestrated effort to recruit new members. Rather, new members often seek out existing groups because they are looking for people with similar beliefs and interests, and it is these common interests that facilitate the development of friendships (Borgeson & Valeri, 2017). These friendships can be established in person, in cyberspace, or some combination of the two. In cyberspace, discussions about music and videos can often facilitate the development of friendships, which heightens commitment to the group (Borgeson & Valeri, 2017).

Hate groups and terrorist groups also facilitate liking by associating themselves with familiar products (Bierley, McSweeney, & Vannieuwkerk;1985; Lott & Lott, 1965). As discussed in the Music, Video, and Computer Games section, terrorists have created their own version of some popular video games. But they also created their own promotional advertisements by altering small sections of these video games to inspire youth to join their cause and to raise the moral of their own followers. For example, ISIS made their own promotional advertisement by editing a section of "Grand Theft Auto" so that it shows a plane flying into one of the World Trade Center Towers while the background audio features someone yelling "Allah Akbar" (Gta V isis version, n.d.; Tassi, September 20, 2014). Another popular image among ISIS fighters in Syria was from the video game "Call of Duty." In the ISIS image from this game, two soldiers with rifles are pictured with the caption "This Is Our Call of Duty: And We Respawn in Jannah [Paradise]" (Hall, November 1, 2014). A group of British jihadists fighting for ISIS also created several online promotions that were based on well-known images or sayings. For example, in one poster like promotion showing a laptop with an assault rifle across the keyboard, they morphed the expression "YOLO, You Only Live Once" into "YODO, You Only Die Once, Why Not Make It Martyrdom" (Wright, February 5, 2014).

COMMITMENT AND CONSISTENCY

Using social judgment theory, we can also see how the initial opinion expressed by an individual can be used to open the door to further persuasion. Research reported by Sherif and Hovland (1961) suggests that a person's own attitudes serve as a frame of reference when judging information. According to social judgment theory (Eagly & Chaiken, 1993; Sherif & Hovland, 1961; Sherif, Taub, & Hovland, 1958), people evaluate new information along a continuum that ranges from acceptance to rejection, with an area of non-commitment in between those two end points. Information that falls within an individual's latitude of acceptance or in their latitude of non-commitment but close to their latitude of acceptance is evaluated positively, and is judged to be more similar to the person's own attitude than it really is. This facilitates acceptance and assimilation of the new information with existing attitudes. In contrast, information that falls within an individual's latitude of rejection or in their latitude of non-commitment but close to their latitude of rejection is negatively evaluated, and is judged to be more discrepant with the person's own attitudes than it really is. This inhibits attitude change, and the information is rejected.

The extremist group or terrorist group can use the information provided by the potential recruit in his/her initial post, tweet, or other communication or information about the site on which the individual is posting as an indication of what the individual views as acceptable and shape their response so that it falls within or close to the individual's latitude of acceptance. Proceeding gradually, the recruiter can expand the individual's latitude of acceptance to include beliefs that are more extreme and are consistent with that of their extremist group or terrorist organization. Both Al Qa'idy and cults, as discussed by Hassan (2015), suggest that the reshaping of ideas and beliefs should occur gradually. "The material that will make up the new identity is doled out gradually. . . . 'Tell the new member only what they are ready to accept . . . these people (potential recruits) are spiritual babies. Don't tell them more then they can handle' . . . spoon feed them" (Hassan, 2015, p. 129).

Social judgment theory also explains why the webpages of hate groups with more banal sounding names and toned down messages appeal to some individuals while the webpages of hate groups with more direct and "in your face" names and content appeal to others. People tend to migrate to the webpages whose content falls within or close to their latitude of acceptance

(Borgeson & Valeri, 2004). The authors of these webpages can then gradually move their followers to more extreme positions, or as an individual's views become more extreme, he/she will migrate to webpages, social media, etc., with more extreme positions.

The extremist group or terrorist group can also use the initial communication of an individual as the basis for building commitment to the group by getting the recruit to say or do things that are consistent with the initial statement and then gradually increase the size of their demands. This process is commonly referred to as "foot-in-the-door" (Cialdini, 2009). Foot-in-the-door works by getting people to make an initial commitment, often by getting them to agree to a small request, and then making a larger request, one that is consistent with the initial request. Agreement to the small request makes it more likely that the individual will agree to the larger request because doing so is consistent with the individual's own previous actions. Foot-in-the-door is effective because it causes a change in the individual's identity so that the individual comes to see themselves as someone who does/believes in Cause X. In this case, Cause X is that of the extremist group or terrorist group. Commitment to a cause can be heightened by drawing the recruit's attention to his/her own previous statements or actions that were consistent with that of the group's ideology or by labeling the person as a supporter of the group. In Alex's case, she was labeled a "good Muslim."

POLARIZING ATTITUDES

In both Berger's (2015) and Hassan's (2015) models, recruits become isolated from non-supporters. Isolation is a key element of the indoctrination process because it allows the terrorist group's or cult's claims of "we're right and they're wrong" to go unchallenged, creating an illusion of unanimous agreement that facilitates cohesion and conformity among group members (Moghaddam, 2005). While the process may occur more quickly for the new ISIS recruit because he/she is encouraged to isolate him/herself from non-believers, isolation from the mainstream also happens to recruits in other groups as a result of typical interpersonal dynamics. People generally form and maintain friendships with similar others (Berscheid & Walster, 1978; Byrne, 1971). Therefore, as an individual's views begin to change, he/she will begin spending more time with those individuals who share their beliefs and spending less time with people who do not share their beliefs. This is why friends often drift apart when the interests and values of the friends diverge. In cyberspace, where communication can occur virtually, around-the-clock, and oftentimes freely via blog posts, Twitter, and Skype, it is especially easy to find and surround oneself with like-minded individuals so that one becomes immersed in these friendships. The result is that the individual becomes isolated from anyone with contrary views and is surrounded by like-minded individuals.

Hate groups and terrorist groups, by their very nature, are instrumental in making the beliefs of new recruits more extreme because the groups act as incubators for extremism. Unlike the typical work or social group where there are a wide range of beliefs and opinions, the norms of all the terrorist/hate group members are already all located at one extreme of the continuum. Group polarization, which occurs through persuasion, comparison, and differentiation, serves to drive the new recruit to even more extreme views and actions (Blaskovich, Ginsburg, & Howe, 1975; Burnstein & Vinokur, 1973; Codol, 1975; Fraser, Gouge, & Billig., 1971; Mackie & Cooper, 1984; Sanders & Baron, 1977; Vinokur & Burnstein, 1974). The new recruit will hear only arguments at one extreme, and in order to gain acceptance, will shift his/her beliefs to be consistent with the group's norms. If the new recruit wishes to gain prestige or demonstrate exceptional commitment to the group, he/she will take a position or take actions that are consistent with that of the group's norms but more extreme.

THE ILLUSION OF CONSENSUS

As just discussed, when an individual is surrounded by only like-minded individuals, they are exposed to a limited range of beliefs. Therefore, it starts to seem as if everyone shares the group's beliefs, after all everyone the recruit knows agrees. The new recruit fails to consider that there is only consensus because the only opinions he/she is being exposed to are those of group members. Thus, widespread consensus is an illusion. Even though consensus is an illusion, it still has a powerful impact on the attitudes and behaviors of the recruit, making it more likely that the recruit will conform to the group's behaviors (Festinger, 1954; Surowiecki, 2004)

ISIS, in their magazine, *Dabiq*, would recount stories of people making hijrah to the Islamic State to suggest to readers that doing so was quite common and therefore make it more likely that the reader would attempt to move to the Islamic State. Similarly, through a regular feature in both *Dabiq* and *Rumiyah* magazines entitled "Among the Believers Are Men," these stories would present the story of an individual who desired to be martyred and was then killed and imply that is was everyone's dream to do so. For example, in one such story, the protagonist is described as "yearning to return to the battlefield, and this yearning . . . intensified as he witnessed the brothers around him all attaining shahadah one after another" (*Rumiyah Magazine*, November 11, 2016, p. 15).

AUTHORITY

Finally, terrorist groups and hate groups will often seek to gain credibility for their beliefs by claiming that their ideology and practices are derived from religious beliefs or books or are consistent with those of religious leaders. Many white supremacist or white nationalist groups base their white supremacist claims on Christian Identity doctrine or by associating themselves with Nordic mythology and Odinism (see chapter 4 on Christian Identity). Islamic extremists make reference to the Qur'an, Sharia, hadiths, and notable Islamic scholars (see chapter 5 on Islamist terror in America; the Al Qa'idy training manual referenced; or any issue of *Inspire*, *Dabiq*, or *Rumiyah*) to justify their beliefs and practices. Sovereign citizens, depending on their bent, base their claims on the Magna Carta, the Constitution of the United States, Admiral Law, the teaching of Noble Drew Ali, or the leadership of the "Empress" Verdiacee "Tiara" Washitaw-Turner Goston El-Bey (see chapter 6 on the Sovereign Citizens Movement). The power of authority lies in the fact that we have been taught to unthinkingly defer to authority because doing so is correct (Foushee, 1984; Galanti, 1993; Milgram, 1974).

In summary, hate groups and terrorist groups have become as savvy as professional advertisers in the tactics they use to promote their ideology and persuade people of their righteousness. How can their efforts be combatted?

Should Hate Speech Be Banned?

Given all of the strategies used by extremist groups and terrorist groups used to persuade people of the righteousness of their cause as well as their extensive efforts to distribute their message, is society's only recourse against these groups banning their message?

Banning hate speech might seem like a good idea, but will it stop hate? As mentioned previously, attempts to ban hate speech online tend to push purveyors of hate to invent more creative ways to deliver their message rather than to give up promoting their beliefs or to stop hating. If a hate group or terrorist's website is banned, the site organizers may try to relist their site using a different name, find another site host, tone down their overt message enough to avoid censorship, or move off the surface web. The result is that the purveyors of hate are forced to work harder in order to deliver their message. Extensive research on self-perception theory (Bem, 1967, 1972; Burger & Caldwell, 2003) and effort justification (Aronson & Mills, 1959) suggests that this will cause those who hate to cling more strongly to their own message, further entrenching them in their beliefs. Consistent with these theories, when the purveyors of hate look at their own behaviors, they will think, if I worked this hard to get my message out, I must really believe it.

Will banning hate speech prevent others from hating or thwart the attempts of the purveyors of hate to recruit new members to these groups? Given the reasons why people hate (Valeri, in press) and the variety of recruitment strategies used by hate groups, it is not only unlikely that attempts to ban hate will be successful but also that attempts to limit access to hate messages will either keep people from hating or from finding information and groups consistent with their beliefs.

There are at least five reasons why hate speech should not be banned. The first is that free speech is vital to democracy, it "is the lifeblood of democracy and an indispensable element of freedom . . . it is the guarantor of civil society. It protects the press, the academy, religion, political parties, and nonprofit associations" (Cole, September 28, 2017). The American Civil Liberties Union (ACLU) is perhaps one of the best sources of information on free speech, its importance to democracy, and why free speech needs to be defended (see www.aclu.org/issues/free-speech for a full discussion). The need to defend free speech is as important today as it was in the past. Esseks (August 9, 2017) as well as others (Cole, September 28, 2017; Herman, November 20, 2015; Rowland, April 20, 2017; April 25, 2017) make clear why defending free speech today is still so vital. Esseks (August 9, 2017) notes several examples of recent attacks on free speech, including one by the Washington Metropolitan Area Transit Authority to ban the ACLU from "put[ting] up ads that show the text of the First Amendment (yes, really) in English, Spanish, and Arabic" (Esseks, August 9, 2017). Esskes also provides several historical examples of the First Amendment being used to defend the rights of people involved in the Civil Rights movements, including the "fight for women's rights. . . . When Virginia made it a crime to publish an ad stating, 'Unwanted Pregnancy—Let Us Help You' . . . it was the First Amendment that protected the right of the public to receive such information" (Esskes, August 9, 2017). It is clear from these examples why it is important to defend free speech, including the speech of people whose views are unpopular or different from our own.

The second reason against banning hate speech, including, and perhaps especially, hate speech in cyberspace is that doing so makes it more difficult for law enforcement and counterterrorist organizations to monitor these groups. Neumann (2012) recommended that rather than banning extremist groups and their messages from cyberspace that terrorist online communications should be exploited. Information available on the Internet from the terrorists themselves can be used to "detect shifts in intentions and priorities, pick up on arguments, cleavages, fault lines, and new tactics . . . identify the people who are involved in . . . radicalization and recruitment [and] in foiling terrorist plots and preventing terrorist attacks" (Neumann, 2012, p. 41). In addition to using the information available in cyberspace to gather information on the terrorist themselves, their recruitment strategies, and plans, the information available on cyberspace can also provide a rich source of evidence for prosecutors.

As a psychologist, I can think of three additional reasons why banning hate speech and terrorist messages is not a good solution. The first reason has to do with scarcity and the psychological reactance that occurs when constraints are placed on our ability to have something. When something becomes less available, people tend to want it more whether it is love, detergent, or information (Cialdini, 2009; Driscoll, Davis, & Lipetz, 1972; Mazis, 1975; Mazis, Settle, & Leslie, 1973; Worchel, & Arnold, 1973; Worchel, Arnold, & Baker, 1975; Worchel, Lee, & Adewole, 1975). Research by Worchel, Arnold, and Baker (1975) reveals the strength of psychological reactance. These researchers found that banning information, even counter-attitudinal information such as the banning of a speech opposing coed dorms, can make people, in this case college students, desire that information more and be more accepting of it. Consistent with this, attempts to ban the messages of hate groups and terrorist groups will only increase both the desire to access this information and acceptance of it. As Cialdini (2009) notes

> Perhaps the authors of this country's [the United States] Constitution were acting as much as sophisticated social psychologists as staunch civil libertarians when they wrote the remarkably permissive free speech provision of the First Amendment. By refusing to restrain freedom of speech, they may have been trying to minimize the chance that new political notions would win support via the irrational course of psychological reactance.
>
> (Cialdini, 2009, pp. 210–211)

Furthermore, as we have seen with the Dailystormer and groups like ISIS and Al Qaeda, attempts to ban them from the surface web are never completely successful. Rather, it causes them to come up with new names or go elsewhere. The result is that people who are searching for information from these groups will be forced to invest more time and effort in finding them. As previously discussed, self-perception theory and effort justification suggest that this will cause individuals who are searching for this information to work harder to find it and, as a result, to believe more strongly in the message. Lastly, while some groups may move to the Dark Web or keep changing their names, other groups will tone done their message enough so that they are not censored. Doing so may result in the posted information falling into the latitude of acceptance or non-commitment of a greater number of people. This could start these individuals down the path of accepting more extreme positions, especially if they either show up for an event hosted by one of these groups or if they have to become a member of the group in order to access additional information. In either case, the person may look at their behavior, I came to this meeting or I joined this group, and consistent with self-perception assume that they must agree with the position advocated. Furthermore, a naïve individual who finds themselves on the webpage of an extremist group with a toned-down image or "soft sell" approach to hate may not recognize the extremist agenda hidden in the web content and accept the information as fact (Borgeson & Valeri, 2004; Valeri & Borgeson, 2005).

So, rather than banning the speech of hate groups and terrorist groups, what should be done? The ACLU and, more recently, Neumann (December 2012) and Cimmino (June 24, 2016) have suggested countering these messages.

Counter-Messaging

Neumann (December 2012) outlines several strategies for countering online radicalization. Neumann notes that most people who are radicalized online maintain in-person relationships. Therefore, countering online radicalization begins by teaching people, parents, educators, medical providers, religious leaders, and children themselves, the signs of online radicalization. Just as parents, educators, medical providers, and others are taught to identify signs of abuse or how to protect children from online or in-person threats, we need to teach these same individuals how to protect youth from online radicalization and also to recognize the signs of online radicalization.

People who join extremist groups, whether they are hate groups or terrorist groups, are looking for something in their lives. Alternatives to hate groups and terrorist organizations need to exist, they need to be known, and they need to be welcoming. While there are many civic, school related, and religious groups available, communities may need to develop more. Also, the presence and voices of these alternative groups need to be heard online and off. The difficulty for many of these groups, whether it's a scouting group, sports team/club, volunteer fire department, etc., is that delivering appealing messages takes knowledge and resources. For many of these groups, self-promotion or recruitment is not their forte, so these skills and resources need to be developed.

In addition to offering alternatives to hate groups and terrorist organizations, actions to counter the messages and recruitment efforts of these groups can also be undertaken. The messages of these groups can be directly challenged in cyberspace with " . . . messages that aim to 'mock . . . or undermine their credibility'; contrast . . . violent extremists' grandiose claims and the reality and/or consequences of their actions; or positive alternatives that cancel out or negate the violent extremists' ideology or lifestyle" (Neumann, December 2012, p. 34). Furthermore, recruitment efforts by hate groups and terrorist organizations may be directly challenged by " . . . go[ing] to the virtual places where extremist messages are being purveyed and engage actual and potential violent extremists in dialogue and discussion" (Neumann, December 2012, p. 35).

In February 2016, Monika Bickert (Beloff, March 2, 2016), the head of global policy management at Facebook, addressed the Policy Forum at The Washington Institute. During that address, Bickert discussed Facebook's efforts to ensure that terrorist groups are not using Facebook as a recruitment platform. Bickert said that not only does Facebook not allow members of terrorist groups or violent organizations to have a presence on their site, something they manage by barring these individuals from the site, removing users who violate their policies, or removing specific content in instances when there is not sufficient cause to close an account, but that they also promote speech that counters the messages of these groups. In order to make counter-speech more effective, Facebook conducted research with Demos, a British think tank, to determine what made counter-speech effective. This research revealed three factors important to effective counter-speech. Message format, especially the inclusion of visual image coupled with conciseness, is key to success. Message tone also impacts message success. Positive and constructive messages were found to be more effective than attack messages. Finally, for a message to be effective, the speaker must be appropriate to the audience. For example, celebrities or another young person tend to be more effective than government officials or other authority figures if the message is for a young adult/youth audience. In closing, Bickert noted that because cyberspace is constantly evolving, the tactics used by Facebook and other organizations used to counter those of violent extremists also need to be continually updated.

Conclusion

Extremist groups, including violent extremist groups, are determined to promote their agenda and recruit new members. These groups have become quite savvy in using any and all means to deliver their message. Furthermore, they have honed the tactics used by professional advertisers to promote their cause. While banning hate speech does not appear to be either a desirable or effective solution that leaves countering the messages and efforts of violent extremists. As discussed in the preceding section on counter-messaging, to do so effectively requires the efforts of individuals as well as both public and private organizations.

REFERENCES

Alexander, H. (September 22, 2013). Tweeting terrorism: How al-Shabaab live blogged he Nairobi terrorist attack. *The Telegraph*. Retrieved from www.telegraph.co.uk/news/worldnews/africaandindianocean/kenya/10326863/Tweeting-terrorism-How-al-Shabaab-live-blogged-the-Nairobi-attacks.html

Al Qa'idy, A. A. (n.d.). A course in the art of recruiting: A graded, practical program for recruiting via individual da'wa.

Aronson, E. & Mills, J. (1959). The effect of severity of initiation on liking for a group. *Journal of Abnormal and Social Psychology, 59*, 177–181.

Astor, M., Caron, C., & Victor, D. (August 13, 2017). A guide to the Charlottesville aftermath. *New York Times*. Retrieved from www.nytimes.com/2017/08/13/us/charlottesville-virginia-overview.html?mcubz=0

Baumeister, R. F. & Leary, M. R. (1995). The need to belong: Desire for interpersonal attachments as a fundamental human motivation. *Psychological Bulleting, 117*, 497–529.

Becker, P. J., Byers, B., & Jipson, A. (March, 2000). The contentious American debate: "The first amendment and internet-based hate speech." *International Review of Law, Computers and Technology, 14*, 33–39.

Beirich, H. (Summer, 2014). White homicide worldwide. *Southern Poverty Law Center*. Retrieved from www.splcenter.org/sites/default/files/d6_legacy_files/downloads/publication/white-homicide-worldwide.pdf

Beloff, J. (March 2, 2016). Internet security and privacy in the age of the Islamic State. Policy Analysis. The Washington Institute. Retrieved from http://www.washingtoninstitute.org/policy-analysis/view/internet-security-and-privacy-in-the-age-of-the-islamic-state

Bem, D. J. (1967). Self-perception theory: An alternative explanation of cognitive dissonance phenomena. *Psychological Review, 74*, 183–200.

Bem, D. J. (1972). Self-perception theory. In L. Berkowitz (Ed.), *Advances in experimental social psychology* (Vol. 6, pp. 1–62). New York: Academic Press.

Berger, J. M. (June 16, 2014). How ISIS games Twitter. *The Atlantic*. Retrieved from www.theatlantic.com/international/archive/2014/06/isis-iraq-twitter-social-media-strategy/372856/

Berger, J. M. (2015). Tailored online interventions: The Islamic State's recruitment strategy. *CTC Sentinel, 8*, 19–23. Retrieved from https://ctc.usma.edu/tailored-online-interventions-the-islamic-states-recruitment-strategy/

Berger, J. M. (September 2016). Nazis vs. ISIS on Twitter: A comparative study of white nationalist and ISIS online social media networks. Program on Extremism. George Washington University, Washington, DC. Retrieved from https://cchs.gwu.edu/files/downloads/Nazis%2520v.%2520ISIS%2520Final_0.pdf

Berger, J. M. & Morgan, J. (March 2015). The ISIS Twitter census: Defining and describing the population of ISIS supporters on Twitter. The Brookings Project on U.S. Relations with the Islamic World. Analysis Paper, No. 20. Center for Middle East Policy, The Brookings Institution. Retrieved from https://www.brookings.edu/wp-content/uploads/2016/06/isis_twitter_census_berger_morgan.pdf

Berscheid, E. & Walster, E. (1978). *Interpersonal attraction*. Reading, MA: Addison-Wesley.

Bierley, C., McSweeney, F. K., & Vannieuwkerk, R. (1985). Classical conditioning preferences of stimuli. *Journal of Consumer Research, 12*, 316–323.

Blaskovich, J., Ginsburg, G. P., & Howe, R. C. (1975). Blackjack and the risky shift. II: Monetary stakes. *Journal of Experimental Social Psychology, 11*, 224–232.

Bodine-Baron, E., Helmus, T.C., Magnuson, M., & Winkelman, Z. (2016). *Examining ISIS support and opposition networks on Twitter*. Santa Monica, CA: Rand Corporation.

Borgeson, K. & Valeri, R. M. (2004). Faces of hate. *Journal of Applied Sociology, 21*(2), 99–111.

Borgeson, K. & Valeri, R. M. (2005). Examining differences in skinhead ideology and culture through an analysis of skinhead websites. *Michigan Sociological Review, 19*, 45–62.

Borgeson, K. & Valeri, R. M. (2017). *Skinhead history, identity, and culture*. New York: Routledge.

Bouchard, K. (January 30, 2017). Ku Klux Klan fliers shock residents of Freeport, Augusta Neighborhoods. *Portland Press Herald*. Retrieved from https://www.pressherald.com/2017/01/30/kkk-fliers-disturb-residents-of-freeport-neighborhood/

Bright Planet (March 27, 2014). Cleaning up confusion: Deep web vs. dark web. Retrieved from https://brightplanet.com/2014/03/clearing-confusion-deep-web-vs-dark-web/

Burger, J. M. & Caldwell, D. F. (2003). The effects of monetary incentives and labeling on the foot-in-the-door effect: Evidence for a self-perception process. *Basic and Applied Social Psychology, 25*, 235–241.

Burnstein, E. & Vinokur, A. (1973). Testing two classes of theories about group-induced shifts in individual choice. *Journal of Experimental Social Psychology, 9*, 123–137.

Byrne, D. (1971). *The attraction paradigm*. New York: Academic Press.

Calamur, K. (February 5, 2016). Twitter shuts down 125,000 ISIS related accounts. *The Atlantic*. Retrieved from www.theatlantic.com/international/archive/2016/02/twitter-isis/460269/

Callimachi, R. (June 27, 2015). ISIS and the lonely young American. *New York Times*. Retrieved from www.nytimes.com/2015/06/28/world/americas/isis-online-recruiting-american.html

Carlson, N. (April 13, 2011). The real history of Twitter. *Business Insider*. Retrieved from www.businessinsider.com/how-twitter-was-founded-2011-4?op=1

Cialdini, R. (2009). *Influence: Science and practice* (5th Ed.). Boston, MA: Pearson Education, Inc.

Cimmino, J. (June 24, 2016). Countering online radicalization. *Foreign Policy Initiative Bulletin*.

Codol, J. P. (1975). On the so called 'superior conformity of the self' behavior: Twenty experimental investigations. *European Journal of Social Psychology, 5*, 457–501.

Cole, D. (September 28, 2017). Why we must still defend free speech. *The New York Review of Books*. Retrieved from www.nybooks.com/articles/2017/09/28/why-we-must-still-defend-free-speech/

Cook, B. (n.d.). *Watcher on the Tower and the Washington State Ku Klux Klan: Seattle Civil Rights and Labor History Project*. University of Washington. Retrieved from http://depts.washington.edu/civilr/kkk_wot.htm

Coveners League (n.d.). Stormfront. Retrieved from http://covenersleague.com/recommended-links/stormfront

Crocker, B. (August 26, 2017, updated August 29, 2017). White supremacist forum site Stormfront seized by domain host. *Knoxville News Sentinel*. Retrieved from www.knoxnews.com/story/news/2017/08/26/white-supremacist-forum-site-stormfront-seized-domain-hosts/604902001/

Davis, A. (August 2, 2016). Neo-Nazi group plans event in Potter County. *The Bradford Era*. Retrieved from www.bradfordera.com/news/neo-nazi-group-plans-event-in-potter-county/article_3c6dc492-585a-11e6-9d59-ff42f-ocffbc5.html

Davis, A. (August 30, 2016). Potter County becoming hotbed of white supremacist activity. *The Bradford Era*. Retrieved from www.bradfordera.com/news/potter-county-becoming-hotbed-of-white-supremacy/article_dd1c3c62-6e52-11e6-89ab-b3c744a3af99.html

Dovidio, J. F., Gaertner, S. I., Shnabel, N., Saguy, T., & Johnson, J. (2010). Recategorization and prosocial behavior: Common in-group identity and a dual identity. In S. Stürmer & M. Snyder (Eds.), *The psychology of prosocial behavior: Group processes, intergroup relations, and helping* (pp. 191–207). Hoboken, NJ: Wiley Blackwell.

Downloading hate (1999, November 13). *Economist, 353*, 30–31.

Driscoll, R., Davis, K. K., & Lipetz, M. E. (1972). Parental interference and romantic love: The Romeo and Juliet effect. *Journal of Personality and Social Psychology, 24*, 1–10.

Eagly, A. H. & Chaiken, S. (1993). *The psychology of attitudes*. Philadelphia, PA: Harcourt Brace Jovanovich College Publishers.

Ebdrup, N. (October 10, 2012). How Nazis turn youth into extremists. *Science Nordic*. Retrieved from http://sciencenordic.com/how-nazis-turn-youths-extremists

Eckholm, E. (December 27, 2015). ISIS influence on web prompts second thoughts on First Amendment. *New York Times*. Retrieved from www.nytimes.com/2015/12/28/us/isis-influence-on-web-prompts-second-thoughts-on-first-amendment.html

Esseks, J. (August 9, 2017). How could you represent someone like Milo Yiannopoulos? *American Civil Liberties Union*. Retrieved from www.aclu.org/blog/free-speech/how-could-you-represent-someone-milo-yiannopoulos

Festinger, L. (1954). A theory of social comparison processes. *Human Relations, 7*, 117–140.

Foushee, M. C. (1984). Dyads and triads at 35,000 feet. *American Psychologists, 39*, 885–893.

Fraser, C., Gouge, C., & Billig, M. (1971). Risky shifts, cautious shifts, and group polarization. *European Journal of Social Psychology, 1*, 7–30.

Galanti, G. A. (1993). Reflections on brainwashing. In M. D. Langone (Ed.), *Recovery from cults* (pp. 85–103). New York: Norton.

Greenberg, J., Solomon, S., & Pyszzynski, T. (1997). Terror management theory of self-esteem and cultural worldviews: Empirical assessments and conceptual refinements. *Advances in Experimental Social Psychology, 26*, 61–139.

Gta V isis version (n.d.). Retrieved from www.youtube.com/watch?v=d2VCW1m2oKw

Hall, M. (November 1, 2014). 'This is our call of duty': How ISIS is using video games. *Salon*. Retrieved from www.salon.com/2014/11/01/this_is_our_call_of_duty_how_isis_is_using_video_games/

Hankes, K. (November 21, 2014). White power music was in trouble: But then racist bands discovered iTunes, and now they're back in business. Music, Money, and Hate (2014 Winter Issue). *Southern Poverty Law Center*. Retrieved from www.splcenter.org/fighting-hate/intelligence-report/2014/music-money-hate

Hankes, K. & Zhang, S. (February 22, 2017). A waning storm: Once the world's most popular white nationalist website, Stormfront is running out of steam. Hatewatch. Southern Poverty Law Center. Retrieved from https://www.splcenter.org/hatewatch/2017/02/22/waning-storm-once-world%E2%80%99s-most-popular-white-nationalist-website-stormfront-running-out

Hassan, S. (2015). *Combatting cult mind control*. Newton, MA: Freedom of Mind Press.

Herman, S. N. (November 20, 2015). The power of speech. American Civil Liberties Union. Retrieved from www.aclu. org/blog/free-speech/power-speech

Hern, A. (August 23, 2017). The dilemma of the dark web: Protecting neo-Nazis and dissidents alike. *The Guardian.* Retrievedfromwww.theguardian.com/technology/2017/aug/23/dark-web-neo-nazis-tor-dissidents-white-supremacists-criminals-paedophile-rings

Inspire Magazine (Summer 1431, 2010). How to use Asrar al-Mujahideen: Sending and receiving encrypted messages. *Inspire Magazine.* Al-Malahem Media.

Internet World Stats (n.d.). Internet users in the world by region—June 30, 2017. *Internet World Stats: Usage and Population Statistics.* Retrieved from www.internetworldstats.com/stats.htm

Jan, T. (August 16, 2017). PayPal escalates the tech industries war on white supremacy. *The Washington Post.* Retrieved from www.washingtonpost.com/news/wonk/wp/2017/08/16/paypal-escalates-the-tech-industrys-war-on-white-supremacy/?utm_term=.8ca84c957e11

Kasuba, J. (February 15, 2017). KKK fliers distributed in Riverview neighborhood on Valentine's Day. *News-Herald.* Retrieved from www.thenewsherald.com/news/kkk-fliers-distributed-in-riverview-neighborhood-on-valentine-s-day/article_667e371d-a9dc-5e05-b300-9748662a06be.html

Katz, R. (July 14, 2016). Almost any messenger app will do—If you're ISIS. *Motherboard.* Retrieved from https:// motherboard.vice.com/en_us/article/kb7n4a/isis-messaging-apps

Klan Watch Project (2011). Ku Klux Klan: A history of racism and violence. Southern Poverty Law Center. Retrieved from https://www.splcenter.org/sites/default/files/Ku-Klux-Klan-A-History-of-Racism.pdf

Leary, M. R. (Ed.) (2001). *Interpersonal rejection.* New York: Oxford University Press.

Leary, M. R. & Baumeister, R. F. (2000). The nature and function of self-esteem: Sociometer theory. *Advances in Experimental Social Psychology, 32,* 1–62.

Levine, M., Prosser, A., Evans, D., & Reicher, S. (2005). Identity and emergency intervention: How social group membership and inclusiveness of group boundaries shape helping behavior. *Personality and Social Psychology Bulletin, 31,* 443–453.

Los Angeles Times (January 19, 2015). Residents find KKK propaganda around Santa Ana neighborhood. *Los Angeles Times.* Retrieved from www.latimes.com/local/lanow/82576742-157.html

Lott, A. J., & Lott, B. E. (1965). Group cohesiveness as interpersonal attraction: A review of relationship with antecedent and consequent variables. *Psychological Bulletin, 64,* 259–309.

Ludwig, J. (November 17, 2014). From white American youth to life after hate: Former racist skinhead vocalist pens memoir about his road to peace. *Interviews, Noisey.Vice.Com.* Retrieved from https://noisey.vice.com/en_us/article/from-white-american-youth-to-life-after-hate-former-racist-skinhead-vocalist-pens-memoir-about-his-road-to-peace

Mackie, D. & Cooper, J. (1984). Attitude polarization: Effects of group membership. *Journal of Personality and Social Psychology, 46,* 575–85.

Marshall, A. (November 9, 2014). How Isis got its anthem. *The Guardian.* Retrieved from www.theguardian.com/music/2014/nov/09/nasheed-how-isis-got-its-anthem

Maslow, A. H. (1968). *Toward a psychology of being.* New York: Van Nostrand.

Maslow, A. H. (1970). *Motivation and personality.* New York: Harper & Row.

Mazis, M. B. (1975). Antipollution measures and psychological reactance theory: A field experiment. *Journal of Personality and Social Psychology, 31,* 654–666.

Mazis, M. B., Settle, R. B., & Leslie, D. C. (1973). Elimination of phosphate detergents and psychological reactance. *Journal of Marketing Research, 10,* 390–395.

Mekhennet, S. (August 31, 2011). German officials alarmed by ex-rapper's new message: Jihad. *New York Times.* Retrieved from www.nytimes.com/2011/09/01/world/europe/01jihadi.html

Milgram, S. (1974). *Obedience to authority: An experimental view.* New York: Harper & Row.

Moghaddam, F. M. (2005). Cultural preconditions for potential terrorist groups: Terrorism and societal change. In F. M. Moghaddam & A. J. Marsella (Eds.), *Understanding terrorism: Psychological roots, consequences, and interventions* (pp. 103–118). Washington, DC: American Psychological Association.

Nance, M. & Sampson, C. (2017). *Hacking ISIS: How to destroy the cyber jihad*. New York: Skyhorse Publishing.

Neumann, P. (December 2012). Countering online radicalization in America. Homeland Security Project: National Security Program: Bipartisan Policy Center. Retrieved from https://bipartisanpolicy.org/wp-content/uploads/sites/default/files/BPC%20_Online%20Radicalization%20Report.pdf

O'Neil, P. H. (June 23, 2015). The online security of white supremacists. *The Daily Dot*. Retrieved from www.dailydot.com/layer8/white-supremacist-stormfront-opsec-encryption/

O'Neil, P. H. (April 13, 2016). ISIS recommends list of secure-messaging apps amid heated U.S. encryption debate. *The Daily Dot*. Retrieved from www.dailydot.com/layer8/isis-telegram-encryption-messenger-recommendations/

Pieslak, J. (2015). *Radicalism & music: An introduction to the music cultures of al-Qa'ida, racist skinheads, Christian-affiliated radicals, and eco-animal rights militants*. Middletown, CT: Wesleyan University Press.

Razran, G. H. S. (1938). Conditional away social bias by the luncheon technique. *Psychological Bulletin, 35,* 693.

Razran, G. H. S. (1940). Conditional response changes in ratings and appraising sociopolitical slogans. *Psychological Bulletin, 37,* 481.

Regan, D. T. (1971). Effects of a favor and liking on compliance. *Journal of Experimental Social Psychology, 7,* 627–639.

Rind, B. & Strohmetz, D. B. (2001). Effect on restaurant tipping of a helpful message written on the back of customers' checks. *Journal of Applied Social Psychology, 32,* 398–412.

Rowland, L. (April 20, 2017). Donald Trump has free speech rights, too. American Civil Liberties Union. Retrieved from www.aclu.org/blog/free-speech/donald-trump-has-free-speech-rights-too

Rowland, L. (2017). We all need to defend speech we hate. American Civil Liberties Union. Retrieved from www.aclu.org/blog/free-speech/we-all-need-defend-speech-we-hate *Rumiyah Issue 3*. Among the Believers Are Men.

Rumiyah Magazine (November, 11, 2016). Among the believers are men: Abu' Abdillah al-Britani. *Ruminyah Magazine*.

Sanders, G. S. & Baron, R. S. (1977). Is social comparison irrelevant for producing choice shifts? *Journal of Experimental Social Psychology, 13,* 303–314.

Schafer, J. R. & Navarro, J. (March, 2003). The seven stage hate model: The psychopathology of hate groups. *FBI Law Enforcement Bulletin*.

Schulberg, J., Liebelson, D., & Craggs, T. (October 3, 2017). The neo-Nazis are back online. *Huffington Post*. Retrieved from www.huffingtonpost.com/entry/nazis-are-back-online_us_59d40719e4b06226e3f46941

Seiter, J. S. (2007). Ingratiation and gratuity: The effect of complementing customers on tipping behavior in restaurants. *Journal of Applied Social Psychology, 37,* 478–485.

Selk, A. (August 16, 2017). A running list of companies that no longer want the Daily Stormer's business. *The Washington Post*. Retrieved from www.washingtonpost.com/news/the-switch/wp/2017/08/16/how-the-alt-right-got-kicked-offline-after-charlottesville-from-uber-to-google/?utm_term=.a9a326e5720f

Seymat, T. (August 10, 2014). How nasheeds became the soundtrack of jihad. *Euronews*. Retrieved from www.euronews.com/2014/10/08/nasheeds-the-soundtrack-of-jihad

Shane, S. (August 27, 2015). The lessons of Anwar al-Awlaki. *New York Times*. Retrieved from www.nytimes.com/2015/08/30/magazine/the-lessons-of-anwar-al-awlaki.html

Sherif, M. & Hovland, C. J. (1961). *Social judgment: Assimilation and contrast effects in communication and attitude change*. New Haven, CT: Yale University Press.

Sherif, M., Taub, D., & Hovland, C. I. (1958). Assimilation and contrast effects of anchoring stimuli on judgements. *Journal of Experimental Psychology, 55,* 150–155.

Smirke, R. (October 10, 2014). Jihadi rap: Understanding the subculture. *Billboard*. Retrieved from www.billboard.com/articles/news/6273809/jihadi-rap-l-jinny-abdel-majed-abdel-bary

Speyer, L. (January 18, 2017). Despicable antisemitic cyber attack at Tennessee campus outrages Jewish student community. *The Algemeiner*. Retrieved from www.algemeiner.com/2017/01/18/despicable-antisemitic-cyber-attack-at-tennessee-campus-outrages-jewish-student-community/

SPLC (December 8, 2014). iTunes pulls hate music following SPLC report, Amazon and Spotify slow to act. *News*. Retrieved from www.splcenter.org/news/2014/12/08/itunes-pulls-hate-music-following-splc-report-amazon-and-spotify-slow-act

SPLC (March 9, 2015). iTunes drops hate music, but Spotify and Amazon still selling: Intelligence report (2015 Spring issue). Southern Poverty Law Center. Retrieved from www.splcenter.org/fighting-hate/intelligence-report/2015/itunes-dumps-hate-music-spotify-and-amazon-still-selling

SPLC (August 29, 2017). Waning storm: Stormfront.org loses its domain. *Hatewatch*. Retrieved from https://www.splcenter.org/hatewatch/2017/08/29/waning-storm-stormfrontorg-loses-its-domain

Stormfront Forum (July 4, 2016). 2016 Australian Ian Stuart Memorial Concert - Blood & Honour and Southern Cross Hammerskins. Retrieved from https://www.stormfront.org/forum/t1166141/

Strohmetz, D. B., Rind, B., Fisher, R., & Lynn, M. (2002). Sweetening the till: The use of candy to increase restaurant tipping. *Journal of Applied Social Psychology, 32*, 300–309.

Stuster (April 29, 2013). 9 Disturbingly good jihadi raps: OK maybe not so 'good'. *Foreign Policy*. Retrieved from http://foreignpolicy.com/2013/04/29/9-disturbingly-good-jihadi-raps/

Surowiecki, J. (2004). *The wisdom of crowds*. New York: Doubleday.

Tassi, P. (September 20, 2014). ISIS uses 'GTA 5' in teen recruitment video. *Forbes*. Retrieved from www.forbes.com/sites/insertcoin/2014/09/20/isis-uses-gta-5-in-new-teen-recruitment-video/#553e5fe0681f

Taylor, J. (January 25, 2017). Spread the message of white consciousness. *American Renaissance*. Retrieved from www.amren.com/commentary/2017/01/spread-message-white-consciousness/

Telegram (n.d.). Telegram: A new era of messaging. Retrieved from https://telegram.org/

United States of America v Ali Shukri Amin (June 11, 2015). Case 1:15-cr-00164-CMH Document 7 filed in the United States District Court for the Eastern District of Virginia Alexandria Division. Retrieved from www.justice.gov/opa/file/477366/download

Valeri, R. M. (in press). Why do we hate? In R. M. Valeri & K. Borgeson (Eds.), *Hate crimes: Victims, motivations and typologies*. Durham, NC: Carolina Academic Press.

Valeri, R. M. & Borgeson, K. (2005). Identifying the face of hate. *Journal of Applied Sociology, 22*, 91–104.

Valeri, R. M. & Borgeson, K. (2016). Sticks and stones: When the words of hatred become weapons, a social psychological perspective. In S. Harding & M. Palasinski (Eds.), *Global perspectives on youth gang behavior, violence, and weapons* (pp. 101–132). Hershey, PA: IGI Global.

Valeri, R.M., Sweazy, N. & Borgeson, K. (2017). An analysis of skinhead websites and social networks, a decade later. *Michigan Sociological Review, 31*, 77–106.

Vinokur, A. & Burnstein, E. (1974). Effects of partially shared persuasive arguments on group-induced shifts: A group problem solving approach. *Journal of Personality and Social Psychology, 29*, 305–315.

Wakin, D. J. (May 18, 2003). Aftereffects: Beirut; Video game created by militant group mounts simulated attacks against Israeli targets. *New York Times*. Retrieved from www.nytimes.com/2003/05/18/world/aftereffects-beirut-video-game-created-militant-group-mounts-simulated-attacks.html?mcubz=1

Watcher on the Tower (September 1, 1923). The Royal Riders initiate another large class. In *Watcher on the Tower* (p. 4). Seattle Civil Rights and Labor History Project, University of Washington. Retrieved from http://depts.washington.edu/civilr/kkk_rrrr.htm

Weinberg, L. (2008). *Global terrorism*. Oxford: Oneworld Publications.

Whitegenocideproject.com (n.d.). Retrieved from http://whitegenocideproject.com/pro-white-terminology/

Winds of Paradise (n.d.). 'Winds of Paradise' part 3. Retrieved from https://archive.org/details/winds-of-heaven-3

Wootson, C. R., Jr. (October 15, 2016). 'It will be a bloodbath': Inside the Kansas militia's plot to ignite a religious war. *The Washington Post.* Retrieved from www.washingtonpost.com/news/post-nation/wp/2016/10/15/it-will-be-a-bloodbath-inside-the-kansas-militia-plot-to-ignite-a-religious-war/?utm_term=.31df7db38cd6

Worchel, S. & Arnold, S. E. (1973). The effects of censorship and the attractiveness of the censor on attitude change. *Journal of Experimental Social Psychology, 9,* 365–377.

Worchel, S., Arnold, S. E., & Baker, M. (1975). The effect of censorship on attitude change: The influence of censor and communicator characteristics. *Journal of Applied Social Psychology, 5,* 229–239.

Worchel, S., Lee, J., & Adewole, A. (1975). Effects of supply and demand on ratings of object value. *Journal of Personality and Social Psychology, 32,* 906–914.

Wright, S. (February 5, 2014). Fanatics in Syria vow to bring terror home to the UK: Terrorists say they will attack public transport and financial centers. *The Daily Mail.* Retrieved from www.dailymail.co.uk/news/article-2552626/Fanatics-Syria-vow-bring-terror-UK-Terrorists-vow-attack-public-transport-financial-centres.html

Chapter 8

Killing Alone

Can the Work Performance Literature Help Us Solve the Enigma of Lone Wolf Terrorism?

Joel A. Capellan

Overview

- Over the years, researchers have identified a number of important recurring patterns and characteristics in lone wolf terrorism.
- Despite seemingly knowing the constellation of recurring factors that may set individuals on a path to radicalization and subsequent lone wolf terrorism, we lack a clear understanding of how these fit together.
- The construct of employees with "lone wolf tendencies" is relevant to the study of lone wolf terrorism in that it places an analytical emphasis on a key turning point in their radicalization and subsequent careers as terrorists—the decision to work alone.
- Additionally, I also argue that the construct of lone wolf tendencies may itself be a risk factor for radicalization and ideologically motivated lone-actor violence.
- By projecting the work performance literature onto the field of lone wolf terrorism, the construct of employees with lone wolf tendencies begins to act as an organizing principle to the constellation of causes found in the phenomenon of lone wolf terrorism.

Introduction

In recent years, lone wolf terrorism has become a top concern for U.S. government officials. The U.S. Department of Homeland Security (DHS) announced that domestically radicalized individuals posed the most dangerous threat to the national security of the United States (DHS, 2009). This is particularly the case for right-wing extremist groups, which according to the report, are actively recruiting by playing on the fear of an economic apocalypse, the institution of sharia law on U.S. soil, and illegal immigration. However, the threat also comes from across the ideological spectrum, with jihad-inspired groups like Al-Qaeda and ISIS, which have also taken to the Internet to spread their extremist ideologies. Across the ideological spectrum, extremist organizations are encouraging individuals to engage in decentralized terror campaigns by acting alone in the commission of violent acts for ideological purposes (Bates, 2012).

These recruiting tactics have been successful in reaching and radicalizing vulnerable individuals around the world, but specifically in the United States. Research consistently shows that not only is the incidence of lone wolf terrorism higher in the United States than in other industrialized countries, but also the frequency of such attacks has been increasing since the 1950s (Hewitt, 2003; Spaaij, 2010). In 2009 alone, 43 American citizens or residents affiliated with jihadi extremist groups were charged or convicted of terrorism crimes in the U.S. or elsewhere. The plots that have been successfully executed, however, only measure part of the threat, as the statistics do not account for the plots that were thwarted by law enforcement. Dahl (2011) identified 176 terrorist plots against American targets from 1987 to 2010. Given how difficult it is to identify lone wolf terrorists, accounting for these foiled plots also fails to capture the extent of the threat, as many plots go undetected until it is too late. Take for instance, Major Nidal Malik Hasa, a U.S. Army trained soldier and psychiatrist who radicalized among his fellow soldiers, who ultimately committed one of the worst ideologically motivated mass shootings in US history when he shot 30 people, killing 13, at Fort Hood military base in 2009.

The surge in the occurrence and insidious nature of lone wolf terrorism has sparked scholarly research on the incidence, motivations, and patterns of this phenomenon. This body of research has identified a number of important recurring patterns and characteristics—from depression, personality disorders, and mental illness to thwarted professional goals, social isolation, and externalization of blame. Despite seemingly knowing the constellation of recurring factors that may set individuals on a path to radicalization and subsequent lone wolf terrorism, we lack a clear understanding of how these fit together. In other words, we lack an organizational principle that can elevate our understanding from knowing the recurring risk factors to being able to specify potential pathways into lone wolf terrorism.

In this chapter, I posit that perhaps the answer to the enigma of lone wolf terrorism lies in the one aspect shared by all lone wolves—the decision to work alone. By definition, all lone wolf terrorists decided to plan and engage in violence alone, without getting formally involved with terrorist networks that would have happily given guidance and material support. This decision is not random, as it may represent systematic attitudinal, psychological, and sociological differences between lone wolf and group-based terrorists. Therefore, examining why individuals prefer to work alone may be the key to understanding lone wolf terrorism as a phenomenon in its own right, related to, but qualitatively different from, group-based terrorism. To better understand this choice, I rely on the work performance literature, particularly the research around the construct of "employees with lone wolf tendencies." The parallels with lone wolf terrorism suggest that the construct of lone wolf tendencies may capture those systematic differences, and therefore explain why individuals take different terrorist paths. Additionally, I argue that the construct of lone wolf tendencies may act as an organizational principle to the constellation of causes of lone wolf terrorism.

Defining Lone Wolf Terrorism

At its most basic level, science is predicated in our ability to define the things we study. Whether it be planets, democracy, war, peace, or in our case lone wolf terrorism, establishing a clear and consistent definition is a prerequisite to any theoretical and empirical examination of this phenomenon. Unfortunately, there is no universally accepted definition of lone wolf terrorism (Spaaij & Hamm, 2015). This is not to say, however, that these definitional variations represent vast schisms in our understanding of the core elements of this phenomenon. Quite the contrary, most definitions would agree that lone wolf terrorism involves violence planned and executed by an individual or a number of individuals (i.e. cell/wolf pack) for ideological or political purposes (Becker, 2014; Spaaij, 2010; Spaaij & Hamm, 2015). However, there are disagreements as to the number of individuals that can be involved in the attack, the independence of activity, and the autonomy of the decision-making process. See Borum et al. (2012), Pantucci (2011), and Spaaij (2015) for an excellent discussion of these dimensions.

The variations in definitions of this phenomenon have resulted in different, but overlapping populations being studied. For instance, under the concept of lone wolf terrorism, researchers have included and analyzed non-ideological attacks (Simon, 2013); small terrorist cells consisting of less than four people (Hewitt, 2003); offenders with formal links to and under the command of terrorist organizations (Gill et al., 2014); and, of course, offenders that have self-radicalized, planned, and executed terrorist attacks alone (Becker, 2014). Naturally, these variations have created discrepancies in our understanding of lone wolf terrorism, discrepancies that cannot be easily reconciled precisely because we do not know if these are due to definitional, methodological choices or real variation within this population.

Despite the confusion, it is important to acknowledge that the considerable variation in how scholars conceptualized lone wolf terrorism has also had a positive impact on the literature. Mainly, it has forced experts to acknowledge and critically discuss the many differences found within the phenomenon of lone wolf terrorism (see Borum et al., 2012). This discussion is necessary not only from a theoretical perspective but also from a policy perspective, as different types of lone wolves may have different patterns, explanations, and situational contexts that require unique responses from law enforcement officials (Gruenewald et al., 2014). Additionally, the operational variations of lone wolf terrorism have also forced researchers to clearly define what they mean by lone wolf terrorism.

In this chapter, I draw from the works of the *Instituut voor Veiligheids-en Crisismanagenebt* (COT, 2007), Pantucci (2011), Gruenewald et al. (2014), and Borum et al. (2012) to conceptualize lone wolf terrorism. In their respective works, these authors have identified a continuum of lone wolves based on offenders' levels of connection to, direction, and support from formal terrorist organizations or networks. On one end of the spectrum, you have *isolated lone wolves*. These individuals have no formal affiliation, nor have they received any type of support, material or otherwise, from extremist organizations or networks. They radicalized, planned, and executed their attacks alone. On the other end, you have *connected lone wolves*. While they also operate alone, connected lone wolves belong to formal terrorist organizations or networks. Consequently, they are under the direct influence of a leader who provides instruction and support during the planning stage.

The theoretical discussion in this chapter is concerned only with isolated lone wolf terrorists. That is, ideologically driven attacks perpetrated by persons who operate individually; have no formal ties to terrorist organizations or networks; and whose tactics and methods are absent of direct outside support, command, or direction.

Research on Lone Wolf Terrorism

While lone wolf terrorism is not a new phenomenon, it is a relatively rare occurrence (Moskalenko & McCauley, 2011). Spaaij (2010) identified 72 lone wolf terrorist attacks in 15 countries from 1968 to 2007. During this time period, these attacks made up 1.28% of all recorded terrorist incidents. Even in the United States, where lone wolf terrorism is significantly more prevalent than in other Western countries (Spaaij, 2010), a very small minority of terrorism victims in the U.S. are killed by unaffiliated individuals (Hewitt, 2003). The rare nature of these events has made it difficult for researchers to systematically collect information on characteristics, motivations, and methods of these offenders. As a result, most studies on the subject have been based on anecdotal evidence (Gruenewald, 2011). Even after 9/11, the bulk of the studies were not empirical. According to Silke (2004), only 3% of the terrorism studies between 1970 and 2003 were empirical. However, a string of new empirical studies (Hewitt, 2003; Gill et al., 2014; Gruenewald, 2011; Gruenewald & Pridemore, 2012; Gruenewald et al., 2013; Spaaij, 2010) and data collection efforts (e.g. the Extremist Crime Database) have allowed researchers to slowly contextualize much of the anecdotal evidence and enhance our understanding of this phenomenon. Following is a synopsis of the things we know and the questions yet to be answered.

DEMOGRAPHIC AND BACKGROUND CHARACTERISTICS

Lone wolf terrorism is not inherent to one ideology or region of the world. Rather, the threat extends across the political spectrum and beyond geo-political boundaries. Lone wolf terrorists have committed heinous atrocities under the mantel of white supremacy, black nationalism, *Jihad*, and other groups across the United States and the world (Hewitt, 2003; Gill et al., 2014; Gruenewald et al., 2013; Spaaij, 2010). Given this ideological and geographic diversity, it is not surprising that a singular demographic profile does not exist for all lone wolves (McCauley et al., 2013; Spaaij, 2010). The only demographic characteristic shared by nearly all lone wolf terrorists is gender. Studies have consistently shown that the overwhelming majority (over 90%) of all lone wolf terrorist attacks are committed by men (Gill et al., 2014; Gruenewald et al., 2013; Spaaij, 2010). Beyond gender, however, the demographic characteristics that these offenders embody are as diverse as the motivations and ideologies that fuel them.

Research on group-based terrorism supports the idea that terrorists are generally wealthier and better educated than the populations from which they came (Krueger & Pischke, 1997; Lee, 2011). While there is not much data on their socio-economic backgrounds, studies on lone wolf terrorists suggest that lone wolves do not tend to come from economically deprived or socially disadvantaged backgrounds (McCauley et al., 2013). While their socio-economic background may be more privileged than most, the success of their forbearers has not translated into their personal lives. For instance, in their study of 109 lone wolf terrorists around the world, Gill et al. (2014) found that while generally having high educational achievements, lone wolf terrorists tended to be unemployed (40%). They also found that those who were employed (about 50%) mainly worked in the service (23%), construction (4.5%), and administrative (4.5%) sectors. Similar levels of unemployment have been found among lone wolf terrorists in the U.S. (Gruenewald et al., 2013). In addition to their socio-economic backgrounds, significant numbers of lone wolf terrorists, both around the world and in the U.S., served in the military and had a history of drug abuse and aggressive behavior (Gill et al., 2014; Gruenewald et al. 2013).

PSYCHOLOGICAL AND PERSONALITY CHARACTERISTICS

Relative to their group-based counterparts, lone wolf terrorists have exhibited a significantly higher rate of psychological disturbances and mental illnesses. For instance, in a cross-national study, Spaaij (2010) found substantive psychological problems among lone wolf terrorists. Of the five case studies, he found four to suffer from severe depression, three were diagnosed with personality disorder, one with compulsive disorder, and one with anxiety disorder. In a similar cross-national study, Gill et al. (2014) also found that 31% of lone wolf terrorists had a history of mental illness and personality disorder. Importantly, they found that isolated lone wolves (i.e. individuals without command and control links) were significantly more likely to suffer from mental illness and personality disorders than individuals with command and control links (i.e. connected lone wolves). These findings have also been corroborated in the United States. Hewitt (2003) found that the level of psychological disturbances among unaffiliated terrorists in the United States was high. Similarly, in perhaps the most comprehensive and methodologically sound study of its kind, Gruenewald et al. (2013) found that disconnected far-right lone wolves were significantly more likely to suffer from mental illness than lone wolves with a formal affiliation to far-right extremist organizations.

In addition to mental illness, disconnected lone wolf terrorists also exhibit a high degree of what Spaaij (2010) calls "social ineptitude." In other words, they tend to be withdrawn and awkward in social situations (Moskalenko & McCauley, 2011; Nijboer, 2012). As a result, they are generally unable to form meaningful relationships with those around them and therefore have very few friends (Spaaij, 2010). Gill et al. (2014) found that loners are social outsiders: 37% lived alone at the time of the attack, and 53% were socially isolated. Similar patterns have also been found in the United States. Springer (2009) found that the inability of these offenders to form and maintain meaningful relationships was so pervasive that it prevented them not only from having friends and establishing romantic relationships but also from joining extremist organizations. For instance, Timothy McVeigh and Terry Nichols were ostracized by the Michigan Militia because they advocated for violence.

MOTIVATIONS AND RADICALIZATION

It is not clearly understood why an individual would risk, and often sacrifice, his own life in order to attack people whom he has never met for an ideological cause. Radicalization refers to the process in which individuals or groups come to adopt extreme political, religious, or ideological views that increasingly justify violence (Moskalenko & McCauley, 2011). There are myriad channels from which normal individuals may become radicalized and decide to act (see McCauley & Moskalenko, 2008). Two channels, however, are particularly relevant to isolated lone wolf terrorists. The first one is personal grievance. Individual victimization is perhaps the most commonly cited explanation for terrorism. For instance, in 2013, Christopher Dorner hunted and killed five Orange County police officers in a series of attacks that lasted 9 days. In his manifesto, Dorner confessed to be motivated by the racial discrimination that eventually led to his firing from law enforcement.

Of course, individuals need not be personally victimized to be radicalized. There are countless examples of lone wolf terrorists being radicalized by political grievance or moral outrage from the perceived mistreatment of groups of people (McCauley & Moskalenko, 2008). The second channel of radicalization involves identification and projection, as the individual must identify with the plight of people he does not know personally and project blame onto others as a psychological justification for committing violence. For example, Robert Lewis Dear, Jr., was morally outraged by the legalization and prevalence of abortions in the United States. In his mind, he was a "warrior for babies" and Planned Parenthood was the enemy because, according to him, "they sold baby parts." Dear had never been victimized by Planned Parenthood, and no one in his family had ever undergone an abortion. However, he was able to identify with the perceived suffering of unborn children and project the blame on Planned Parenthood. This process led him to kill three and injure eight victims in an attack on a Planned Parenthood clinic in Colorado Springs.

THE ENIGMA OF LONE WOLF TERRORISM

As this very short review on the lone wolf literature highlights, there is a constellation of motivational, ideological, demographic, psychological, and social factors that may drive individuals into a path of radicalization and, ultimately, lone-actor violence. The possible combination and interactions of individual, ideological, and sociological causes are nearly endless. And therein lies the enigma of lone wolf terrorism. We seem to know all the recurring patterns and characteristics of these individuals, yet we do not have a clear understanding of how they all fit together. In other words, we lack an organizational principle that allows us to make sense of the known constellation of determinants of lone wolf terrorism.

In this chapter, I argue that the answer to the enigma of lone wolf terrorism may very well lie in the name itself—*lone* wolf. All isolated lone wolf terrorists, radicalized, planned, and committed the attacks alone. Their preference to work alone, whether it be by choice or by an inability to work with others, may very well be the organizing principle we need to make sense of the complex constellation of recurring patterns and risk factors to ideologically motivated lone-actor violence. This is by no means the first time that social ineptitude or social isolation has been identified as a potential risk factor. As noted, social ineptitude is a recurring pattern in all isolated lone wolf terrorists. From a social control perspective, a lack of social life facilitates a self-radicalization process as it isolates the individual from agents of control (i.e. family, friends, wife) (McCauley & Moskalenko, 2008). This detachment and isolation create a void in their lives that may leave them vulnerable to violent ideologies and allow for radicalization and planning to go virtually undetected.

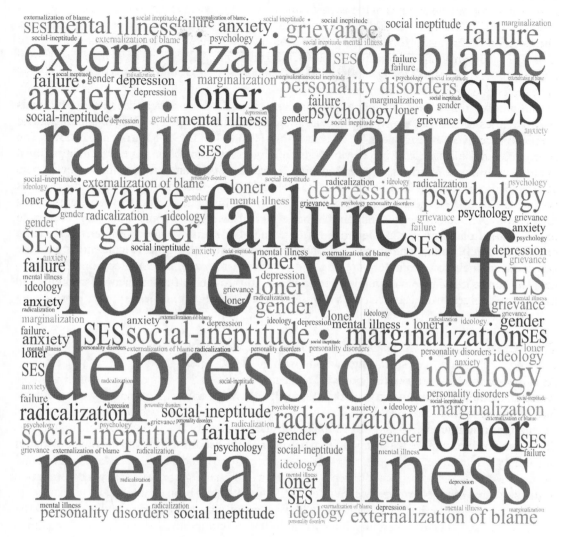

FIGURE 8.1 | A Constellation of Causes

In this chapter, however, I make a more specific argument. I posit that the inability of an individual to work with others may be a significant risk factor in violent radicalization and, ultimately, in lone wolf terrorism. Of course, the inability to work with others is related to social ineptitude, but as noted in the next section, it is only one component of what is known in the field of work/school performance as individuals with lone wolf tendencies (LWTs). In the pages that follow, I describe the concept of lone wolf tendencies in the context of work and school, and also discuss the research surrounding this construct. Importantly, I discuss how the research on employees with lone wolf tendencies may have inadvertently tapped into a construct that can help us better understand lone wolf terrorism in the United States.

Employees With Lone Wolf Tendencies

Employees with lone wolf tendencies (LWTs) like to work alone. Naturally, these individuals are not enthusiastic about expending time and effort on building interpersonal relationships and cooperating with others in a work or school setting (Blau & Boal, 1987; Barr et al., 2005; Dixon et al., 2003; Mulki et al., 2007). Their preference to work alone may be driven by their personal inability to establish interpersonal relationships, as well as a distrust of others and a proclivity to see others as less capable and ineffective (Barr et al., 2005). At best, employees with lone wolf tendencies lack any concern for positive work relationships with others. At worst, employees with LWTs do things their way and tend to focus on their own goals, which often run contrary to organizational mandates and procedures (Mulki et al., 2007). Either way, these behaviors create resentment and ill will among employees, and as a consequence, these individuals end up socially isolated from their coworkers.

The construct of lone wolf tendencies is measured through self-assessment of attitudes and behaviors. This construct is based on a seven-item Likert scale that has been empirically validated by Dixon et al. (2003). The scale included the following items:

1. Given the choice, I would rather work alone than work with others.
2. I prefer solitude over social interactions with acquaintances.
3. For me, working with others poses a threat to my success.
4. I am more successful when I work by myself than with others.
5. Working with others is a hassle.
6. I have little tolerance when others make mistakes.
7. I don't like attending team meetings where I have to listen to the simple-minded ideas of others.

In the work and school performance literature, lone wolves have been characterized as extremely intelligent, creative individuals that possess high levels of job involvement (Mulki et al., 2007). That is, they are task-oriented and highly committed to completing the tasks that have been assigned to them. Despite high levels of job involvement, however, employees with LWTs tend to lack loyalty to the organization and its goals (Ingram et al., 1991).

Individuals with lone wolf tendencies generally suffer from lower levels of *organizational citizen behavior* (OCB). No social system can survive solely upon its blueprints of prescribed behavior (Katz, 1964). In order for social systems to thrive, its "citizens" must engage in voluntary, prosocial, and altruistic behaviors that lubricate the machinery that creates social cohesion (Smith et al.,1983). OCB is a multidimensional concept comprised of *helping, courtesy,* and *sportsmanship. Helping* behaviors are selfless acts of consideration that emphasize interpersonal harmony (Mulki et al., 2007). *Courtesy* is often described as individual efforts to prevent and deescalate problems and conflicts. Courteous employees are sensitive to the effects that interpersonal problems will have on others and so are willing to resolve conflicts and build a healthy organizational climate (Borman & Motowidlo, 1997). *Sportsmanship* is the willingness to tolerate actions and outcomes that fall short of one's expectations. Individuals with high levels of sportsmanship not only maintain a positive attitude when dealing with others' shortcomings but also open to criticism or rejection of their own ideas (Podsakoff et al., 2000). Therefore, individuals with high levels of OCB voluntarily engage in activities that are not required and that aim at benefiting the collective good.

Empirical research shows that, all else equal, employees with LWTs score significantly lower in OCBs compared to their counterparts (Barr et al., 2005; Mulki et al., 2007). Specifically, Mulki et al. (2007) found that high ratings in LWTs negatively impact all elements of OCB: *helping*, *courtesy*, and *sportsmanship* behaviors. Similar to Barr et al. (2005), Mulki et al. (2007) also found that employees with lone wolf tendencies suffered from lower levels of task performance. Importantly, they found that this effect is entirely mediated OCB. This is a really important finding as it suggests that many of life's outcomes (in this case work performance) do not only depend on individual performance but also on one's ability to establish healthy interpersonal relationships. Furthermore, lone wolf tendencies are also significantly associated with lower levels of job satisfaction and higher levels of turnover intentions (Mulki et al., 2007).

OCB has been empirically linked to a number of important personality traits. For instance, Mahdiuon et al. (2010) examined the relationship between OCB and the Big Five personality traits: *neuroticism* (long-term tendency to easily experience negative emotions such as depression, anxiety, fear, and sadness—it is essentially a measure of emotional stability), *extroversion* (long-term tendency to enjoy being with people and participating in social gatherings), *openness* (tendency to enjoy new things), *agreeableness* (tendency to be compassionate and cooperative, rather than suspicious and antagonistic), and *conscientiousness* (a tendency to be disciplined, organized, and dependable). They found that individuals with high levels of organizational citizen performance also enjoy higher levels of *extroversion, openness, agreeableness*, and *conscientiousness*. Conversely, lower levels of OCB are linked to higher levels of *neuroticism*. In addition to the Big Five personality traits, higher levels of organizational citizen behavior have been linked to high levels of *collectivism* (the tendency to be concerned for the well-being of others, as opposed to oneself), and higher levels of *external locus of control* (the tendency to believe that one's successes and failures result from factors outside one's control). While the personality predictors of lone wolf tendencies have not been empirically examined, the operationalization of lone wolf tendencies embody many of the aforementioned personality traits. It is possible that the relationship between these personality traits and OCB is mediated, at least in part, by the construct of lone wolf tendencies.

The construct of employees with lone wolf tendencies is relevant to the study of lone wolf terrorism in two important regards. First, it places an analytical emphasis on a key turning point in their radicalization and subsequent career as terrorists—the decision to work alone. While seemingly inconsequential, the one characteristic shared by all isolated lone wolf terrorists that makes them unique from other types of terrorists is that they have all radicalized, prepared, and conducted their attacks alone. This choice may be quite significant in our understanding of lone wolf terrorism since dictates whether a radicalized individual formally joins an extremist organization and engages in group-based terrorism, or stays alone and patiently prepares to engage in ideologically motivated lone-actor violence. This choice is not random. It may reflect a lack of interest in or inability to work with others. Studies on the subject consistently show lone wolf terrorists to be loners, often to the point of social ineptitude (Spaaij, 2010). Additionally, the degree of isolation seems to be inversely related to how connected they are to formal terrorist organizations or networks, with isolated lone wolves suffering from higher levels of social isolation, followed by connected lone wolves and group-based terrorists, respectively (see Gill et al., 2014; Gruenewald et al., 2013). In this regard, the construct of employees with lone wolf tendencies may explain this very important decision.

Second, research on employees with lone wolf tendencies shows that this construct does not exist in a vacuum, but rather captures a series of personality, social, and psychological traits. As noted, individuals with LWTs do not care for or enjoy social interactions; they think of themselves as better or smarter than other employees, and as such have little interest in the thoughts of others or the patience for their mistakes.

If these characteristics sound familiar in the context of ideologically driven violence, it is because these are common traits found in lone wolf terrorism. Like employees with lone wolf tendencies, lone wolf terrorists are also highly intelligent, creative, and committed individuals (Simon, 2013). They think outside the box. Despite lacking resources, training, and external support, they are able to plan and execute very elaborate attacks. No lone wolf terrorist embodies these characteristics better than Ted Kaczynski (a.k.a. the Unabomber), a Harvard and University of Michigan trained mathematician that would later plot and execute a nationwide bombing campaign. Paralleling the concept of employees with lone wolf tendencies, lone wolf terrorists also tend to be narcissistic, often suffering from delusions of grandeur. These individuals are distrusting of others, often to the point of paranoia (see Auchincloss & Weiss, 1992). One defining aspect of their personality is their fundamentalist belief systems and complete and utter intolerance for any facts or perspectives that differ—even in the slightest—from those beliefs (Reid Meloy & Yakeley, 2014). Their intolerance is so pervasive that it drives them into deeper levels of isolation. For instance, Buford Furrow, an anti-Semite, quit an Aryan Nations group in Idaho because their membership requirements were "too permissive." This plunged him into a deeper cycle of isolation and violent radicalization that would end his marriage and ultimately culminate in the shooting at a Jewish daycare center in California.

Undoubtedly, there is a parallel between the concept of OCB and what we may call "societal" citizen behavior. Indeed, the organization in which one works is but a microcosm of the society in which it is embedded. In order for both to thrive, society's "citizens" must engage in voluntary, prosocial, and altruistic behaviors for the common good. In sociology, this concept is known as social capital theory (Putmam, 1995). Similar to OCB, social capital is a construct based on *trust*, *volunteerism*, *sociability*, and *togetherness* (see Narayan & Cassidy, 2001). In the context of work, individuals with lone wolf tendencies generally have lower levels of OCB, which explains why they tend to have lower levels of task performance and higher levels of dissatisfaction with organization. In the context of terrorism, lone wolves inherently have lower levels of social capital or "societal" citizen behavior. Their violent attacks are, in essence, acts of rebellion against conventional society. Lone wolf terrorists are distrustful and isolated, and as a consequence do not engage in prosocial activities. In addition to social ineptitude, their lower levels of social capital may also explain why lone wolf terrorists tend to have life-long histories of thwarted occupational goals (Reid Meloy & Yakeley, 2014). Research on social capital theory demonstrates that individuals with a higher degree of network structure enjoy higher levels of career success (Seibert et al., 2001). In other words, career success does not only depend on one's skills, but also on the extent and strength of interpersonal networks. This mediating effect explains Gill et al. (2014) finding that given their high educational achievement, lone wolf terrorists are disproportionally unemployed and underemployed.

The long history of occupational and romantic failures, in a society where the ideal is to be married, have kids, own a home, and have financial stability, creates a great deal of strain, which in turn leaves them vulnerable to extremist ideologies. As Spaaij (2010) notes, these ideologies provide a psychological mechanism of externalization, allowing them to channel their personal frustrations and failures and project blame onto other members of society. This "othering" process desensitizes and dehumanizes the "enemy," providing a psychological justification for committing violence. It is important to note that the presence of an extremist ideology is not a necessary condition for violence. Research on ideological and non-ideological mass shooters suggests that both phenomena are caused by the same underlying social and psychological processes (Capellan, 2015). Therefore, what looks like seemingly different phenomena (i.e. lone wolf terrorism, assassinations, and mass shootings) are part of a larger phenomenon of lone-actor, grievance-fueled violence (see McCauley et al., 2013). The only tangible difference between these individuals is the channels they latch onto to externalize their frustrations. Ideology is one of many channels.

The construct of employees with lone wolf tendencies is useful to the study of terrorism not only because it places an emphasis on the crucial decision these individuals make to act alone and therefore engage in lone wolf terrorism, but also because it may help us understand why they get to that point in the first place. Undoubtedly, the parallels between the construct of employees with lone wolf tendencies and lone wolf terrorists may help us decipher the enigma of lone wolf terrorism. If we apply our understanding of the construct of lone wolf tendencies within the work performance literature to the recurring characteristics and patterns of lone wolf terrorism, then the constellation of causes begins to take a recognizable shape (see Figure 8.2).

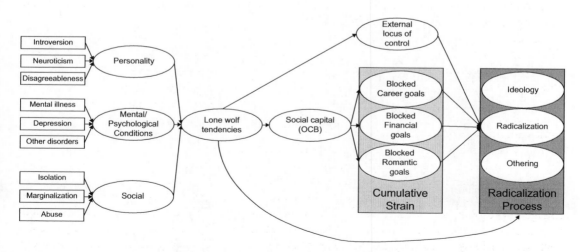

FIGURE 8.2 | Lone Wolf Tendencies (LWTs) as an Organizing Principle

The recurring social, psychological, and personality characteristics contribute to the construct of lone wolf tendencies. The work performance literature tells us that individuals with lone wolf tendencies score lower in OCB; similarly, the terrorism literature also suggests that these individuals will have lower levels of social capital (the societal counterpart to OCB). Low levels of social capital, or network density, may in turn lead to blocked career, financial, and romantic goals. The strain from these blocked goals over time will accumulate, and coupled with an external locus of control, leave individuals vulnerable to radicalization and possibly violence.

Conclusion

In this chapter, I employed the construct of lone wolf tendencies and the broader work performance literature to bring light to a very important, yet understudied, point in the life of a lone wolf terrorist—the decision to plan, prepare, and execute a terrorist attack alone, without command structure or material support. As argued, this choice is not random. Rather, it represents systematic attitudinal, psychological, and sociological differences between lone wolf and group-based terrorists. The construct of lone wolf tendencies may capture those systematic differences and therefore explain why individuals take different terrorist paths. Additionally, I also argue that the construct of lone wolf tendencies may itself be a risk factor for radicalization and ideologically motivated lone-actor violence. While seemingly implausible, the construct of lone wolf tendencies, in its relationships with personality and psychological conditions, as well as life outcomes, has many parallels with recurring patterns and characteristics of lone wolf terrorists. By projecting the work performance literature onto the field of lone wolf terrorism, the construct of employees with lone wolf tendencies begins to act as an organizing principle to the constellation of causes found in the phenomenon of lone wolf terrorism.

It is important to note, however, that much of the discussion in this chapter is based on conjecture. While the connections between the construct of lone wolf tendencies and lone wolf terrorists are strong, this does not mean that the underlying mechanisms specified in this chapter are real. Therefore, future research should begin to apply the literature on work performance to the field of lone wolf terrorism. The first step is measurement. Researchers should first operationalize the construct of lone wolf tendencies for a non-work/school-specific setting. Second, once we have a validated measure of this construct, researchers must start correlation analyses to test the various relationships specified here. We must examine the social, psychological, and personality determinants of the LWT construct. Then, researchers must test the relationships between this construct and some of the recurring characteristics and outcomes identified in the lone wolf terrorism literature. For instance, future research should study the association between LWTs and external locus of control. Importantly, researchers must examine the association between LWTs and social capital. And if there is a relationship, does social capital mediate the effects of lone wolf tendencies on life outcomes such as career and financial goals? Additionally, case studies can also shed light on the decision of lone wolf terrorists to act alone. Particularly, researchers should focus on the determinants of that decision. The construct of lone wolf tendencies would suggest that the choice was driven by an inability or lack of interest in working with others. However, it could have also been driven by a lack of opportunity to work with others. The answer to these important questions could significantly enhance our understanding of the lone wolf terrorism phenomenon.

REFERENCES

Auchincloss, E. L., & Weiss, R. W. (1992). Paranoid character and the intolerance of indifference. *Journal of the American Psychoanalytic Association, 40*(4), 1013–1037.

Barr, T. F., Dixon, A. L., & Gassenheimer, J. B. (2005). Exploring the "lone wolf" phenomenon in student teams. *Journal of Marketing Education, 27*(1), 81–90.

Bates, R. A. (2012). Dancing with wolves: Today's lone wolf terrorists. *The Journal of Public and Professional Sociology, 4*(1), 1–14.

Becker, M. (2014). Explaining lone wolf target selection in the United States. *Studies in Conflict & Terrorism, 37*(11), 959–978.

Blau, G. J., & Boal, K. B. (1987). Conceptualizing how job involvement and organizational commitment affect turnover and absenteeism. *Academy of Management Review,* 288–300.

Borman, W. C., & Motowidlo, S. J. (1997). Task performance and contextual performance: The meaning for personnel selection research. *Human Performance, 10*(2), 99–109.

Borum, R., Fein, R., & Vossekuil, B. (2012). A dimensional approach to analyzing lone offender terrorism. *Aggression and Violent Behavior, 17*(5), 389–396.

Capellan, J. A. (2015). Lone wolf terrorist or deranged shooter? A study of ideological active shooter events in the United States, 1970–2014. *Studies in Conflict & Terrorism.*

COT. (2007, July). Lone-wolf terrorism: Case study for work package 3: Citizens and governance in a knowledge-based society. The Netherlands: TTSRL.

Dahl, E. J. (2011). The plots that failed: Intelligence lessons learned from unsuccessful terrorist attacks against the United States. *Studies in Conflict & Terrorism, 34*(8), 621–648.

Dixon, A. L., Gassenheimer, J. B., & Feldman Barr, T. (2003). Identifying the lone wolf: A team perspective. *Journal of Personal Selling & Sales Management, 23*(3), 205–219.

Gill, P., Horgan, J., & Deckert, P. (2014). Bombing alone: Tracing the motivations and antecedent behaviors of lone-actor terrorists. *Journal of Forensic Sciences, 59*(2), 425–435.

Gruenewald, J. (2011). A comparative examination of homicides perpetrated by far-right extremists. *Homicide Studies, 15,* 177–203.

Gruenewald, J., Chermak, S., & Freilich, J. D. (2014). Far-right lone wolf homicides in the United States. *Studies in Conflict & Terrorism, 36*(12), 1005–1024.

Gruenewald, J., Freilich, J. D., & Chermak, S. (2013). Distinguishing "loner" attacks from other domestic extremist violence. *Criminology & Public Policy, 12*(1), 65–91.

Gruenewald, J., & Pridemore, W. A. (2012). A comparison of ideologically-motivated homicides from the extremist crime database and homicides from supplementary homicides report using multiple imputations by chained equations to handle missing values. *Journal of Quantitative Criminology, 28,* 141–162.

Hewitt, C. (2003). *Understanding terrorism in America: From the Klan to al Qaeda.* New York: Psychology Press.

Ingram, T. N., Lee, K. S., & Lucas, G. H. (1991). Commitment and involvement: Assessing a salesforce typology. *Journal of the Academy of Marketing Science, 19*(3), 187–197.

Katz, D. (1964). The motivational basis of organizational behavior. *Behavioral Science, 9*(2), 131–146.

Krueger, A. B., & Pischke, J.-S. (1997). A statistical analysis of crime against foreigners in unified Germany. *Journal of Human Resources, 32*(1), 182–209.

Lee, A. (2011). Who becomes a terrorist? Poverty, education, and the origins of political violence. *World Politics, 63*(2), 203–245.

Mahdiuon, R., Ghahramani, M., & Sharif, A. R. (2010). Explanation of organizational citizenship behavior with personality. *Procedia-Social and Behavioral Sciences, 5,* 178–184.

McCauley, C., & Moskalenko, S. (2008). Mechanisms of political radicalization: Pathways toward terrorism. *Terrorism and Political Violence, 20*(3), 415–433.

McCauley, C., Moskalenko, S., & Van Son, B. (2013). Characteristics of lone-wolf violent offenders: A comparison of assassins and school attackers. *Perspectives on Terrorism, 7*(1).

Moskalenko, S., & McCauley, C. (2011). The psychology of lone-wolf terrorism. *Counselling Psychology Quarterly, 24*(2), 115–126.

Mulki, J. P., Jaramillo, F., & Marshall, G. W. (2007). Lone wolf tendencies and salesperson performance. *Journal of Personal Selling & Sales Management, 27*(1), 25–38.

Narayan, D., & Cassidy, M. F. (2001). A dimensional approach to measuring social capital: Development and validation of a social capital inventory. *Current Sociology, 49*(2), 59–102.

Nijboer, M. (2012). A review of lone wolf terrorism: The need for a different approach. *Social Cosmos, 3*(1), 33–39.

Pantucci, R. (2011). *A typology of lone wolves: Preliminary analysis of lone Islamist terrorists.* London: The International Centre for the Study of Radicalization and Political Violence.

Podsakoff, P. M., MacKenzie, S. B., Paine, J. B., & Bachrach, D. G. (2000). Organizational citizenship behaviors: A critical review of the theoretical and empirical literature and suggestions for future research. *Journal of Management, 26*(3), 513–563.

Putnam, R. D. (1995). Bowling alone: America's declining social capital. *Journal of Democracy, 6*(1), 65–78.

Reid Meloy, J., & Yakeley, J. (2014). The violent true believer as a "lone wolf": Psychoanalytic perspectives on terrorism. *Behavioral Sciences & the Law, 32*(3), 347–365.

Seibert, S. E., Kraimer, M. L., & Liden, R. C. (2001). A social capital theory of career success. *Academy of Management Journal, 44*(2), 219–237.

Silke, A. (2004). The road less travelled: recent trends in terrorism research. *Research on terrorism: trends, achievements and failures,* 186–213.

Simon, J. D. (2013). *Lone wolf terrorism: Understanding the growing threat.* Amherst, NY: Prometheus Books.

Smith, C. A., Organ, D. W., & Near, J. P. (1983). Organizational citizenship behavior: Its nature and antecedents. *Journal of Applied Psychology, 68*(4), 653.

Spaaij, R. (2010). The enigma of lone wolf terrorism: An assessment. *Studies in Conflict & Terrorism, 33*(9), 854–870.

Spaaij, R., & Hamm, M. S. (2015). Key issues and research agendas in lone wolf terrorism. *Studies in Conflict & Terrorism, 38*(3), 167–178.

Springer, N. R. (2009). *Patterns of Radicalization: Identifying the Markers and Warning Signs of Domestic Lone Wolf Terrorism in our Midst.* Unpublished Master's thesis, Naval Postgraduate School, Monterey, CA.

U.S. Department of Homeland Security. (2009). *Right wing extremism: Current economic and political climate fueling resurgence in radicalization and recruitment.* Washington, DC: Office of Intelligence and Analysis Assessment. Retrieved from: http://fas.org/irp/eprint/rightwing.pdf.

Pathways to Terrorism*

Mark Hamm

Addressing a Singapore conference during the early days of the Obama administration, U.S. Defense Secretary Robert Gates warned that the West was vulnerable to a dual threat of al-Qaeda terrorism from both European and American recruits. He added his concern that there also was "the development of violent, extremist networks" within Western nations.[1] This assessment is valuable because it draws attention to both international and domestic dangers posed by Islamic extremists. Yet the assessment does not go far enough—entirely overlooked is the white supremacy movement. In fact, the major domestic terrorism unit in the United States, the Department of Homeland Security (DHS), abandoned its efforts to gather intelligence on white supremacy groups in 2009 following a firestorm of criticism by lawmakers of the political right who accused the DHS of painting all conservatives as potential domestic terrorists.[2] Domestic plots are not included in the presidential daily briefings on terrorism or in interagency threat assessments within the federal government.[3] This is a big mistake—at least that is what history suggests. Racist antigovernment groups have been responsible for nearly all of the successful terrorist attacks in America since the early 1980s.[4] After years of dormancy, the movement is experiencing a revival brought on by the election of President Obama, rising unemployment, and the contentious debate over U.S. immigration policy. The bombing of government buildings and the killing of scores of young people at a summer camp in Norway during the summer of 2011 has, however, focused new attention around the world on the subculture of right-wing activists, stimulating debate over the focus of counterterrorism policy.

Four emerging threats are examined in the following cases. One looks at the white supremacy movement and another examines the threat posed by Somali gangs. In 2009, forty-two people were indicted on terrorist-related crimes in the United States, fourteen of them for recruiting Somalis into jihad.[5] The other two cases interrogate the threat of lone-wolf terrorists—one influenced by Prison Islam and the other inspired by an Internet-recruiting campaign by Anwar al-Awlaki.

A case-study approach is appropriate here because it not only has the ability to analyze a small number of cases, but also has the capacity to discover the sequence of individual trajectories, or "turning points," leading to terrorism. The case-study approach also can examine the extent to which these turning points were embedded in experiences deriving from prison social networks, clandestine communication systems, radical religious beliefs, and leadership competences—all of which can enable the transformation of an individual's violent tendencies into terrorist causes. The sociologist Howard Becker argues that case studies focus on process, or "the temporal dimension in which phenomena occur in specific settings."[6] According to Becker, social processes form a narrative analysis that has a story to tell. As we shall see, there is considerable variance in what is known about the following stories. That is a problem common to all terrorism research and it is unfortunate because the lack of available information prevents the writing of biographies that can reveal the underlying causes of radicalization. "Until we can answer basic questions about the trajectories radicalized individuals have followed," observes the veteran terrorism scholar Brian Jenkins, "our ability to understand and counter radicalization will be severely limited."[7] Yet to the extent that processes of radicalization contained within the subsequent accounts are similar across time and place, then perhaps something may be said about the common denominators of prison-based terrorism.

* * *

Ruben Luis Leon Shumpert (case 32) was born in Seattle, Washington, in 1977 to a Hispanic mother and an African American father. Reflecting on his upbringing in a court filing years later, Shumpert wrote, "My life has been peppered with substance abuse, crime, and hardships so severe it would have completely destroyed most people."[8] Emblematic of his adaptation to these hardships, when Shumpert was twelve years old he bought a gun and tattooed a large cross on his arm demonstrating his love for Jesus. Although Shumpert claimed that his background "neither defines [him] nor is it a contributing factor to [his] current situation," these two personal obsessions—guns and religion—would play a crucial role in what lay ahead for him.

As a teenager, Shumpert was arrested and remanded to juvenile detention on a firearms violation. With his release, the stage was set for a series of life-course events that would become turning points along Shumpert's pathway to terrorism. These events were made possible by four interrelated social networks.

Network 1: The Prison

According to Shumpert's statement to the court, by the age of twenty he had become a prosperous Seattle drug dealer. He bought expensive cars, assault rifles, and a house complete with surveillance cameras.[9] In 1998, Shumpert was arrested and convicted of drug trafficking and sentenced to the Monroe State Prison near Everett, Washington. He learned to cut hair in prison, and he is likely to have associated mainly with other minority inmates. Shortly before his release on August 6, 2002, Shumpert converted from the Catholic faith to Sunni Islam. Like most Islamic converts, Shumpert chose a Muslim name to mark his new symbolic birth to the religion: Amir Abdul Muhaimeen. He was then twenty-five years old.

Network 2: The Barbershop

Returning to Seattle, Shumpert gave up substance abuse and drug dealing and vowed to stay away from guns. He quickly became destitute and homeless, though, and sought shelter in a local mosque. There he met a man who owned the Crescent Cuts Barbershop, located in a ramshackle two-story building at 7821 Rainier Avenue South—a low-income black community on the city's south side. Shumpert went to work at Crescent Cuts (Crescent being the symbol of Islam), thereby putting to use both the skill and the religion he had learned in prison. As in many African American communities, the barbershop was a neighborhood gathering place. According to a federal court document, "The shop served as a casual meeting place for . . . like-minded individuals, mostly African American men with criminal histories who had converted to Islam, either in prison or after contact later with prison converts."[10] Sensing the potential for terrorist recruitment among these prison-based Muslims in the year following 9/11, the Seattle office of the FBI developed an undercover informant—a convicted felon who was paid $3,000 a month by the FBI—to monitor activities inside the barbershop.[11]

According to FBI testimony, "conversations at the barber shop often turned to militancy and the need to be ready for jihad against the 'kafir,' or non-believers. The acquisition of firearms was a frequent topic of conversation in that connection."[12] Among those involved in these conversations were members of a local Somali street gang. There are no fewer than three versions of Shumpert's radicalization; it is possible that all three played a role. A source close to Shumpert insists that it was through the Somali gang that Shumpert was introduced to the Takfir wal Hijrah movement (the *takfir* doctrine involves declaring other Muslims to be apostates), a breakaway group from Egypt's Muslim Brotherhood that would also influence both Ayman al-Zawahiri and the Madrid train-bomber Jamal Ahmidan, the Chinaman.[13] The FBI, however, asserted that Shumpert was radicalized by an older Somali American named Abraham Sheik Mohamed, thought to be a moderate Salafist and former member of a terrorist group in Somalia, who was then the presiding imam at Rainier Valley's Abu-Bakr Mosque.[14] For his part, Shumpert claimed that he was introduced to "radical Islam" by the FBI informant.[15]

The investigation went on for three years (from 2002 to 2005), during which time Shumpert became more attuned to world events and emerged as the most outspoken member of the barbershop group. He was also its most religiously devout. By this point Shumpert typically dressed in a white robe, wore a Muslim prayer cap and a beard, and had developed a prayer mark or a "raisin" in the middle of his forehead, the mark of a pious Muslim who grinds his forehead into the ground during prayer. Shumpert also got married, became a father, opened a homeless shelter, and conducted clothing drives for the poor. He also took part in interfaith dialogues at several churches and synagogues, and he volunteered at a shelter for troubled youth. Shumpert was an asset to his community. "I went from forcefully taking from people to quietly giving to people," as he would write.[16] Yet on one occasion Shumpert gave the FBI informant a counterfeit $100 bill. At another time, he sold the informant a handgun. Meanwhile, barbershop discussions about the war in Iraq were likely at fever pitch. Shumpert described his grievance like this: "Look at Iraq. Nineteen extremists kill over 3,000 Americans on 9/11 and over 30,000 Iraqis are killed as an indirect result. . . . The extremist commits an act of terror and the Muslim community always pays the price. So, many of us, in many different ways, have joined the fight against this evil ideology."[17] For Shumpert, the root cause of post-9/11 terrorism was terrorism perpetrated by the United States of America.

At length, Shumpert met several men who had recently returned from Chechnya. They gave Shumpert some jihadist videos (praising the 9/11 hijackers, the Taliban, al-Qaeda, and Chechen suicide bombers) and Shumpert began showing these videos to his customers at Crescent Cuts, including children as young as eleven years old.[18] According to the informant, as these videos played the group adopted the rallying cry "Black Hawk Down!' in reference to the shooting down in 1993 of a U.S. military helicopter in Somalia and the killing of its crew. Shumpert also made available to his customers such terrorist training manuals as *The Terrorist's Cookbook* and *The Minimanual of the Urban Guerrilla*.[19] With his grievance at an all-time high and reminiscent of the Chinaman's attitude prior to the bombings in Madrid, Shumpert announced that he was going to Iraq to fight alongside Abu Musab al-Zarqawi.[20] Yet before he could do so, on April 15, 2005, Shumpert was arrested for beating a man during a barbershop dispute and was locked up in Seattle's King County Jail. Before Shumpert could post bail, the FBI unsealed charges in federal court accusing him of passing counterfeit money and being a felon in possession of a firearm. The FBI then opened a second investigation, this one charging Shumpert with inciting terrorism and conducting military training inside the barbershop.

Network 3: The Jail

The FBI questioned Shumpert about his involvement with al-Qaeda and Osama bin Laden and about his intentions to carry out terrorist attacks against the United States. This proved fruitless for the FBI and its terrorism investigation of Shumpert ground to a halt. Meanwhile, scores of Seattle residents came to Shumpert's defense. Some signed a petition supporting leniency, and others wrote letters to the U.S. Attorney, saying that Shumpert was a positive influence in their community. This, too, came to no avail. Shumpert was still looking at a two-year federal prison sentence, leading Shumpert to take his most drastic step toward terrorism. In King County, Shumpert met a group of Somali inmates who advised him to accept a plea agreement, pleading guilty on the counterfeiting charge in exchange for dropping the assault and firearms violations, allowing Shumpert to be released on bond so that he could flee America and join the cause of jihad in Somalia.[21] He would do just that.

On May 20, 2006, after a year in custody, Shumpert was released on his own recognizance and ordered to reside in a halfway house until his sentencing on July 9. Reporters would later claim that Shumpert was ordered to surrender his passport as well; yet there is no indication that he did so or even that Shumpert had a passport.[22] A more likely scenario is provided by terrorists who were later associated with Shumpert. They contend that, while at the halfway house, Shumpert used his former jailhouse contacts to acquire a forged passport.[23] When Shumpert failed to appear for his July sentencing, the FBI raided a Somali grocery that once housed Crescent Cuts in an unsuccessful attempt to arrest him.

Network 4: The Transnational Terrorist Community

Shumpert had already jumped bail and fled the country, flying to Somalia via Dubai. Upon his arrival at the Mogadishu airport, Shumpert was met by members of al-Shabaab, a militia of violent Islamist guerrillas at war against Somalia's weak U.S.-backed transitional government because it is not based on Islam. In 2007, al-Shabaab established a strict *shariah* code (Islamic law) and, to enable recruitment, its own media division featuring jihadist videos complete with English rap lyrics. A year later, they were joined by al-Qaeda terrorists wanted in connection with the 1998 embassy bombings in Kenya and Tanzania. At this point, al-Shabaab and al-Qaeda become one. "We are negotiating how we can unite into one [with al-Qaeda]," said a senior al-Shabaab leader at the time. "We will take our orders from Sheik Osama bin Laden because we are his students."[24] Accordingly, al-Shabaab was designated as a terrorist organization by the U.S. State Department.[25] Renowned for its "summary justice" against government officials and innocent Sufi Muslims, al-Shabaab had in recent years committed a series of arsons, bombings, kidnappings, beheadings, amputations, and a mortar attack against a plane carrying a U.S. congressman.[26] Soon al-Shabaab would wage an assassination attempt against U.S. Secretary of State Hillary Clinton during her 2008 visit to Nairobi, Kenya.[27]

In preparation for jihad, al-Shabaab arranged for Shumpert to purchase an AK-47 assault rifle and took him to a training camp where he was issued the Shabaab insignia to wear on his uniform—the patch featured a green circle with a yellow banner on top reading, in Arabic, "the Movement of the Shabaab Mujahideen." The center of the image includes a map of the Horn of Africa, an open Koran, and two crossed AK-47s. For Shumpert, it could have been a personal medallion.

Shumpert was not the only American Muslim recruited by al-Shabaab during these years—yet he was the only American recruit who *was* not a Somali—representing a recruiting innovation for al-Shabaab. Between 2007 and 2009, at least twenty young Somali American men left Minnesota to attend al-Shabaab's training camps.[28] On October 29, 2007, Shirwa Ahmed, a twenty-seven-year-old Somali American college student from Minneapolis, blew himself up near Mogadishu in one of five simultaneous suicide bombings attributed to al-Shabaab, thereby becoming the first American suicide bomber anywhere.[29] It is conceivable that Shumpert used the same pipeline that brought Ahmed from Minnesota to Somalia and that would later bring the Minneapolis suicide bomber Farah Mohamed Beledi (case 50).[30]

On November 18, 2007, Shumpert placed a call from Somalia to an FBI special agent, Robert Walby, in Seattle, taunting Walby by saying that he was in Somalia and would not be returning to the United States. In the background, Walby could hear men chanting "Allah Akbar" ("God is Great"), often used by jihadists as a terrorist battle cry. On November 27, Shumpert placed a second call to Walby, this time making a direct threat, saying that he and the agent were now sworn enemies. "He then added," Walby testified, "that he and his Muslim associates would destroy everything the United States stood for."[31]

The rest of the story is sketchy. According to a Shabaab statement, sometime in 2008 Shumpert's brigade traveled to Adale, about 150 kilometers north of Mogadishu, where Shumpert was shot in the back during a battle with Ethiopian soldiers and evacuated with the wounded to

Mogadishu for treatment.[32] After his recovery in early 2009, the militia retreated to a forest near Mogadishu. Within al-Shabaab's ranks at this point was a counterterrorism informant attached to AFRICOM, the U.S. military command for Africa.

While living in the forest, a small group boarded a boat during another fight with Ethiopian rivals, destination unknown. Acting on intelligence from the informant, the group was targeted by a U.S. rocket attack, killing three. Soon after, Joseph Lieberman, the chairman of the Senate Homeland Security Committee, announced that Ruben Shumpert was among the dead.[33]

Three features of Shumpert's story resonate with the major takeaways from the database analysis. First, Shumpert's association with al-Shabaab occurred at the height of the Iraq War, during the peak years of prison-based terrorism, suggesting that Shumpert was part of a global anti-Western terrorist movement rooted in the prison experience. Evidence of this movement is found in an al-Shabaab interview with Ayman al-Zawahiri on the fourth anniversary of 9/11. "I take this opportunity to address our prisoners," said Zawahiri. "We have not forgotten you. We are still committed to the debt of your salvation . . . until we shatter your shackles."[34] Al-Shabaab would shatter the shackles of Ruben Shumpert and set him free to fight jihad in Somalia. Second, each of the social networks that Shumpert was involved with—from the prison to the barbershop; from the jail to al-Shabaab—served to facilitate the transformation of Shumpert's existing violent tendencies into a terrorist cause. Radicalization behind bars was not his only pathway to terrorism. Finally, although Shumpert's pathway was inspired by several religious orientations, it was the amorphous social movement called the Salafi-Jihad that led him to terrorism.

* * *

Another takeaway from the database is that, as incredible as it may seem, inmates are capable of waging terrorist plots from behind bars without assistance from outsiders. Such a tactic has long been common knowledge among prisoners. Prison intelligence officers routinely discover inmate plots to send crude explosive devices to governors, congressmen, and even presidents, yet none of them have been successful. Al-Qaeda tacticians are fully aware of this potential. In 2011, New York City police arrested a Muslim convert who had used an al-Qaeda article called "How to Build a Bomb in the Kitchen of Your Mom" to construct a pipe bomb using match heads, Christmas lights, and a converted clock, yet it, too, was unsuccessful.[35] The following case represents a classic example of prison terrorism that achieved its desired results.

Marc Harold Ramsey (case 38) was born to a Caucasian mother and an African American father in Detroit on March 1, 1969. The couple divorced a year later, leaving the infant with his mother in their Detroit home. As he grew up, two behavioral patterns emerged that would ultimately play a crucial role in Ramsey's criminality. On one hand, Ramsey developed an intense interest in military affairs; on the other, he came to resolve family problems with violence. The latter problem first arose in 1977 when eight-year-old Ramsey set his mother's house on fire in an attempt to kill his abusive stepfather as he slept. Still, Ramsey was an outstanding student and an accomplished athlete. At thirteen, he was accepted into a military academy where he earned straight A's; later, Ramsey became an all-state baseball player. During these years Ramsey also maintained contact with his biological father, a Vietnam War veteran who worked as a nuclear engineer for the U.S. Department of Energy in Maryland.[36]

Following in his father's footsteps, after graduating from high school Ramsey enlisted in the Air Force. Yet trouble soon darkened his door. Unable to manage his financial affairs, Ramsey began writing bad checks and was arrested for larceny. Prior to his trial, he went AWOL, only to be captured and court-martialed for desertion. After serving three years in a military brig, Ramsey returned to his Air Force duties but once again fell on hard times when his three-year-old daughter was killed in a drive-by shooting in East Chicago, Indiana. Again he went AWOL and tracked down the man who murdered his daughter with the intent of killing him. And with that, the stage was set for Ramsey's entry into a terrorism trajectory that occurred within two social networks.

Network 1: The Prison

As a result of Ramsey's decision to avenge his daughter's death, he was sentenced to twenty-two years in the Indiana Department of Correction on kidnapping charges. It was here that Ramsey was introduced to the Moorish Science Temple. "I made a tour of nearly all the prisons in Indiana," Ramsey recalled. "And at each one I ran into more and more brothers who taught me about Moorish Science."[37] Accordingly, at the age of twenty-five he converted through the proselytizing efforts of a Moorish elder. In this tradition, Marc Harold Ramsey became Akeem Ramsey El.

In prison, Ramsey gained the reputation of a devout Muslim with an avid interest in military history. His views were shaped by the writings of Malcolm X and Louis Farrakhan, as well as newspaper articles and television coverage of America's role in the Middle East. Like many observers of Middle Eastern affairs, Ramsey found America's involvement in the region to be fraught with contradiction. "The 'do as I say not as I do' approach by our government loathes me [*sic*]," he explained. "The only nation in the world to ever use an atomic bomb on another country wants to tell another country you can't. Not you *should* not use one but you *cannot* even have the technology. And I don't even [want to] begin the issue of US supporting violations of international law committed by Israel."[38]

Ramsey became known to the U.S. Secret Service during the presidency of George W. Bush. Writing from an Indiana prison, Ramsey sent Bush and Vice President Dick Cheney a series of threatening letters, fulminating about their mishandling of Middle Eastern affairs. "He is on record with us and he is known as a prolific letter writer," a Secret Service spokesman would later say.[39] It was also during this time that Ramsey's father became critically ill due to his exposure to Agent Orange in Vietnam. Ramsey would later explain that his father's illness was "very important in the motives of some of my actions."[40]

Network 2: The Jail

Ramsey was released from prison in 2006, and he then relocated to Denver, Colorado. On September 17, 2007, however, Ramsey was arrested for felony menacing, second-degree assault, and being a fugitive from justice. Unable to post a $350,000 bond, Ramsey was locked up in the Arapahoe County Detention Center where he was subsequently charged with assaulting another prisoner and a guard, making Ramsey a high-security inmate.[41]

A year later, a U.S. Army scientist committed suicide as federal prosecutors were preparing to indict him in connection with the 2001 anthrax mailings that killed five people in the aftermath of 9/11. This event, which gained national media attention, had an intense effect on the already politically conscious Marc Ramsey, taking him far beyond the traditions of Moorish Science.

On August 20, 2008, Ramsey wrote a letter to the presumptive Republican presidential candidate John McCain. Before sealing it, Ramsey placed a white powder substance inside the envelope. He mailed the letter to McCain's campaign headquarters in Centennial, Colorado, and he affixed his name, inmate number, and location of the jail on the envelope—as required on all outgoing mail from the facility.

At 3 p.m. the following day, Ramsey's letter arrived at the headquarters (the Senator was in Sedona, Arizona, that day). "Senator McCain, IFF [*sic*] you are reading this then you are already DEAD!" the letter began. "Unless of course you can't or don't breathe." The letter attacked the government because it had taken care of McCain—an injured Vietnam War vet—but not of Ramsey's ailing father who had served in Vietnam during the same period as McCain. "You're not the only one that was in the jungle, buddy," Ramsey wrote. "When election time comes we're going to need somebody to take care of the soldiers. Not somebody who wants another war."[42] Ramsey's letter—signed "Allahu Akbar, Akeem Ramsey El"—was a terrorist threat veiled in war protest.

The Secret Service was notified, prompting a twelve-hour HAZMAT alert involving more than a hundred officials from the FBI, the National Guard, the Arapahoe County Sheriff's Office, and the U.S. Postal Service. Five McCain staff members were taken to area hospitals as a precautionary measure and twelve were quarantined. Testing later determined that the white substance inside the envelope was not anthrax or another lethal substance; however, the identity of the substance was never disclosed.

The Secret Service quickly traced the letter to inmate Akeem Ramsey El at the Arapahoe County Detention Center, due to the simple fact that his name and address were on the envelope. On August 22, a Denver television crew was allowed to interview Ramsey inside a holding pen at the jail. Speaking straight into the camera, Ramsey said that he was "a terrorist sympathizer." Ramsey later gave a more detailed explanation for his crime. "The VA [Veterans Administration] would do nothing [for my father]. It was then that I believed, as I still do, that something must be done. Soldiers were being returned home from Iraq every day in the same condition as my father or worse. . . . Vietnam strikes 40 years later and Senator McCain was trying to [use] Vietnam as a springboard to the Oval Office."[43] In 2009 Ramsey was sentenced to thirty months in federal prison on terrorism charges related to his executed threat against McCain.[44]

Not only does Marc Ramsey represent a classic case of the stand-alone prison terrorist but his pathway classically demonstrates the importance of inmate leadership. In his case, as with Abu Musab al-Zarqawi at Jordan's Suwaqah prison a decade earlier, Ramsey's passage through criminality led to the meeting of an inmate imam (the Moorish elder in Indiana), which served as a crucial first step along his pathway to terrorism. Ramsey's case is also consistent with other features of the database. His violence was triggered by events surrounding the Iraq War; by moving beyond Moorish Science teachings—Nobel Drew Ali said nothing about the use of political violence—he embraced a form of Prison Islam. His tactic, the use of imitation anthrax, is another innovation in the field of prison-based terrorism.

* * *

The next case also resonates with the database analysis. It highlights the roles of extremist religion and inmate social networks as crucial to the radicalization process in the peak years of prison-based terrorism. But it is distinguished from the preceding two cases due to the outstanding question it raises for national security.

Shawn Robert Adolf (his real name, case 34) was born in 1974, probably in Greeley, Colorado. Other than being Caucasian, nothing more is known of his early life.[45] Court records show that Adolf's first criminal offense occurred in 1993 when he pled guilty to two burglary charges in Weld County, Colorado. In time, two social networks would provide turning points for his pathway to terrorism.

Network 1: The Prison

In 1997, a Denver court sentenced twenty-three-year-old Adolf to eight years in state prison for possession/sales of a controlled substance, weapons charges, and grand theft. Sources indicate that by the time Adolf entered prison he was a member of the Sons of Silence, a "1%" motorcycle gang based in Colorado Springs. (Within biker subcultures, it is believed that 99 percent live within the boundaries of the law; the remaining 1 percent is the outlaw element.) According to gang investigators, in prison the Sons of Silence are linked via the methamphetamine trade to both the Aryan Brotherhood and the Aryan Nations; the latter was an influential neo-Nazi organization classified as a terrorist threat by the FBI.[46] Investigators also agree that religion plays an important role in the meaning and purpose of these white supremacy groups, indicating that Adolf was influenced by either Christian Identity or Odinism/Asatru. An Aryan Nations prison gang member summarized these influences in an interview with a researcher from the Southern Poverty Law Center: "Most of the guys are into Asatru, but then we also have guys who are into Christian Identity, so it varies. Overall, it's about brotherhood. It's about blood, not religion. Well, actually, dope comes first. The meth. Then the brotherhood. That's the reality."[47]

Network 2: The Domestic Terrorist Organization

Adolf was paroled in 2001 but was soon arrested in Weld County on two third-degree assault charges. Known to local law enforcement as Shawn "Trouble" Adolf, he was released on bail and told to follow orders from his parole officer. Court records show that by 2007 Adolf had eight warrants out for him on various felonies around Colorado, including burglary, aggravated motor vehicle theft, and skipping out on a $1 million bond. One of these crimes involved the theft of a travel trailer, which served as Adolf's home and mobile meth lab as he moved from campground to campground through Colorado and Texas, possibly with his wife. (Records show that one Shawn R. Adolf and Sarah Williamson were issued a marriage license on July 18, 2007.[48]) Adolf was placed on the most-wanted list of the Weld County Sheriff's Department, prompting an investigator to say she feared that Adolf would eventually kill a police officer. "I've been a cop for 18 years," she said, "and he was not your typical bad guy."[49]

In the summer of 2008, several thousand federal and local law-enforcement agents descended on downtown Denver in preparation for massive protest marches and traffic jams at the Democratic National Convention. Their primary concern was that Senator Barack Obama's nomination would draw tens of thousands of demonstrators, including antiwar protestors and anarchists carrying on the widespread vandalism and window smashing that marked the 1999 World Trade Organization conference in Seattle. "The magnitude of the event has expanded," said the Denver mayor John Hickenlooper three weeks before the convention. "It's bigger and more profound than we expected. . . . What worries me is we don't know what we don't know."[50] These were not idle words. On the eve of the convention, it became clear that local officials were unprepared for the task before them. Of the security arrangements, one local journalist remarked, "It makes you think something is about to happen." Another journalist called the security situation "a cluster-fuck."[51] Denver streets represented a full-on police state, complete with miles of concrete barricades, black-clad SWAT teams, hovering helicopters, horse-mounted police in riot gear, and designated "freedom cages" set up to accommodate the right to free speech. As it turns out, none of this was necessary for preventing the convention's most serious threat.

At 1:37 a.m., on August 24, the day before the convention began, a lone police officer in the Denver suburb of Aurora spotted a blue Dodge pickup driving erratically. The officer pulled the truck over and, while checking the identification of the driver, twenty-eight-year-old Tharin Gartrell, discovered that the driver's license was suspended and that Gartrell was on probation for possessing methamphetamine. Inside the truck, the officer found what appeared to be a mobile meth lab, along with ammunition, a bulletproof vest, fake ID cards, wigs, walkie-talkies, and two bolt-action rifles, one being a loaded Ruger Mark II .22-250-caliber field rifle with a hunting scope and bipod shooting stand attached—a weapon commonly used in the West for killing prairie dogs and other disease-carrying pests. Gartrell was arrested and questioned about the weapons. He said he had no knowledge of the guns but that the truck belonged to his cousin, Shawn Adolf.

Adolf was arrested a short time later after jumping out of a sixth-story hotel window and breaking his ankle. When taken into custody, Adolf was wearing a Sons of Silence t-shirt, body armor, and a ring emblazoned with a swastika. Around one wrist he wore a handcuff key. Adolf admitted to being under the influence of methamphetamine.[52] An underage female, who had taken drugs with Adolf and his gang at the hotel, told investigators that Adolf had talked about killing Senator Obama. "No nigger should ever live in the White House," he said.[53] A third man—an Aryan Nations member as was Gartrell—also rolled over on Adolf, telling the Secret Service that Adolf had threatened to kill Obama on a prior occasion. Adolf had come to Denver, he said, to "go out in a blaze of glory" by killing Obama with a sniper rifle and telescopic scope from a distance of 750 yards during Obama's acceptance speech at Denver's Mile High Stadium on August 28, the fortieth anniversary of Martin Luther King's historic "I Have a Dream" speech.[54] The assassination was to be a "suicide mission" whereby Adolf would hide the Ruger rifle inside a hollowed-out television video camera, a method he had learned about in *The Bodyguard*, the 1992 Kevin Costner and Whitney Houston movie.

Moreover, the Secret Service had enough evidence to establish probable cause to believe that the three Aryan Nations members were conspiring to kill Barack Obama—a terrorist conspiracy with significant precedent in the database. During the 1992 presidential race, Richard Guthrie and Peter Langan (cases 6 and 7) were pursued by the Secret Service for plotting to assassinate President George H. Bush during a campaign swing through Georgia. Guthrie and Langan were affiliated with the Aryan Nations of Ohio at the time, and both had converted to Christian Identity in prison years earlier.[55] Likewise, after converting to Identity at the Arizona State Prison, Gary Yarbrough (case 4) would play a role in the Order's 1984 assassination of the Jewish radio talk show host Alan Berg in Denver.

Adolf's weapon, the Ruger rifle, also has a long history of use by violent extremists of the radical right. Richard Wayne Snell of the revolutionary white supremacist group the Covenant, the Sword and the Arm of the Lord, used a Mini-14 Ruger to kill a black state trooper in southwestern Arkansas in 1984, and he then fought it out with police across the border in Oklahoma. Snell was a movement hero in the eyes of Timothy McVeigh; Snell was executed on April 19, 1995, the same day McVeigh bombed the Oklahoma City Federal Building. McVeigh owned a .223-caliber Ruger assault rifle and the Aryan Republican Army committed its bank robberies with the same piece of weaponry.[56] Not only is the gun dependable and easy to load and fire, but it also has achieved nothing less than a fetishism within the American radical right: the weapon has been endowed with an aura based on its reverent status. It was reportedly for this very reason that the perpetrator of the mass killing spree in Norway, Anders Behring Breivik, chose as his weapon the Ruger .233-caliber assault rifle. In his 1,500-page manifesto, which was discovered after the attacks, Breivik wrote that he resorted to the assault rifle after discovering that he could not purchase enough ammonium nitrate fertilizer to build a weapon of mass effect terrorism like the one used by McVeigh in Oklahoma City. "Times are changing," Breivik wrote, "and the possibilities which were available to us during the time of Mr. Timothy McVeigh are no longer present."[57] Breivik's lawyer would later say that his client believed the massacre was necessary to save Norway and Europe from Muslims and to punish politicians who had embraced multiculturalism.

Shawn Adolf was locked up in the Arapahoe County Detention Center on a $1 million bond. On November 6, 2009, he pled guilty to federal weapons charges in connection with his assassination attempt against Barack Obama, and he faces up to thirty years in federal prison. As of 2011, Adolf was incarcerated in the Bent County Correctional Facility in southern Colorado. His actions in Denver reverberate with a number of characteristics familiar to other white supremacists in the database, none more obvious than his fanatical dedication to a cause—a necessary precondition for terrorism. Yarbrough, once again, was "not your standard criminal."[58] Following Langan's dramatic 1996 shootout with the FBI, leading to his capture, an agent said, "Someone who pulls a gun on twenty-two FBI agents is one nasty character. One nasty dude."[59] Shawn Adolf "was not your typical bad guy."

Shortly after the Norway massacres, President Obama released an updated national counterterrorism strategy. Although al-Qaeda was still considered the primary threat to U.S. security, the administration had clearly revisited the white supremacy issue. "Throughout our history," Obama wrote, "misguided groups—including international and domestic terrorist organizations, neo-Nazis and anti-Semitic groups—have engaged in horrific violence to kill our citizens and threaten our way of life. . . . As a government, we are working to prevent all types of extremism that leads to violence."[60] Crucial to this prevention strategy, as the Adolf case shows, is a clear understanding of the social networks that support prisoner radicalization and terrorism.

* * * *

Essentially, the debate over prisoner radicalization turns on a matter of logic. Criminologists who find no threats are working from a deductive model by attempting to estimate the *prevalence* of radicalization within the general U.S. prison population. With that population now soaring above the two million mark, this approach is like looking for a needle in the haystack. Criminologists who do recognize a threat work from an inductive model by focusing on actual *incidents* of prisoner radicalization and terrorism. They begin with a handful of needles and try to find consistencies in how they were made.

This research has discovered several consistencies, beginning with the importance of extremist religion as part of a cycle of ideologically motivated violence. This is not necessarily a direct cause-and-effect relationship where a young man goes off to prison, converts to a radical religion, and then becomes a terrorist. Prisons do not manufacture terrorists like a factory; if so, they are doing a lousy job. The process is more complicated than that. It seems to begin with conversion to a religious ideology that the convert himself may not fully understand. This is followed by other decisive turning points—both inside prison and out—that are sequenced yet progressive, with one turning point leading to another. Such an idea was eloquently theorized decades ago by Albert Cohen:

> The history of a violent incident is the history of an interaction process. The intention and the capacity for violence do not pop out, like a candy bar out of a vending machine. They take shape over time. One event calls forth, inhibits, or deflects another; it invites, provokes, abets, tempts, counsels, soothes, or turns away wrath. Every violent episode, whether it is an altercation between friends, a mugging, or a riot is the product of such an interactive history.[61]

Robert Sampson and John Laub, the winners of the 2011 Stockholm Prize in Criminology for their work on life-course theory, apply such an interactive process to the influence of prison, arguing that "the effect of confinement may be indirect and operative in a developmental, cumulative process that reproduces itself over time. . . . Its indirect effect may well be criminogenic (positive) as structural labeling theorists have long argued."[62] From the life-course perspective, Ruben Shumpert is seen as a common criminal who would have never become involved with the transnational terrorist organization al-Shabaab had he not gone to jail, because there he met Somali inmates who were sympathetic to their cause. For it was through these jailed Somalis that Shumpert not only took up the jihadist banner, but also obtained the forged passport that allowed him to become an international fugitive. This was a major turning point for Shumpert but it was not his only one. Shumpert may have never gone to jail in the first place were it not for the associations he formed at the barbershop; the most important association he formed was with an FBI informant. It follows that Shumpert may have never gone to work at the Islamic barbershop had he not converted to Islam in prison. And Shumpert may have never converted to Islam in prison had he not been dealing with substance abuse issues upon his arrival there. An often overlooked aspect of Sageman's research is that some mujahedeen had prior histories of drug abuse and had joined the jihad specifically to abandon their hedonistic lifestyles. "This was the appeal of Salafi Islam for many of the converts," Sageman concludes. "However, after joining the jihad, they returned to petty crime—without the drug abuse—in support of the cause."[63]

Yet Shumpert's involvements with these social networks do not tell the whole story of his pathway to terrorism. According to a 2006 poll by the Pew Research Center, some 5 percent of American Muslims expressed a positive view of al-Qaeda, due mainly to their disapproval of the Iraq War.[64] Shumpert was one of them. Shumpert was profoundly affected by the war because he saw it as an assault on Islam. This is a common theme among Shumpert's generation of anti-American jihadists, one that is documented time and again in terrorism research. J. M. Berger, for one, argues that the U.S. invasion of Iraq on the basis of unfounded claims about weapons of mass destruction "has provided jihadist ideologues with all the ammunition they need to deflect the question of 'who started' [the war]. No future change in the course of U.S. policy can fully erase the impact of that mistake."[65]

Sampson and Laub leave no doubt about the potential influence of such sociopolitical events on adult criminality. "The idea is that turning points in the adult life course matter," they argue, "and that a change in life direction may stem from macro-level events largely beyond individual control (e.g., *war*, depression, natural disaster, revolutions)."[66] Evidence gathered by New York University's Center on Law and Security shows that the Iraq War served as a recruiting tool for al-Qaeda, increasing the number of fatal attacks by jihadists around the world by more than one-third in the three years following the invasion of Iraq.[67] Shumpert's terrorist development was, therefore, a combination of turning points involving micro- and macro-level events, a phenomenon acknowledged in research showing that there is not a single "conveyer belt" to terrorism. Rather, the radicalization process involves a complex interaction of multiple pathways, including personal victimization, political grievance, and the influence of radical group dynamics.[68] A similar pattern is found in the other cases as well.

Marc Ramsey would have never waged his anthrax hoax against John McCain had McCain not stepped onto the world stage as a U.S. presidential candidate. This brought McCain's Vietnam War record into sharp relief against Ramsey's feelings about his father's failing health as a result of Vietnam. The personal became the political for Marc Ramsey—who had a personal history of solving family problems with violence—and that was his major turning point toward terrorism. Yet were he not confined to jails and prisons for his entire adult life, thereby depriving him of social bonding with noncriminals, Ramsey may have never begun his threatening letter-writing campaign against public officials. And had he not abandoned the basic teachings of Moorish Science and set out on his own path of Prison Islam, Ramsey may have never acted upon his intense hatred of U.S. Middle Eastern policy and its consequences for Muslims.

Like Shumpert and Ramsey, Shawn Adolf was a career criminal whose pathway to terrorism was fomented in the crucible of a macro-level political event: the ascendency of Barack Obama. Yet Adolf is distinguished from the others due to the unresolved question his criminality raises for U.S. security: how does an assassination attempt against America's first black president form? In Adolf's case, it began in prison when he joined the Aryan Nations with its racist religious creed. This was Adolf's first turning point. His second turning point occurred by dint of the fact that Adolf's affiliation with this domestic terrorist organization not only endured beyond his time in prison but also more than likely intensified due to Adolf's chronic and persistent use of methamphetamine. This is all too reminiscent of James Earl Ray's behavior leading up to the assassination of Martin Luther King.

But Adolf does share a final characteristic with the others. In each case, there was a long-lasting relationship between a terrorist-in-waiting and law enforcement officials. Shumpert was known to the Seattle FBI for nearly five years before he fled the country to join al-Shabaab, leading one to question whether Shumpert was encouraged and therefore entrapped by overly zealous FBI agents. Ramsey's string of vitriolic prison letters to politicians was well known to the Secret Service years before he became a high-profile inmate at the Denver jail. Adolf's violent tendencies had been feared by the Weld County Sheriff's Department for the better part of a decade. In other words, in each case law enforcement had ample warning of the terrorist event to come. Conceivably, preventive measures could have been taken. All of this raises a compelling question: to what extent does the socially imbalanced relationship between would-be terrorists and law-enforcement officials constitute a developmental process that can be generalized to other cases of terrorism?

* * *

For years, prisoners have used what James Aho calls the *politics of righteousness* as justification for ideologically motivated violence. It is nothing new. This research provides no evidence suggesting that terrorism is widespread among radicalized prisoners (it is not prevalent). To be sure, the identification of only fifty-one terrorists out of millions of inmates who have passed through prisons over the past half-century belies an obsession with the spectacular few. Then again, this is logical. Research shows that recruitment methods used by terrorists are not designed to yield a high number of recruits.[69] In general terms, this study does support security concerns about the prison as an operational base for radicalization and terrorism. The research shows that the largest increase in terrorist incidents committed by radicalized prisoners has occurred since the 9/11 attacks—a period paralleling the remarkable growth of Islam behind bars. It is also an era marked by public indifference about the terrorist threat posed by white supremacists.

Prison-based terrorists are typically radicalized during their early twenties through friendship and kinship networks featuring charismatic leaders. Others are radicalized through torture. In the United States, these terrorists belong primarily to small homegrown groups yet they are often motivated by foreign organizations, including al-Qaeda, highlighting the trouble with using such formulaic distinctions as "international" and "homegrown" terrorism. Shumpert's participation in international terrorist activity, for instance, would have never been possible without the help of homegrown extremists.

Prison-based terrorists exhibit a reputable level of competence in carrying out their attacks. A clashing viewpoint suggests that U.S. prisoners are criminally incompetent and have never executed a successful act of terrorism. The criticism is not only factually mistaken but it represents a myopic view of the global threat posed by the radicalization of contemporary prison populations. Recent developments indicate that national security concerns must extend beyond U.S. prisons.

Events occurring in foreign prisons have created serious challenges to American-led NATO military operations in Southeast Asia, the Middle East, and Africa. There have been several prison breaks in Yemen in recent years, leading to the escape of more than sixty inmates, including al-Qaeda members, some of whom were involved in the USS *Cole* attack.[70] According to a report by the Combatting Terrorism Center at West Point, Iraq's prison system has become the new cradle of jihadist propaganda, leading to the reconstitution of al-Qaeda in Iraq following the death of Abu Musab al-Zarqawi.[71] Afghanistan's prison population has exploded, from six hundred prisoners in 2001 to about nineteen thousand in 2011, creating appalling conditions of confinement and widespread detainee abuse.[72] A 2011 report by the United Nations found evidence of routine human rights abuses and torture at detention centers in Afghanistan; in some cases, detainees were beaten with rubber hoses, hung from hooks, and had their genitals twisted to extract confessions.[73] There has also been a rash of escapes. Two bold Taliban attacks on Afghanistan's Sarposa Prison in 2008 and 2010 freed nearly 1,400 insurgents.[74] Another five hundred Taliban broke out of a Kandahar prison in 2011. The threat posed by Pakistan's prisons is even more ominous. The nation's prison system has the capacity to hold around twenty thousand convicts, yet they currently incarcerate close to one hundred thousand, of whom half are Islamic extremists linked to the Taliban or al-Qaeda. Children as young as ten years old are mixed in with hardened criminals and religious militants, creating the potential for a new generation of jihadists to carry on bin Laden's ideas for years to come.[75]

There is for Americans, however, an even more compelling case to be made about the global reach of prisoner radicalization. Osama bin Laden's chosen biographer has described Ayman al-Zawahiri—radicalized not in a U.S. prison but in an Egyptian prison—as the "real brains" behind al-Qaeda, an analysis that appeared in numerous post-9/11 accounts.[76] Some twenty years elapsed between Zawahiri's torture in Egyptian custody and his terrorist campaign against America. This significant time lag is not a cause to dismiss Zawahiri's three years in Egypt's notorious prisons. To the contrary, it only confirms Sampson and Laub's argument that the criminogenic effect of confinement is a "cumulative process" that reproduces itself over time. For ex-convicts, the prison experience lingers for the rest of their lives.

* * *

But that was al-Qaeda of old and today the West faces another kind of enemy—the lone-wolf terrorist, an unaffiliated individual who nevertheless often draws on beliefs and ideologies of validation generated and transmitted by extremist movements.[77] "The biggest concern we have right now," said President Obama in an interview shortly before the tenth anniversary of 9/11, "is the lone wolf terrorist."[78] It is exemplified in the final case discussed here, Carlos Bledsoe (case 49).[79]

Carlos Leon Bledsoe was born to middle-class African American parents of Baptist persuasion in Memphis, Tennessee, on July 9, 1985. In his youth, Bledsoe attended school and church and worked a series of menial jobs. He also admired the work of Martin Luther King and had hung a picture of the great civil rights leader on his bedroom wall. But then he drifted toward the gang life, leading to several school suspensions. After graduating from high school, Bledsoe left Memphis for Nashville where he enrolled at Tennessee State University. In 2003, prior to his eighteenth birthday and while still a student at Tennessee State, Bledsoe's emerging criminality became more violent. He was arrested for possession of a chrome-plated set of brass knuckles, which he had used to pulverize a woman's car window after she rammed into a vehicle Bledsoe was riding in. As Bledsoe smashed out the window, he shouted, "Bitch, I'm gonna kill you. . . . Get out. . . . I'm gonna kill you when I get your address." The case was processed out of court by juvenile authorities.

A year later, during a routine traffic stop Bledsoe was found with some marijuana, two shotguns, a switchblade knife, and a Russian-made SKS semiautomatic rifle with a chambered bullet. Facing a fourteen-year sentence on weapons charges, Bledsoe was given a plea arrangement whereby all but the switchblade violation was dropped in exchange for one year of probation. Curiously, the switchblade charge was dismissed and Bledsoe was never assigned a probation officer. Even so, the experience frightened Bledsoe and he set out to change his life. He found new friends and began an intense study of religion. Questioning his Baptist faith, Bledsoe was initially drawn to Judaism. He visited a couple of orthodox synagogues and was given some pamphlets to read but was turned away, because, in Bledsoe's telling of it, he was black. So he turned to Islam and converted to the faith at Nashville's al-Farooq mosque in 2004 when he was nineteen. Shortly thereafter, the picture of Martin Luther King came down from his wall.

By 2007, Bledsoe had become an observant Muslim and had legally changed his name to Abdulhakim Mujahid Muhammad. (The middle name, Mujahid, or "holy warrior," is not a common name among Muslims.[80]) Yet he had changed more than his name. In September, Bledsoe flew to Yemen, arriving there on the sixth anniversary of 9/11. He found a job teaching English at a British school in Aden, South Yemen, studied Arabic and Islamic law, and entered into an arranged marriage with a local woman. Who Bledsoe met during his time in Aden is the subject of debate, but in a subsequent letter to the press he discussed the influence of a terrorist network, stating that he was "asked many times to carry out a martyrdom operation in America."[81]

On November 14, 2008, Bledsoe was arrested at a roadside checkpoint for failing to carry the proper government documents for his travel. Found in his possession was a fake Somali passport, an explosives manual, a cellphone with numbers for wanted terrorists in Saudi Arabia, and a computer jump drive containing literature from Anwar al-Awlaki, the Yemen-based American Islamic cleric. Awlaki had been released from a Yemen prison a year earlier for his involvement in an al-Qaeda plot to kidnap a U.S. military attaché and he was then beginning to have a major influence on English-speaking jihadists internationally, including the would-be Illinois courthouse bomber Michael Finton, the underwear bomber Umar Farouk Abdulmutallab, and Nidal Hasan whose November 2009 massacre at Fort Hood, Texas, would come to define *opposition to the U.S. military* as the new face of lone-wolf terrorism in America.[82]

Bledsoe's plan had been to travel to Somalia for training in bomb building, perhaps with al-Shabaab, but he ended up imprisoned in Yemen's Political Security Organization, where he was interviewed by representatives from the U.S. embassy. According to Bledsoe's later statement to the court, he was also interviewed by an FBI agent. During his months in custody, Bledsoe met fellow Muslim detainees from Germany, Britain, Somalia, and Cameroon. Some were allegedly beaten, tortured, and sodomized by their interrogators in Bledsoe's presence. Although Bledsoe was an extremist before his imprisonment, the experience amplified his violent tendencies and brought him to a turning point. As Bledsoe later told a psychiatrist, his time in the Yemen prison provoked him to launch a jihad against America.

Bledsoe was deported to the United States in January 2009, purportedly through the intervention of the U.S. Justice Department, and he resettled with his father in Memphis where he went to work in his family's tour-bus company. Sources indicate that Bledsoe was placed on a terrorism watch list once he landed in the United States.[83] Other sources indicate that the FBI's Joint Terrorism Task Force had investigated him. In any event, several months later Bledsoe moved to Little Rock, Arkansas, where he opened a new office for the family business. On May 20, CNN reported the story of a foiled terrorist attack on New York synagogues and military aircraft by men who had converted to Islam in prison (cases 43, 45, and 47). It was around this time that Bledsoe's plan for killing took shape. Bledsoe made a martyrdom video for his wife back in Yemen, stockpiled ammunition, bought several firearms, and took target practice at a construction site. One of the guns he purchased was a .22-caliber rifle, bought over the counter at a Wal-Mart. Bledsoe would claim that the reason he made this purchase was to determine whether the FBI was following him. When Wal-Mart did not put a hold on the firearm purchase, Bledsoe was home free to pursue two ideas. "Plan A" was to assassinate three Jewish rabbis with Molotov cocktails. "Plan B" was to assassinate U.S. military personnel. He chose the latter.

On June 1, Bledsoe loaded his black Ford Explorer with six hundred rounds of ammunition, homemade silencers, the .22 rifle, and his SKS semiautomatic carbine. He drove to a Little Rock army recruiting center where he spotted two soldiers in fatigues smoking cigarettes near the entrance. Bledsoe opened fire from his vehicle, spending multiple rounds from the semiautomatic, killing one soldier and wounding another. Bledsoe sped away, intent on making the 150-mile drive to Memphis where he would switch cars, but he made a wrong turn into a construction zone where he was captured by a patrolman. As Bledsoe was being placed in the cruiser, he told the officer, "It's a war going on against Muslims, and that's why I did it!"

On January 12, 2010, with images of the underwear bomber still flashing on television screens across America, Bledsoe sent the presiding judge in his case a letter pleading guilty to one count of capital murder and fifteen counts of terrorist acts. "I'm affiliated with al-Qaeda in the Arabian Peninsula (al-Qaeda in Yemen)," he wrote. "This was a Jihadi attack on infidel forces." Months later, AQAP's English-language online magazine, Inspire, acknowledged the organization's strategic shift to lone-wolf terrorism by encouraging American Muslims to "fight jihad on U.S. soil," rather than attempting to travel overseas for training. The article extolled the virtues of random shootings and praised the killings by Nidal Hasan and Abdulhakim Mujahid Muhammad. As of 2011, Bledsoe was locked in solitary confinement at an Arkansas county jail after attacking a guard with a metal shank. As Bledsoe stabbed the guard, he shouted, "I got your white boy ass. Allah!"

* * *

The gestation period between Bledsoe's radicalization in a Yemen prison and his act of terrorism in Arkansas was roughly five months, shorter than Ayman al-Zawahiri's by an order of magnitude. (The human carnage left behind was also distinguished by an order of magnitude.) What is most at issue here is intention, however, not time lapses. Bledsoe's moral outrage over the treatment of Muslims in Yemen led him to make the ideological leap to armed jihad in America. Little Rock was to have been only the beginning. Armed with hundreds of rounds of ammunition, multiple firearms, a box of Molotov cocktails, and cellphones, Bledsoe's plan had been to commit mass murder at army recruiting centers from Memphis to Richmond, Kentucky, and then to go on to the nation's capital. From there his plan was to bomb synagogues throughout the northeast. Bledsoe is hardly unique. Shumpert's intention was to assist al-Shabaab in its ruthless campaign of summary justice against U.S.-supported government officials and Sufi Muslims in Somalia. The purpose of Marc Ramsey's anthrax hoax was to obstruct a U.S. presidential campaign. Shawn Adolf wanted nothing less than to kill Barack Obama. A common denominator propelled each man's trajectory toward terrorism: each had, in one way or another, been radicalized through prison social networks. Shumpert and his Somali homeboys in the King County Jail, Ramsey and the Moorish brothers of the Indiana prisons, Adolf and the Aryan Nations of Colorado, Bledsoe and the tortured Muslims in Yemen—all of these social networks facilitated the transformation of violent propensities into terrorist causes.

Along with a sense of brotherhood and a compelling ideology disseminated through folk knowledge, literature, videos, and (for Bledsoe) the Internet, what these social networks offered their supporters were two long-standing psychological preconditions for mass killing, used to spectacular effect by Hitler and Goebbels: the dehumanization of the victim and the symbolic elevation of the executioner to a position of moral sanctity.[84] Internalizing these preconditions, extremists began to think of themselves as soldiers. The verbal dehumanization of the "other" is evident in Shumpert's fight not against American citizens but against "everything America stood for." Ramsey addressed his victim as if he were "already DEAD." Adolf wanted to prevent a "nigger" from occupying the White House by killing him with a weapon made for the eradication of vermin. Bledsoe didn't stick a white male guard but his "white boy ass," followed immediately by the invocation "Allah!"—or the symbolic elevation of his violence to an expression of moral sanctity. Other verbal cues of moral sanctity: Bledsoe's "Jihadi attack on infidel forces" was retaliation against a "war against Muslims"; Adolf wanted to "go out in a blaze of glory" on the anniversary of Martin Luther King's famous civil rights speech; U.S. Middle Eastern policy "loathed" Ramsey (don't even get him started on Israel), signing off with the battle cry, "Allahu Akbar"; Shumpert was locked in a life-or-death battle against an "evil ideology."

Overall, the case studies indicate that terrorism is triggered by internal turning points revolving around individual grievances, and by external turning points beyond the individual's control. All of this is encapsulated in social networks. Social networks provide both an underlying structure and a grammar for extremists to connect with one another. In each case, social networks were there when criminals recruited themselves into the role of terrorists as a personal response to evolving world events, offering support, resources, and, in the case of Shumpert and Bledsoe, traditional knowledge on local customs in strange and distant lands. Social networks provide the pathways for moving from individual grievances to identification with radical political agendas to the abandonment of politics for violence exclusively. In the end, then, it is not just time that matters but timing and who you hang out with, both literally and virtually. And it is for this reason that life-course criminology matters to the study of terrorism. It provides a portal through which we may understand how people *evolve* into terrorists.

Life-course criminology may also provide a better understanding of how prisoners evolve into radicals. What prison conditions would inspire an inmate to set foot on the pathway to radicalization? Previous research offers few answers; ironically, what is usually missing from these studies is an investigation of prisons themselves. That subject is taken up next through an ethnographic study of prisoners who converted to Islam and white supremacy faiths while in custody. An ethnographic approach also allows for a more thorough investigation of the strategies employed by prison radicals to convert individual grievances into collective action: kinship networks, clandestine communication systems, and charismatic leadership.

NOTES

* Chapter 9 refers to a database which can be found in Appendix 1: The Prisoner Radicalization/Terrorism Database of Hamm, M. (2013). *The spectacular few.* New York: New York University Press.

1 Quoted in Sciolino and Schmitt, "A Not Very Private Feud over Terrorism."

2 "Southern Poverty Law Center," *SPLC Report* (Summer 2011): 1.

3 Barton Gellman, "How the G-Man Got His Groove Back: Inside Bob Mueller's 10-Year Campaign to Fix the FBI," *Newsweek*, May 9, 2011.

4 Andrew Blejwas, Anthony Griggs, and Mark Potok, "Terror from the Right," *Intelligence Report* (Southern Poverty Law Center) (Summer 2005): 33–46.

5 Jenkins, *Would-Be Warriors.*

6   Howard S. Becker, "The Epistemology of Qualitative Research," in Charles C. Ragin and Howard S. Becker (eds.), *What Is a Case? Exploring the Foundations of Social Inquiry* (New York: Cambridge University Press, 1995), p. 208.

7   Jenkins, *Would-Be Warriors*, p. 6.

8   Letter from Amir Abdul Muhaimeen (Ruben Shumpert) to U.S. District Judge Marsha J. Pechman, June 5, 2006.

9   Ibid.

10 *USA v. Ruben Luis Leon Shumpert*, CR04-494MJP.

11 Paul Shukovsky, "14 Arrested in Raids by Terror Task Force," *Seattle Post Intelligencer*, November 19, 2004, accessed at www.seattlepi.com/news/article/14-arrested-in- raids-by-terror-task-force-1159972.php.

12 *USA v. Shumpert*.

13 Al-Shabaab, "Stories from the Muhajireen: Ruben Shumpert," accessed at http://revolution.thabaat.net/?p=741; Mark S. Hamm, *Terrorism as Crime: From Oklahoma City to Al-Qaeda and Beyond* (New York: New York University Press, 2007).

14 Paul Shukovsky, "Sheik Depicted as a Danger," *Seattle Post-Intelligencer*, February 10, 2006.

15 Letter to Judge Pechman.

16 Ibid.

17 Ibid.

18 *USA v. Shumpert*.

19 Shukovsky, "Sheik Depicted as Dangerous."

20 Al-Shabaab, "Stories from the Muhajireen."

21 Ibid.

22 "Seattle Case Raises Question about War on Terror," CNN.com, December 18, 2006.

23 Al-Shabaab, "Stories from Muhajireen."

24 Edmund Sanders, "Conditions May Be Ripe for Al Qaeda to Gain in Somalia," *Los Angeles Times*, August 25, 2008.

25 John Lee Anderson, "The Most Failed State: Letter from Mogadishu," *New Yorker*, December 14, 2009.

26 Andrea Elliott, "A Call to Jihad, Answered in America," *New York Times*, July 12, 2009.

27 Bruce Loudon, "Islamists Plotted to Kill Clinton in Nairobi Hotel," *The Australian*, September 8, 2009.

28 Berger, *Jihad Joe*.

29 FBI Director Robert S. Mueller III, speech before the Council on Foreign Relations (Washington, DC, January 23, 2009).

30 The pipeline is thought to have run from Minneapolis to Mexico to Mogadishu. See Laura Yuen, "Family IDs Minn: Man Allegedly behind Somali Suicide Bombing," Minnesota Public Radio, June 7, 2011.

31 *USA v. Ruben Luis Leon Shumpert*, Magistrate's Docket No. 06-631 M.

32 Al-Shabaab, "Stories from the Muhajireen."

33 Spencer S. Hsu and Carrie Johnson, "Somali Americans Recruited by Extremists," *Washington Post*, March 11, 2009.

34 Quoted in Eric Vogt, "Terrorists in Prison: The Challenges Facing Corrections," *Inside Homeland Security*, no date, accessed at www.icpa.ca/tools/download/622/Terrorists_in_Prison.pdf.

35 Russ Buettner, "Manhattan Man Indicted in Pipe Bomb Case," *New York Times*, February 29, 2012.

36 Letter to the author from Marc Ramsey, September 15, 2010.

37 Ibid.

38 Ibid., emphasis in original.

39 Associated Press, "Officials: Threat to McCain Colorado Office," *Press release*, August 22, 2008.

40 Letter to author from Marc Ramsey.

41 CBS News, "Inmate Charged for McCain Office Threat," August 22, 2008.

42 Ibid.

43 Letter to author from Marc Ramsey.

44 Howard Pankratz, "Inmate Sentenced for White Powder McCain Threat," *Denver Post*, March 3, 2009.

45 My attempts to correspond with Adolf were unsuccessful.

46 U.S. Department of Justice, *Outlaw Motorcycle Gangs in the United States* (Washington, DC.: n.d.).

47 Quoted in David Holthouse, "Killer Kindred," *Intelligence Report,* Southern Poverty Law Center 137 (2010): p. 27.

48 This overall narrative is a composite based on various news articles in the *Greeley Tribune.*

49 John Piazza, "Feds: Trio of Would-Be Obama Assassins Not Much of 'Threat'," *New York Daily News,* August 27, 2008.

50 David Johnston and Eric Schmitt, "Denver Police Brace for Convention," *New York Times,* August 5, 2008; *Convention,* a documentary by AJ Schnack (Sundance Films, 2009).

51 *Convention.*

52 Mark Hosenball, "A Racial Plot?," *Newsweek,* August 27, 2008.

53 Frank Cardona, "Obama-Plot Figure Sentenced," *Denver Post,* January 30, 2009.

54 *USA v. Shawn Robert Adolf.*

55 Hamm, *In Bad Company.*

56 Ibid.

57 Andrew Gumbel, "Seeds of Terror in Norway," *Los Angeles Times,* July 28, 2011.

58 Aho, *Politics of Righteousness,* p. 66.

59 Mark S. Hamm, "Apocalyptic Violence: The Seduction of Terrorist Subcultures," *Theoretical Criminology* 8 (2004): 329.

60 Barack Obama, *Empowering Local Partners to Prevent Violent Extremism in the United States,* The White House, August 2011, p. 1.

61 Albert K. Cohen, "Prison Violence: A Sociological Perspective," in Albert K. Cohen, George F. Cole, and Robert G. Bailey (eds.), *Prison Violence* (Lexington, Mass: D. C. Heath, 1976), p. 8.

62 Robert J. Sampson and John H. Laub, "A Life-Course Theory of Cumulative Disadvantage and the Stability of Delinquency," in Alex Piquero and Paul Mazerolle (eds.), *Life-Course Criminology: Contemporary and Classic Readings* (Belmont, Calif.: Wadsworth, 2001), p. 159.

63 Sageman, *Understanding Terror Networks,* p. 82.

64 Pew Research Center, *Muslim Americans: Middle Class and Mostly Mainstream* (Washington, D. C.: Pew Research Center, 2007).

65 Berger, *Jihad Joe,* p. 209.

66 Robert J. Sampson and John R. Laub, "Socioeconomic Achievement in the Life Course of Disadvantaged Men: Military Service as a Turning Point," *American Sociological Review* 61 (1996): 347, emphasis added.

67 Cited in Bergen, *Longest War.*

68 Clark McCauley and Sophia Moskalenko, "Mechanisms of Political Radicalization: Pathways toward Terrorism," *Terrorism and Political Violence* 20 (2008): 415–433.

69 Sageman, *Understanding Terror Networks.*

70 Bergen, *Longest War; New York Times,* June 22, 2011.

71 Myriam Benraad, "Prisons in Iraq: A New Generation of Jihadists?" *CTC Sentinel* (December 2009): 16–18.

72 Ray Rivera, "Afghan Jails Are Accused of Torture," *New York Times,* September 9, 2011.

73 Alissa J. Rubin, "Afghan Jails Again Get Detainees from NATO," *New York Times,* February 16, 2012.

74 "Taliban Fighters Escape in Mass Afghan Prison Break," *The Telegraph,* April 25, 2011.

75 Interview with confidential sources, 2011.

76 Ayub Khan, "Interview with Hamid Mir: Bin Laden Biographer," Islamonline.net, October 23, 2001, accessed at http://www.islamonline.net/servlet/Satellite?c=Article_C&pagename=Zone-English-Muslim_Affairs/MAELayout&cid=1156077760398.

77 Ramon Spaaij, "The Enigma of Lone Wolf Terrorism: An Assessment," *Studies in Conflict and Terrorism* 33 (2010): 854–870.

78 "Obama: 'Lone Wolf' Terror Attack Biggest Concern," *Time*, August 16, 2011.

79 The following composite is drawn from Competency Evaluation for Abdulhakim Mujahid Muhammad, Arkansas Department of Human Services, Arkansas State Hospital, Forensic Report, July 20, 2010; Kristina Goetz, "When Carlos Bledsoe Became Abdulhakim Mujahid Muhammad," *Memphis Commercial Appeal*, November 14, 2010.

80 Bergen, *Longest War*.

81 Goetz, "When Carlos Bledsoe Became Abdulhakim Mujahid Muhammad."

82 Mark S. Hamm, "Lone Wolves on the Rise: The New Threat of Lone Terrorists, from the Unabomber to the Standalone Jihadist," International Centre for Counter-Terrorism—The Hague, 2010, http://www.icct.nl/events_past_vervolg.php?id=14; Jenkins, *Would-Be Warriors*.

83 Because the case has not yet gone to trial, relevant investigative documents remain sealed.

84 Aho, *Politics of Righteousness*.

Part IV

Effects of Terrorism

Chapter 10

Terrorism and Fear

"Terrorists Want a Lot of People Afraid— Not a Lot of People Dead"

Tom Monahan and Robin Maria Valeri

Overview

- What is the purpose of terrorism? Whether it is it to kill people, gain the public's attention, or cause people to be fearful is discussed.
- The physiological response to fear known as the fight-or-flight response and the health implications of prolonged activation of this response are explained.
- Risk assessment and the impact of the availability heuristic and the affect heuristic on risk perception are examined.
- The specific impact of risk assessment on individual behaviors is presented.
- Research examining the impact of the media on the public's development of posttraumatic stress disorder (PTSD) is discussed.
- Finally, the impact of fear of terrorism on acceptance of terrorism-related policies is examined.

What Do Terrorists Want?

Brian Michael Jenkins once famously said, "Terrorists want a lot of people *watching*, not a lot of people dead" [italics added] (2009, p. 83). Terrorists want people watching the violent act to instill fear and influence their behavior. Influencing behavior is central to the definition of terrorism and is what differentiates a terrorist act from a mere criminal act. Title II of U.S. Code, Section 2656f(d), defines terrorism as "premeditated, politically motivated violence perpetrated against non-combatant targets by subnational groups or clandestine agents, usually intended to influence an audience." The FBI defines terrorism as "the unlawful use of force or violence against persons or property to intimidate or coerce a government, the civilian population, or any segment thereof, in furtherance of political or social objectives." (Federal Bureau of Investigation, 2002).

The central elements in each of these definitions are influence and intimidation. The chosen means by which terrorists influence and intimidate an audience is violence, another key element of the definition. Jenkins argues that terrorists don't view a body count as a measure of success, but rather whether the news of the violent terrorist act reaches a broader audience. To reach the ultimate objective of influence and intimidation, the emotion of fear must be generated, with the plausible expectation that this fear will result in producing the desired influence on the intended audience. The United Nations embraces this explanation, claiming in the Geneva Declaration on Terrorism that "the distinguishing feature of terrorism is fear, and this fear is stimulated by threats of indiscriminate and horrifying forms of violence directed against ordinary people everywhere" (United Nations, 1987).

This chapter examines how terrorists leverage and maximize fear to achieve their strategic objectives, and how terrorism risk is perceived by considering both the availability heuristic and affect heuristic. We consider how the fear of terrorism influences individual behaviors such as vacation travel destination decisions and office space rental, as well as group behaviors such as American civil liberties vis-à-vis national counterterrorism policies and governmental budget and spending priorities. Finally, we present evidence to suggest that Jenkins' aforementioned assertion could be modified to say, "Terrorist want a lot of people *afraid*—not a lot of people dead."

Existing research suggests that fear can be persuasive. While it was once believed that arousing high levels of fear was not conducive to attitude change (Janis & Feshbach, 1953), more recent research reveals that high levels of fear can change attitudes and behaviors (de Hoog, Stroebe, & de Wit, 2007). Research showed, however, that for fear to influence and change behavior, the message recipient needs to be provided with an effective strategy for coping with their fear or else they tend to ignore the message (de Hoog, Stroebe, & de Wit, 2007; Keller, 1999; Leventhal, 1970; Rogers, 1983)

At least one researcher (Lewis, 2000) notes that using fear-based reactions as a measurement of a terrorists' success would result in otherwise spectacular terrorist events to be considered abject failures of terrorism. "Public opinion data show . . . conclusively that the bombing of the Murrah Federal Building [in Oklahoma City] did not provoke personal apprehension and therefore, failed as an act of terrorism, despite the incalculable human anguish it inflicted" (Lewis, 2000). Terrorism expert Lawrence Wright also disputes Jenkins' claim, "The spectacular violence that characterized al-Qaeda's attacks was not a means to a goal—it **was** the goal. Success was to be measured by body count, not by political change" [emphasis added] (Wright, 2016). But Wright is indirectly contradicted by Osama bin Laden. In a recorded tape released by Al-Jazeera, bin Laden proclaimed: "We are continuing this policy of bleeding America to the point of bankruptcy" (CNN, 2004). This sentiment was echoed in a 2013 message by al-Qaeda leader Ayman al- Zawahiri, who said, "We should bleed America economically by provoking it to continue in its massive expenditure on its security, for the weak point of America is its economy, which has already begun to stagger due to the military and security expenditure" (Cowell, 2013).

The Physiology of Fear

Most of us have experienced the emotion of fear. But what is fear and how does it impact our bodies? Fear is as an "unusually unpleasant feeling that arises as a normal response to realistic danger" (Marks, 1987, p. 5). It occurs automatically and instantly in response to a threat

(LeDoux, 1996). The emotion of fear is associated with automatic physiological changes in the body often referred to as the "fight-or-flight" response (Cannon, 1932). As part of the fight-or-flight response, adrenal hormones are secreted and heart rate speeds up, increasing circulation. Blood flow is directed to the muscles that help us fight or flee. Additionally, the pupils dilate, respiration increases, and perspiration increases, all of which combine to facilitate an individual fighting or fleeing from a threat.

With regard to terrorism, when one is confronted by a terrorist, being fearful and experiencing the concurrent physiological responses could save your life. But research also reveals that exposure to a terrorist event, either directly or through the media, can result in the development of posttraumatic stress disorder (PTSD), the symptoms of which may persist for years after the event (Brackbill et al., 2009; Galea et al., 2002; Schlenger et al., 2002; Schuster, et al., 2001; Silver, Holman, McIntosh, Poulin, & Gil-Rivas, 2002). Furthermore, if the possibility of a terrorist attack or news stories related to terrorism produce fear, especially prolonged fear, this can have negative health implications (Sapolsky, 2007; Selye, 1936, 1956, 1973). Long-term activation of the fight-or-flight response can result in negative physiological effects such as coronary disease and can also lead to negative behaviors and emotions associated with stress such as becoming aggressive, giving up, or becoming depressed (Dougall & Swanson, 2011; Holman et al., 2008; Kim, Plumb, Gredig, Rankin, & Taylor, 2008;).

Fear and How Heuristics Influence the Perception of Terrorism Risk

In addition to fear causing emotional and physiological responses, it also impacts our thinking. Two cognitive biases that drive the public's evaluation of risk and influence decision-making are the availability heuristic and the affect heuristic. A heuristic is a shortcut, or rule of thumb, that people rely on to quickly process information and make a decision.

The availability heuristic is the tendency for people to estimate the likelihood of an event based upon the ease with which they can recall a specific instance. Because vivid events are more readily called to mind than "boring" statistical facts, people are more likely to overestimate the likelihood of the frequently broadcasted event and base their decision on that, rather than on the statistics (Loewenstein, Weber, Hsee, & Welch, 2001; Slovic, 2000; Tversky & Kahneman, 1973). "For example, the impact of seeing a house burning . . . is probably greater than the impact of reading about the fire in the local paper" (Tversky & Kahneman, 1982: p. 11). Perhaps a more apt illustration of the availability heuristic is the image of the airplanes flying into the World Trade Center being repeatedly broadcasted and viewed by millions for months and years, and the measurable impact it has on human behaviors.

In addition to activating the availability heuristic as it relates to the perception of fear, by exploiting mass media coverage, terrorists not only draw attention to the acts they perpetrate, demonstrating their strength, power, and resourcefulness, but they also concurrently erode trust in the government's ability to protect its people from violence. In contrast to other violent criminals, who take great measures to conceal their identities from the pursuing government, terrorists proudly take credit for their criminal acts, seemingly in conflict with their best interests, reinforcing the notion that the terrorists are beyond the reach of, and more powerful than, the government.

The Availability and Affect Heuristics and the Mass Media

The mass media has been described as the life-sustaining "oxygen" of terrorism (Dettmer, 2004), and Hoffman suggests that modern terrorism began only after the development of satellite television broadcasting in late 1968—further suggesting that it is not coincidental that in the ensuing 30 years, the United States became the number one target of terrorist attacks in the world (Hoffman, 2006, p. 178). Hoffman goes on to explain how terrorists no longer require the complicity of the mass media to communicate with the world. The advent of the Internet and digital communications allows terrorist groups to control every aspect of their message, "determining content, context, and medium . . . targeting precisely the audience (or multiple audiences) they seek to reach" (Hoffman, 2006, p. 198). Indeed, al-Qaeda (as-Sahab) and the Islamic State (al-Hayat) have established media productions companies whose capabilities rival those of established Western outlets.

So, if the availability heuristic is a primary driver of terrorism fear and fear-caused behavioral changes, why is it that other fear-producing phenomena do not result in these types of behavioral change? Why is it that Americans will happily climb behind the steering wheel of an automobile and drive to a summer vacation destination after cancelling air travel, when statistics clearly show that automobile accidents are one of the leading causes of fatalities in the United States? The affect, or dread, heuristic might be one explanation.

In the 16 years since September 11, 2001, approximately 3100 Americans have been killed by terrorist acts within the United States (National Consortium for the Study of Terrorism and Responses to Terrorism, 2017). Contrast this number of fatalities with the number of persons killed in automobile accidents in a single year—33,594 in 2014 (Center for Disease Control, 2016, p. 12); yet, we readily climb behind the steering wheel of our automobiles. Indeed, research established that by avoiding air travel, more people died on the highways in the 3 months following 9/11 than died on the four hijacked airplanes (Gigerenza, 2004). Another health crisis that is causing deaths at a rate much higher than terrorism is opioid abuse. "Opioids—prescription and illicit—are the main driver of drug overdose deaths. Opioids were involved in 33,091 deaths in 2015, and opioid overdoses have quadrupled since 1999" (Centers for Disease Control and Prevention, 2016). One explanation for the difference in perceived risk is the affect heuristic. United States Congressman Thomas Lantos complained during the Iranian hostage crisis, "focusing on individual tragedies, interviewing the families of people in anguish, in horror, in nightmare, completely debilitates national policymakers from making rational decisions in the national interest" (Schmid, 1989). Joseph Stalin explained it in perhaps the darkest of terms, "A single death is a tragedy. A million deaths is a statistic" (Bartlett, 2002).

"Simply put, [the affect heuristic is manifested when] ordinary people use their feelings to estimate risk. In general, the public's assessment of risk utilizes an intuitive, emotional process that deems highly dreaded, unusual, or uncontrolled events as more probable. . . . Thus, those threats that are most feared (i.e. evaluated as the most dreadful and unfamiliar) are actually perceived as greater risks" (Breckenridge & Zimbardo, 2007, pp. 121–122). The Islamic State maximized the impact of the affect heuristic of fear when it broadcasted the grotesque decapitation of hostages James Foley and Steven Sotloff, and the Jordanian pilot burning to death in caged captivity. While very few victims of terrorism are killed in such horrific ways, the affect heuristic causes us to overestimate the probability that it could happen to us, maximizing our terror and advancing the Islamic State's goal.

To demonstrate the impact of the affect heuristic on the perceived risk of terrorism, research has demonstrated that other fear-invoking phenomena do not have the same fear-producing impact as terrorism. Recall that terrorism is particularly effective when terrorists leverage the mass media, reaching an audience far beyond the target of terrorist violence and triggering the availability heuristic. Crime, natural disasters, and public health crises are all fear-inducing phenomenon that result in broad media coverage, yet research shows that the fear-produced behaviors resulting from these phenomena are confined to the affected area only, with no external impact (Monahan, 2013).

In 2016, Chicago experienced a 63% increase in criminal homicides, with 762 deaths reported (Rosenberg-Douglas & Briscoe, 2017), in comparison to the 468 homicides in 2015 (Sanburn, 2016). Concurrent with this crime trend, tourism dropped, with nine fewer conventions being held in the city and 187,000 fewer hotel room nights booked (Channick, 2016). While homicides in Las Vegas also surged 31% to a record high in 2016, unlike Chicago, tourism did not decline in Las Vegas; instead, it increased by 1.5% over the previous year. Supporting the premise that the availability heuristic plays a major role in the stimulation of fear, the relative lack of national and international media exposure focused on murders in Las Vegas as compared to Chicago could explain this disparity in tourist volume. Nonetheless, the increase in homicides in Las Vegas did negatively influence tourism as the 2016 spike in homicides does coincide with a noticeably smaller increase in tourism when compared to previous years. Tourism in Las Vegas did increase slightly in 2016—a mere 1.5% bump over the previous year—compared with 2.8% and 3.7% gains in 2015 and 2014, respectively (Las Vegas Convention and Visitors Authority, 2017). While not universal, any negative impact on tourism was localized to some of those areas that were impacted by the increase of violent crime (homicides) and not generalized to cities without a rise in violent crime.

When it comes to estimating the risk of a terrorist event, the availability and affect heuristics combine synergistically, causing most people to overestimate terrorism risk, and act in a manner consistent with this overestimate. Not only does fear cause us to overestimate risk, it also makes us more risk averse. Consistent with the fight-or-flight response, the individual behaviors influenced by the fear of terrorism include the personal decision to purchase weapons (fight), alter their travel plans, or change office rental locations (flight). These terrorism fear-influenced decisions impact both the individual and the nation's economy.

Fear of Terrorism and Its Influence on Individual Human Behavior

In addition to measuring concerns about a possible terrorist attack, Gallup Polls have also examined whether people have changed their behaviors, asking "As a result of the events on September 11, would you say that you are now less willing to . . . " (Jones, September 8, 2011). In a poll taken on September 14 and 15, 2001, only a few days after the September 11 attacks, 30%of respondents said they were less willing to attend an event with thousands of people and 43% said they were less willing to fly. Ten years after the attacks, in a July 15–17, 2011, poll, the number of people less willing to attend a mass gathering had only decreased slightly to 27%, while the number of people less willing to fly had dropped to 24% (Jones, September 8, 2011).

While people say they are less willing to fly, a comparison of Gallup poll data on air travel collected in August 2000 with that of data from a December 2008 poll shows that air travel has returned to pre-9/11 levels (Jones, September 8, 2011). In August 2000, 45% of Americans said they had flown in the past 12 months, taking an average of 1.8 round trips. In December 2008, 43% of Americans said they had flown in the past 12 months, taking an average of 1.7 round trips.

So, although air travel has returned to pre-9/11 levels, the percentage of people who say that 9/11 has permanently changed how they live their lives has remained relatively constant when comparing a 2002 poll in which 25% of respondents said that the attacks had permanently changed how they lived their lives to an August 2011 poll in which 28% of respondents said the same (Jones, September 8, 2011). With roughly a quarter of Americans saying that 9/11 has changed how they personally live their lives, in the August 2011 poll, 58% said they think it has permanently changed how Americans live their lives, an increase from 49% in 2002 (Jones, September 8, 2011).

The Gallup Poll results suggest that Americans changed their behaviors after the September 11, 2001, attacks in several ways, including, but not limited to, changing their travel plans and avoiding crowded places. These changes were driven by the fear of future terrorist events. In addition to these Gallup Poll results, researchers have also examined how fear of terrorism has changed individuals' behaviors and the financial impact of these changes.

Research by Torabi and Seo (2004) examined how fear of terrorism impacted individuals' behaviors 10 to 12 months after the September 11 attacks. As noted by the researchers, behavioral changes are important to study for two reasons. First, because "behavioral changes tend to be more enduring and stable than psychological and emotional changes [and second, because] behavioral changes as a result of the 9-11 attacks [help] reveal individuals' relatively stable perceptions about terrorist threats" (Torabi & Seo, 2004, p. 180). To complete the study, 807 adults from across the United States were interviewed and asked questions regarding behavior changes they had made as a result of the September 11 attacks. Questions included whether the respondent had turned to prayer, gathered emergency supplies, donated money or blood, moved to another neighborhood, improved home security, purchased a weapon, limited outside activities, avoided contact with people of another race, and/or changed their mode of transportation.

Twenty-five percent of respondents said that they had limited their outside activities because they were afraid of more terrorist attacks; however, this number dropped to approximately 7% when participants were asked if they were still limiting their outside activities 10 to 12 months after the attacks. Twenty-three percent of respondents said that they had changed their mode of transportation because of the attacks—significantly more women and African Americans than men and whites reported doing so. Twelve percent of respondents reported that they had improved their home security since the attacks; significantly more African Americans and Hispanics reported doing so than did white respondents. Also, 10% of respondents reported considering purchasing a weapon, with significantly more men than women and significantly more people aged 18–44 versus 45–64 considering doing so. These latter four behavior changes are driven by individuals' perceptions of risk.

Fear influences individual behaviors, such as leisure travel decisions, which in turn have an external economic impact, as demonstrated by the airline and tourism industries following the September 11, 2001, attacks. According to *The Fiscal Times* (September 9, 2011),

> Airlines, in a weak financial position before the attacks, lost $7 billion in 2001 as business and leisure travel declined. In the decade through 2010, passenger carriers posted a cumulative loss of $63 billion. The travel industry estimates hotels, restaurants, retailers and others lost more than $600 billion in revenue over the last decade as international visitors stayed away from the U.S. Las Vegas and Reno, Nev., and Myrtle Beach, S.C., were among the cities that lost business and jobs.

Because of the decline in air travel immediately following the attacks, the number of jobs in the air transportation industry fell by 10% nationally in the fourth quarter of 2001 (Bram, Orr, & Rapaport, 2002). At LaGuardia Airport and John F. Kennedy International Airport, the job loss rate was twice the national average, or 20%, with approximately 11,000 total jobs lost at these two airports (Bram, Orr, & Rapaport, 2002). In addition to the employment and economic losses suffered by the air transportation industry, Blalock, Kadiyali, and Simon (2009) estimate that one hidden cost of the September 11, 2001, attacks was the approximately 2300 additional lives that were lost in traffic incidents, which resulted from people choosing to drive rather than fly. Fortunately, the increase in road traffic fatalities decreased over time and disappeared by October 2003. While the researchers note that their analyses do not allow them to discern whether people chose driving versus air travel because of fear of flying resulting from concerns about terrorism or because of the increased inconvenience of flying due to airport security. Research by Blalock, Vrinda, and Simon (2007) suggests that the inconvenience resulting from increased airport security has caused some people to choose the riskier but more convenient option of driving over flying. Based on these findings, the authors suggest that officials need to increase the public's confidence in the safety of air and rail travel while minimizing the inconvenience of increased security.

As mentioned, the travel industry also suffered financial losses after the September 11, 2001, attacks. Bram and colleagues (2002) reported that the hotel industry in New York City lost 6000 jobs or 15% of its workforce between September 2001 and March 2002, with the majority of those jobs (5000 jobs) lost in October 2001. During that same time period, the number of jobs in the hotel industry fell by 4% nationally. Fortunately for hotel workers in New York City, in April 2002, the number of jobs in the hotel industry rose by 4000. The restaurant and bar industry in New York City, but not nationally, also experienced large fluctuations in employment after September 11 (Bram, Orr, & Rapaport, 2002). An estimated 9000 jobs (6%) were lost in October. But employment rates returned to their pre- 9/11 level by December 2001 (Bram, Orr, & Rapaport, 2002). Similar declines in tourism and hotel occupancy rates were experienced in Madrid after the March 11, 2004, attacks, in London after the July 7, 2005, attacks, and in Paris after the January 7, 2015, and November 13, 2015, attacks (Hospitality ON, January 21, 2015; February 18, 2015; November 16, 2015). These declines are consistent with research that suggests tourism and travel are particularly sensitive to fear caused by terrorism (Abadie & Gardeazabal, 2003; Crain

& Crain, 2006; Drakos & Kutan, 2003; Enders & Sandler, 2008; Enders, Sandler, & Parise, 1992; Mansfield, 1996).

Tourists make purchasing decisions based on the relative safety of the travel destination. One study suggests that a country might benefit from a terrorist attack on its neighbor because such activity causes tourists to change their travel plans, perhaps deciding instead to travel to a presumably safer neighboring country (Mansfield, 1996). However, another study concluded that neighboring countries may be considered a substitute tourist destination only in the short term because terrorism tends to result in a negative impact in tourism demand for the wider region (Drakos & Kutan, 2003). For example, Enders, Sandler, and Parise (1992), in a study examining the impact of terrorism on tourism in the areas of Greece, Italy, and Austria concluded that terrorism negatively impacted both the country attacked and its neighboring countries. In fact, the September 11, 2001, attacks impacted the travel industry worldwide. During the last 4 months of 2001, there was an 11% drop in travel worldwide with the Americas (–24%) and the Middle East (–30%) experiencing the greatest declines (Hospitality ON, November 19, 2015). It was not until 2004 that travel in the United States returned to pre-9/11 levels (Hospitality ON, November 19, 2015).

A more recent report by the World Travel and Tourism Council (WTTC) suggests that at the global level, the tourism and travel industry may be fairly resilient to terrorism (WTTC, March 20, 2017). In their 2016 report, the WTTC noted that global tourism grew by 3.3% in 2016 and, for the sixth year in a row, outpaced the global economy, contributing US$7.6 trillion to the global GDP. Consistent with what was previously stated, consumers are still traveling but "are switching to destinations they perceive to be 'safer'" (WTTC, March 20, 2017, p. 1). For those countries that have experienced a terrorist attack, the WTTC notes "the new data shows that in countries where attacks have happened, visitor exports, which is money spent by foreign visitors in a country, has suffered. The impacts of the initial attacks are compounded by inaccurate or extended travel advisories, and consumer reaction to seek perceived 'safer' places for their vacations" (WTTC, March 20, 2017, p. 1). For example, after the terrorist attacks in Sousse, Tunisia, on June 26, 2015, the Tunisian Central Bank reported that foreign visitors to the country fell by 44% (Hospitality ON, September 1, 2015).

There is also evidence to support the counter-argument that there is no relationship between terrorism and tourism. For example, the terrorist attack on December 2, 2015, in San Bernardino, California, a mere 60 miles from Los Angeles, did not seem to have a meaningful impact on tourism in Los Angeles, as tourist volume jumped 4% in 2016 (Martin, 2017).

Fear also changed individual behaviors beyond just the travel and tourism industry. The New York City area, the United States, and global commercial real estate markets suffered financial losses from the September 11, 2001, attack. In New York City, the attacks destroyed 3% of Manhattan's office space and made another 3% temporarily unusable. The law of supply and demand dictates that vacancies should decline with reduced supply and rents should increase commensurate with demand for space (Bram, Orr, & Rapaport, 2002). However, the opposite occurred. Vacancy rates, which had already been rising prior to the attacks, continued to increase while rents decreased (Bram, Orr, & Rapaport, 2002). Bram and colleagues (2002) suggest that this was because firms that already had available vacant space sublet to those in need and because many hotels repurposed space to serve as temporary offices. Research by Dermisi (2009) suggests that the September 11, 2001, attacks impacted office markets in other cities as well. Dermisi examined the impact of fear of terrorism and economic recession that occurred after 9/11 on office rents and vacancies in trophy buildings (Sears Tower, Aon Center, and John Hancock Center), Class A (well constructed, well managed, good infrastructure, visually appealing, and in good locations), and Class B buildings (tend to be older construction, but well managed and well maintained) in the city of Chicago. The city of Chicago was chosen for analyses because of its concentration of high-rise office buildings (Sears Tower, Aon Center, and John Hancock Center) less than 2 miles from each other, its concentration of key financial and economic functions, and its increase in vacancy rates after 9/11. Data were analyzed from 1997 through 2005. Their results indicate that vacancy rates increased significantly in all three building types examined. But only trophy buildings experienced a significant decrease in rental rates. Dermisi suggests that the changes in vacancy rates and rental rates that occurred after 9/11 resulted from a combination of factors that included fear of future terrorist attacks, the addition of new Class A office space in Chicago, a sluggish economy, and a lack of tenants moving into the downtown area.

Obviously, travel and tourism, and commercial office space, are not the only markets impacted by terrorism. But these two industries were highlighted to show how fear may influence the decisions of individuals, which may in turn affect the economy. Certainly the events of 9/11 impacted the economy in the short term. But are there long-term economic effects of terrorism? An article in *Economists*, published shortly after the November 2015 attacks in Paris, suggests that the economic effects of terrorism are minimal (Buttonwood, November 16, 2015). In the United States, the stock market recovered within a month of the 9/11 attacks, and the US's GDP growth may have been reduced by half a percentage point. After the London attacks in July 2005, the UK markets recovered in just days. The author suggests that terrorist attacks "may cause a short-term disruption to economic life; people may decide not to visit town centres for a few days. But this generally means they postpone their consumption rather than abandon it; economic activity is simply shifted from one period to the next" (Buttonwood, November 16, 2015). The article does note that the effects of terrorism can have a much larger impact on economies that are dependent on international tourists, such as that of Tunisia and Egypt. It also warns that costly counterterrorism measures could be a drain on economic growth. Finally, the article concludes that if terrorism were to become endemic, as was the case in Northern Ireland, rather than sporadic, the economic impact could be more drastic.

Fear also influences interpersonal relationships and how we respond to others. Terror management theory suggests that as the threat of terrorism causes us to think about our own death, it should also cause us to bolster and defend our own cultural worldviews by rewarding and revering those who uphold them, while punishing those who oppose or transgress against them (Greenberg, Pyszczynski, & Solomon, 1986; Pyszczynski, Solomon, & Greenberg, 2005; Pyszczynski et al., 1996; Rosenblatt, Greenberg, Solomon, Pyszczynski, & Lyon, 1989). The results of terror management research reveal that when one's own death is made salient, people will physically distance themselves from, give harsher punishments to, and aggress against those with opposing worldviews (Greenberg et al., 1990; Greenberg, Simon, Porteus, Pyszczynski, & Solomon, 1995). This would explain why Americans support the harsh treatment of terrorists and anyone who is a threat to America, and why Americans support and revere the people who represent America. Research by Landau et al. (2004) reveals that, for example, presidential approval ratings increased after mortality salience was increased, either experimentally or following government-issued terror warnings (Landau et al. 2004; Willer, 2004).

Fear of Terrorism and Mass Media Exposure

If we accept Brian Michael Jenkins' proposition to be true: "Terrorists want a lot of people watching, not a lot of people dead" (Jenkins, 2009, p. 83), then it logically follows that the global mass media will have a large role in determining how many people are watching. It also draws attention to the fact that individuals do not have to be directly impacted by a terrorist event in order to be affected by it. Rather, exposure to an event and its aftermath, gained through television or other forms of media, can generate fear. Goodin (2006) noted, "in the eighteen months following the 9/11 attacks, between 15% and 30% of the public continued to name terrorism as the nation's most important problem—and the fluctuations closely track[ed] the frequency of television news stories concerning terrorism." This finding is supported by both correlational and experimental research.

Rohner and Frey employed a simple game theoretical model using the world's two dominant newspapers (the *New York Times* and the Swiss *Neue Zurcher Zeitung*), and concluded that a causal relationship exists between terrorism and mass media. "Terrorist attacks are a particular form of communication by terrorist groups. The media are used as a platform for securing a broad dissemination of the terrorists ideology. . . . There is a common-interest-game, whereby both parties adjust their actions according to the actions of the other player" (Rohner & Frey, 2007, p. 142).

In the opening section on fear, the results of research on the development of PTSD resulting from the September 11 attacks were discussed briefly (Ahern et al., 2002, 2004; Brackbill et al., 2009; Galea et al., 2002; Schlenger et al., 2002; Schuster et al., 2001; Silver, Holman, McIntosh, Poulin, & Gil-Rivas, 2002). As expected, people who are directly impacted by a traumatic event such as terrorism can develop PTSD. The results also suggest that exposure to media coverage of these events can exacerbate the development or symptoms of PTSD in those who are directly impacted by terrorism. Furthermore, results suggest that people whose only exposure to the events of September 11 was through the media can develop symptoms of PTSD (Suvak, Maguen, Litz, Silver, & Holman, 2008).

These findings are supported by experimental research (Bourne, Mackay, & Holmes, 2013; Slone, 2000). Research by Slone (2000) suggest that exposure to terrorist threats can increase anxiety. In this research, Slone had 237 research participants watch footage of Israeli news that either depicted terrorist threats or no terrorist threats. After viewing the footage, participants completed questionnaires to assess their anxiety. Consistent with expectations, participants who viewed the terrorism-related news reported significantly higher levels of anxiety.

Research by Bourne, Mackay, and Holmes (2013) not only reveals that watching a traumatic film can result in flashbacks, a symptom of posttraumatic stress disorder, but also that when watching a traumatic film that included both control scenes and potentially intrusive scenes that could lead to flashbacks, different areas of the brain were activated when viewing those potentially intrusive scenes that later produced (versus failed to produce) flashbacks.

Holman, Garfin, and Silver (2013) examined the impact of media exposure versus direct exposure on the development of acute stress symptoms that appear in the weeks after a traumatic event. The traumatic event examined was the Boston Marathon Bombing on April 15, 2013. The researchers also sought to examine the impact of cumulative exposure, through both the media and direct exposure, to several traumatic events. The events included were the September 11, 2001, terrorist attacks, Superstorm Sandy (which hit the United States on October 29, 2012), and the Sandy Hook Elementary School shootings (December 14, 2012). As the researchers note, it is important to examine the effects of cumulative exposure to traumatic events because cumulative exposure increases an individual's risk for the development of a psychiatric disorder over the course of their lifetime. For the study, the researchers conducted an Internet-based survey between April 29 and May 13, 2013, with 846 residents of Boston, 941 residents of New York City, and 2,888 Americans living in the rest of the United States. As expected, people with direct exposure to the Boston Marathon Bombings experienced acute stress but not high acute stress. Whereas people who viewed 6 or more hours of daily media coverage of the Boston Marathon Bombings for the week after the bombing reported significantly more symptoms of high acute stress than either people with direct exposure to the Boson Marathon bombings or people who reported minimal media exposure. Acute stress symptoms were also reported by people with direct exposure to the deliberate and violent attacks of September 11 or to the Sandy Hook school shooting but not to Superstorm Sandy. Given that acute stress reactions may lead to the development of long-term mental and physical illness, it is important to consider the health implications of these findings and the media's role in creating trauma-related distress. While it is important for people to remain informed of important developments that could impact them while a threat is ongoing, as was the case for Bostonians during the lockdown and search for one of the Boston Marathon bombers, perhaps encouraging people outside the directly affected area to limit their media exposure could help curtail the development of acute stress symptoms and the resulting mental and physical health problems that develop from media exposure alone.

Terrorists are well aware of the psychological damage they create. In his communications with Taliban leader, Mullah Omar, Osama bin Laden noted, "Newspapers mentioned that a recent survey showed that seven out of every ten Americans suffer psychological problems following the attacks on New York and Washington" (Cullison, 2004).

In addition to the mental health issues that result from terrorism, physical injuries and physical health problems occur as well. Enders and Olson (n.d.), in a paper examining the direct and indirect costs of terrorism, state that the "direct costs of terrorism include the loss of life, the injuries and the personal suffering resulting from a terrorist attack" (p. 22). The researchers then present and discuss models for calculating the economic cost resulting from loss of life and physical and psychological injuries. Enders and Olson "note that this measure of direct costs excludes the costs of pain and suffering to those injured in a terrorist attack. It also excludes the dollar value of the fear engendered by terrorists" (p. 23). This last statement highlights the fact that fear caused by the threat of terrorism can not only impact mental and physical health but also the financial well-being of both the individual and the nation.

Fear and Vulnerability

As discussed previously, perceived fear may or may not be based in actual risk of harm. Criminologists have established that the group most afraid of crime, elderly women, are statistically the least likely to be victims of crime (Skogan & Maxfield, 1981). Conversely, the group most likely to be victimized by crime, young men, is the least fearful (Skogan, 1986). The conclusion drawn is that perceived or real vulnerability is the primary factor in stimulating fear of crime.

Similarly, there appears to be a small but consistent percentage of people who are very worried about a possible terrorist attack and also a small but consistent percentage of people who are not very worried about a terrorist attack. Given these findings, researchers have sought to examine who is more concerned about a possible terrorist attack. Research by Huddy, Feldman, Capelos, and Provost (2002) conducted in the months just after the September 11 attacks revealed demographic differences in who is afraid. Respondents reported their perceptions of personal/family risk of terrorism and national risk of terrorism. This research revealed that women were significantly more fearful than men of both personal/family risk of terrorism and national risk of terrorism. Perceptions of personal threat, but not national threat, were also predicted by education, race, political affiliation, and proximity to the attacks. Perceptions of personal threat, but not national threat, were related to engaging in precautionary behaviors while perceptions of national threat, but not personal threat, were related to a pessimistic economic outlook for the country.

Eisenman and colleagues (2009) examined whether groups who were typically more vulnerable to disasters—people with mental disabilities and physical disabilities, or members of minority groups—reported greater fear of terrorism and avoided more things they wanted to do because of fears of terrorism than other people. Their results reveal that people who reported a serious mental illness were significantly more likely to worry about terrorism and more likely to avoid things because of terrorism-related fears than people without a mental illness. Latinos were also more likely than whites to report greater worry about terrorism and avoid things that they wanted to do. Both African Americans and people who were disabled reported avoiding more things that did whites. These finding are consistent with Huddy and colleagues (2002) results, which suggested that some demographic groups, in this case those who are typically more vulnerable, may be disproportionately impacted by the threat of terrorism than other groups.

Fear of Terrorism and Its Influence on Group Behaviors

As stated previously in this chapter, influence and intimidation of a government, a society, or a segment of society is central to the definition of terrorism. Having examined how fear influences the individual and individual behaviors, we now consider how the fear of terrorism influences group behaviors and drives governmental policies and doctrine.

We have discussed the oversized reach of terrorist acts and the disproportionate impact on individuals as it relates to fear. We have discussed the availability and affect heuristics that contribute to the incongruence between the perceived likelihood of being victimized by terrorism and the statistical improbability of being so victimized. Perhaps the best known example of how the fear of terrorism drove United States domestic and foreign policy is the Cheney doctrine—also known as the "One-Percent Doctrine" (Suskind, 2006). According to Suskind, following the 9/11 attacks, Vice President Richard Cheney decided that regardless of the statistical probability of a hostile nation or a terrorist group employing a weapon of mass destruction—even if that probability is only 1%—the United States government must act and prepare as if it were a virtual certainty. "It's not about our analysis, as Cheney said, it's about our response." (Suskind, 2006, p. 62). Critics of the George W. Bush administration will charge that this doctrine led to U.S. domestic policies such as the USA PATRIOT Act and the military action in Iraq—widely regarded as one of the worst foreign policy decisions in American history.

The 9/11 attacks on New York and Washington, D.C. stimulated such a level of fear that it changed the behavior of Americans as it relates to counterterrorism policies and the protection of civil liberties. Researchers conducted a national survey and found that as the public senses a greater threat from terrorism, there was an increased willingness to restrict some protections of civil rights and civil liberties (Davis & Silver, 2004). A longitudinal study found that public support for restricting civil liberties to combat terrorism peaked in the days immediately following 9/11, with this public support gradually tapering off over then next year (Kuzma, 2004). Risk experts John Mueller and Mark Stewart note, "Although allowing emotion to overwhelm sensible analysis is both understandable and common among ordinary people, it is not appropriate for officials charged with—and responsible for—keeping them safe" (Mueller & Stewart, 2014). Yet, some would argue that civil liberties were indeed sacrificed, pointing to the surveillance activities of the United States government.

To better understand the role of fear and fear-inducing heuristics in the formulation of public policy, let's examine the difference between the governmental policies related to terrorism and the public health crisis of opioid overdose deaths. It is easy to conjure up an image of an airliner flying into a skyscraper, the building collapsing on itself, killing everyone inside. This image is highly available to our imagination because we have that video clip seared into our brain, after seeing it countlessly replayed on the news and in historical documentaries. Conversely, it is difficult to envision ourselves, or a loved one, so completely addicted to an opioid and dying from an accidental overdose of heroin. Everyday there is a news report of a terrorist attack somewhere in the world. Rarely does the news report on an opioid death—feeding the availability heuristic.

The affect heuristic is the emotional process that "deems highly dreaded, unusual, or uncontrolled events as more probable" (Breckenridge & Zimbardo, 2007, 121). We consider a terrorist attack to be outside our control, yet consuming the first dose of an opioid is widely considered to be a conscious choice and within our control. Thus, the affect heuristic creates the "shortcut" to a disproportionate fear of terrorism in contrast to the far more likely outcome of opioid addiction.

As demonstrated by the evidence showing that the sense of vulnerability has a direct correlation on the fear of crime and terrorism, the media magnifies the unpredictable vulnerability of the symbolic "Average Joe" victimized in a terrorist attack, yet rarely reports on the opioid overdose victim. Families, embarrassed to acknowledge the drug abuse of the decedent, quietly bury their loved ones without flag-draped coffins and bagpipes, outside the view of TV cameras.

Aside from his declaration that "terrorists want a lot of people watching, not a lot of people dead," Jenkins also asserts, "Terrorism is theatre" (Jenkins, 1974). Psychiatrist Dr. Frederick Hacker further explained, "terrorists seek to frighten and, by frightening, to dominate and control. They want to impress. They play to and for an audience, and solicit audience participation" (Hacker, 1976). With this premise, coupled with the understanding of the heuristics of fear and the individual and group behavioral changes caused by fear, we make our central claim: "Terrorists want a lot of people scared—not a lot of people dead."

REFERENCES

Abadie, A. & Gardeazabal, J. (2003). The economic costs of conflict: A case study of the Basque Country. *The American Economic Review, 93*, 113–132.

Ahern, J., Galea, S., Resnick, H., Kilpatrick, D., Bucuvalas, D., Gold, J., & Vlahov, D. (2002). Television images and psychological symptoms after the September 11 attacks. *Psychiatry, 65*, 289–300.

Ahern, J., Galea, S., Resnick, H., & Vlahov, D. (2004). Television images and probable posttraumatic stress disorder after September 11: The role of background characteristics, event exposures, and perievent panic. *Journal of Nervous Mental Disorders, 192*, 217–226.

Bartlett's Familiar Quotations 686. (17th ed., Little, Brown & Co. 2002).

Blalock, G., Kadiyali, V., & Simon, D. H. (2009). Driving fatalities after 9/11: A hidden cost of terrorism. *Applied Economics, 41*, 1717–1729.

Blalock, G., Vrinda, K., & Simon, D. H. (2007). The impact of post-9/11 airport security measures on the demand for air travel. *Journal of Law and Economics, 50*, 731–755.

Bourne, C., Mackay, C. E., & Holmes, E. A. (2013). The neural basis of flashback formation: The impact of viewing trauma. *Psychological Medicine, 43*, 1521–1532.

Brackbill, R. M., Hadler, J. L., DiGrande, L., Ekenga, C. C., Fargel, M. R., Friedman, S., Perlman, S. E., Stellman, S. D., Walker, D. J., Wu, D., Yu, S., & Thorpe, L. E. (2009). Asthma and posttraumatic stress symptoms 5 to 6 years following exposure to the World Trade Center terrorist attack. *Journal of the American Medical Association, 32*, 502–516.

Bram, J., Orr, J., & Rapaport, C. (2002). Measuring the effects of the September 11 attack on New York City. *Federal Reserve Bank of New York Economic Policy Review, 8*, 5–20.

Breckenridge, J. & Zimbardo, P. (2007). The strategy of terrorism and the psychology of mass-mediated fear. In B. Bongar, L. Brown, L. Beutner, J. Breckenridge, & P. Zimbardo (Eds.), *Psychology of terrorism*. Oxford: Oxford University Press.

Buttonwood. (November 16, 2015). Why terrorism has a limited impact on markets. *The Buttonwood Blog, the Economist*. Retrieved from www.economist.com/blogs/buttonwood/2015/11/investing

Cannon, W. B. (1932). *The wisdom of the body*. New York, NY: Norton.

Centers for Disease Control and Prevention. (2016). *Drug Overdose Death Data*. Retrieved from www.cdc.gov/drugoverdose/data/statedeaths.html

Channick, R. (January 13, 2016). Can Chicago tourism overcome image of crime, police brutality? *Chicago Tribune*. Retrieved from www.chicagotribune.com/business/ct-chicago-tourism-image-0112-biz-20160112-story.html

CNN. (November 1, 2004). *Bin Laden: Goal Is to Bankrupt the U.S*. Retrieved August 10, 2012, from www.cnn.com/2004/WORLD/meast/11/01/binladen.tape

Cowell, A. (September 13, 2013). Attack U.S., Qaeda Chief Tells Muslims in a speech. *The New York Times*. Retrieved September 17, 2013, from www.nytimes.com/2013/09/14/world/al-qaeda-leader-ayman-al-zawahiri-urges-muslims-to-attack-america.html?_r=0

Crain, N. & Crain, W. M. (July 2006). Terrorized economies. *Public Choice, 128*(1/2), 317–349.

Cullison, A. (September 2004). Inside al-Qaeda's hard drive. *Atlantic Monthly*, 55–70.

Davis, D. & Silver, B. (January, 2004). Civil liberties vs. security: Public opinion in the context of the terrorist attacks on America. *American Journal of Political Science, 48*(1), 28–46.

Dermisi, S. V. (2009). The impact of terrorism fears on downtown real estate Chicago office market cycles. *Journal of Real Estate Portfolio Management, 13*, 57–73.

de Hoog, N., Stroebe, W., & de Wit, J. B. F. (2007). The impact of vulnerability to and severity of a health risk on processing and acceptance of fear-arousing communications: A meta-analysis. *Review of General Psychology, 11*, 258–285.

Dettmer, J. (2004). Supplying terrorists the "oxygen of publicity". In T. J. Badey (Ed.), *Annual editions: Violence and terrorism, 2004/2005* (pp. 136–137). Guilford, CT: McGraw-Hill/Duskin.

Dougall, A. L. & Swanson, J. N. (2011). Physical health outcomes of trauma. In R. J. Contrada & A. Baum (Eds.), *Handbook of stress science: Biology, psychology, and health*. New York, NY: Spring Publishing Company.

Drakos, K. & Kutan, A. M. (2003). Regional effects of terrorism on tourism in three Mediterranean countries. *Journal of Conflict Resolution, 47*, 621–641.

Eisenman, D. P., Gilk, D., Ong, M., Zhou, Q., Tseng, C., Long, A., Fielding, J., & Ash, S. (2009). Terrorism related fear and avoidance behavior in a multiethnic urban population. *American Journal of Public Health, 99*, 168–174.

Enders, W. & Olson, E. (n.d.) Measuring the economic costs of terrorism. Department of Economics, Finance, and Legal Studies, Culverhouse College of Commerce and Business Administration, University of Alabama, Tuscaloosa, Alabama.

Enders, W. & Sandler, T. (2008). Causality between transnational terrorism and tourism: The case of Spain. *Terrorism, 14*, 49–58.

Enders, W., Sandler, T., & Parise, G. F. (1992). An econometric analysis of the impact of terrorism on tourism. *Kyklos, 45*, 531–554.

Federal Bureau of Investigation, Counterterrorism Threat Assessment and Warning Unit. (2002). *Terrorism in the United States 2000/2001*. FBI Publication 0308. Washington, DC: U.S. Department of Justice, p. 3.

Fiscal Times, The. (September 9, 2011). The economic cost of 9/11: Three industries still recovering. *The Fiscal Times*. Retrieved from www.thefiscaltimes.com/Articles/2011/09/09/Economic-Cost-of%20 9-11-Three-Industries-Still-Recovering

Galea, S., Ahern, J., Resnick, H., Kilpatrick, D., Bucuvalas, M., Gold, J., & Vlahov, D. (2002). Psychological sequelae of the September 11 terrorist attacks in New York City. *New England Journal of Medicine, 346*, 982–987.

Gigerenza, G. (2004). Dread risk, September 11, and fatal traffic accidents. *Psychological Science, 151*(4), 286–287.

Goodin, R. E. (2006). What's wrong with terrorism? *Columbia Law Review, 119*.

Greenberg, J., Pyszczynski, T., & Solomon, S. (1986). The causes and consequences of the need for self-esteem: A terror management theory. In R. F. Baumeister (Ed.), *Public self and private self* (pp. 189–212). New York: Springer-Verlag.

Greenberg, J., Pyszczynski, T., Solomon, S., Rosenblatt, A., Veeder, M., Kirkland, S., & Lyon, D. (1990). Evidence for terror management theory: II. The effects of mortality salience reactions to those who threaten or bolster the cultural worldview. *Journal of Personality and Social Psychology, 58*, 308–318.

Greenberg, J., Simon, L., Porteus, J., Pyszczynski, T., & Solomon, S. (1995). Evidence of a terror management function of cultural icons: The effects of mortality salience on the inappropriate use of cherished cultural symbols. *Personality and Social Psychology Bulletin, 21*, 1221–1228.

Hacker, F. (1976). *Crusaders, criminals, crazies: Terror and terrorism in our time*. New York: Norton, p. xi.

Hoffman, B. (2006). *Inside terrorism* (2nd Ed.). New York: Columbia University Press.

Holman, E. A., Garfin, D. R., & Silver, R. C. (2013). Media's role in broadcasting acute stress following the Boston Marathon bombings. *Proceedings of the National Academy of Sciences of the United States of America, 111*, 93–98.

Holman, E. A., Silver, R. C., Poulin, M., Andersen, J., Gil-Rivas, R., & McIntosh, D. N. (2008). Terrorism, acute stress, and cardiovascular health: A 3-year national study following the September 11th attacks. *Archives of General Psychiatry, 65*, 73–80.

Hospitality ON. (January 21, 2015). Paris: Terrorist attacks continue to raise concern in the hotel industry. *Hospitality ON*. Retrieved from http://hospitality-on.com/en/news/2015/01/21/paris-terrorist-attacks-continue-to-raise-concern-in-the-hotel-industry/

Hospitality ON. (February 18, 2015). Activity in Paris, the aftershock of the terrorist attacks is dwindling but leisure demand remains weak. *Hospitality ON*. Retrieved from http://hospitality-on.com/en/news/2015/02/18/

activity-in-paris-the-aftershock-of-the-terrorist-attacks-is-dwindling-but-leisure-demand-remains-weak/#ixzz4mvcAnmFq

Hospitality ON. (September 1, 2015). Tunisia: Hotel activity remains slow after the attacks. *Hospitality ON.* Retrieved from http://hospitality-on.com/en/news/2015/09/01/tunisia-hotel-activity-remains-slow-after-the-attacks/

Hospitality ON. (November 16, 2015). Terrorist attacks in Paris: Impact on the hotel industry. *Hospitality ON.* Retrieved from http://hospitality-on.com/en/news/2015/11/16/terrorist-attacks-in-paris-impact-on-the-hotel-industry/

Hospitality ON. (November 19, 2015). Overview of the impact of 9/11 on America's hotel industry. *Hospitality ON.* Retrieved from http://hospitality-on.com/en/news/2015/11/19/overview-of-the-impact-of-9-11-on-americas-hotel-industry/

Huddy, L., Feldman, S., Capelos, T., & Provost, C. (2002). The consequences of terrorism: Disentangling the effects of personal and national threat. *Political Psychology, 23*(3), 485–509.

Janis, I. L. & Feshbach, S. (1953). Effects of fear arousing communications. *Journal of Abnormal and Social Psychology, 48*, 78–92.

Jenkins, B. M. (1974). International terrorism: A new mode of conflict. In D. Carlton & C. Schaerf (Eds.), *International terrorism and world security* (p. 16). London: Croom Helm, 1975.

Jenkins, B. M. (2009). In Genevieve Lester, "societal acceptability of domestic intelligence". In B. Jackson (Ed.), *The challenge of domestic intelligence in a free society*. Santa Monica: RAND Corporation.

Jones, J. M. (September 8, 2011). One in four Americans say lives permanently changed by 9/11. *Gallup.* Retrieved from www.gallup.com/poll/149366/One-Four-Americans-Say-Lives-Permanently-Changed.aspx?g_source=&g_medium=&g_campaign=tiles

Keller, P. A. (1999). Converting the unconverted: The effect of inclination and opportunity to discount health-related fear appeals. *Journal of Applied Psychology, 84*, 403–415.

Kim, S., Plumb, R., Gredig, Q., Rankin, L., & Taylor, B. (2008). Medium-term post-Katrina health sequalae among New Orleans residents: Predictors of poor mental and physical health. *Journal of Clinical Nursing, 17*, 2335–2342.

Kuzma, L. (2004). Security vs. liberty: 9/11 and the American public. In W. Crotty (Ed.), *The politics of terror: The U.S. response to 9/11* (pp. 160–190). Boston: Northeastern University Press.

Landau, M. J., Solomon, S., Greenberg, J., Cohen, F., Pyszczynski, T., Arndt, J., Miller, C. H., Ogilvie, D. M., & Cook, A. (2004). Deliver us from evil: The effects of mortality salience and reminders of 9/11 on support for President George W. Bush. *Personality and Social Psychology Bulletin, 30*, 1136–1150.

Las Vegas Convention and Visitors Authority. (2017). *2016 Las Vegas Year-to-Date Executive Summary.* Retrieved from www.lvcva.com/includes/content/images/media/docs/ES-YTD-2016.pdf

LeDoux, J. E. (1996). *The emotional brain.* New York: Simon & Schuster

Leventhal, H. (1970). Findings and theory in the study of fear communications. In L. Berkowitz (Ed.), *Advances in experimental social psychology* (Vol. 5, pp. 119–186). New York: Academic Press.

Lewis, C. W. (2000). The terror that failed: Public opinion in the aftermath of the bombing in Oklahoma City. *Public Administration Review, 60*(3), 201–210.

Loewenstein, G. F., Weber, E. U., Hsee, C. K., & Welch, N. (2001). Risk as feelings. *Psychological Bulletin, 127*, 267–286.

Mansfield, Y. (1996). Wars, tourism and the 'Middle East' factor. In A. Pizam & Y. Mansfield (Eds.), *Tourism, crime and international security issues* (pp. 265–278). New York: Wiley and Sons.

Marks, I. (1987). *Fears, phobias, and rituals: Panic, anxiety, and their disorders.* New York: Oxford University Press.

Martin, H. (January 11, 2017). Los Angeles County brings in a record-high number of tourists in 2016. *Los Angeles Times.* Retrieved from www.latimes.com/business/la-fi-tourism-numbers-2010111-story.html

Monahan, T. (2013). Terrorism and tourism: Incorporating the economic spillover impact of terrorism into the DHS risk formula. Master's Thesis, Naval Postgraduate School, Monterey, CA.

Mueller, J. & Stewart, M. (September 10, 2014). Responsible counterterrorism policy. *Cato Institute Policy Analysis*, 255, 2.

National Consortium for the Study of Terrorism and Responses to Terrorism (START). (2017). *Global Terrorism Database*. University of Maryland. Retrieved from www.start.umd.edu/gtd/

Pyszczynski, T., Solomon, S., & Greenberg, J. (2005). *In the wake of 9/11: The psychology of terror*. Washington, DC: American Psychological Association.

Pyszczynski, T., Wicklund, R. A., Floresku, S., Koch, H., Gauch, G., Solomon, S., & Greenberg, J. (1996). Whistling in the dark: Exaggerated consensus estimates in response to incidental reminders of mortality. *Psychological Science*, 7, 332–336.

Rogers, R. W. (1983). Cognitive and psychological processes in fear appeals and attitude change: A revised theory of protection motivation. In J. Cacioppo & R. Petty (Eds.), *Social psychophysiology: A sourcebook* (pp. 153–176). New York: Guilford.

Rohner, D. & Frey, B. (2007). Blood and ink! The common-interest-game between terrorists and the media. *Public Choice*, 133, 129–145.

Rosenberg-Douglas, K. & Briscoe, T. (January 2, 2017). 2016 ends with 762 homicides: 2017 opens with fatal Uptown gunfight. *Chicago Tribune*. Retrieved from www.chicagotribune.com/news/local/breaking/ct-two-shot-to-death-in-uptown-marks-first-homicide-of-2017–20170101-story.html

Rosenblatt, A., Greenberg, J., Solomon, S., Pyszczynski, T., & Lyon, D. (1989). Evidence for terror management theory I: The effects of mortality salience on reactions to those who violate or uphold cultural values. *Journal of Personality and Social Psychology*, 57, 681–690.

Sanburn, J. (January 2, 2016). Chicago shootings and murders surged in 2015. *Time*. Retrieved from http://time.com/4165576/chicago-murders-shootings-rise-2015/

Sapolsky, R. M. (2007). Stress, stress related disease, and emotion regulation. In J. J. Gross (Ed.), *Handbook of emotion regulation*. New York, NY: Oxford University Press.

Schlenger, W. E., Caddell, J. M., Ebert, L., Jordan, B. K., Rourke, K. M., Wilson, D., Thalji, L., Dennis, J. M., Fairbank, J. A., & Kulka, R. A. (2002). Psychological reactions to terrorist attacks: Findings from the national study of Americans' reactions to September 11. *Journal of the American Medical Association*, 288, 581–588.

Schmid, A. P. (October, 1989). Terrorism and the media: The ethics of publicity. *Terrorism and Political Violence*, 1(4), 589.

Schuster, M. A., Stein, B. D., Jaycox, L. H., Collins, R. L., Marshall, G. N., Elliott, M. N., Zhou, A. J., Kanouse, D. E., Morrison, J. L., & Berry, S. H. (2001). A national survey of stress reactions after the September 11, 2001 terrorist attacks. *New England Journal of Medicine*, 345, 1507–1512.

Selye, H. (1936). A syndrome produced by diverse nocuous agent. *Nature*, 138, 32.

Selye, H. (1956). *The stress of life*. New York, NY: McGraw-Hill.

Selye, H. (1973). The evolution of the stress concept. *American Scientist*, 61, 672–679.

Silver, R. C., Holman, E. A., McIntosh, D. N., Poulin, M., & Gil-Rivas, V. (2002). Nationwide longitudinal study of psychological responses to September 11. *Journal of the American Medical Association*, 288, 1235–1244.

Skogan, W. (1986). Fear of crime and neighborhood change. In A. Reiss & M. Tonry (Eds.), *Communities and crime, Volume 8 of crime and justice: A review of research* (p. 210). Chicago: The University of Chicago Press.

Skogan, W. & Maxfield, M. (1981). *Coping with crime: Individual and neighborhood reactions* (Vol. 124). Beverly Hills, CA: Sage Publications, pp. 74–77.

Slone, M. (2000). Responses to media coverage of terrorism. *Journal of Conflict Resolution*, 44(4), 508–522.

Slovic, P. (2000). *The perception of risk*. London: Earthscan.

Suskind, R. (2006). *One percent doctrine: Deep inside America's pursuit of its enemies since 9/11*. New York: Simon and Schuster.

Suvak, M., Maguen, S., Litz, B. T., Silver, R. C., & Holman, E. A. (2008). Indirect exposure to the September 11 terrorist attacks: Does symptom structure resemble PTSD? *Journal of Traumatic Stress, 21,* 30–39.

Torabi, M. R. & Seo, D. (2004). National study of behavioral and life changes since September 11. *Health Education and Behavior, 31,* 179–192.

Tversky, A. & Kahneman, D. (1973). Availability: A heuristic for judging frequency and probability. *Cognitive Psychology, 5,* 207–232.

Tversky, A. & Kahneman, D. (1982). Judgment under uncertainty: Heuristics and biases. In Kahneman, D., Slovic, P. & Tversky, A. (Eds.), *Judgment under uncertainty: Heuristics and biases* (Vol. 3). New York: Cambridge University Press.

United Nations. (May 29, 1987). Geneva declaration on terrorism. Paper presented at the United Nations General Assembly, Geneva, Switzerland.

Willer, R. (2004). The effects of government-issued terror warnings on presidential approval ratings. *Current Research in Social Psychology, 10*(1), 1–12.

World Travel and Tourism Council (WTTC). (March 20, 2017). Resilience is key as impact of terrorism on tourism becomes clearer. *WTTC Report.* Retrieved from www.wttc.org/media-centre/press-releases/press-releases/2017/resilience-is-key-as-impact-of-terrorism-on-tourism-becomes-clearer-wttc-report/

Wright, L. (August 2, 2004). The terror web. *The New Yorker,* 40–47. Retrieved from http://classes.maxwell.syr.edu/PSC783/The_Terror_Web.pdf

Chapter 11

Conclusion

An End to Terrorism

Robin Maria Valeri

Will terrorism end? Terrorism is not a new phenomenon, nor are the motivations for terrorism. But, because cyberspace, which includes the Internet, telecommunications networks, and computer systems (White House, 2008), is available to almost anyone anywhere, terrorists now have the ability to easily and inexpensively promote, recruit, and take credit for terrorist activities at a global level. As mentioned in *Fear and Terrorism* (Ch. 10), "terrorists want a lot of people watching" (Jenkins, 2009, p. 83) so that they can cause fear and use that fear to influence behaviors. Cyberspace offers terrorists a global audience.

More recently, terrorists are finding ways to use cyberspace to commit acts of terrorism remotely. Their efforts include "denial of service" attacks, "doxing," and cyber sabotage (Brown, October 7, 2016). Thus, changes in cyberspace have allowed terrorists to change how they operate and have facilitated their activities, which in turn has required and continues to require civilians, law enforcement, the justice system, the military, and governments to adapt their prevention, detection, defense, and prosecution strategies to deal with the threats posed by terrorists. Given that technologies will continue to evolve, this ripple effect suggests a somewhat dark future in which the lives of individuals and nations will begin to revolve around safeguarding themselves from terrorism. But is the future so bleak?

There are many assumptions hidden in the dismal future described here. The first assumption is that terrorism will continue to flourish or, at a minimum, will continue. The second is that technology will continue to evolve. The third is that technological innovations will give terrorists an advantage over everyone else. And the fourth is that all we, non-terrorists, can do is react.

Will terrorism continue? Call me pessimistic, but my guess is that the answer to this question is "yes," terrorism will continue even if the political and religious motivations for terrorism might change from those discussed in the first six chapters of this book. Almost 30 years ago, I read Weinberg and Davis's (1989) book *Introduction to Political Terrorism*. Those authors posed a similar question, "If terrorism is to end, what will or does the process look like" (p. 194). According to Weinberg and Davis, there are several reasons why terrorist groups come to an end. Terrorist groups may be defeated by governmental authorities. Some terrorist groups may "end" because they change their strategy from terrorism to something legitimate, joining a political party, forming their own political party, or using the law to their advantage. They may also be defeated by the very groups whose causes they are purportedly defending, if these groups, disgusted by the atrocities committed in their name, turn against the terrorists. Finally, terrorist groups may also simply fizzle away. Young people lured to terrorist groups by the promise of action, adventure, and fame may drift away once they are faced with the nitty-gritty reality that everyday life in a terrorist organization is not all that glamorous.

The question then becomes what can individuals, communities, and nations do to facilitate each of these. The first two reasons as to why terrorism may end require military and political interventions. While the latter two reasons can be facilitated by nations, they can also be achieved through grassroots efforts. But whatever actions are taken to stop terrorism, those actions need to occur in the physical world as well as in cyberspace.

With regard to governmental authorities defeating terrorism, this now requires waging war and engaging in counter terrorism efforts in both the physical world and cyberspace. After the September 11, 2001, attacks, the counterterrorism efforts of the United States included the creation of the Department of Homeland Security. Counterterrorism efforts also require businesses to improve their security measures in the physical world and citizens to be more vigilant about noticing and reporting signs of terrorism. In addition to countering terrorism, governments can also engage their military to fight terrorists. Assuming the United States military already has the knowledge and ability to wage war in the physical world, it means that they must continue to develop strategies for protecting and defending the nation against cyber-warfare/cyber-terrorism.

What does this entail? Given that we, individually and collectively, are all becoming more dependent on technologies and that these technologies continue to evolve, so too must the safeguards to protect ourselves and our nation in cyberspace. Unfortunately, too many of us have not taken cyber-security seriously, and so it's not always a matter of someone, whether motivated by crime, hate, or terrorism, breaking through our cyber defenses but simply walking through the cyber equivalent of an open door or window. For example, the recent Equifax scandal revealed that the company had not only suffered a major security breach because it had failed to install a software patch that had been available for over a month, but that the company suffers from other security weaknesses stemming from their continued reliance on old software (Fox-Brewster, September 8, 2017; Newman, September 14, 2017).

While many hackers are using their computer savvy to engage in cyber-crime for profit, other groups such as Anonymous are engaged in "hactivism" as a form of civil disobedience in which they blend hacking and activism for a social cause (Bergal, January 11, 2017). In 2015, Brookings (November 13, 2015) reported that the group Anonymous was waging a cyber-war against the Islamic State. Brookings reported that one member of #OpISIS "summed up the anti-Islamic State position simply 'Taking away the free speech from a group that is advocating the end of free speech is delicious fun'" (Brookings, November 13, 2015). Another more recent example of hactivism was the largely unsuccessful hack on North Carolina's website as a means of protesting the state's transgender bathroom law, which required individuals to use the bathroom consistent with the gender on their birth certificate. Other hactivists, such as those targeting the state of Michigan, to draw attention to the water crisis in Flint, and Missouri, to protest the fatal police shooting of an unarmed African-American teenager Michael Brown, were somewhat more successful (Bergal, January 11, 2017; Williams, May 18, 2016). While IT professionals for each state were able to counter the hackers' efforts, the hacking and counter-hacking measures did cost these states money. More recently, Anonymous claims to have shut down the websites of Ku Klux Klan groups and neo-Nazi groups, and to have "outed" member of these groups by posting their names and pictures online after the white supremacist rally in Charlottesville, Virginia, in August 2017 (McGoogan & Molloy, August 14, 2017).

This "outing" of people by hackers is referred to as "doxing," releasing the personal information, home addresses, and phone numbers of individuals online. Ardit Ferizi, aka Th3Dir3ctorY, who was the first person convicted of cyber-terrorism in the United States engaged in doxing (US Department of Justice, September 13, 2016; Wilber, September 23, 2016). In 2015, Ferizi hacked into the computers of an American company, culled through the personally identifiable information (PII) of its customers, and compiled a list of names and addresses of over 1,300 United States military and government personnel. He then gave this information to a leader in ISIS who, on August 11, 2015, posted a tweet that contained the PII information of these individuals along with the statement "we are . . . passing on your personal information to the soldiers of the khilafah, who soon with the permission of Allah will strike at your necks in your own lands!" (US Department of Justice, September 13, 2016). It is because of attacks like these that cybersecurity professionals worry that

> as hactivists get more sophisticated, the consequences could become more serious. Instead of potentially affecting citizen services such as revenue collection or driver's license renewals for a brief period . . . hactivists could do far greater damage by knocking out the electric grid, water systems, or other untilites.
>
> (Bergal, January 11, 2017)

In fact, in 2013, Hamid Firoozi allegedly hacked into a dam in Rye Brook, New York, and obtained water level and temperature information (Kutner, March 30, 2016). Had the system not been in maintenance mode, Firoozi would have been able to operate the floodgate remotely (Kutner, March 30, 2016).

To help prevent and detect cyberattacks, the United States government and military have taken steps to ensure the nation's cybersecurity. The Department of Homeland Security works with other agencies to help protect America's infrastructure, secure federal networks, and detect and prevent cybercrime. Efforts at ensuring the nation's cyber defenses are also reflected in the fact that, in 2005, the United States Air Force updated its mission to include cyberspace. Their mission statement now reads "The mission of the United States Air Force is to deliver sovereign options for the defense of the United States of America and its global interests—to fly and fight in Air, Space, and Cyberspace" (Moseley, December 7, 2005). On February 9, 2016, the Obama Administration announced a Cybersecurity National Action Plan (The White House, February 9, 2016) aimed at "enhancing cybersecurity capabilities within the Federal Government and across the country." Just recently, in May 2017, the United States Air Force announced the start of its cyber squadron initiative (McCrae, May 2017). Obviously the government's efforts to combat cyberwarfare and cyberterrorism are not limited to those discussed here. But like them, private businesses, organizations, and individuals all need to ensure that their cybersecurity is up-to-date to deter cyberattacks. Fortunately, there are companies who specialize in cybersecurity. We just have to take advantages of the services they provide.

The second reason that terrorism ends is because some terrorist groups decide to use lawful means to accomplish their goals and/or become (part of) legitimate organizations or political parties. Because many terrorist groups have organizational structures that allow them to function in a manner similar to legitimate organizations, governments may be able to facilitate their transformation to legitimacy by engaging in the same types of negotiations that they would use with legitimate organizations to achieve peace. Moghaddam (2005) notes that "radical groups that engage in dialogue tend to become incorporated within the larger discourse, and to eventually help shape the discourse, as well as to become influenced by it themselves" (p. 110). This suggests that a key to ending terrorism as well as preventing it would be ensuring that there are legal means for making change within a society and that it is clear to all members of that society that those avenues for making change are open to them (Moghaddam, 2005).

Enabling?

If we move on to the possibility that some groups "defended by" terrorists might be appalled by the actions of terrorists purportedly taken on their behalf, one means of defeating the terrorists might be to encourage members of those groups to speak out against the terrorists. For example, after the rally by white supremacists in Charlottesville, Virginia, on August 11 and 12, 2017, which led to the death of a protestor, many American's found ways to show that the beliefs and actions of the white supremacists did not represent them. For example, at a "free speech" rally the following weekend in Boston, thousands of people came to peacefully protest the Charlottesville rally (Lowery & Pazzanese, August 19, 2017).

In addition to member of the "defended" group speaking out against the terrorists, another powerful voice comes from former members of the terrorist group. Neumann (2015), in a report on defectors from the Islamic State, notes that the testimony of defectors from these groups can be a powerful tool used to prevent others from joining because "no one has more credibility in challenging the IS narrative and giving a realistic impression of the group and the totalitarian society it seeks to create than the people who have experienced it" (p. 6). According to the narratives of the defectors, they left the Islamic State because they "felt a sense of outrage about IS' [Islamic State] extreme brutality, violence and abuse against the very people it claimed to defend . . . " (Neumann, 2015, p. 6).

As noted, defection of members is another factor that can lead to the collapse of a terrorist group. While some avenues for exiting these groups exist such as Life After Hate (www.lifeafterhate.org), leaving a terrorist group can be mentally and/or physically difficult and even dangerous. As both Hassan (2015) and Neumann (2015) note, leaving these groups can be psychologically difficult because members, as part of their indoctrination, have come to believe that the group represents the "true faith." Joining these groups often requires members to turn their backs on family and friends, and in some cases, give up all of their possession. This can make leaving the terrorist group or extremist group all the more difficult because the defector is faced with the reality that he/she will have to (re)build relationships and rebuild their lives. Leaving can also be dangerous. The terrorist group, extremist group, or cult may try to injure or kill the defector, and if the defector is able to escape from these groups, he/she may even face legal ramifications from the nation to which they are returning. For these reasons, Neumann (2015) recommends that governments remove disincentives for defection, aid the defectors in their resettlement, help to ensure their safety, and provide a means for defectors to go public with their stories.

Finally, in the chapters on recruitment and radicalization (Chapters. 7, 8, and 9), the reasons why individuals join terrorists' groups are discussed. These reasons include a need to belong, a search for purpose or meaning in life, or a desire for excitement and adventure. The first two reasons have been used by both cults and terrorist groups to recruit members. While the latter reason, a desire for excitement or adventure, has not only led youth to join terrorist groups but also to engage in hate crimes (Valeri & Brown, in press). Given that one obvious way to reduce terrorism is to prevent people from becoming terrorists, individuals and organizations need to find ways of fulfilling these needs. So, if one of the reasons that youth join terrorist groups is because they are seeking excitement, then schools, youth-focused organizations, and communities need to ensure that such opportunities are available and make every effort to be welcoming and inclusive to all youth so that they become engaged in these organizations and activities (Valeri & Brown, in press). With regard to the first two reasons for joining a terrorist organization, a search for belonging or meaning, community groups, whether it's through schools, civic organizations, or religious institutions, need to provide people of all ages with a sense of belonging as well as a way to find purpose and meaning in their lives. These suggestions focus on the actions that individuals and organizations can take in the physical world to prevent someone from joining a terrorist organization. Chapter 7, From *Declarations to Deeds*, offers further suggestions for combatting the cyber recruitment tactics used by terrorists, as does the Department of Homeland Security (DHS). A key focus of DHS is countering violent extremism. DHS provides myriad resources to communities so that they can counter violent extremism (see www.dhs.gov/countering-violent-extremism).

In summary, communities can take measures to prevent terrorism if they engage in efforts to make people resilient to the recruitment attempts of terrorists; help individuals learn to recognize when they, or someone they know, are being recruited; or help them resist these attempts by turning to their families and friends for support. Finally, it requires developing strategies to counter the recruitment efforts of terrorists. But individuals also need to take responsibility for themselves. As Hassan notes,

> Throughout the world, millions of people are searching to find purpose and meaning in their lives. . . . People must learn to know themselves and take responsibility for their own beliefs, values, and behavior. They must also develop and use social support networks to connect them to the resources of the greater community, and to help them to enjoy the fulfillment that comes with healthy, interdependent, mature relationships.
>
> (Hassan, 2013, pp. xx–xxi)

In conclusion, while terrorism may continue and technology will most certainly continue to develop, we as individuals and as communities can use the same resources available to terrorists to be proactive in building stronger and healthier communities because the best way to stop terrorism is by preventing its causes.

REFERENCES

Bergal, J. (January 11, 2017). 'Hactivists' increasing target local and state government computers. *Huffington Post*. Retrieved from www.huffingtonpost.com/entry/hacktivists-increasingly-target-local-and-state-government_us_587651e8e4b0f8a725448401

Brookings, E. T. (November 13, 2015). Anonymous vs. the Islamic state. *Foreign Policy*. Retrieved from http://foreignpolicy.com/2015/11/13/anonymous-hackers-islamic-state-isis-chan-online-war/

Brown, D. S. (October 7, 2016). The cyber war against terrorism. *Technopedia*. Retrieved from www.techopedia.com/2/31916/security/the-cyber-war-against-terrorism

Cyber Security Enhancement Act of 2002 (H.R.3482). Retrieved from www.congress.gov/bill/107th-congress/house-bill/3482

Fox-Brewster, T. (September 8, 2017). A brief history of Equifax security fails. *Forbes*. Retrieved from www.forbes.com/sites/thomasbrewster/2017/09/08/equifax-data-breach-history/#4e9d9b62677c

Hassan, S. (2013). *Freedom of Mind: Helping Loved Ones Leave Controlling People, Cults and Beliefs*. Newton, MA: Freedom of Mind Press.

Hassan, S. (2015). *Combatting Cult Mind Control*. Newton, MA: Freedom of Mind Press.

Jenkins, B. M. (2009). In Genevieve Lester, "societal acceptability of domestic intelligence". In B. Jackson (Ed.), *The Challenge of Domestic Intelligence in a Free Society*. Santa Monica, CA: RAND Corporation.

Kutner, M. (March 30, 2016). Alleged dam hacking raises fears of cyber threats to infrastructure. *Newsweek*. Retrieved from www.newsweek.com/cyber-attack-rye-dam-iran-441940

Lowery, W. & Pazzanese, C. (August 19, 2017). Boston 'free speech' rally ends early amid flood of counterprotestors: 27 people arrested. *Washington Post*. Retrieved from www.washingtonpost.com/news/post-nation/wp/2017/08/19/thousands-expected-at-boston-free-speech-rally-and-counter-protest/?utm_term=.12fe840d9b24

McCrae, J. (May, 2017). Cyber squadron initiative: Arming airmen for the 21st century battle. *U.S. Air Force News*. Retrieved from www.af.mil/News/Article-Display/Article/1174583/cyber-squadron-initiative-arming-airmen-for-21st-century-battle/

McGoogan, C. & Molloy, M. (August 14, 2017). Anonymous shuts down neo-Nazi and KKK websites after Charlottesville rally. *The Telegraph*. Retrieved from www.telegraph.co.uk/technology/2017/08/14/anonymous-shuts-neo-nazi-kkk-websites-charlottesville-rally/

Moghaddam, F. M. (2005). Cultural preconditions for potential terrorist groups: Terrorism and societal change. In F. M. Moghaddam & A. J. Marsella (Eds.), *Understanding Terrorism: Psychological Roots, Consequences, and Interventions* (pp. 103–118). Washington, DC: American Psychological Association.

Mosely, T. M. (December 7, 2005). Letter to the Airmen of the United States Air Force. Retrieved from www.24af.af.mil/Portals/11/documents/About_Us/AFD-111003-050.pdf?ver=2016-04-26-113014-917

Neumann, P. R. (2015). Victims, perpetrators, assets: The narratives of Islamic State defectors. The International Center for the Study of Radicalization and Political Violence. Retrieved from http://icsr.info/wp-content/uploads/2015/09/ICSR-Report-Victims-Perpertrators-Assets-The-Narratives-of-Islamic-State-Defectors.pdf

Newman, L. H. (September 14, 2017). Equifax officially has no excuse. *Wired*. Retrieved from www.wired.com/story/equifax-breach-no-excuse/

United States Department of Justice. (September 23, 2016). ISIL-linked Kosovo hacker sentenced to 20 years in prison. *Justice News*. Retrieved from www.justice.gov/opa/pr/isil-linked-kosovo-hacker-sentenced-20-years-prison

Valeri, R. M. & Brown, A. (in press). From bullying to brutality: Hate crimes and hate incidents at schools and universities. In R. M. Valeri & K. Borgeson (Eds.), *Hate Crimes: Victims, Motivations and Typologies*. Durham, NC: Carolina Academic Press.

Weinberg, L. B. & Davis, P. B., (1989). *Introduction to Political Terrorism*. New York: McGraw Hill.

White House. (2008). *National Security Presidential Directive 54/Homeland Security Presidential Directive 23, Cybersecurity Policy*. Retrieved from https://fas.org/irp/offdocs/nspd/nspd-54.pdf

White House. (February 9, 2016). *Fact Sheet: Cybersecurity National Action Plan*. Retrieved from https://obamawhitehouse.archives.gov/the-press-office/2016/02/09/fact-sheet-cybersecurity-national-action-plan

Wilber, D. Q. (September 23, 2016). Hacker from Kosovo who aided the Islamic State is sentenced to 20 years in U.S. prison. *Los Angeles Times*. Retrieved from www.latimes.com/nation/la-na-hacker-islamic-state-20160923-snap-story.html

Williams, K. B. (May 18, 2016). Anonymous targets NC government over bathroom law. *The Hill*. Retrieved from http://thehill.com/policy/cybersecurity/280322-anonymous-targets-north-carolina-government-over-bathroom-law

Index

Note: Figures in bold indicate a table on the corresponding page.